JUST A BITE

EGON RONAY'S

PGtips

1987 GUIDE

Light Meals and Snacks
to suit all pockets
and palates

*including All the Fun of the Fare
a colour section for families*

Establishment research conducted by a team of full-time professional inspectors, who are trained to achieve common standards of judgement with as much objectivity as this field allows. Their professional identities are not disclosed until they seek information from the management after paying their bills. The Guide is independent in its editorial selection and does not accept advertising, payment or hospitality from establishments covered.

Egon Ronay's Guides
Second Floor, Greencoat House
Francis Street, London SW1P 1DH

Editor Moyra Fraser
Copy editor Julanne Arnold
Chief copywriter & crossword compiler Peter Long
Research editors Michèle Roche
                 Coreen Williams
Editorial contributor Joy Langridge
Publisher William Halden
Sponsorship consultants Spero Marketing Consultants Ltd

Design of introductory pages and colour section Michael Leaman
Illustrations Margaret Leaman
Cover design Michael Leaman & Spero Communications

Cartography by Intermap PS Ltd. All road maps are based on the Ordnance Survey Maps, with the permission of the Controller of HM Stationery Office. Crown copyright reserved.

Town plans produced by the Cartographic Department, Publishing Division of the Automobile Association

The contents of this book are believed correct at the time of printing. Nevertheless, the publisher can accept no responsibility for errors or omissions or changes in the details given.

Distributed in the United Kingdom by the Publishing Division of The Automobile Association, Fanum House, Basingstoke, Hampshire RG21 2EA and overseas by the British Tourist Authority, Thames Tower, Black's Road, London W6 9EL.

ISBN 0 86145 406 5

AA Ref 54713

Typeset in Great Britain by William Clowes Ltd, Beccles and London
Printed in Great Britain by Cox & Wyman Ltd, Reading

CONTENTS

HOW TO USE
THIS GUIDE

TYPES OF ESTABLISHMENT
For this Guide the inspectors have a brief to look for establishments serving good snacks and light meals. These snacks could be anything from a scone and a sandwich to a slice of quiche, a salad, a hot main course or perhaps something in the sushi line or ditto with dim sum. Establishments where the food is judged outstanding are shown with a star.

PRICES
Prices are quoted for two typical items or for the cost of a set tea where applicable. These prices were valid at the time of inspection but may have risen a little since then. Minimum charges per person are usually indicated in the entry.

LICENSING AND OPENING HOURS
It is indicated if an establishment is unlicensed. Opening hours given refer specifically to times when the snacks described are available. For example, a restaurant offering just a bite at lunchtime does not have its evening hours listed if there is only a full dinner menu, but reference may be made to this in the entry. As far as possible it is indicated which dishes are served throughout opening hours and which form part of a special lunch, tea or other menu. Many establishments have flexible hours because of their small size or remote location, and it is thus safest to check opening times.

PARKING
Details of the nearest convenient parking are given.

ORDER OF LISTINGS
London entries appear first and are in alphabetical order by establishment name. Listings outside London are in alphabetical order by location within the regional divisions of England, Scotland, Wales, the Channel Islands and the Isle of Man.

MAP REFERENCES
Entries contain references to the map section in the middle of the Guide or to a town plan printed along with the entries.

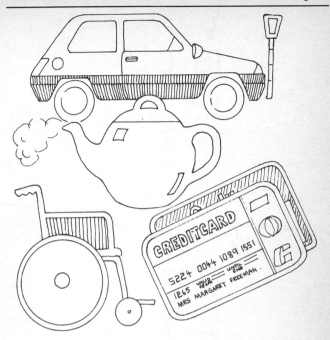

SYMBOLS

★   Outstanding food

☕   A good cup of tea (see also page 20)

☺   Good cheeseboard (see also page 28 for cheeseboards considered outstanding)

LVs Luncheon Vouchers accepted (see also page 39)

Credit Credit cards accepted

P   Nearest convenient spot for car parking

♿   Considered by the management as suitable for wheelchairs

WC A clean lavatory with soap, towels, paper and running water

BROOKE BOND & JUST A BITE

Brooke Bond is delighted to be associated with this popular and highly regarded Guide to establishments where families can enjoy a reasonably priced meal and a beverage such as a cup of tea in pleasant surroundings.

When our founder, Arthur Brooke, was a young man, tea was expensive and the quality was rarely up to scratch. Armed with an extensive knowledge of tea-blending techniques taught to him by his father, Brooke concentrated on premium blends, selecting exact proportions from the best of several teas. The result was an exciting new range of teas that didn't vary in quality from one week to the next. So in 1869 the enterprising Arthur Brooke added an impressive-sounding 'Bond' to his name and opened the first Brooke Bond tea shop.

This formula has served the company well. For today, as one of the UK's premier food organisations, Brooke Bond provides the country with much of its sustenance, including some 60 million cups of tea a day! – which is why the link with Egon Ronay's Just a Bite Guide is such a natural one.

Our products are renowned for their high and consistent quality. And so in its own way is this authoritative book. We hope you will long continue to enjoy both.

John R. Nicolson

John R. Nicolson
Marketing Manager

INTRODUCTION

Changing of the guard is successful if it is executed smoothly, with organised precision, and if it is imperceptible to the outside world. This is exactly how the change in the publishers of this Guide has taken place.

I am particularly pleased that the publisher's philosophy continues to place quality above all other considerations. The traditional, stringent criteria of judgement have been applied by the inspectors and the thoroughness of their inspections has been maintained. A guide is always as good and as reliable as its inspectors.

A further guarantee of continuity is that most of the previous key staff – inspectors, editors, writers and researchers – have been taken over with the Guide and are directed by a publisher as dedicated as I have been.

All this is a remarkable achievement if one considers the nature of a guide publishing operation, far more complex and demanding than is generally supposed. Starting from scratch every year, drawing up terms of reference for the research, the almost military organisation of inspectors, the gruelling task of vetting the inspectors' long and detailed reports, attending to them clerically and – most important – evaluating them to arrive at a just classification of establishments, not to mention the task of marketing and sales, are vital parts of the machinery necessary to enable a reader to choose a reliable dining venue or a good room for the night.

As you will see, the changing of the guard is a success.

Egon Ronay

WAVE GOODBYE
TO THE SCONE...

If any dish personifies this 'Just a Bite' Guide it is the Scone.

Whether plain or fruited, served with butter or thick clotted cream, accompanied by strawberry jam or other home-made preserves, it remains our inspectors' favourite tea-time treat.

Scones are quick and easy to make and are a traditional part of every afternoon menu. Cooked well, they almost guarantee a favourable mention in the inspectors' reports.

But this year has been different. Among the hundreds of visits there have been tastings of scones described as 'dehydrated', 'tasteless', 'hard' and 'brittle' or even 'scones that could have been bounced off the wall'.

Whatever has happened to our favourite afternoon delight – the centrepiece for countless Dorset, Devon and other cream teas and the item that is guaranteed to make tourists' mouths water?

It isn't that the owners of our restaurants, tea rooms and coffee shops or their chefs have suddenly lost the traditional skills that have made Britain famous for its baking. Or that their customers have lost their taste for afternoon tea.

The culprit is a gleaming, electronic interloper from Japan – the microwave oven. Once a novelty, tucked away in the kitchens and used with discretion, it now sits proudly centre-stage in restaurants, its timing bell producing applause from the waiting customers every time it rings.

Like its predecessors, the video, the calculator, the computer, we have not yet learned to put it in its place. Caterers have become hypnotised by its gadgetry and the scone is only one of its victims. At this rate, like the soft, light texture of the scone itself, afternoon tea will evaporate and with it one of the many pleasures of the traditional British holiday scene.

There is nothing better than a scone fresh out of the oven – a traditional oven I mean. If it is reheated in a microwave then it requires split-second timing – and that's the trouble. Far too many of the places we have visited this year are using microwaves that are designed for domestic use once or twice a day but not for constant all-day catering.

And even worse it was quite clear from our research that staff and management are confused and untrained in how to use them. The result is that scones, bread and other varied delights emerge dried up or tasteless, or both.

Microwave

The other problem is us. For some unfathomable reason we seem to have decided that everything we eat, whether it's for afternoon tea or any other meal, must be warm.

So we demand warm scones, warm bread, warm quiches, warm everything. Once again, the microwave steps into action. What's easier for cafés than popping the scones back into the oven for a minute and reheating them? And if they are not all eaten and the next customer arrives, popping them back in yet again.

So often that explains the angry comments from the inspectors.

Of course, the opposite can happen. Wine bars were the first to fall in love with the microwave in the Seventies: we all remember moussaka and lasagne appearing under the arc lights – hot on the edges, soggy and cold in the middle.

This year there is evidence that wine bars are reorganising and are learning how to use the microwave better – on good days we found:

superb salmon mayonnaise (fish is one texture that does respond kindly to the microwave), Scottish fish soup and a textbook French onion soup.

At one delightful olde-worlde restaurant one of our inspectors chose his quiche from a display of several varieties, sat down to be served and then watched horrified when his portion was placed in the microwave. The restaurant almost suffered the instant penalty of non-appearance in this Guide. Instead, when the quiche arrived it was faultless. Its spell in the microwave had been timed to perfection – but this inspector's experience was the exception to prove the rule.

This 'everything must be warm' craze is also leading to a growth in the 'cook today, serve tomorrow' syndrome. If the customers constantly demand the warm glow of food that has been heated up, then why should café owners bother to be up at four in the morning to make sure it is baked that day?

Or even – and we have met this a few times this year – why do restaurants serve yesterday's heated-up bread and scones when there is a baker's shop a few minutes down the road selling freshly baked produce?

The answer is to use – or misuse – the microwave.

Just to spin the dial, switch on and walk away is not enough. We have tasted too many of the results of this to know that is not the way. Bread and scones with their low water content are just the first to suffer.

One of the attractions of so many of the successful entries in this 'Just a Bite' Guide is the cheerful staff who serve at tables in seaside and rural locations. They are usually recruited locally, with smiles making up for lack of expertise. However, if owners insist on installing one of the 50 brands of microwaves now on offer to caterers, they must accompany it with staff training and supervision. Otherwise, our tea rooms and traditional restaurants will lose their reputation for care and pride in the traditions of fine food and instead will become linked with the worst practices of fast food.

And if this electronic blight continues the British Scone could well sink without trace – and with it Devon and Dorset teas. And wasn't it a product similar to the microwave that was launched in America with that infamous advertising slogan 'From the team that brought you Pearl Harbour'?

This could give the phrase yet another new meaning.

William Halden, Publisher

JUST A BITE
PLACE of the YEAR

This year a new award for the Just a Bite Place of the Year is introduced to recognise general all-round excellence in terms of what an establishment sets out to do, whether it be just a snack or a light meal.

A short list has been drawn up from the hundreds of entries in the Guide, and the three nominees are listed on the following pages. At the Guide's launch the winner will be announced and presented with a specially designed Wedgwood plaque.

Elland, West Yorkshire
BERTIE'S BISTRO

Michael Swallows cooks with abundant skill and flair to bring this well-run bistro way above the ordinary. He changes his menu every week, so his regulars never run out of new and tempting things to try, and the last spoonful of white wine syllabub is as delightful as the first taste of chicken and spinach terrine or a perfectly executed watercress sauce. Further pluses are the appealing period decor, the comely waitresses and the very friendly, helpful owner.

Congleton, Cheshire
ODD FELLOWS
WINE BAR & BISTRO

Character, atmosphere, accomplished cooking and a remarkable cellar with an outstanding selection of Italian wines – all this is offered by brothers Neil and Ashley Kirkham in splendid Regency-style premises. Hot dishes span the globe, from roghan josh to Mexican pork casserole; soups are subtle yet full of flavour; super salads centre round anything from rare roast beef to herrings in Madeira sauce. Vegetarians and healthy eaters aren't forgotten, while budding Billy Bunters can dive into delicious desserts.

London *MANDEER*

The cooking in this Indian vegetarian restaurant provides an object lesson in the use of spices and seasoning. All sorts of goodies are available on the à la carte menu, or you can sample the multiple delights of a thali, a traditional set meal. Everything comes freshly prepared, piping hot and full of flavour. Dishes without spices, and complete meals without garlic or onion, are cooked on separate stoves with their own utensils – a fine example of the care they take here.

Egon Ronay's
Minutes
from the Motorway
M25 AROUND
LONDON GUIDE

Newly compiled for 1987, this colourful guide spotlights over 200 carefully selected eating places within easy reach of London's orbital motorway.

Everything from starred restaurants and country pubs to the best tearooms and wine bars.

Special features include detailed area maps.

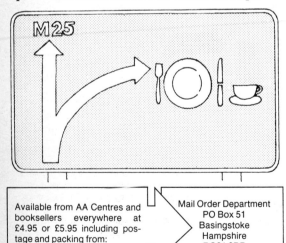

Available from AA Centres and booksellers everywhere at £4.95 or £5.95 including postage and packing from:

Mail Order Department
PO Box 51
Basingstoke
Hampshire
RG21 2BR

STARRED ENTRIES

LONDON

Brasserie at L'Escargot, W1
Le Cochonnet, Maida Vale, W9
Cranks Health Food Restaurant, W1
Dorchester Hotel, Promenade, W1
Inn on the Park Lounge, W1
Inter-Continental Hotel, Coffee
  House, W1
Joy King Lau, WC2
Justin de Blank, W1
Maison Bertaux, W1
Mandeer, W1
Mulford's Wine Bar, W6
The Savoy, Thames Foyer, WC2

ENGLAND

Ambleside, Cumbria: Rothay Manor
Ambleside, Cumbria: Sheila's Cottage
Bamburgh, Nthmb: Copper Kettle
Barden, N Yorks: Low House Farm
Berkhamsted, Herts: Cook's Delight
Billingshurst, W Sussex: Burdock
  Provender
Bolton Abbey, N Yorks: Bolton Abbey
  Tea Cottage
Borrowdale, Cumbria: Lodore Swiss
  Hotel Lounge
Brighton, E Sussex: Food for Friends
Brighton, E Sussex: Mock Turtle
Broadway, H & W: Collin House Hotel
Canterbury, Kent: Sweet Heart Patis-
  serie
Chichester, W Sussex: Clinch's Salad
  House

Cockermouth, Cumbria: Quince &
  Medlar
Congleton, Ches: Odd Fellows Wine
  Bar & Bistro
Corse Lawn, Glos: Corse Lawn
  House
Coventry, W Mid: Trinity House Hotel,
  Herbs Restaurant
Dartington, Devon: Cranks Health
  Food Restaurant
Devizes, Wilts: Wiltshire Kitchen
Eastbourne, E Sussex: Byrons
Eastbourne, E Sussex: Nature's Way
Elland, W Yorks: Bertie's Bistro
Faversham, Kent: Recreation Tavern
Ipswich, Suffolk: Orwell House
Kew, Surrey: Original Maids of Hon-
  our
Leamington Spa, Warks: Mallory
  Court
Leintwardine, H & W: Selda Coffee
  Shop
Ludlow, Shrops: Hardwicks
Lustleigh, Devon: Primrose Cottage
Lympstone, Devon: River House
Lynton, Devon: Lee Cottage
Lyonshall, H & W: Church House
Marlborough, Wilts: Polly
Melmerby, Cumbria: Village Bakery
Oxford, Oxon: Heroes
Oxford, Oxon: Munchy Munchy
Plumtree, Notts: Perkins Bar Bistro
Selworthy, Som: Periwinkle Cottage
  Tea Rooms

Sheffield, S Yorks: Just Cooking
Sheffield, S Yorks: Toff's Restaurant & Coffee House
Skipton, N Yorks: Herbs Wholefood & Vegetarian Restaurant
Tiverton, Devon: Hendersons
Trebarwith Strand, Corn: Old Millfloor
Tunbridge Wells, Kent: Downstairs at Thackeray's
Ullswater, Cumbria: Sharrow Bay Country House Hotel
Warminster, Wilts: Vincent's
Whitby, N Yorks: Magpie Café
Yarm, Clev: Coffee Shop

SCOTLAND
Aberfeldy, T'side: Country Fare Coffee House
Cullipool, S'clyde: Longhouse Buttery
Dulnain Bridge, H'land: Muckrach Lodge Hotel
Edinburgh, Loth: Handsel's Wine Bar
Edinburgh, Loth: Kalpna
Edinburgh, Loth: Laigh Kitchen
Inverness, H'land: Brookes Wine Bar

Knipoch, S'clyde: Knipoch House Hotel
Taynuilt, S'clyde: Shore Cottage
Wester Howgate, Loth: Old Howgate Inn, Coach House
Whitehouse, S'clyde: Old School Tearoom

WALES
Aberaeron, Dyfed: Hive on the Quay
Cardiff, Mid-Glamorgan: Armless Dragon
Caernarfon, Gwynedd: Bakestone
Llangollen, Clwyd: Gales Wine & Food Bar
Newport, Dyfed: Cnapan

CHANNEL ISLANDS
Gorey, Jersey: Jersey Pottery Restaurant

ISLE OF MAN
Ballasalla, Isle of Man: La Rosette

TEA PLACE
OF THE YEAR

It's seven years since our good tea symbol [❤] first appeared, and at that time few establishments were serving tea that was anything but distinctly ordinary. Today high-quality teas are the norm for caterers just as for more and more people drinking tea at home. Speciality teas like Darjeeling, Earl Grey and Lapsang Souchong are appearing with increasing regularity, along with teas subtly flavoured with a variety of fruits and herbs. Afternoon tea, in particular, is one of Britain's great traditions, and it's nice to be able to report that it once again thrives.

The Tea Place of the Year award, initiated six years ago, is presented annually to a tea place in Britain that is judged to make and serve an outstanding cup of tea and also to offer superb cakes, scones, sandwiches and similar fare.

In the search for the Tea Place of the Year, Egon Ronay's Guide inspectors drink and munch their way through innumerable cups of tea and plates of pastries to arrive at their recommendations for the award. The award for 1987 goes to the Church House, at Lyonshall in Hereford and Worcester.

Lyonshall,
Hereford & Worcester
CHURCH HOUSE

Edwardian recipes are used for the lovely cakes and pastries served at teatime in this delightful guest house. The choice couldn't be simpler – just cakes, scones and tea, except by prior booking for a set tea with finger sandwiches. The baking, by local girls, is quite outstanding, and the tea room itself, which is decked out in pretty Edwardian fashion, overlooks a scene of pastoral peace. In an adjoining crafts shop Eileen Dilley continues the theme with her Edwardian-style blouses and accessories.

AFTERNOON TEAS

The following establishments offer set afternoon teas, including what our inspectors judge a good cuppa.

LONDON

Athenaeum Hotel, Windsor Lounge, W1
Bonne Bouche Pâtisserie, W1
Brown's Hotel Lounge, W1
Christys Healthline, W1
Dorchester Hotel, Promenade, W1
Goring Hotel Lounge, SW1
Grosvenor House, Park Lounge, W1
Harrods Georgian Restaurant & Terrace, SW1
Harvey Nichols, Harveys at the Top, SW1
The Heal's Restaurant, W1
Hyatt Carlton Tower, Chinoiserle, SW1
Hyde Park Hotel, Park Room, SW1
Inn on the Park Lounge, W1
Inter-Continental Hotel, Coffee House, W1
London Marriott Hotel, Regent Lounge, W1
Le Meridien Piccadilly, W1
Muffin Man, W8
Richoux, SW3 & W1
The Ritz, Palm Court, W1
Royal Festival Hall, Riverside Café, SE1
The Savoy, Thames Foyer, WC2
Sheraton Park Tower Restaurant, SW1
Tea-Time, SW4
Waldorf Hotel, Palm Court Lounge, WC2
Westbury Hotel Lounge, W1

ENGLAND

Abbots Bromley, Staffs: Marsh Farm Tea Room
Alfriston, E Sussex: Singing Kettle
Alnwick, Nthmb: Maxine's Kitchen
Alston, Cumbria: Brownside Coach House
Alstonefield, Staffs: Old Post Office Tea Room
Ambleside, Cumbria: Rothay Manor
Amersham, Bucks: Fripp's
Ashbourne, Derbys: Spencers of Ashbourne
Ashburton, Devon: Ashburton Coffee House
Ashford-in-the-Water, Derbys: Cottage Tea Room
Avebury, Wilts: Stones Restaurant
Axminster, Devon: New Commercial Inn
Aysgarth Falls, N Yorks: Mill-Race Teashop
Bakewell, Derbys: Marguerite & Stephanie
Barden, N Yorks: Howgill Lodge
Barden, N Yorks: Low House Farm
Barnard Castle, Durham: Priors Restaurant
Bath, Avon: Canary
Bath, Avon: Pump Room
Beer, Devon: Old Lace Shop
Biddenden, Kent: Claris's Tea Shop
Billingshurst, W Sussex: Burdock Provender
Bishop's Waltham, Hants: Casey's

Blanchland, Nthmb: White Monk Tea Room

Bleasdale, Lancs: Bleasdale Post Office Tea Room

Bolton Abbey, N Yorks: Bolton Abbey Tea Cottage

Boot, Cumbria: Brook House Restaurant

Borrowdale, Cumbria: Lodore Swiss Hotel Lounge

Bournemouth, Dorset: Carlton Hotel Lounge

Bowness on Windermere, Cumbria: Laurel Cottage

Brighton, E Sussex: Food for Friends

Brighton, E Sussex: Mock Turtle

Bristol, Avon: Wild Oats II

Broad Chalke, Wilts: Cottage House

Broadway, H & W: Coffee Pot

Caldbeck, Cumbria: Swaledale Watch

Canterbury, Kent: Sweet Heart Patisserie

Castle Cary, Som: Old Bakehouse

Castle Combe, Wilts: Manor House Hotel

Castle Hedingham, Essex: Colne Valley Railway Restaurant

Castleton, Derbys: Rose Cottage Café

Castleton, N Yorks: Castleton Tea Rooms

Chagford, Devon: Coffee Pot

Cheddar, Som: Wishing Well Tea Rooms

Chester, Ches: Abbey Green

Chester, Ches: Chester Grosvenor Lounge

Clacton-on-Sea, Essex: Montague Hill China Cup Café

Clare, Suffolk: Ship Stores

Collier Street, Kent: Butcher's Mere

Compton, Surrey: Old Congregational Tea Shop

Dedham, Essex: Essex Rose Tea House

Dorking, Surrey: Burford Bridge Hotel Lounge

Dunster, Som: Tea Shoppe

Easingwold, N Yorks: Truffles

East Budleigh, Devon: Grasshoppers

Falmouth, Corn: Secrets

Findon, W Sussex: Tea House

Framlingham, Suffolk: Tiffins

Froghall, Staffs: The Wharf Eating House

23

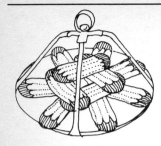

Frome, Som: Settle
Gaydon, Warks: Gaydon Lodge
Gittisham, Devon: Combe House Hotel
Great Torrington, Devon: Rebecca's
Great Torrington, Devon: Top of the Town
Guildford, Surrey: Richoux
Hailsham, E Sussex: Homely Maid
Harrogate, N Yorks: Bettys
Harrogate, N Yorks: Chimes Tea Room
Hastings, E Sussex: Judge's
Hathersage, Derbys: Country Fayre Tea Room
Hawkshead, Cumbria: Minstrel's Gallery
Henfield, W Sussex: Norton House
Henley-on-Thames, Oxon: Henley Tea Shop
Herstmonceux, E Sussex: Cleavers Lyng
Herstmonceux, E Sussex: Praise the Lord
Holmfirth, W Yorks: Wrinkled Stocking
Hurst Green, Lancs: Whitehall
Ilkley, W Yorks: Bettys
Keswick, Cumbria: Underscar Hotel
Kew, Surrey: Original Maids of Honour
Lamberhurst, Kent: The Down
Leamington Spa, Warks: Mallory Court

Leeds, W Yorks: Reed's Café
Leintwardine, H & W: Selda Coffee Shop
Luccombe Chine, I of W: Dunnose Cottage
Lustleigh, Devon: Primrose Cottage
Lyme Regis, Dorset: Golden Cap
Lyonshall, H & W: Church House
Magham Down, E Sussex: Ye Old Forge
Marlborough, Wilts: Polly
Marlow, Bucks: Burgers
Melmerby, Cumbria: Village Bakery
Middlewood, H & W: Burnt House Barn
Midsomer Norton, Avon: Mrs Pickwick
Minstead, Hants: Honey Pot
Montacute, Som: Montacute House Restaurant
New Romney, Kent: Country Kitchen
Newport, I of W: God's Providence House
Northallerton, N Yorks: Bettys
Oakham, Leics: Oakham Gallery
Offham, E Sussex: Old Post House
Otley, W Yorks: Chatters Tea Shoppe
Oxford, Oxon: Browns
Oxford, Oxon: Randolph Hotel Lounge
Painswick, Glos: Cup House
Penshurst, Kent: Fir Tree House Tea Rooms
Poole, Dorset: Inn à Nutshell
Pulborough, W Sussex: Chequers Hotel
Ringmer, E Sussex: Coffee House
Ringwood, Hants: Old Brown House
Romsey, Hants: Cobweb Tea Rooms
Romsey, Hants: Latimer Coffee House
Ross-on-Wye, H & W: Walford House Hotel
St Margaret's at Cliffe, Kent: Roses
St Michael's Mount, Corn: Sail Loft
Salisbury, Wilts: Mainly Salads

Salisbury, Wilts: Michael Snell
Scunthorpe, Humb: Bees Garden
Coffee Lounge
Seale, Surrey: Herbs
Selworthy, Som: Periwinkle Cottage
Tea Rooms
Settle, N Yorks: Car & Kitchen
Shipston on Stour, Warks: Bell Inn
Shipston on Stour, Warks: Kerry
House Tea Rooms
Shoreham-by-Sea, W Sussex:
Cuckoo Clock
Sidbury, Devon: Old Bakery
Spilsby, Lincs: Buttercross
Restaurant
Stamford, Lincs: George of Stamford
Stamford, Lincs: Mr Pips Coffee Shop
& Restaurant
Stockbridge, Hants: Old Dairy
Stow-on-the-Wold, Glos: Ingram's
Stratford-upon-Avon, Warks: Truffles
Olde Tea Shoppe
Sutton Scotney, Hants: Riverside Tea
Garden
Tewkesbury, Glos: Wintor House
Tissington, Derbys: Old School Tea
Rooms
Trebarwith Strand, Corn: House on
the Strand
Trebarwith Strand, Corn: Old Millfloor
Ullswater, Cumbria: Sharrow Bay
Country House Hotel
Walberswick, Suffolk: Potters
Wheel
Wareham, Dorset: Annies
Whitby, N Yorks: Magpie Café
Winchelsea, E Sussex: Finch of
Winchelsea
Winchelsea, E Sussex: Winchelsea
Tea Rooms
Winchester, Hants: Wessex Hotel
Coffee Shop
Windermere, Cumbria: Langdale
Chase Hotel
Windermere, Cumbria: Miller Howe
Hotel

Windsor, Berks: Windsor Chocolate
House
Woodstock, Oxon: Feathers Hotel
Lounge
Woodstock, Oxon: Linden Tea
Rooms
Woodstock, Oxon: Vanbrughs
Worthing, W Sussex: Mr Pastry
Yarm, Clev: Coffee Shop
Yarmouth, I of W: Jireh House
Yeovil, Som: Trugs
York, N Yorks: Bettys
York, N Yorks: Taylors Tearooms

SCOTLAND

Dryburgh Abbey, Bdrs: Orchard
Tearoom
Falkland, Fife: Kind Kyttock's Kitchen
Isle of Gigha, S'clyde: Gigha Hotel
Moffat, D & G: Beechwood Country
House Hotel

WALES

Aberdovey, Gwynedd: Old Coffee
Shop
Caernarfon, Gwynedd: Bakestone
Chepstow, Gwent: Willow Tree
Eglwysfach, Dyfed: Ty'n-y-Cwm Tea
Rooms
Llanrwst, Gwynedd: Tu-Hwnt-i'r-Bont
Llanycefn, Dyfed: Llain Llogin
Tynant, Clwyd: Bronnant Tea Shop
Wrexham, Clwyd: Bumbles Coffee
Shop

CHANNEL ISLANDS

St Anne's, Alderney: Gossip Coffee
Shop
Gorey, Jersey: Jersey Pottery
Restaurant
St Brelade's Bay, Jersey: Hotel
l'Horizon

The Dairy Crest Symbo

DAIRY CREST FOODS, the leading manufacturer of cheese in Britain, has joined with Egon Ronay's Guide to identify 'Just a Bite' establishments where the quality and presentat of cheese is excellent.

The inspectors for Egon Ronay's Guides have awarded the Dairy Crest Symbol of Excellence for standards which project the many characteristics and qualities of cheese. And these will be evident however cheese is served, whether as part of a tasty lunch-time snack or on an appetising cheese board.

The inspectors will also be awarding the Dairy Crest Symbol of Excellence to establishments in the two other major guides, the Hotels & Restaurants Guide and the Pub Guide. For all these awards the inspectors are particularly interested in those who, like Dairy Crest Foods, are applying the highest quality standards.

Wherever you see the Dairy Crest Symbol of Excellence, you will be sure that particular attention has been given to:

f Excellence...

QUALITY OF TASTE – through careful selection, expert handling and correct storage

QUALITY OF CHOICE – by offering traditional cheeses as well as new and local varieties

QUALITY OF VISUAL APPEAL – by using colour, texture and shape to create a mouth-watering and attractive presentation

QUALITY OF INFORMATION – by enthusiastically passing on knowledge and understanding

Dairy Crest Foods' own excellent cheeses include soft cheeses such as Lymeswold, White Lymeswold, Melbury and Medley; the reduced-fat Tendale range as well as prize-winning Cheddars, Stilton and the full range of English and Welsh traditional regional cheeses.

DAIRY CREST

OUTSTANDING CHEESEBOARDS

The following places offer a good selection of well-kept and nicely presented cheeses.

LONDON
Le Bistroquet, NW1
Bubbles Wine Bar, W1
Cork and Bottle, WC2
Cuddeford's Wine Bar, SE1
Ebury Wine Bar, SW1
Gyngleboy, W2
Le Metro, SW3
Odette's Wine Bar, NW1
Le Tire Bouchon, W1

ENGLAND
Canterbury, Cogan House
Cirencester, Fleece Hotel, Shepherd's Wine Bar
Congleton, Odd Fellows Wine Bar & Bistro
Hailsham, Waldernheath Country Restaurant
Horsforth, Stuarts Wine Bar
Hungerford, Bear, Kennet Room
Ross-on-Wye, Walford House Hotel
Stamford, George of Stamford
Stevenage, De Friese Coffee Shop
Stretton, Ram Jam Inn
Stroud, Mother Nature
Thame, Mallards
Upper Slaughter, Lords of the Manor
Wallingford, Lamb Wine Vaults
Winchester, Mr Pitkin's Wine Bar

SCOTLAND
Dulnain Bridge, Muckrach Lodge Hotel
Edinburgh, Handsel's Wine Bar
Glasgow, De Quincey's/Brahms & Liszt
Knipoch, Knipoch House Hotel

WALES
Cardiff, Champers

OPEN AIR EATING

LONDON

Anna's Place, NI
Aspava, W1
L'Autre Wine Bar, W1
Balls Brothers (Wine Bar), EC4
Bar du Musée, SE10
Blake's Wine & Food Bar, WC2
Blenheim's, NW8
Bolton's Wine Bar, SW10
Bonne Bouche Pâtisserie, W1
Boos (Wine Bar), NW1
Brasserie, SW17
La Brasserie, SW3
Bubbles Wine Bar, W1
Café Delancey, NW1
Café Fish des Amis du Vin, SW1
Café Pastiche, SW6
Café Pélican, WC2
Café St Pierre Brasserie, EC1
Charco's Wine Bar, SW3
Chequers, NW1
Cherry Orchard, E2
Le Cochonnet, W9
Crêperie, W1
Di's Larder, SW11
Earth Exchange, N6
Efes Kebab House, W1
Falafel House, NW3
Fino's Wine Cellar, North Row, W1
Flamingo (Wine Bar), SW1
Govindas, W1
Granary, W1
Gyngleboy, W2
Hard Rock Café, W1
Harvey Nichols, Harveys at the Top, SW1
Hoults (Wine Bar), SW17

Justin de Blank at General Trading Company, SW1
Lincoln's Inn Wine Bar, WC2
Lou Pescadou, SW5
Macarthurs, SW13
Manna, NW3
Methuselah's (Wine Bar), SW1
Mother Huffs, NW3
No 77 Wine Bar, NW6
Oliver's, W14
Ormes Wine Bar & Restaurant, SW4
Pasta Connection, SW3
Pâtisserie Parisienne, W8
Le Plat du Jour, NW1
Punters Pie, SW11
Raoul's, W9
Ravenscourt Park Tea House, W6
Raw Deal, W1
Soho Brasserie, W1
Spirals Wine Bar & Restaurant, NW3
Twenty Trinity Gardens, SW9
Verbanella Pasta Bar, W1
Wilkins Natural Foods, SW1
Wine Gallery, SW3, SW10, W11

ENGLAND

Abbots Bromley, Staffs: Marsh Farm
Alfriston, E Sussex: Drusillas
Alston, Cumbria: Brownside Coach House
Alstonefield, Staffs: Old Post Office
Altrincham, Greater Manchester: Gander's
Ambleside, Cumbria: Rothay Manor
Ambleside, Cumbria: Zeffirellis
Amersham, Bucks: Willow Tree
Ashtead, Surrey: Bart's

Avebury, Wilts: Stones Restaurant
Bakewell, Derbys: Green Apple
Bamburgh, Nthmb: Copper Kettle
Banham, Norfolk: Banham
  Bakehouse
Barden, N Yorks: Howgill Lodge
Bath, Avon: Bath Puppet Theatre
Bath, Avon: Beaujolais Restaurant
Bath, Avon: Moon & Sixpence
Berkhamsted, Herts: Cooks Delight
Berwick upon Tweed, Nthmb: Wine
  Bar
Biddenden, Kent: Claris's Tea Shop
Billingshurst, W Sussex: Burdock
  Provender
Birmingham, W Mid: La Galleria
Birmingham, W Mid: La Santé
Bishop's Lydeard, Som: Rose
  Cottage
Bishop's Waltham, Hants: Casey's
Bolton Abbey, N Yorks: Bolton Abbey
  Tea Cottage
Boot, Cumbria: Brook House
Borrowdale, Cumbria: Lodore Swiss
  Hotel Lounge
Bournemouth, Dorset: Carlton Hotel
Bourton-on-the-Water, Glos: Small
  Talk Tea Room
Bowdon, Ches: Griffin
Bowness on Windermere, Cumbria:
  Laurel Cottage
Bowness on Windermere, Cumbria:
  Trattoria Pizzeria Ticino
Braithwaite, Cumbria: Book Cottage
Bridgnorth, Shrops: Sophie's
Bridgwater, Som: Nutmeg
Bristol, Avon: Arnolfini Café-Bar
Bristol, Avon: Wild Oats II
Broad Chalke, Wilts: Cottage House
Broadway, H & W: Collin House Hotel
Bury St Edmunds, Suffolk:
  Beaumonts
Cambridge, Cambs: Waffles
Canterbury, Kent: Crotchets
Canterbury, Kent: Il Vaticano Pasta
  Parlour

Canterbury, Kent: Sweet Heart
  Patisserie
Carlisle, Cumbria: Hudson's Coffee
  Shop
Castle Cary, Som: Old Bakehouse
Castle Combe, Wilts: Manor House
Castleton, Derbys: Rose Cottage
Castleton, N Yorks: Castleton Tea
  Rooms
Cattawade, Essex: Bucks Wine Bar
Chatham, Kent: Simson's Wine Bar
Cheltenham, Glos: Choirs Tea Rooms
Cheltenham, Glos: Langtry Pâtisserie
  & Tea Rooms
Cheltenham, Glos: Montpellier Wine
  Bar & Bistro
Cheltenham, Glos: Retreat (Wine Bar)
Chester, Ches: Abbey Green
Chester, Ches: Pierre Griffe Wine Bar
Chichester, W Sussex: St Martin's
  Tea Rooms
Chichester, W Sussex: Savourie
Chipping Campden, Glos: Kings Arms
  Hotel, Saddle Room
Chipping Norton, Oxon: Nutters
Cirencester, Glos: Fleece Hotel,
  Shepherds Wine Bar
Clare, Suffolk: Ship Stores
Collier Street, Kent: Butcher's Mere
Compton, Surrey: Old Congregational
  Tea Shop
Congleton, Ches: Odd Fellows Wine
  Bar & Bistro
Coniston, Cumbria: Bridge House
Corse Lawn, Glos: Corse Lawn
  House
Dartington, Devon: Cranks Health
  Food Restaurant
Dent, Cumbria: Dent Crafts Centre
Derby, Derbys: Lettuce Leaf
Devizes, Wilts: Wiltshire Kitchen
Dodd Wood, Cumbria: Old Sawmill
Dorchester, Dorset: Potter In
Dorking, Surrey: Burford Bridge Hotel
Dorstone, H & W: Pump House Tea
  Room

Easingwold, N Yorks: Truffles
Emsworth, Hants: Cloisters
Eton, Berks: Eton Wine Bar
Exeter, Devon: Clare's Restaurant
Falmouth, Corn: Secrets
Faversham, Kent: Recreation Tavern
Findon, W Sussex: Tea House
Frome, Som: Settle
Gaydon, Warks: Gaydon Lodge
Gittisham, Devon: Combe House
Glastonbury, Som: Rainbow's End
Grange-in-Borrowdale, Cumbria: Grange Bridge Cottage
Grange-over-Sands, Cumbria: At Home
Grantham, Lincs: Knightingales
Grasmere, Cumbria: Coffee Bean
Grasmere, Cumbria: Rowan Tree
Great Barton, Suffolk: Craft at the Suffolk Barn
Guildford, Surrey: Richoux
Hailsham, E Sussex: Waldernheath Country Restaurant
Hastings, E Sussex: Brant's
Hawes, N Yorks: Cockett's Hotel
Henfield, W Sussex: Norton House
Hereford, H & W: Fodder
Herstmonceux, E Sussex: Cleavers Lyng
High Lorton, Cumbria: White Ash Barn
Holmfirth, W Yorks: Wrinkled Stocking
Hope, Derbys: Hopechest
Hungerford, Berks: Bear, Kennet Room
Huntingdon, Cambs: Old Bridge Hotel
Hurst Green, Lancs: Whitehall
Ipswich, Suffolk: Belstead Brook Hotel Lounge
Kendal, Cumbria: The Moon
Kendal, Cumbria: Nutters
Kendal, Cumbria: Waterside Wholefoods
Kenilworth, Warks: Castle Green Tea Shop

Kents Bank, Cumbria: Abbot Hall
Keswick, Cumbria: Underscar Hotel
Lamberhurst, Kent: The Down
Lancaster, Lancs: Libra
Leamington Spa, Warks: Mallory Court
Ledbury, H & W: Verzons Country Hotel Bistro
Leeds, W Yorks: Flying Pizza
Lewes, E Sussex: Mike's Wine Bar
Limpsfield, Surrey: Limpsfield Brasserie
Lincoln, Lincs: Wig & Mitre
Lower Basildon, Berks: Cottage Restaurant & Tea Rooms
Luccombe Chine, I of W: Dunnose Cottage
Ludlow, Shrops: Hardwicks
Lustleigh, Devon: Primrose Cottage
Lynton, Devon: Lee Cottage
Lyonshall, H & W: Church House
Lytchett Minster, Dorset: Slepe Cottage Tea Rooms
Magham Down, E Sussex: Ye Old Forge
Mawgan, Corn: Yard Bistro
Mentmore, Beds: Stable Yard Craft Gallery & Tea Room
Midsomer Norton, Avon: Mrs Pickwick
Minstead, Hants: Honey Pot
Moreton-in-Marsh, Glos: Market House
Newark, Notts: Gannets
Newbury, Berks: Crafty Cat
Newcastle upon Tyne, Tyne & Wear: Mather's
Newhaven, E Sussex: Kenya Coffee House
Norwich, Norfolk: Britons Arms
Offham, E Sussex: Old Post House
Otley, W Yorks: Chatters Tea Shoppe
Oxford, Oxon: Browns
Oxford, Oxon: St Aldate's Church Coffee House

Painswick, Glos: Cup House
Painswick, Glos: Painswick Hotel
Penrith, Cumbria: Bluebell Tearoom
Penshurst, Kent: Fir Tree House
Plumtree, Notts: Perkins Bar Bistro
Portsmouth (Southsea), Hants:
    Rosie's Vineyard (Wine Bar)
Pulborough, W Sussex: Chequers
    Hotel
Richmond, Surrey: Mrs Beeton
Richmond, Surrey: Refectory
Richmond, Surrey: Wildefoods
    Wholefood Café
Ringwood, Hants: Old Brown House
Romsey, Hants: Cobweb Tea Rooms
Romsey, Hants: Latimer Coffee
    House
Ross-on-Wye, H & W: Walford House
Rottingdean, E Sussex: Old Cottage
    Tea Rooms
Rottingdean, E Sussex: Rottingdean
    Pâtisserie
Rowlands Castle, Hants: Coffee Pot
Ryton-on-Dunsmore, Warks: Ryton
    Gardens Café
St Albans, Herts: Kingsbury Mill
    Waffle House
St Margaret's at Cliffe, Kent: Roses
St Mary's, Corn: Tregarthens Hotel
Salisbury, Wilts: Michael Snell
Seale, Surrey: Herbs
Selworthy, Som: Periwinkle Cottage
Shipston on Stour, Warks: Bell Inn
Shipton, N Yorks: Beningbrough Hall
Shoreham-by-Sea, W Sussex:
    Cuckoo Clock
Sidbury, Devon: Old Bakery
Spetisbury, Dorset: Marigold Cottage
    Tea Rooms
Spilsby, Lincs: Buttercross
    Restaurant
Stamford, Lincs: George of Stamford
Stevenage, Herts: De Friese Coffee
    Shop
Stonham Aspal, Suffolk: Stonham
    Barns

Stow-on-the-Wold, Glos: Wyck Hill
    House
Stratford-upon-Avon, Warks: Slug &
    Lettuce
Stratford-upon-Avon, Warks: Truffles
    Olde Tea Shoppe
Stretton, Leics: Ram Jam Inn
Sutton Scotney, Hants: Riverside Tea
    Garden
Tarr Steps, Som: Tarr Farm
Tetbury, Glos: Calcot Manor
Thames Ditton, Surrey: Skiffers
Tissington, Derbys: Old School Tea
    Rooms
Tiverton, Devon: Hendersons
Totnes, Devon: Planters
Totnes, Devon: Willow
Trebarwith Strand, Corn: House on
    the Strand
Trebarwith Strand, Corn: Old Millfloor
Tunbridge Wells, Kent: Buster
    Browns
Tunbridge Wells, Kent: Delicious
Tunbridge Wells, Kent: Downstairs at
    Thackeray's
Tutbury, Staffs: Corn Mill Tea
    Room
Upper Slaughter, Glos: Lords of the
    Manor Hotel
Walton on the Naze, Essex: Naze
    Links Café
Wansford-in-England, Cambs:
    Haycock Hotel Lounge
Wantage, Oxon: Vale & Downland
    Museum Centre
Wareham, Dorset: Annies
Warminster, Wilts: Jenner's
Warminster, Wilts: Vincent's
Waterperry, Oxon: Waterperry
    Gardens Tea Shop
Wells, Som: Good Earth
Westbourne, Dorset: Hollywood!
Williton, Som: Blackmore's Bookshop
    Tea Room
Windermere, Cumbria: Langdale
    Chase Hotel

Windermere, Cumbria: Miller Howe
Windsor, Berks: Dôme
Wokingham, Berks: Setters Bistro
Woodstock, Oxon: Feathers Hotel
    Lounge & Garden Bar
Woodstock, Oxon: Linden Tea
    Rooms
Wool, Dorset: Rose Mullion Tea
    Rooms
Woolpit, Suffolk: The Bakery
Worcester, H & W: Natural BreaK
    (Hopmarket)
Worthing, W Sussex: Fogarty's
Yarm, Clev: Coffee Shop
Yeovil, Som: Clarries
York, N Yorks: Gillygate Wholefood
    Café
York, N Yorks: St Williams College
    Restaurant

SCOTLAND

Aberfeldy, T'side: Country Fare
    Coffee House
Arisaig, H'land: Old Library Lodge &
    Restaurant
Buckie, Gram'n: Old Monastery
Colbost, H'land: Three Chimneys
Dirleton, Loth: Open Arms Hotel
Dulnain Bridge, H'land: Muckrach
    Lodge Hotel
Edinburgh, Loth: Laigh Kitchen
Edinburgh, Loth: Waterfront Wine Bar
Falkirk, Central: Healthy Life
Isle of Gigha, S'clyde: Gigha Hotel
Kentallen of Appin, H'land: Holly Tree
Kilchrenan, S'clyde: Taychreggan
    Hotel
Kildonan, H'land: Three Rowans Tea
    Shop & Restaurant
Kincraig, H'land: Boathouse
Knipoch, S'clyde: Knipoch Hotel
Lamlash, S'clyde: Glenscorrodale
    Farm Tearoom
Moffat, D & G: Beechwood Country
    House Hotel
New Abbey, D & G: Abbey Cottage

Newcastleton, Bdrs: Copshaw
    Kitchen
Peebles, Bdrs: Kailzie Garden
    Restaurant & Tea Room
Pitlochry, T'side: Luggie Restaurant
Powmill, T'side: Powmill Milk Bar
Selkirk, Bdrs: Philipburn House Hotel
Tayvallich, S'clyde: Tayvallich Inn
Tomintoul, Gram'n: Glenmulliach
    Restaurant
Ullapool, H'land: Ceilidh Place
Wester Howgate, Loth: Old Howgate
    Inn, Coach House

WALES

Aberaeron, Dyfed: Hive on the Quay
Cardiff, Mid-Glamorgan: Sage
Chepstow, Gwent: Willow Tree
Eglwysfach, Dyfed: Ty'n-y-Cwm Tea
    Rooms
Hay-on-Wye, Powys: Granary
Keeston, Dyfed: Keeston Kitchen
Llangollen, Clwyd: Gales Wine & Food
    Bar
Llanycefn, Dyfed: Llain Llogin
Machynlleth, Powys: Centre for
    Alternative Technology
Menai Bridge, Gwynedd: Jodies
Newport, Dyfed: Cnapan
Wolf's Castle, Dyfed: Wolfscastle
    Country Hotel

CHANNEL ISLANDS

St Anne's, Alderney: Gossip Coffee
    Shop
St Peter Port, Guernsey: Flying
    Dutchman Hotel
Gorey, Jersey: Jersey Pottery
    Restaurant
St Brelade's Bay, Jersey: Hotel
    l'Horizon

ISLE OF MAN

Douglas, Isle of Man: L'Experience

WHOLEFOOD & VEGETARIAN RESTAURANTS

LONDON

Beehive, 11a Beehive Place, SW9
Chequers, 18 Chalk Farm Road, NW1
Cherry Orchard, 241 Globe Road, E2
Christys Healthline, 122 Wardour Street, W1
Country Life, 1 Heddon Street, W1
Cranks, 17 Great Newport Street, W1
Cranks, 9 Tottenham Street, W1
Cranks Health Food Restaurant, 8 Marshall Street, W1
Di's Larder, 62 Lavender Hill, SW11
Dining Room, Winchester Walk, off Cathedral Street, SE1
Diwana Bhelpoori House, 114 Drummond Street, NW1; 121 Drummond Street, NW1; 50 Westbourne Grove, W2
Earth Exchange, 213 Archway Road, N6
East West Restaurant, 188 Old Street, EC1
Fallen Angel, 65 Graham Street, N1
First Out, 52 St Giles High Street, WC2
Food for Health, 13 Blackfriars Lane, EC4
Food for Thought, 31 Neal Street, WC2
Govindas, 9 Soho Street, W1
Harrods, Health Juice Bar, Knightsbridge, SW1
Mandeer, 21 Hanway Place, Tottenham Court Road, W1
Manna, 4 Erskine Road, NW3
Millward's, 97 Stoke Newington Church Street, N16
Neal's Yard Bakery & Tea Room, 6 Neal's Yard, Covent Garden, WC2
Neal's Yard Bakery at the Ecology Centre, 45 Shelton Street, WC2
Nuthouse, 26 Kingly Street, W1
Raj Bhelpoori House, 19 Camden High Street, NW1
Rani, 3 Long Lane, N3
Ravenscourt Park Tea House, Ravenscourt Park, W6
Ravi Shankar, 135 Drummond Street, NW1
Raw Deal, 65 York Street, W1
Sabras, 263 High Road, Willesden Green, NW10
Slenders, 41 Cathedral Place, Paternoster Square, EC4
Suruchi, 18 Theberton Street, N1
Wholemeal Vegetarian Café, 1 Shrubbery Road, SW16

Wilkins Natural Foods, 61 Marsham Street, SW1
Windmill Wholefood Restaurant, 486 Fulham Road SW6
Woodlands Restaurant, 77 Marylebone Lane, W1; 37 Panton Street, SW1;
 402a High Road, Wembley, Middx

ENGLAND
Altrincham, Greater Manchester: Nutcracker Vegetarian Restaurant
Ambleside, Cumbria: Harvest
Ambleside, Cumbria: Zeffirellis
Ashtead, Surrey: Bart's
Avebury, Wilts: Stones Restaurant
Aylesbury, Bucks: Wild Oats
Barnard Castle Co. Durham: Priors Restaurant
Berkhamsted, Herts: Cook's Delight
Birmingham, W Mid: Gingers
Birmingham, W Mid: La Santé
Birmingham, W Mid: Wild Oats
Bournemouth, Dorset: Flossie's
Bournemouth, Dorset: Salad Centre
Bowness on Windermere, Cumbria: Hedgerow
Brighton (Hove), E Sussex: Blossoms
Brighton, E Sussex: Food for Friends
Brighton, E Sussex: Saxon's
Bristol, Avon: Wild Oats II
Bury St Edmunds, Suffolk: Beaumonts
Cambridge, Cambs: Nettles
Castle Cary, Som: Old Bakehouse
Cauldon Lowe, Staffs: Staffordshire Peak Arts Centre

Chester, Ches: Abbey Green
Chichester, W Sussex: Clinch's Salad House
Chichester, W Sussex: St Martin's Tea Rooms
Christchurch, Dorset: Salads
Cockermouth, Cumbria: Quince & Medlar
Coventry, W Mid: Trinity House Hotel, Herbs Restaurant
Croydon, Surrey: Hockneys
Croydon, Surrey: Munbhave
Dartington, Devon: Cranks Health Food Restaurant
Derby, Derbys: Lettuce Leaf
Eastbourne, E Sussex: Ceres Health Food Restaurant
Eastbourne, E Sussex: Nature's Way
Glastonbury, Som: Rainbow's End Café
Gosforth, Tyne & Wear: Girl on a Swing
Grantham, Lincs: Knightingales
Hastings, E Sussex: Brant's
Hereford, H & W: Fodder
Hereford, H & W: Marches
Hythe, Kent: Natural Break
Ipswich, Suffolk: Marno's Restaurant
Kendal, Cumbria: Eat Fit
Kendal, Cumbria: Waterside Wholefoods
Lancaster, Lancs: Libra
Leicester, Leics: Blossoms
Ludlow, Shrops: Olive Branch
Much Wenlock, Shrops: Scott's Coffee & Wholefood Shop
Newcastle upon Tyne, Tyne & Wear: Madeleine's
Northenden, Greater Manchester: Nut 'n' Meg

Norwich, Norfolk: Café La Tienda
Nottingham, Notts: Ten
Penrith, Cumbria: Bluebell Tearoom
Poole, Dorset: Inn à Nutshell
Portsmouth (Southsea), Hants: Country Kitchen
Richmond, Surrey: Richmond Harvest
Richmond, Surrey: Wildefoods Wholefood Café
Ryton-on-Dunsmore, Warks: Ryton Gardens Café
Salisbury, Wilts: Mainly Salads
Shrewsbury, Shrops: Delany's
Skipton, N Yorks: Herbs Wholefood & Vegetarian Restaurant
Stockport, Greater Manchester: Coconut Willy's
Stroud, Glos: Mother Nature
Swindon, Wilts: Acorn Wholefoods
Tiverton, Devon: Angel Foods
Totnes, Devon: Willow
Tunbridge Wells, Kent: Pilgrims
Ware, Herts: Sunflowers
Wareham, Dorset: Annies
Warley, W Mid: Wild Thyme
Warminster, Wilts: Jenner's
Wells, Som: Good Earth
Worcester, H & W: Natural Break
Worthing, W Sussex: Hannah
Worthing, W Sussex: Nature's Way Coffee Shop
Yeovil, Som: Trugs
York, N Yorks: Gillygate Wholefood Café

SCOTLAND

Edinburgh, Loth: Country Kitchen
Edinburgh, Loth: Helios Fountain
Edinburgh, Loth: Henderson's Salad Table
Edinburgh, Loth: Kalpna
Falkirk, Central: Healthy Life
Peebles, Bdrs: Sunflower
St Andrews, Fife: Brambles

WALES

Cardiff, Mid-Glamorgan: Sage
Carmarthen, Dyfed: Waverley Restaurant
Machynlleth, Powys: Centre for Alternative Technology
Machynlleth, Powys: Quarry Shop
Newport, Dyfed: Cnapan
Newport, Gwent: Happy Carrot Bistro
Newtown, Powys: Jays

Egon Ronay's
PUB GUIDE 1987

TO BAR FOOD AND ACCOMMODATION IN BRITISH PUBS AND INNS

- The best British bar snacks and meals
- Highly selective
- Surprising gastronomic finds at low prices
- Pubs that welcome children
- Homely, clean and pleasant bedrooms
- Excellent breakfasts

Plus pubs specially selected for atmosphere and historic interest.

Available from AA Centres and booksellers everywhere at £4.95 or £5.95 including postage and packing from:

Mail Order Department
PO Box 51
Basingstoke
Hampshire
RG21 2BR

LUNCHEON VOUCHERS ACCEPTED

LONDON
Aspava, W1
L'Autre Wine Bar, W1
Balls Brothers, EC2 & EC4
Beehive, SW2
Bentley's Wine Bar & Oyster Bar, W1
Blake's Wine & Food Bar, WC2
Blooms, NW11 & E1
Bonne Bouche Pâtisserie, W1
Bubbles Wine Bar, W1
Canton, WC2
Cherry Orchard, E2
Christys Healthline, W1
City Friends, EC4
Country Life, W1
Cranks, WC2 & W1
Cranks Health Food Restaurant, W1
Crêperie, W1
Criterion Brasserie, W1
Da Gianbruno, W6
Daly's Wine Bar, WC2
Daquise, SW7
Diwana Bhel-Poori House, W2 & NW1
Downs Wine Bar, W1
East West Restaurant, EC1
Efes Kebab House, W1
Fallen Angel, N1
Fino's Wine Cellar, WC2 & W1
First Out, WC2
Flamingo, SW1
Food for Health, EC4
Food for Thought, WC2
Garbanzo Coffee House, EC1
Geale's, W8
Gino's, W5
Govindas, W1
Granary, W1
Gurkhas Tandoori, W1
Hat Shop, W12
Jeeves Wine Cellar, W1
Justin de Blank, W1
Justin de Blank at General Trading
  Company, SW1

Kitchen Yakitori, W1
Lincoln's Inn Wine Bar, WC2
Lindas, W9
Lok Ho Fook, W1
Loon Fung, W1
Lou Pescadou, SW5
Macarthurs, SW13
Maha Gopal, W1
Maison Bertaux, W1
Maison Bouquillon, Le Montmartre, W2
Maison Pechon Pâtisserie Française, W2
Mandeer, W1
Marine Ices, NW3
Maxim, W7 & SW1
Muffin Man, W8
National Gallery Restaurant, WC2
Neal's Yard Bakery & Tea Room, WC2
Neal's Yard Bakery at the Ecology
  Centre, WC2
New Shu Shan, WC2
Nosherie, EC1
Nuthouse, W1
Palings Wine Bar, W1
Parsons, SW10
Pasticceria Amalfi, W1
Pasticceria Cappucetto, W1
Pâtisserie Valerie, W1
Pavilion Wine Bar, EC2
Raj Bhelpoori House, NW1
Raoul's, W9
Ravenscourt Park Tea House, W6
Ravi Shankar, NW1
Raw Deal, W1
Richoux, W1 & SW3
Rouxl Britannia, Le Café, EC2
Royal Festival Hall, Riverside Café, SE1
Sabras, NW10
Sagarmatha, NW1
Seashell, NW1 & E8
Slenders, EC4
Soho Brasserie, W1
Sweetings, EC4

Swiss Centre, Swiss Imbiss, W1
Le Tire Bouchon, W1
Trattoria Imperia, WC2
Tuxedo Junction, NW6
Verbanella, SW3
Verbanella Pasta Bar, W1
Village Delicatessen & Coffee Shop, W14
Wilkins Natural Foods, SW1

ENGLAND
Alstonefield Old Post Office
Altrincham, Ganders
Ashford, Il Cardinale Pasta Parlour
Aylesbury, Wild Oats
Bath, Canary
Bath, The Walrus & The Carpenter
Berkhamstead, Cook's Delight
Bexhill, Trawlers
Billericay, Webber's Wine Bar
Birmingham, Boots Time for a Break
Birmingham, Drucker's
Birmingham, La Galleria Wine Bar
Bournemouth, Coriander
Bournemouth, Flossies & Bossies
Bournemouth, Salad Centre
Bradford, Pizza Margherita
Braintree, Braintree Curry Palace
Bridgwater, Nutmeg
Brighton, Food for Friends
Brighton, Goodies
Bristol, Arnolfini Café-Bar
Bristol, Edwards
Bristol, Rainbow Café
Bristol, Wild Oats II
Bromley, Hollywood Bowl
Burnley, Butterfingers
Bury St Edmunds, Beaumonts
Canterbury, Crochet's
Canterbury, Il Vaticano Pasta Parlour
Canterbury, JV's City Brasserie
Canterbury, Pizza Place
Carlisle, Hudson's Coffee Shop
Castle Combe, Manor House Hotel
Chatham, Simson's Wine Bar
Cheam, Superfish
Cheltenham, Langtry
Cheltenham, Montpellier Wine Bar
Cheltenham, Promenade Pâtisserie
Cheltenham, Retreat
Chester, Abbey Green

Chester, Farmhouse
Chester, Pierre Griffe Wine Bar
Chichester, Chats Brasserie
Chichester, Clinch's Salad House
Chislehurst, Mrs Bridges' Kitchen
Christchurch, Salads
Clitheroe, The Castle
Croydon, Hockneys
Dartington, Cranks
Derby, Lettuce Leaf
Dorking, Burford Bridge Hotel Lounge
East Molesey, Superfish
Eastbourne, Ceres Health Food
   Restaurant
Eastbourne, Nature's Way
Eastleigh, Piccolo Mondo
Ewell, Superfish
Exeter, Clare's Restaurant
Exeter, Cooling's Wine Bar
Grays, R. Mumford & Son
Great Torrington, Rebecca's
Great Yarmouth, Friends Bistro
Guildford, Richoux
Harrogate, Bettys
Hastings, Brant's
Hastings, Judge's
Henley-on-Thames, Barnaby's
Hereford, Marches
Ipswich, Marno's Restaurant
Ipswich, Tackets
Kendal, Corner Spot Eating House
Kew, Wine & Mousaka
Lancaster, Potters Coffee House
Leamington Spa, Regency Fare
Leeds, Ike's Bistro
Leeds, Reed's Café
Leeds, Strawberryfield Bistro
Leicester, Blossoms
Leicester, Peacock Alley
Leintwardine, Selda Coffee Shop
Lewes, Lunch Counter
Lewes, Pattisson's Coffee Shop
Lincoln, Wig & Mitre
Liverpool, Armadillo Restaurant
Liverpool, Everyman Bistro
Liverpool, La Grande Bouffe
Liverpool, Mandarin
Lytham, Lytham Kitchen
Manchester, Woo Sang
Manchester, Yang Sing
Market Harborough, Taylor's
Midsomer Norton, Mrs Pickwick

Morden, Superfish
Newcastle upon Tyne, Mather's
Newcastle upon Tyne, Roulade Crêperie & Brasserie
Newmarket, Jane's Wine Bar
Northampton, Lawrence's
Norwich, Waffle House
Nottingham, Alice's Restaurant
Nottingham, Café Punchinello
Nottingham, New Orleans Diner
Nottingham, Pagoda
Oxford, Go Dutch
Oxford, St Aldate's Coffee House
Parkgate, Champers
Poole, Inn a Nutshell
Portsmouth, Country Kitchen
Reading, Wine Butts
Richmond, Richmond Harvest
Salisbury, Mainly Salads
Salisbury, Mo's
Seaford, Trawlers
Sheffield, Toff's
Shipston-on-Stour, Bell Inn
Shoreham-by-Sea, Cuckoo Clock
Shrewsbury, Delany's
Southampton, La Lupa 4
Southampton, La Margherita
Southampton, Piccolo Mondo I
Stevenage, De Friese Coffee Shop
Stockport, Coconut Willy's
Stratford-upon-Avon, Pinocchio
Surbiton, Fortunes
Surbiton, Liberty Bell
Swindon, Acorn Wholefoods
Tiverton, Red Fox

Tolworth, Superfish
Tunbridge Wells, Buster Browns
Tunbridge Wells, Delicious
Tunbridge Wells, Downstairs at Thackeray's
Tunbridge Wells, Pilgrims
Tunbridge Wells, Pizza Piazza
Walton on the Naze, Naze Links Café
Warwick, Bar Roussel
West Byfleet, Superfish
Westbourne, Hollywood
Winchester, Cloisters
Winchester, Wessex Hotel
Woodlands, Three Cranes
Worcester, Heroes
Worcester, Natural Break
Worthing, Nature's Way Coffee Shop
Yeovil, Clarries
Yeovil, Trugs
York, York Wholefood Restaurant

SCOTLAND
Buckie, Old Monastery
Edinburgh, Country Kitchen
Edinburgh, Henderson's Salad Table
Falkirk, Coffee Cabin
Glasgow, Tom Sawyer's

WALES
Aberystwyth, Connexion
Wrexham, Bumbles Coffee Shop

ISLE OF MAN
Castletown, Golf Links Hotel

SUNDAY EATING IN BRITAIN'S MAJOR CENTRES

LONDON
Ajanta, W12   noon–2.30 & 6–midnight
Aspava, W1   noon–midnight
Athenaeum Hotel, Windsor Lounge, W1   24 hours
Bar du Musée, SE10   noon–3 & 6.30–11
La Bersagliera, SW3   12.30–3 & 7–midnight
Bill Stickers, W1   noon–3am
Le Bistroquet, NW1   noon–6 & 7–11
Blake's Wine & Food Bar, WC2   11.45–10
Blenheim's, NW8   noon–3 & 7–midnight
Blooms, E1   11.30–10
Blooms, NW11   noon–9.30
Bolton's Wine Bar, SW10   noon–2
Bon Ton Roulet, SE24   12.30–3
Bonne Bouche Pâtisserie, W1   9–6
Brasserie, SW17   noon–3 & 7–11
La Brasserie, SW3   10am–midnight
Brown's, W1   8.30am–12.30am
Le Café du Jardin, WC2   noon–10
Café Pacifico, WC2   noon–2.45 & 7–10.45
Café Pélican, WC2   11am–2am
Canton, WC2   24hours
Carriages, SW1   (summer only) 11.30–2.30 & 5.30–10.30
Chequers, NW1   10am–12.30am
Chiang Mai, W1   noon–3 & 6–11
Chicago Pizza Pie Factory, W1   noon–10.30
Chicago Rib Shack, SW7   noon–11
Chuen Cheng Ku, W1   11am–11.30pm
La Cloche, NW6   noon–3 & 7–midnight
Le Cochonnet, W9   noon–2.45 & 7–10.45
Cork & Bottle Wine Bar, WC2   noon–2 & 7–10.30
Da Gianbruno, W6   Noon–3 & 6–11.30
Daquise, SW7   10am–11.30pm
Diwana Bhel-Poori House (114 Drummond St) NW1   noon–10
Diwana Bhel-Poori House (121 Drummond St) NW1   noon–midnight
Diwana Bhel-Poori House (50 Westbourne Grove) W2   noon–11

Dorchester Hotel, Promenade, W1   9am–1am
Downs Wine Bar, W1   noon–2.30 & 7–10.30
Draycott's (Wine Bar) SW3   11–2.30 & 7–10.30
Earth Exchange, N6   noon–4 & 6–10.30
East West Restaurant, EC2   11–3
Ebury Wine Bar, SW1   noon–2.45 & 6.30–10.30
Equatorial, W1   noon–3 & 6–11
Fallen Angel, W1   12.30–9
Gachons, SE10   11–5.30
Gino's (Wine Bar) W5   7–11.30
Goring Hotel Lounge, SW1   10–6
Govindas, W1   12.30–3.30
Green Cottage, NW3   noon–11.30
Grill St Quentin, SW13   noon–4 & 7–11
Grosvenor House, Park lounge, W1   3–5.30
Grosvenor House, Pavilion Espresso Bar, W1   7am–10.30pm
Gurkhas Tandoori, W1   noon–3 & 6–midnight
Hard Rock Café, W1   noon–12.15am
Harry Morgan's, NW8   noon–10
Hoults (wine bar) SW17   12.30–2.45 & 7–10.30
Hung Toa, W2   noon–11
Hyatt Carlton Tower, Chinoiserie, SW1   8am–1am
Hyde Park Hotel, Park Room, SW1   8am–11am & 4–6
Ikkyu, W1   7pm–10.30pm
Inn on the Park, W1   9am–1pm
International Hotel, Coffee House, W1   7am–2am
Ipphei, NW3   12.30–3 & 6–10.30
Jade Garden, W1   noon–10.30
Joe Allen, WC2   noon–midnight
Joy King Lau, WC2   11–10.30
Julie's Bar, W11   11–10.30
L.S. Grunts Chicago Pizza Co., WC2   noon–9
Lantern, NW6   noon–3 & 7–midnight
Laurent, NW2   noon–2 & 6–11
Ley-On's, W1   11.30am–11.30pm
Lok Ho Fook, W1   noon–1am
London Marriott Hotel, Regent Lounge, W1   24 hours
Loon Fung, W1   noon–12.30am
Louis Pâtisserie (Harben Parade) NW3   9–6
Louis Pâtisserie (Heath Street), NW3   9.30–6
Macarthurs, SW13   12.30–11.30
Maha Gopal, W1   noon–3 & 7–11.30
Maison Bouquillon, Le Montmarte, W2   8.30am–9.30pm
Maison Pechon Pâtisserie Française, W2   10–5
Manna, NW3   6.30–midnight
Marine Ices, NW3   11–9 (winter till 7)

Matono, W1   6pm–midnight
Maxim (wine bar), W7   noon–2 & 7–10.30
Maxim (wine bar), SW1   11.30–2.30 & 6.30–10.30
Le Meridien Piccadilly, W1   8am–2am
Millwards, N16   noon–midnight
Mulford's Wine Bar, W6   noon–3 & 7–10.30
Nakamura, W1   6–10.30
National Gallery Restaurant, WC2   2pm–5pm
New Kam Tong, W2   noon–11.15
New Loon Fung, W1   11–10.30
New Shu Shan, WC2   noon–midnight
No 77 Wine Bar, NW6   7–10.30
Old Heidelberg Pâtisserie, W4   7–10.30
Oliver's, W14   noon–4.20 & 6.15–10.20
Ormes Wine Bar & Restaurant, SW4   noon–2.30 & 6.30–11
Parsons, SW10   noon–midnight
Pasta Underground, NW1   noon–3 & 6–11
Pasticceria Amalfi, W1   10.30am–11pm
Pasticceria Cappuccetto, W1   7.30am–8pm
Pâtisserie Parisienne, W8   10–6
The Peck Provender, N1   11–10.30
Le Petit Prince, NW5   7pm–11.30pm
Pigeon, SW6   noon–3 & 7–midnight
Poons, WC2   noon–11.30
Portman Hotel, Portman Corner, W1   11am–midnight
Punters Pie, SW1   noon–3 & 7–11.30
Raffles, NW6   noon–midnight
Raj Bhelpoori House, NW1   noon–11.30
Rani, N3   12.30–2 & 6–10.30
Raoul's, W9   8.30–6.30
Ravenscourt Park Tea House, W6   10–6
Ravi Shankar, NW1   noon–11
Richoux (Brompton Rd) SW3   10–7
Richoux (Piccadilly), W1   10am–11.30pm
Richoux (South Audley St), W1   10am–11.30pm
The Ritz, Palm Court, W1   10–2, 3.30–5.30 & 6–10.30
Royal Festival Hall, Riverside Café, SE1   10–10
Royal Lancaster Hotel Lounge, W2   11–11
Sabras, NW10   12.30–9.15
Sagarmatha, NW1   noon–2.45 & 6–11.45
The Savoy, Thames Foyer, WC2   10am–midnight
Sheraton Park Tower Restaurant, SW1   6.30am–midnight
Smollensky's Balloon, W1   noon–10.30
Spirals Wine Bar & Restaurant, NW3   noon–3 & 7–11
Spread Eagle, SE10   noon–3
Suruchi, N1   noon–3 & 6–11

Swiss Centre, Swiss Imbiss, W1   11.30–9
Tea-Time, SW4   10–7
Topkapi, W1   noon–midnight
Tui, SW7   12.30–3 & 7–10.30
Tuxedo Junction, NW6   12.30–3 & 7–10.30
209 Thai Restaurant, W8   noon–3 & 6–10.30
Victoria & Albert Museum, New Restaurant, SW7   2.30–5.30
Village Delicatessen & Coffee Shop, W14   10–2
Waldorf Hotel, Palm Court Lounge, WC2   3.30–6.30
Westbury Hotel Lounge, W1   10am–11pm
Whole Meal Vegetarian Restaurant, SW16   noon–10.30
Windmill Wholefood Restaurant, SW6   11–7
Wine Gallery, SW10   noon–3 & 6–11
Wine Gallery, W11   noon–3 & 6 midnight
Woodlands Restaurant, SW1   noon–3 & 6–11
Woodlands Restaurant, W1   noon–3 & 6–11
Woodlands Restaurant, Wembley   noon–3 & 6–11
Zen W3, NW3   noon–11.30

BATH
Bath Puppet Theatre   10–5.30
Canary   11–6
Moon & Sixpence (wine bar)   noon–2 & 7–10.30
Number Five   11.30–2.30 (November–May)
Pump Room   10–5.30
The Walrus & the Carpenter   6–11

BIRMINGHAM
Bobby Browns in Town   6–11
New Happy Gathering   noon–11.45

BRIGHTON
Allanjohn's   10.30–3
Blossoms   noon–2.15
Cripes   noon–2.30 & 6–11.30
Food for Friends   11.30–10
Pie in the Sky   noon–2.30 & 6.30–11.30
Samsons   6–11.30

BRISTOL
Arnolfini Café Bar   noon–10.30
Wild Oats 11   10–10

CAMBRIDGE
Upstairs   6.30–11
Waffles   9.30–2.30 & 6–10

CARDIFF
Champers 7pm–12.30am

EDINBURGH
Brasserie Saint Jacques   12.30–2
Helios Fountain   noon–2.30 & 4–11.30
Henderson's Salad Table   9–9 (Festival season)

GLASGOW
Joe's Garage   noon–midnight
Loon Fung   noon–11.30
Tom Sawyers   noon–2.30 & 6.30–10

LEEDS
Flying Pizza   12.30–3 & 6–11
Ike's Bistro   noon–2 & 5.30–11

LIVERPOOL
Mandarin   5.30–11.30
Streets   noon–7

MANCHESTER
Pizzeria Bella Napoli   6.30–11.3
Pizzeria Italia   6.30–11.30
Venezia Trattoria   6–midnight
Woo Sang   noon–11.45
Yang Sing   noon—11.30

OXFORD
Browns   noon–11.30
Go Dutch   noon–11
Randolph Hotel Lounge   3–6

STRATFORD UPON AVON
Slug & Lettuce   noon–1.30 & 7–9.30
Truffles Old Tea Shoppe   noon–5.30

YORK
Bettys   9–9
St William's College Restaurant   noon–5
Taylors Tea Rooms   9–7

LATE NIGHT EATING IN BRITAIN'S MAJOR CENTRES

The following establishments are open after 11 pm, daily unless otherwise indicated

LONDON
Ajanta, W12
Aspava, W1
Athenaeum Hotel, Windsor Lounge, W1
L'Autre Wine Bar, W1   Mon–Sat
La Bersagliera, SW3
Bill Stickers, W1
Le Bistroquet, NW1   Mon–Sat
Blenheim's, NW8
La Brasserie, SW3
Brasserie at L'Escargot, W1   Mon–Sat
Brown's Hotel Lounge, W1
Café Delancey, NW1   Mon–Sat
Café Fish Des Amis du Vin, SW1   Mon–Sat
Le Café du Jardin, WC2   Mon–Sat
Café Pacifico, WC2   Mon–Sat
Café Pélican, WC2
Caffe Venezia, W1   Mon–Sat
Camden Brasserie, NW1   Mon–Sat
Canton, WC2
Chequers, NW1
Chiang Mai, W1   Mon–Sat
Chicago Pizza Pie Factory, W1   Mon–Sat
Chicago Rib Shack, SW7   Mon–Sat
Christys Healthline, W1   Mon–Sat
Chuen Cheng Ku, W1
City Friends, EC4   Mon–Sat
La Cloche, NW6
Le Cochonnet, W9   Thur–Sat
Da Gianbruno, W6

Daquise, SW7
Diwana Bhel-Poori House (121 Drummond St), NW1
Dorchester Hotel, Promenade, W1
Downs Wine Bar, W1   Mon–Sat
Efes Kebab House, W1   Mon–Sat
Equatorial, W1   Mon–Sat
Falafel House, NW3   Mon–Sat
First Out, WC2   Mon–Sat
Fridays Tex-Mex, WC2   Mon–Sat
Geale's, W8   Tues–Fri
Gino's (wine bar), W5
Green Cottages, NW3
Grill St Quentin, SW13   Mon–Sat
Grosvenor House, Pasta, Vino e Fantasia, W1   Mon–Sat
Gurkhas Tandoori, W1
Hard Rock Café, W1
Hyatt Carlton Tower, Chinoiserie, SW1
Inn on the Park, Lounge, W1
Inter-Continental Hotel, Coffee House, W1
Jeeves Wine Cellar, W1   Mon–Sat
Joe Allen, WC2
Joy King Lau, WC2   Mon–Sat
Julie's Bar, W11   Mon–Sat
L.S. Grunts Chicago Pizza Co. WC2   Mon–Sat
Lantern, NW6
Ley-On's, W1
Lok Ho Fook, W1
London Marriott Hotel, Regent Lounge, W1
Loon Fung, W1
Lou Pescadou, SW5
Macarthurs, SW13
Maha Gopal, W1
Manna, NW3
Matono, W1
Mélange, WC2   Mon–Sat
Le Meridien Piccadilly, W1
Millwards, N16
New Kam Tong, W2
New Shu Shan, WC2
No 77 Wine Bar, NW6   Thurs–Sat
Nontas, NW1   Mon–Sat
Parsons, SW10
Pasta Connection, SW3   Mon–Sat
Pasta Fino, W1   Mon–Sat
Le Petit Prince, NW5
Pigeon, SW6

Poons (Leicester Street), WC2   Mon–Sat
Poons (Lisle Street), WC2   Mon–Sun
Portman Hotel, Portman Corner, W1
Punters Pie, SW1
Raffles, NW6
Raj Bhelpoori House, NW1
Sagarmatha, NW1
The Savoy, Thames Foyer, WC2
Sheraton Park Tower Restaurant, SW1
Soho Brasserie, W1   Mon–Sat
Spirals Wine Bar & Restaurant, NW3   Mon–Sat
Swiss Centre, Swiss Imbiss, W1   Mon–Sat
Topkapi, W1
Trattoria Imperia, WC2   Mon–Sat
Tuxedo Junction, NW6   Mon–Sat
Verbanella, SW3   Mon–Sat
Villa Estense, SW6   Mon–Sat
Wine Gallery, SW3   Mon–Sat
Wine Gallery, SW10   Mon–Sat
Wine Gallery, W11
Zen W3, NW3

BATH
Beaujolais Restaurant   Fri–Sat

BIRMINGHAM
New Happy Gathering

BRIGHTON
Al Duomo   Mon–Sat
Cripes
Pie in the Sky
Samsons

CAMBRIDGE
Upstairs   Fri–Sat
Waffles   Sat

CARDIFF
La Brasserie   Mon–Sat
Champers

EDINBURGH
Helios Fountain
Waterfront Wine Bar   Mon–Sat

GLASGOW
Café Gandolfi   Mon–Sat
Joe's Garage
Loon Fung

LEEDS
Flying Pizza   Mon–Sat
Salvo's   Mon–Sat

LIVERPOOL
Everyman Bistro   Mon–Sat
Mandarin

MANCHESTER
Pizzeria Bella Napoli
Pizzeria Italia
Venezia Trattoria
Woo Sang
Yang Sing

OXFORD
Browns

STRATFORD UPON AVON
Pinocchio   Mon–Sat

WHERE
TO EAT
ON AND OFF
MOTORWAYS

LONDON

JUNCT

6   BRICKET WOOD   ¼ mile   Oakwood Tea Room

Oakwood Road. Take the A405 towards St Albans. Oakwood Road is second turning to the right.
Set teas are popular at this friendly place, and the range of home baking is impressive, from scones and gâteaux to lunchtime specials like steak and kidney pie.
Petrol Esso Garage, Old Watford Road

JUNCT

15   NORTHAMPTON   3½ miles   Lawrence's Coffee House

35 St Giles Street. Take the A508 into the town centre and follow signs to the Riding car park.
Crusty rolls and slices of quiche, Danish pastries, lemon meringue pie and chocolate sponge slice – the snacks here are very enjoyable, and the window display makes it hard to pass by.
Petrol Bells, Bedford Road

JUNCT

20   MARKET HARBOROUGH 10 miles Taylor's Fish Restaurant

10 Adam & Eve Street. Take the A427 into Market Harborough. Turn right at first traffic lights and immediately filter left to turn into Adam & Eve Street.
Restaurant and self-service cafeteria, both offering the same choice of excellent fish and chip dishes. Among the selection you'll find cod, haddock, plaice and skate, plus scampi and sometimes even crab.
Petrol Coventry Road Service Station, Coventry Road

JUNCT

21 & 22   LEICESTER FOREST EAST   Welcome Break Motorway Services

Between junctions 21 & 22.
Standards of food and hygiene are commendable at this motorway complex, as is the wide choice, from burger bar, pie parlour and fish bar to self-service cafeteria and even a restaurant.
Petrol Service Area

JUNCT

25   DERBY   *8 miles*   Lettuce Leaf ▶

21 Friar Gate. Take the A52 towards town centre, which runs into Friar Gate.

Consult the blackboard for the day's specials at this little wholefood restaurant – they could include things like celery hot pot and vegetables provençale. The regular menu offers omelettes, grills, toasties and salads, plus nice sweets.

Petrol The 211 Garage, Ashbourne Road

JUNCT

26   NOTTINGHAM   *4 miles*   Brasserie St Marie ▶

30 High Pavement. Take the A610 to city centre. Follow the Maid Marian Way to Castle Gate, which runs into High Pavement.

Omelettes are a favourite snack at this bright modern brasserie. Other items range from spicy merguez sausages to fricassee of pigeon and creamy sauced mussels.

Petrol Derby Road Service Station, Derby Road

JUNCT

33   SHEFFIELD   *5 miles*   ★   Just Cooking ▶

16 Carver Street. Take the A630, then A57 into city centre to Charter Square near City Hall.

The long lunchtime brings many delights here, typified by cheese and mushroom quiche or a lamb and apricot casserole bursting with flavour. Also delicious salads and super sweets.

Petrol Murco Service Station, Pond Street

JUNCT

33   SHEFFIELD *5 miles* ★   Toffs Restaurant & Coffee House ▶

23 Matilda Street. Take the A630, then A57 into city centre. Follow signs for The Moor.

Summery surroundings in which to enjoy star-quality snacks. Super lunchtime dishes include lovely wholemeal quiches, mushroom tartlet and chicken casserole. Lovely sweets, too, and cakes in the morning.

Petrol Murco Service Station, Pond Street

JUNCT

47   LEEDS   *1 mile*   Reed's Café ▶

64 Albion Street. Follow the signs for city centre. Once in City Square follow signs for Infirmary. Turn right at Town Hall and then second right again.

There's a good choice of baking, including éclairs, fruit cake and Danish pastries, at this cosy tea room above a chocolate shop. Also sandwiches and salads. Fine teas and coffees.

Petrol Commercial Garage, Swinegate

LEEDS

M4

2   KEW   *1 mile*   ★   **Original Maids of Honour Shop**

288 Kew Road. Take the A4, then turn on to the A307 and follow the signs to Kew Bridge.
Baking of the highest class has brought far-reaching fame to this marvellous tea shop. Cream slices, brandy snaps and the scrumptious Maids of Honour touch on a galaxy of delights.
Petrol Chiswick Flyover Service Station, 1 Great West Road

5   ETON   *2½ miles*   **Eton Wine Bar**

82 High Street. Take B470 towards Slough. Follow signs for Eton.
Neat, friendly and informal, with a menu that shows imagination. Some typical delights, smoked salmon and spinach mousse, cold cucumber and mint soup, veal and almond casserole served with super turmeric rice.
Petrol Datchet Green Motors, Datchet

10   WOKINGHAM   *4½ miles*   **Setters Bistro**

49 Peach Street. Take the A329(M), signposted to Wokingham, then follow the A329.
The blackboard tempts lunchtime visitors with tasty specials like garlic mushrooms, liver and bacon or lamb curry. Main courses come with very fresh vegetables, and there are some delicious desserts.
Petrol Gowrings Service Station, London Road

11   READING   *4 miles*   **Wine Butts**

61 St Marys Butts. Take A33 into Reading and follow signs for Ramada Hotel. The wine bar is just around the corner.
First-floor wine bar in a town-centre shopping complex. The cooking's very good, the menu varied. Pasta, savoury pies and pâtés are among the favourites.
Petrol Fairfield Motors, Basingstoke Road

13   NEWBURY   *4½ miles*   **Crafty Cat**

5 Inch's Yard, Market Street. Take A34 into town past clock tower and over bridge. Alongside Market Street car park.
Scones and shortbread keep the customers purring at this coffee room. At lunchtime there are baps and hot specials.
Petrol Wheeler's Motors Ltd, London Road

14 HUNGERFORD 3½ miles Bear, Kennet Room

41 Charnham Street. Follow A338 into town centre. Bear is on the left.
Snatch a snack or linger over a full meal at this traditional inn. Typical fare includes fish soup, stuffed aubergines, baked trout and terrine of summer fruit.
Petrol Hungerford Garages, Charnham Street

14 & 15 MEMBURY Welcome Break Motorway Services
Between junctions 14 & 15

Stylish, spacious and clean, this is everything a motorway service area should be. Food, hot and cold, is attractively presented and service is swift.
Petrol Service Area

17 EASTON GREY 5½ miles Easton Grey Restaurant

Take the A429 for about 2 miles, then turn left on road towards Hullavington, which after ½ mile is signposted to Easton Grey. Lovely home-baked cakes, salads, sandwiches, hot dishes like lasagne or chicken à la crème – that's the choice at this summery restaurant in the grounds of Easton Grey House.
Petrol Herbert's Garage, Bristol Road (B4040)

19 BRISTOL 6 miles Arnolfini Café-Bar

Narrow Quay, Prince Street. Take the M32 & follow signs to city centre. Park in NCP at the Unicorn Hotel.
Old dockland warehouses are home for the arts complex of which this is a part. There's a varied menu, from seafood pancake and lamb kebabs to curries, quiches and gooey sweets.
Petrol Princess Service Station, Park Row

19 BRISTOL 6 miles Guild Café-Restaurant

68 Park Street. Take the M32 & follow signs to city centre. Park at Clifton Down multi-storey car park.
A nice feature of this first-floor café is a leafy outdoor area. The basic menu of home-made cakes, biscuits and cheese rolls is supplemented by lunchtime savouries and sweets.
Petrol Princess Service Station, Park Row

M5

JUNCT 4   **BELBROUGHTON**   *3 miles*   **Coffee Pot**

High Street. Take A491 towards Stourbridge, then turn left at Bell End on B4188 to Belbroughton.
A tiny restaurant serving appetising lunchtime fare like prawn, asparagus and smoked salmon pie. Super salads, scrumptious sweets, splendid baking.
Petrol Bell Service Station, Bell End

JUNCT 6   **OMBERSLEY**   *4 miles*   **Ombersley Gallery Tea Room**

Church Terrace. Take A449 towards Kidderminster. Ombersley is signposted to the left.
Biscuits and scones, rhubarb flan and Genoa sponge are among the baked goodies, with pâtés and moussaka for savoury palates in this old-world tea room.
Petrol Old School House Garage, Ombersley

JUNCT 9   **TEWKESBURY**   *4 miles*   **Telfords**

61 High Street. Follow the A438 into Tewkesbury and continue on the A38.
One-course lunches are a snacker's delight at this agreeable little place. Prime produce makes hits of salads and steaks, baked trout, spicy duck pancake and all the rest.
Petrol Graham Wright, Ashchurch Road

JUNCT 9   **TEWKESBURY**   *4 miles*   **Wintor House**

73 Church Street. Follow the A438 into Tewkesbury and continue on the A38.
Sandwiches plain or toasted, soup with croûtons, casseroles, a Sunday roast, set afternoon teas – they all merit a visit to this pleasant beamed restaurant.
Petrol Graham Wright, Ashchurch Road

JUNCT 11   **CHELTENHAM**   *4 miles*   **Langtry Pâtisserie & Tea Rooms**

56 High Street. Take A40 into Cheltenham town centre and follow the one-way system.
Locals and tourists make tracks for this Victorian tea shop to sample the delights of the bakehouse beyond the garden. Savoury snacks, too, and ice cream specialities.
Petrol Lansdown Service Station, Montpellier Terrace

JUNCT

13 & 14

MICHAEL WOOD   **Welcome Break Motorway Services**
Between junctions 13 & 14

A well-run service station restaurant with smart, friendly staff and flowers on the tables. Freshly baked bread, cakes and pastries are all commendable, as are the generously filled sandwiches and savoury pies like chicken and mushroom.
Petrol Service Area

JUNCT

23   **BRIDGWATER**   *4 miles*   **Nutmeg**

8 Clare Street. Take the A38. Follow signs to Bridgwater and take Clink Road. Clare Street is a turning on the left just past the police station.
Cooked breakfasts give the day a good start at this popular café, and later offerings like cakes, sandwiches and a lunchtime hot pot keep up the good work.
Petrol Shell, Bristol Road

JUNCT

25   **TAUNTON**   *2 miles*   **Castle Hotel, Bow Bar**

North Street. Take the A358 and follow signs for town centre and then Wellington, turning right before the Top Rank Club and right by the car park.
It's part of the Castle Hotel, but this tapestry-hung bar has its own entrance. Light lunches offer things like turkey sandwiches, noodles with seafood and minute steak.
Petrol Marshalsea Motors Ltd, Wellington Road

JUNCT

27   **TIVERTON**   *7 miles*   ★ **Hendersons**

18 Newport Street. Take the dual carriageway to Tiverton. At the end of the carriageway turn left at the roundabout and on up the hill into town. Turn left into Newport Street. Hendersons is on the left.
Snackers can do it in style at this super restaurant, where the seasonal menus delight with dishes like green summer pâté, goujons of plaice and veal ragout.
Petrol Bolham Road Petrol Station

EXETER

BIRMINGHAM

17 CONGLETON *7 miles* ★ Odd Fellows Wine Bar & Bistro

20 Rood Hill. Take A534 into Congleton. Turn left at first junction, left again at roundabout and then first right into Rood Hill.

The marvellously imaginative lunchtime and evening menu is matched by suitably skilful cooking, prime ingredients and colourful presentation. Herby salads are especially good, and sweets such as home-made ice cream are smashing.
Petrol Texaco Station, Newcastle Road

19 ALTRINCHAM *6 miles* Gander's

2 Goose Green. Take A556 through Bowden and then the A56 to Altrincham. Turn right at Regent Road (just before overhead footbridge) and continue to the T-junction. Gander's is behind Barclays Bank.

Comfortable wine bar-cum-bistro, with a varied menu that includes soup, club sandwiches, spare ribs and savoury pancakes.
Petrol Bowden Filling Station, Altrincham Road (A56)

19 ALTRINCHAM *6 miles* Nutcracker Vegetarian Restaurant

43 Oxford Road. Take the A556 through Bowden and then the A56 to Altrincham. Turn right at Regent Road (just before overhead footbridge) and continue to the T-junction. Turn right, take lefthand fork and first left into Oxford Road.

A long-time local favourite, this pretty vegetarian restaurant has a counter display of good baking, with savoury items at lunchtime.
Petrol Bowden Filling Station, Altrincham Road (A56)

31 PRESTON *3 miles* Angelo's

31 Avenham Street. Take A59 into town centre.
Pizza and pasta are perennially popular at this bright Italian restaurant, along with chicken, veal and some imaginative starters.
Petrol Key Motors, 38 Garstang Road

JUNCT

34 | **LANCASTER** | *2 miles* | **Dukes Playhouse Restaurant**

Moor Lane. Follow signs for city centre. Turn left off one-way system just after the post office.
Actors, audience and public patronise this theatre restaurant, where the menu co-stars vegetarian and meaty dishes.
Petrol Caton Road Service Station (A683)

JUNCT

34 | **LANCASTER** | *2 miles* | **Libra**

19 Brock Street. Follow signs for city centre. Libra is off the main street, close to Marks & Spencer.
Attractive salads, healthy bakes, vegan cakes in this pleasant vegetarian restaurant that leans to the alternative society.
Petrol Caton Road Service Station (A683)

JUNCT

37 | **KENDAL** | *5 miles* | **Eat Fit**

3 Stramongate. Follow the A684 into town centre.
A self-service restaurant, mainly vegetarian, whose menu includes jacket potatoes, French bread pizzas, lentil loaf, cakes and pastries.
Petrol Blackhall Road Service Station

JUNCT

40 | **PENRITH** | *½ mile* | **Bluebell Tearoom**

Three Crowns Yard. Follow the signs to Penrith and then for Bluebell Lane car park. Tea room is on the other side of car park.
Super cakes and biscuits win the day in this cottage tea room in a bookshop. Honey bread, date slices, plum cake, sticky gingerbread and many others will go with your choice from the marvellous selection of teas and coffees. Good facilities for children.
Petrol Davidsons Garage, Scotland Road

JUNCT

43 | **CARLISLE** | *2 miles* | **Hudson's Coffee Shop**

Treasury Court, Fisher Street. Follow A69 into town centre and towards the cathedral. The coffee shop is a 2 minute walk away.
Delightful little coffee shop where scones, caramel shortbread and chocolate slice make light bites with tea or coffee. Salads, a quiche and hot daily special at lunchtime.
Petrol Country Garage, Hardwick Circus

M25

JUNCT

3   CHISLEHURST   *7 miles*   Mrs Bridges' Kitchen

49 Chislehurst Road. Take A20 and turn left on to A222 to Chislehurst. This becomes Chislehurst Road and Mrs Bridges' Kitchen is on the right close to railway station and the Caves. The emphasis is on simple, satisfying fare at this pleasant café. Farmhouse breakfasts, grills, bumper toasted sandwiches and salads are among the favourites.
Petrol Mobil, Chislehurst Road (opposite café)

JUNCT

6   LIMPSFIELD   *3 miles*   Old Lodge

(For Eastbound Travellers)
High Street. Take A22, then A25 towards Oxted. At first traffic lights turn left on to the B269 (signposted Warlingham); the restaurant is about 100 yards on right. To return to motorway, continue on A25 towards Sevenoaks and take A21 on to junction 5.
Bar snacks at the Old Lodge include a first-rate quiche lorraine, fish and meat pies, chicken kebabs and an enjoyable selection of sweets.
Petrol Old Oxted Service Station (on A25)

JUNCT

18   AMERSHAM   *8 miles*   Willow Tree

1 Market Square. Take A404 through Chorleywood. The restaurant is on right after fourth roundabout (follow signs for Old Amersham).
A delightful, beamy place on the Market Square that beckons all day with super home baking. There are savoury snacks (roast on Sunday) and delicious sweets at lunchtime.
Petrol Elf (on A404 at second roundabout from junction)

JUNCT

30   GRAYS   *5 miles*   R. Mumford & Son

6 Cromwell Road. Take A13 into Grays. At beginning of one-way system turn left. Mumford's is opposite the Thameside Theatre.
Market-fresh fish is lightly battered and carefully cooked in this bright, modern restaurant. Jumbo chips or crisp salads accompany.
Petrol R. T. Rate, Hogg Lane

NEW FOREST

JUNCT

3 ROMSEY   3½ miles   Cobweb Tea Rooms

49 The Hundred. Take M271 signposted to Romsey and then follow A3057 into the town centre.
Fine home baking in a neat little tea room includes scones, coffee cake and chocolate hazelnut torte. Savoury snacks are also available.
Petrol Testwood Motors, Romsey Bypass

JUNCT

3 SOUTHAMPTON   3 miles   Lunch Break

321 Shirley Road. Take M271 towards Southampton. Turn on to A3057 which passes through Shirley; the restaurant is on the left.
Part of a bakery, so there's always a wide selection of fresh cakes and pastries in this self-service restaurant. Cornish pasties and quiches are typical savouries.
Petrol Testwood Motors, Shirley Road (100 yards from restaurant)

JUNCT

6 EASTLEIGH   2 miles   Piccolo Mondo

1 High Street. Take the A335 into Eastleigh.
Home-made herby sausages are a popular dish at this comfortable Italian restaurant, along with pizzas, pasta, veal and chicken. Super ices.
Petrol Texaco, Southampton Road

JUNCT

7 BISHOP'S WALTHAM   6 miles   Casey's

Corner of Bank & Brook Streets. Take A334 to Botley and then for Bishop's Waltham.
Wholesome home cooking in a former granary. There's a good choice of cakes, scones and biscuits with tea or coffee, plus lunchtime savoury items.
Petrol Botley Garage, next to railway station

JUNCT

12 PORTSMOUTH   4 miles   Rosie's Vineyard

87 Elm Grove. Take M275 into Portsmouth and follow signs for Southsea.
Lively wine bar offering tasty hot dishes like moussaka, stuffed trout and paprika pork. Light snacks, too.
Petrol Hendy Lennox Garage, Grove Road

PORTSMOUTH   61

LONDON BY AREAS

BAYSWATER & NOTTING HILL
Diwana Bhel-Poori House, W2
Geale's, W8
Gyngleboy, W2
Hung Toa, W2
Maison Bouquillon, W2
Maison Pechon Pâtisserie
  Française, W2
New Kam Tong, W2
Royal Lancaster Hotel Lounge,
  W2
Wine Gallery, W11

BLOOMSBURY
Cranks, W1
Efes Kebab House, W1
Gurkhas Tandoori, W1
The Heal's Restaurant, W1
Ikkyu, W1
Jeeves Wine Cellar, W1
Mandeer, W1
Pirroni's, W1

CHELSEA & FULHAM
La Bersagliera, SW3
Boltons Wine Bar, SW10
Charco's Wine Bar, SW3
L'Express, SW1
Hiders, SW6
Justin de Blank at General
  Trading Company, SW1
Lou Pescadou, SW5
Parsons, SW10
Pasta Connection, SW3
Pigeon, SW6
Villa Estense, SW6
Windmill Wholefood Restaurant,
  SW6
Wine Gallery, SW3 & SW10

CITY
Balls Brothers, EC2
Balls Brothers, EC4
Bottlescrue, EC1
Café St Pierre Brasserie, EC1
City Friends, EC4
East West Restaurant, EC1
El Vino, EC4
Food for Health, EC4
Garbanzo Coffee House, EC1
Greenhouse, EC3
Mother Bunch's, EC4
Nosherie, EC1
Pavilion Wine Bar, EC2
Le Poulbot Pub, EC2
Rouxl Britannia, Le Café, EC2
Slenders, EC4
Sweetings, EC4

COVENT GARDEN
Le Beaujolais Wine Bar, WC2
Blake's Wine & Food Bar, WC2
Le Café du Jardin, WC2
Café Pacifico, WC2
Daly's Wine Bar, WC2
Fino's Wine Cellar, WC2
Food for Thought, WC2
Friday's, WC2
Joe Allen, WC2
L. S. Grunt's Chicago Pizza Co.,
  WC2
Lincoln's Inn Wine Bar, WC2
Mélange, WC2
Neal's Yard Bakery & Tea Room,
  WC2
Neal's Yard Bakery at the
  Ecology Centre, WC2
The Savoy, Thames Foyer, WC2

Waldorf Hotel, Palm Court
   Lounge, WC2

EAST LONDON
Bloom's, E1
Cherry Orchard, E2
Seashell, E8

KNIGHTSBRIDGE & KENSINGTON
Bill Bentley's Oyster Bar, SW3
La Brasserie, SW3
Chicago Rib Shack, SW7
Daquise, SW7
Draycott's, SW3
Grill St Quentin, SW3
Harrods Circles, SW1
Harrods Georgian Restaurant &
   Terrace, SW1
Harrods Health Juice Bar, SW1
Harvey Nichols, Harveys at the
   Top, SW1
Hyatt Carlton Tower,
   Chinoiserie, SW1
Hyde Park Hotel, Park Room,
   SW1
Maxim (Wine Bar) SW1
Le Métro, SW3
Muffin Man, W8
Pâtisserie Parisienne, W8
Richoux, SW3
Sheraton Park Tower
   Restaurant, SW1

Tui, SW7
209 Thai Restaurant, W8
Verbanella, SW3
Victoria & Albert Museum, New
   Restaurant, SW7

MAYFAIR & MARYLEBONE
Aspava, W1
Athenaeum Hotel, Windsor
   Lounge,W1
L'Autre Wine Bar, W1
Bonne Bouche Pâtisserie, W1
Brown's Hotel, Lounge, W1
Bubbles Wine Bar, W1
Caffe Venezia, W1
Chicago Pizza Pie Factory, W1
Crêperie, W1
Dorchester Hotel, Promenade,
   W1
Downs Wine Bar, W1
Fino's Wine Cellar (North Row),
   W1
Granary, W1
Grosvenor House, Park Lounge,
   W1
Grosvenor House, Pasta, Vino e
   Fantasia, W1
Grosvenor House, Pavilion, W1
Hard Rock Café, W1
Inn on the Park Lounge, W1
Inter-Continental Hotel, Coffee
   Lounge, W1

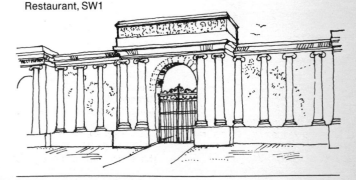

Justin de Blank, W1
Kitchen Yakitori, W1
London Marriott Hotel, Regent
  Lounge, W1
Maha Gopal, W1
Maison Sagne, W1
Matono, W1
Nakamura, W1
Nanten, W1
Paling's Wine Bar, W1
Portman Hotel, Portman Corner,
  W1
Raw Deal, W1
Richoux (South Audley Street),
  W1
Smollensky's Balloon, W1
Topkapi, W1
Verbanella Pasta Bar, W1
Westbury Hotel Lounge, W1
Woodlands Restaurant, W1
Yumi, W1

NORTH & NORTH-WEST LONDON

Almeida Theatre Wine Bar, N1
Anna's Place, N1
Asuka, NW1
Le Bistroquet, NW1
Blenheim's, NW8
Bloom's, NW11
Boos, NW1
Café Delancey, NW1
Camden Brasserie, NW1
Chequers, NW1
La Cloche, NW6
Diwana Bhel-Poori House, NW1
Earth Exchange Collective, N6
Falafel House, NW3
Fallen Angel, N1
Green Cottage, NW3
Harry Morgan's, NW8
Ipphei, NW3
Lantern, NW6
Laurent, NW2
Leith's Good Food, N1
Louis' Pâtisserie, NW3

Manna, NW3
Marine Ices, NW3
Millward's, N16
Mother Huff's, NW3
Nontas, NW1
No. 77 Wine Bar, NW6
Odette's, NW1
Pasta Underground, NW1
The Peck Provender, N1
Le Petit Prince, NW5
Le Plat du Jour, NW1
Raffles, NW6
Raj Bhelpoori House, NW1
Rani, N3
Raoul's, W9
Ravi Shankar, NW1
Sabras, NW10
Sagarmatha, NW1
Seashell, NW1
Solopasta, N1
Spirals Wine Bar & Restaurant,
  NW3
Suruchi, N1
Tuxedo Junction, NW6
Upper Street Fish Shop, N1
Woodlands, Wembley
Zen W3, NW3

ST JAMES'S

Bentley's Wine Bar & Oyster Bar,
  W1
Country Life, W1
Criterion Brasserie, W1
Fino's Wine Cellar (Swallow
  Street), W1
Green's Champagne & Oyster
  Bar, SW1
Le Meridien Piccadilly, W1
Pappagalli's Pizza Inc, W1
Richoux (Piccadilly), W1
The Ritz, Palm Court, W1
Simpson's Wine Bar, W1
Le Tire Bouchon, W1

SOHO & TRAFALGAR SQUARE

Bill Stickers, W1

Brasserie at l'Escargot, W1
Café Fish des Amis du Vin, SW1
Café Pélican, WC2
Canton, WC2
Chiang Mai, W1
Christys Healthline, W1
Chuen Cheng Ku, W1
Cork & Bottle, W2
Cranks, WC2
Cranks Healthfood Restaurant, W1
Equatorial, W1
First Out, WC2
Govindas, W1
Ikeda, W1
Jade Garden, W1
Joy King Lau, WC2
Ley-On's, W1
Lok Ho Fook, W1
Loon Fung, W1
Maison Bertaux, W1
National Gallery Restaurant, WC2
New Loon Fung, W1
New Shu Shan, WC2
Nuthouse, W1
Pasta Fino, W1
Pasticceria Amalfi, W1
Pasticceria Cappuccetto, W1
Pâtisserie Valerie, W1
Poons (Leicester Street), WC2
Poons (Lisle Street), WC2
Shampers, W1
Soho Brasserie, W1
Swiss Centre, Swiss Imbiss, W1
Trattoria Imperia, WC2
Woodlands, SW1

SOUTH-EAST LONDON
Bar du Musée, SE10
Bon Ton Roulet, SE24
Colonel Jasper's, SE10
Cuddiford's Wine Bar, SE10
Davy's Wine Vaults, SE10
Dining Room, SE1
Gachons, SE10

Royal Festival Hall, Riverside, Café, SE1
Skinkers, SE1
Spread Eagle, SE10

SOUTH-WEST LONDON
Beehive, SW2
Brasserie, SW17
Café Pastiche, SW6
Di's Larder, SW11
Hoults, SW17
Macarthurs, SW13
Ormes Wine Bar & Restaurant, SW4
Punters Pie, SW11
Rebato's, SW8
Tea-Time, SW4
Twenty Trinity Gardens, SW9
Whole Meal Vegetarian Restaurant, SW16

VICTORIA & WESTMINSTER
Carriages, SW1
Ebury Wine Bar, SW1
Flamingo, SW1
Goring Hotel Lounge, SW1
Methuselah's, SW1
Tapster, SW1
Wilkins Natural Foods, SW1

WEST LONDON
Ajanta, W12
Le Cochonnet, W9
Da Gianbruno, W6
Gino's, W5
Hat Shop, W12
Julie's Bar, W11
Linda's, W9
Maxim's Wine Bar, W7
Mulford's Wine Bar, W6
Old Heidelberg Pâtisserie, W4
Oliver's, W4
Ravenscourt Park Tea House, W6
Village Delicatessen & Coffee Shop, W14

ESTABLISHMENTS BY COUNTIES

ENGLAND

AVON
Bath   Bath Puppet Theatre
   Beaujolais Restaurant
   Canary
   Jollys, Circles Restaurant
   Moon & Sixpence
   Number Five
   Pump Room
   Rossiter's
   Tarts
   Theatre Vaults
   The Walrus & the Carpenter
Bristol   Arnolfini Café Bar
   Edwards
   Guild Café-Restaurant
   Rainbow Café
   Wild Oats II
Midsomer Norton   Mrs Pickwick

BEDFORDSHIRE
Mentmore   Stable Yard Craft Gallery & Tea
   Room

BERKSHIRE
Eton   Eton Wine Bar
Hungerford   Bear, Kennet Room
Lower Basildon   Cottage Restaurant & Tea
   Rooms
Newbury   Crafty Cat
Reading   Mama Mia
   Wine Butts
Windsor   Angelo's Wine Bar
   Dôme
   Tracks Brasserie
   Windsor Chocolate House
Wokingham   Setters Bistro

BUCKINGHAMSHIRE
Amersham   Fripp's
   Willow Tree
Aylesbury   Wild Oats
Buckingham   Bakery & Austrian Coffee
   Room
Marlow   Burgers

CAMBRIDGESHIRE
Cambridge   Nettles
   Upstairs
   Waffles
Huntingdon   Old Bridge Hotel Lounge
Wansford-in-England   Haycock Hotel
   Lounge

CHESHIRE
Bowdon   Griffin
Bridgemere   Bridgemere Garden World
   Coffee Shop
Cheadle Hulme   Portobello
Chester   Abbey Green
   Chester Grosvenor, Harveys
   Chester Grosvenor Lounge
   Farmhouse
   Pierre Griffe Wine Bar
   60s American Restaurant
Congleton   Odd Fellows Wine Bar & Bistro
Middlewich   Tempters
Parkgate   Chompers
Tarporley   Feathers
Tiverton   Red Fox

CLEVELAND
Yarm   Coffee Shop

CORNWALL
Falmouth   Secrets
Mawgan   Yard Bistro
Polperro   Captain's Cabin
St Mary's   Tregarthens Hotel
St Michael's Mount   Sail Loft
Trebarwith Strand   House on the Strand
   Old Millfloor

CUMBRIA
Alston   Brownside Coach House
Ambleside   Harvest
   Rothay Manor
   Sheila's Cottage
   Zeffirellis
Boot   Brook House Restaurant
Borrowdale   Lodore Swiss Hotel Lounge

Bowness on Windermere Hedgerow
  Laurel Cottage
  Trattoria Pizzeria Ticino
Braithwaite Book Cottage
Caldbeck Swaledale Watch
Carlisle Hudson's Coffee Shop
Cartmel St Mary's Lodge
Cockermouth Quince & Medlar
  Wythop Mill
Coniston Bridge House Café
Dent Dent Crafts Centre
Dodd Wood Old Sawmill
Grange-in-Borrowdale Grange Bridge
  Cottage
Grange-over-Sands At Home
Grasmere Baldry's
  Coffee Bean
  Rowan Tree
Hawkshead Minstrel's Gallery
High Lorton White Ash Barn
Kendal Corner Spot Eating House
  Eat Fit
  Farrers Tea & Coffee House
  The Moon
  Nutters
  Waterside Wholefoods
Kents Bank Abbot Hall Coffee Shop
Keswick Bryson's Tea Rooms
  Mayson's
  Squire's
  Underscar Hotel

Melmerby Village Bakery
Penrith Bluebell Tearoom
Ullswater Sharrow Bay Country House
  Hotel
Wasdale Greendale Gallery Restaurant
Windermere Langdale Chase Hotel
  Miller Howe Hotel

DERBYSHIRE
Ashbourne Ashbourne Gingerbread Shop
  Spencers of Ashbourne
Ashford-in-the-Water Cottage Tea Room
Bakewell Aitch's Wine Bar & Bistro
  Green Apple
  Marguerite & Stephanie
Baslow Cavendish Hotel
Calver Bridge Derbyshire Craft Centre
  Eating House
Castleton Rose Cottage Café
Derby Lettuce Leaf
Edensor Stables Tea Rooms
Hathersage Country Fayre Tea Room
Hope Hopechest
Matlock Strand Restaurant
Tideswell Horsmans Poppies
Tissington Old School Tea Rooms

DEVON
Ashburton Ashburton Coffee House
Axminster New Commercial Inn
Beer Old Lace Shop

Chagford Coffee Pot
Dartington Cranks Health Food
  Restaurant
East Budleigh Grasshoppers
Exeter Clare's Restaurant
  Cooling's Wine Bar
Gittisham Combe House Hotel
Great Torrington Rebecca's
  Top of the Town
Lustleigh Primrose Cottage
Lympstone River House
Lynton Lee Cottage
Sidbury Old Bakery
Tiverton Angel Foods
  Hendersons
Torquay Village Kitchen
Totnes Planters
  Willow

DORSET
Abbotsbury Flower Bowl
Bournemouth Carlton Hotel Lounge
  Coriander
  Flossies & Bossies
  Salad Centre
Bridport Moniques Wine Bar
Christchurch Salads
Dorchester Potter In
Lyme Regis Golden Cap
Lytchett Minster Slepe Cottage Tea
  Rooms
Poole Inn à Nutshell

Spetisbury Marigold Cottage Tea Rooms
Wareham Annies
Westbourne Hollywood!
Wimborne Minster Quinneys
Wool Rose Mullion Tea Rooms

CO. DURHAM
Barnard Castle Market Place Teashop
  Priors Restaurant
Piercebridge George Wine Bar

ESSEX
Billericay Webber's Wine Bar
Braintree Braintree Curry Palace
Castle Hedingham Colne Valley Railway
  Restaurant
Cattawade Bucks Wine Bar
Clacton-on-Sea Montague Hill China Cup
  Café
Colchester Bistro Nine
Dedham Essex Rose Tea House
Grays R. Mumford & Son
Walton on the Naze Naze Links Café

GLOUCESTERSHIRE
Bourton-on-the-Water Small Talk Tea
  Room
Cheltenham Choirs Tea Rooms
  Forrest Wine Bar
  Langtry Pâtisserie & Tea Rooms
  Montpellier Wine Bar & Bistro
  Promenade Pâtisserie
  Retreat

Chipping Campden   Bantam Tea Room
  Kings Arms Hotel, Saddle Room
Cirencester   Brewery Coffee Shop
  Fleece Hotel, Shepherds Wine Bar
Corse Lawn   Corse Lawn House
Moreton-in-Marsh   Market House
Newent   Good News Centre Coffee House
Painswick   Cup House
  Painswick Hotel
Stow-on-the-Wold   Ingram's
  St Edwards Café
  Wyck Hill House
Stroud   Mother Nature
Tetbury   Calcot Manor
Tewkesbury   Telfords
  Wintor House
Upper Slaughter   Lords of the Manor Hotel
Winchcombe   Pilgrims Way Coffee House

GREATER MANCHESTER

Altrincham   Gander's
  Nutcracker Vegetarian Restaurant
Manchester   Pizzeria Bella Napoli
  Pizzeria Italia
  Venezia Trattoria
  Woo Sang
  Yang Sing
Northenden   Nut 'n' Meg
Rochdale   Casa Capri
Stockport   Coconut Willy's

HAMPSHIRE

Bishop's Waltham   Casey's
Eastleigh   Piccolo Mondo
Emsworth   Cloisters
Minstead   Honey Pot
Portsmouth (Southsea)   Country Kitchen
  Rosie's Vineyard
Ringwood   Old Brown House
Romsey   Cobweb Tea Rooms
  Latimer Coffee House
Rowlands Castle   Coffee Pot
Southampton   Lunch Break
  La Lupa 4
  La Margherita
  Piccolo Mondo 1
Stockbridge   Old Dairy Restaurant
Sutton Scotney   Riverside Tea Garden
Winchester   Cloisters
  Mr Pitkin's Wine Bar
  Wessex Hotel Coffee Shop

HEREFORD & WORCESTER

Belbroughton   Coffee Pot

Broadway   Coffee Pot
  Collin House Hotel
  Goblets Wine Bar
Dorstone   Pump House Tea Room
Eardisland   Elms
Hereford   Effy's
  Fodder
  Marches
Ledbury   Applejack Wine Bar
  Feathers Hotel
  Verzons Country Hotel Bistro
Leintwardine   Selda Coffee Shop
Leominster   Granary Coffee House
Lyonshall   Church House
Middlewood   Burnt House Barn
Ombersley   Ombersley Gallery Tea Room
Ross-on-Wye   Meader's
  Walford House Hotel
Worcester   Heroes
  Natural Break

HERTFORDSHIRE

Berkhamsted   Cook's Delight
Bricket Wood   Oakwood Tea Room
St Albans   Kingsbury Mill Waffle House
Stevenage   De Friese Coffee Shop
Ware   Ben's Brasserie Bar
  Sunflowers

HUMBERSIDE

Scunthorpe   Bees Garden Coffee Lounge

ISLE OF WIGHT

Luccombe Chine   Dunnose Cottage
Newport   God's Providence House
Yarmouth   Jireh House

KENT

Ashford   Il Cardinale Pasta Parlour
Biddenden   Claris's Tea Shop
Bromley   Hollywood Bowl
Canterbury   Cogan House English
  Brasserie
  Crochets
  Il Vaticano Pasta Parlour
  JV's City Brasserie
  Pizza Place
  Sweet Heart Patisserie
Chatham   Simson's Wine Bar
Chislehurst   Mrs Bridges' Kitchen
Cliftonville   Batchelor's Pâtisserie
Collier Street   Butcher's Mere
Edenbridge   Buffin's Restaurant
Faversham   Recreation Tavern
Hythe   Natural Break

Lamberhurst   The Down
New Romney   Country Kitchen
Penshurst   Fir Tree House Tea Rooms
Ramsgate   Sands Wine Bar
Rochester   Casa Lina
St Margaret's at Cliffe   Roses
Tunbridge Wells   Buster Browns
  Delicious
  Downstairs at Thackeray's
  Pilgrims
  Pizza Piazza
Westerham   Henry Wilkinson

LANCASHIRE
Bleasdale   Bleasdale Post Office Tea
  Room
Burnley   Butterfingers
Clitheroe   The Castle
Hurst Green   Whitehall
Lancaster   Dukes Playhouse Restaurant
  Libra
  Marinada's
  Potters Coffee House
Lytham   Lytham Kitchen
Poulton-le-Fylde   Anna's Bistro
Preston   Angelo's

LEICESTERSHIRE
Leicester   Blossoms
  Joe Rigatoni
  Peacock Alley
Market Harborough   Taylor's Fish
  Restaurant
Oakham   Oakham Gallery
Stretton   Ram Jam Inn

LINCOLNSHIRE
Grantham   Knightingales
Lincoln   Harveys Cathedral Restaurant
  Wig & Mitre
Louth   Mr Chips
Spilsby   Buttercross Restaurant
Stamford   George of Stamford
  Mr Pips Coffee Shop & Restaurant

MERSEYSIDE
Liverpool   Armadillo Restaurant
  Everyman Bistro
  La Grande Bouffe
  Mandarin
  Streets
  Thatcher's

NORFOLK
Banham   Banham Bakehouse
Great Yarmouth   Friends Bistro
King's Lynn   Antonio's Wine Bar
Norwich   Britons Arms Coffee House
  Café La Tienda
  Mange-Tout Bistro & Coffee Shop
  Waffle House
Swaffham   Red Door

NORTHAMPTONSHIRE
Northampton   Lawrence's Coffee House

NORTHUMBERLAND
Alnwick   Hansel Coffee Shop
  Maxine's Kitchen
Bamburgh   Copper Kettle
Berwick upon Tweed   Kings Arms Hotel,
  Hideaway
  Town House
  Wine Bar
Blanchland   White Monk Tea Room

NOTTINGHAMSHIRE
Newark   Gannets
Nottingham   Alice's Restaurant
  Brasserie St Marie
  Café Punchinello
  Café Royal Brasserie
  New Orleans Diner
  Pagoda
  The Q in the Corner at Ziggi's
  Ten
Plumtree   Perkins Bar Bistro

OXFORDSHIRE
Blewbury   Lantern Cottage
Chipping Norton   Nutters
Goring-on-Thames   Coffee Pot
Henley-on-Thames   Barnaby's Brasserie
  Copper Kettle
  Henley Tea Shop
Oxford   Browns
  Go Dutch
  Heroes
  Munchy Munchy
  Randolph Hotel Lounge
  St Aldate's Church Coffee House
Thame   Mallards
Wallingford   Lamb Coffee Shop
  Lamb Wine Vaults
Wantage   Vale & Downland Museum
  Centre
Waterperry   Waterperry Gardens Tea Shop
Woodstock   Brothertons Brasserie

Feathers Hotel Garden Bar
Feathers Hotel Lounge
Linden Tea Rooms
Vanbrughs

SHROPSHIRE
Bishop's Castle   No 7
Bridgnorth   Sophie's Tea Rooms
Ludlow   Hardwicks
  Olive Branch
  Penny Anthony Restaurant
Much Wenlock   Scott's Coffee &
  Wholefood Shop
Oswestry   Good Companion
Shrewsbury   Cornhouse Restaurant &
  Wine Bar
  Delany's

SOMERSET
Bishops's Lydeard   Rose Cottage
Bridgwater   Bridge Restaurant
  Nutmeg
Castle Cary   Old Bakehouse
  Tramps Wine Bar
Cheddar   Wishing Well Tea Rooms
Dunster   Tea Shoppe

Frome   Old Bath Arms
  Settle
Glastonbury   Rainbow's End Café
Montacute   Montacute House Restaurant
Selworthy   Periwinkle Cottage Tea Rooms
Tarr Steps   Tarr Farm
Taunton   Castle Hotel, Bow Bar
Wells   Cloister Restaurant
  Good Earth
Williton   Blackmore's Bookshop Tea Room
Yeovil   Clarries
  Trugs

STAFFORDSHIRE
Abbots Bromley   Marsh Farm Tea Room
Alstonefield   Old Post Office Tea Room
Cauldon Lowe   Staffordshire Peak Arts
  Centre
Froghall   The Wharf Eating House
Kinver   Berkley's Bistro
Tutbury   Corn Mill Tea Room
Uttoxeter   Ye Olde Pantry

SUFFOLK
Bury St Edmunds   Beaumonts
Clare   Peppermill Restaurant
  Ship Stores

Establishments by counties

Framlingham Tiffins
Great Barton Craft at the Suffolk Barn
Hadleigh Weaver's Bistro
Ipswich Belstead Brook Hotel Lounge
  Marno's Restaurant
  Orwell House
  Tackets
Newmarket Jane's Wine Bar
Stonham Aspal Stonham Barns
Sudbury Ford's
Walberswick Potters Wheel
Woodbridge Wine Bar
Woolpit The Bakery

SURREY
Ashstead Bart's
Cheam Superfish
Compton Old Congregational Tea Shop
Croydon Hockneys
  Munbhave
  Wine Vaults
Dorking Burford Bridge Hotel Lounge
  Superfish
Ewell Superfish
Guildford Richoux
Kew Original Maids of Honour
  Pissarro's
  Wine & Mousaka
Limpsfield Limpsfield Brasserie
Morden Superfish

Richmond Mrs Beeton
  Refectory
  Richmond Harvest
  Wildefoods Wholefood Café
Seale Herbs
Surbiton Fortunes
  Liberty Bell
Thames Ditton Skiffers
Tolworth Superfish
West Byfleet Superfish

EAST SUSSEX
Alfriston Drusillas Thatched Barn
  Singing Kettle
Bexhill Trawlers
Brighton Al Duomo
  Allanjohn's
  Blossoms
  Cripes!
  Food for Friends
  Goodies
  Mock Turtle
  Pie in the Sky
  Samsons
  Saxons
Eastbourne Byrons
  Ceres Health Food Restaurant
  Nature's Way
Hailsham Homely Maid
  Waldernheath Country Restaurant

Hastings Brant's
  Judge's
  Town House
Herstmonceux Cleavers Lyng
  Praise the Lord
Lewes Lunch Counter
  Mike's Wine Bar
  Pattisson's Coffee Shop
Magham Down Ye Old Forge
Newhaven Kenya Coffee House
Offham Old Post House
Ringmer Coffee House
Rottingdean Old Cottage Tea Rooms
  Rottingdean Pâtisserie
Rye Swiss Pâtisserie & Tea Room
Seaford Trawlers
Winchelsea Finch of Winchelsea
  Winchelsea Tea Rooms

WEST SUSSEX
Billingshurst Burdock Provender
Chichester Chats Brasserie
  Clinch's Salad House
  Nicodemus
  St Martin's Tea Rooms
  Savourie
Findon Tea House
Henfield Norton House
Pulborough Chequers Hotel
Shoreham-by-Sea Cuckoo Clock
Worthing Fogarty's
  Hannah
  Mr Pastry
  Nature's Way Coffee Shop

TYNE & WEAR
Gateshead Marks & Spencer, Garden
  Restaurant
Gosforth Girl on a Swing
Newcastle upon Tyne Blackgate
  Restaurant
  Madeleine's
  Mather's
  Roulade Crêperie & Brasserie

WARWICKSHIRE
Atherstone Cloisters Wine Bar & Bistro
  Muffins Salad Bar
Gaydon Gaydon Lodge
Kenilworth Castle Green Tea Shop
  George Rafters
Leamington Spa Mallory Court
  Piccolino's
  Regency Fare
  Ropers

Ryton Ryton Bridge Hotel Bistro
  Ryton Gardens Café
Shipston on Stour Bell Inn
  Kerry House Tea Rooms
Stratford-upon-Avon Pinocchio
  Slug & Lettuce
  Truffles Olde Tea Shoppe
Studley Interesting Things
Warwick Bar Roussel
  Brethren's Kitchen
  Charlottes Tea Rooms
  Piccolino's Pizzeria
  Westgate Arms, Gate Brasserie

WEST MIDLANDS
Birmingham Bobby Browns in Town
  Drucker's
  La Galleria Wine Bar
  Gingers
  New Happy Gathering
  Rackhams Rooftop Restaurant
  La Santé
  Time for a Break
  Wild Oats
Coventry Trinity House Hotel, Herbs
  Restaurant
Solihull Bobby Browns
Warley Wild Thyme

WILTSHIRE
Avebury Stones Restaurant
Bradford-on-Avon Corner Stones
Broad Chalke Cottage House
Castle Combe Manor House Hotel
Devizes Wiltshire Kitchen
Easton Grey Easton Grey Garden
  Restaurant
Marlborough Polly
Salisbury Mainly Salads
  Michael Snell
  Mo's
Swindon Acorn Wholefoods
Warminster Chinn's Celebrated
  Chophouse
  Jenner's
  Vincent's

NORTH YORKSHIRE
Aysgarth Falls Mill-Race Teashop
Barden Howgill Lodge
  Low House Farm
Bolton Abbey Bolton Abbey Tea Cottage
Castleton Castleton Tea Rooms
Easingwold Truffles

Establishments by counties

Harrogate Bettys
  Chimes Tea Room
  Vani's Pizzeria
  William & Victoria Downstairs
  William & Victoria Restaurant
Hawes Cockett's Hotel
Helmsley Crown Hotel
Knaresborough Crumpets Coffee Shoppe
Northallerton Bettys
Pateley Bridge Willow
Ripon Warehouse
Settle Car & Kitchen
Shipton Beningbrough Hall Restaurant
Skipton Herbs Wholefood & Vegetarian
  Restaurant
Whitby Magpie Café
York Bettys
  Gillygate Wholefood Café
  Mulberry Hall Coffee Shop
  St Williams College Restaurant
  Taylors Tea Rooms
  Wholefood Trading Company

SOUTH YORKSHIRE
Sheffield Just Cooking
  Toff's Restaurant & Coffee House
Woodlands Three Cranes Coffee Shop

WEST YORKSHIRE
Bradford Pizza Margherita
Elland Bertie's Bistro
Holmfirth Wrinkled Stocking
Horsforth Stuarts Wine Bar
Ilkley Bettys
Leeds Flying Pizza
  Ike's Bistro
  Reed's Café
  Salvo's
  Strawberryfields Bistro
Otley Chatters Tea Shoppe

SCOTLAND

BORDERS
Dryburgh Abbey Orchard Tearoom
Newcastleton Copshaw Kitchen
Peebles Kailzie Garden Restaurant & Tea
  Room
  Sunflower
Selkirk Philipburn House Hotel

CENTRAL
Balfron Coffee Mill
Falkirk Coffee Cabin
  Healthy Life

DUMFRIES & GALLOWAY
Dalbeattie Coffee & Things
Dumfries Opus Salad Bar
Moffat Beechwood Country House Hotel
New Abbey Abbey Cottage
Stranraer L'Aperitif

FIFE
Falkland Kind Kyttock's Kitchen
St Andrews Brambles
  Pepita's Restaurant

GRAMPIAN
Aboyne Alford House Restaurant
Buckie Old Monastery
Stonehaven George A. Robertson
Tomintoul Glenmulliach Restaurant

HIGHLAND
Arisaig Old Library Lodge & Restaurant
Colbost Three Chimneys
Dulnain Bridge Muckrach Lodge Hotel
Inverness Brookes Wine Bar
Kentallen of Appin Holly Tree
Kildonan Three Rowans Tea Shop &
  Restaurant
Kincraig Boathouse Restaurant
Kingussie Wood'n'Spoon
Kinlochbervie Kinlochbervie Hotel
Strathcarron Carron Restaurant
Tarbet Tigh-na-Mara Seafood Restaurant
Ullapool Ceilidh Place

LOTHIAN
Dirleton Open Arms Hotel Lounge
East Linton Harvesters Hotel, Farmers
  Den
Edinburgh Brasserie Saint Jacques
  Country Kitchen
  Handsel's Wine Bar
  Helios Fountain
  Henderson's Salad Table
  Kalpna
  Laigh Kitchen
  Lune Town
  Waterfront Wine Bar
Wester Howgate Old Howgate Inn, Coach
  House

STRATHCLYDE
Crinan Crinan Coffee Shop
Cullipool Longhouse Buttery
Dunoon Black's Tea Room
Eaglesham Wishing Well Tea Room

Glasgow   Café Gandolfi
  De Quincey's/Brahms & Liszt
  Joe's Garage
  Loon Fung
  Tom Sawyer's
  Ubiquitous Chip
  Warehouse Café
Hardgate   Elle Coffee Shop
Helensburgh   Original Famous Coffee
  House
Isle of Gigha   Gigha Hotel
Kilchrenan   Taychreggan Hotel
Knipoch   Knipoch House Hotel
Lamlash   Carraig Mhor
  Glenscorrodale Farm Tearoom

Largs   Green Shutter Tearoom
  Jacobite Teashop
Milngavie   Famous Coffee House
Taynuilt   Shore Cottage
Tayvallich   Tayvallich Inn
Whitehouse   Old School Tearoom

TAYSIDE
Aberfeldy   Country Fare Coffee House
Dundee   Raffles Restaurant
Glamis   Strathmore Arms
Inchture   Inchture Milk Bar
Pitlochry   Luggie Restaurant
Powmill   Powmill Milk Bar

WALES

CLWYD
Llangollen   Gales Wine & Food Bar
Llanrhaeadr   Lodge
Rossett   Churtons Wine & Food Bar
Tynant   Bronnant Tea Shop
Wrexham   Bumbles Coffee Shop

DYFED
Aberaeron   Hive on the Quay
Aberystwyth   Connexion
Carmarthen   Waverley Restaurant
Eglwysfach   Ty'n-y-Cwm Tea Rooms
Keeston   Keeston Kitchen
Llandeilo   Cawdor Arms Hotel
Llanycefn   Llain Llogin
Newport   Cnapan
Wolf's Castle   Wolfscastle Country Hotel

GWENT
Abergavenny   Coffoodles
Chepstow   Willow Tree
Newport   Happy Carrot Bistro

GWYNEDD
Aberdovey   Old Coffee Shop
Caernarfon   Bakestone
Llandudno   No. 1 Food & Wine Bar
Llanrwst   Tu-Hwnt-i'r-Bont
Menai Bridge   Jodies Wine Bar

MID-GLAMORGAN
Cardiff   Armless Dragon
 La Brasserie
 Champers
 Sage

POWYS
Crickhowell   Cheese Press
Hay-on-Wye   Granary
 Lion's Corner House
Machynlleth   Centre for Alternative
 Technology
 Quarry Shop
Newtown   Jays

WEST GLAMORGAN
Swansea   Home on the Range

CHANNEL ISLANDS

ALDERNEY
St Anne's   Gossip Coffee Shop

GUERNSEY
St Peter Port   Flying Dutchman Hotel

JERSEY
Gorey   Jersey Pottery Restaurant
St Aubin's   Sadler's
St Brelade's Bay   Hotel l'Horizon

ISLE OF MAN
Ballasalla   La Rosette
Castletown   Castletown Golf Links Hotel
Douglas   L'Experience

LONDON

Ajanta

12 Goldhawk Road, W12
01-743 5191
Map 9 A2

Open 12–2.30 & 6–midnight
Closed 25 & 26 December

Chicken vindaloo £2.80   Mixed tandoori £6.30
Credit Access, Amex, Diners, Visa

P street parking   **WC**

First-class cooking raises this friendly Indian restaurant near Shepherd's Bush out of the ordinary – as its many regulars will tell you (booking advised). Moist and tender meats make dishes like chicken tikka, kebabs and pasanda really special; sauces are richly flavoured and subtly spiced from mild to fiery; rice and vegetables are perfectly executed (note the nicely aromatic pilau). *No dogs.*

Almeida Theatre Wine Bar

1a Almeida Street, N1
01-226 0931
Map 10 C1

Open 10.30–2 & 5.30–11
Closed Sun except for special concerts & Bank Holidays when no theatre production

Cheese & fennel hot pot £3.25   Plum crumble 95p
P street parking   **&**   **WC**

Friendly, relaxed and unpretentious surroundings for enjoying tasty snacks and a good choice of wines by bottle or glass. The food is served in enormous portions and ranges from soup, houmus and guacamole to stuffed spuds, flans, vegetable hot pots and barbecued pork chops. Sweets include plum crumble and chocolate fudge cake. From time to time the cuisine of a particular country is featured. *No dogs.* ✑

Anna's Place

90 Mildmay Park, NI
01-249 9379
Map 10 C1

Open 12.30–2.30 & 7.15–10.15
Closed Sun, Mon, Bank Holidays, 1 week Easter, 1 week Christmas & all August

Soup of the day £2.25   Swedish meatballs with vegetables £5.70
P street parking   **WC**

There's a cosy atmosphere at Anna Hegarty's bustling little restaurant specialising in appetising and authentic Swedish fare. Just-a-biters should head for the bar and try smoked reindeer meat with horseradish or spinach and lemon soup for a snack with a difference, or perhaps go for the popular meatballs, smoked chicken or Swedish caviar with sour cream. Lovely sweets, too. More elaborate evening meals in restaurant. Booking advised. *No dogs.*

Aspava

19b Trebeck Street, W1
01-491 8739
Map 11 A2

Open noon–midnight
Closed 25 December

Prawn salad £1.70   Kofte £3.85
LVs

P NCP on Shepherd Street   **WC**

On the corner of Shepherd Market, this tiny restaurant is packed throughout its long opening hours with a friendly crowd hungry for the tasty Middle Eastern food on offer. Taramasalata, houmus and dolmades make delicious starters, while juicy charcoal-grilled kebabs, moussaka and aromatic lamb casserole (all served with rice and salad) are favourite main courses. *No dogs.*

Asuka   *New Entry*

209a Baker Street, NW1
01-486 5026
Map 9 B2

Open noon–2.30 & 6–11
Closed Sat lunch, all Sun, Bank Holidays & 10 days Christmas
Tekamaki sushi £6.50   Assorted sushi £10
Credit Access, Amex, Diners, Visa
P NCP in Glentworth Street or meters & **WC**

Typical decor, complete with a small formal indoor garden, for this Japanese restaurant at the north end of Baker Street. The sushi bar, just up from the smart lobby, offers a regular choice that includes mackerel, tuna, prawns, yellow tail and salmon. The special sushi (ask for it by that name) gives the best and most elaborately prepared selection. Fresh fish arrives every Tuesday and Friday. *No dogs.*

Athenaeum Hotel, Windsor Lounge

116 Piccadilly, W1
01-499 3464
Map 11 A2

Open 24 hours

Scrambled eggs royale £3.50   Afternoon tea £4
Credit Access, Amex, Diners, Visa
P Park Lane Hotel car park in Brick Street & meter parking **WC**

Impeccable service and a delightfully peaceful ambience make this long elegant lounge complete with Greek statues and fern-filled stone vases a most appealing rendezvous. At all times you can enjoy snacks like soup, club sandwiches, smoked salmon and sorbets, while afternoon tea from 3–5.30 brings finger sandwiches, super scones and a couple of pastries. *No dogs.* 🦃

L'Autre Wine Bar

Shepherd Street, W1
01-499 4680
Map 11 A2

Open 12–3 & 5.30–11.30
Closed Sat lunch, all Sun & Bank Holidays

Mediterranean prawns in garlic butter £5.95
Enchiladas frijoles £4.25
LVs *Credit* Access, Visa
P NCP in Carrington Street **WC**

Imagine yourself in Paris at this lively little wine bar with its check-clothed tables and solid wooden benches. Seafood is a speciality, and the generous platters of prawns, herring, cockles, mussels and crab are an irresistible attraction. Appetising alternatives include Mexican tostados and burritos, Auvergne sausage and smoked ham. Finish with some delicious blue Auvergne or chèvre cheese. No children. *No dogs.* 🍷

Balls Brothers (Wine Bar)

6 Cheapside, EC2
01-248 2708
Map 11 C1

Open 11.30–3
Closed Sat, Sun & Bank Holidays

Sandwiches £2.50   Cheese platter £2.50
LVs *Credit* Access, Amex, Diners, Visa

P NCP in Paternoster Row & **WC**

This attractive panelled wine bar is crowded at lunchtime with a regular clientele who appreciate the convivial surroundings, excellent wines and good, simple food. Sandwiches are a favourite choice, generously filled with smoked salmon, ham and fresh pineapple, roast beef with horseradish; there are also salads, well-kept cheeses and a hot daily special like shepherd's pie. No children. *No dogs.* 🍷

Balls Brothers (Wine Bar)

11 Moor House, Moorgate, EC2
01-628 3944
Map 11 C1

Open 11.30–3
Closed Sat, Sun & Bank Holidays

Fillet of beef Wellington £5.25   Monkfish
provençale £4.75
LVs   *Credit* Access, Amex, Diners, Visa
P NCP at London Wall   **WC**

It's best to arrive early or book if you want a seat in the restaurant section of this friendly wine bar, as it's always crowded at lunchtime. The cold buffet of meats, seafood and salads is popular for light meals, while a short menu offers more substantial fare like vegetable soup or potted shrimps followed by, say, a steak or veal escalope Biarritz. Sandwiches only in the wine bar; children in the restaurant only. *No dogs.* ℮

Balls Brothers (Wine Bar)

2 Old Change Court, St Paul's Churchyard,
EC4
01-248 8697
Map 11 C1

Open 11.30–3
Closed Sat, Sun & Bank Holidays
Steak & kidney pie with vegetables £3.65
Smoked turkey salad £4
LVs   *Credit* Access, Amex, Diners, Visa
P Distaff Lane NCP   **WC**

Office workers pack this wine bar in a modern precinct opposite St Paul's at lunchtime, so arrive early to guarantee some elbow space. Substantial sandwiches like garlicky grilled steak served in a baguette are popular, and there are freshly made soups, cold meats and salads, cheeses and hot dishes like cottage pie with vegetables, too. Good selection of wines. No children. *No dogs.* ℮

Bar du Musée

17 Nelson Road, Greenwich, SE10
01-858 4710
Map 10 D2

Open noon–3 & 6.30–11
Closed 25 December

Pumpkin soup with bread £1.50   Chicken Kiev
£3.95
Credit Access, Amex, Diners, Visa
P Burney Street car park   &   **WC**

A cheerful and atmospheric wine bar-cum-bistro just a short stroll from the National Maritime Museum. The menu sticks mainly to familiar dishes capably prepared: garlic mushrooms or smoked mackerel pâté to start, then perhaps a burger, quiche or chicken Kiev. Vegetarians are well provided for (pasta provençale, lentil burgers, meatless Scotch eggs), and there are a few simple sweets like banana mousse and ice cream. Children at lunchtime only. ℮

Le Beaujolais Wine Bar

25 Litchfield Street, WC2
01-836 2277
Map 11 B1

Open 12–3 & 5.30–11
Closed Sat lunch, all Sun, Bank Holidays, 4 days Easter & 4 days Christmas
Montbeliard sausage & lentils £2.95   Boeuf
bourguignonne £3.95
Credit Access
P NCP in St Martin's Lane   **WC**

Tasty snacks come in a limited but tempting variety at this busy, lively little wine bar. Cream of watercress soup and smoked mackerel pâté are typical starters, with tasty main courses like braised ham with peach or French sausage with lentils and sauté potatoes. The charcuterie platter is another popular choice, and there are French cheeses and one or two simple sweets. Enjoyable wines by the glass. *No dogs.* ℮

Beehive

11a Beehive Place, SW9
01-274 1690
Map 10 C3

Open 11–4 (Sat from 10)
Closed Sun & Bank Holidays

Potato & mushroom curry £1.35   Banana &
coconut trifle £1
LVs
P street parking   **WC**

Appetising and imaginative wholefood
dishes based on organically grown produce
are the mainstay of this simple counter-
service restaurant. Snacks like falafel with
pitta bread and tahini sauce have appeal,
while hot lunchtime offerings range from
ratatouille pancakes to Indonesian gado
gado – fresh vegetables and tofu in spicy
peanut sauce. Salads and cakes available all
day, and more elaborate evening meals.
No dogs.

Bentley's Wine Bar & Oyster Bar

11 Swallow Street, W1
01-734 0401
Map 11 A2

Open noon–3 & 5.30–9
Closed Sun & Bank Holidays

Crab bisque £1.75   Seafood pancakes £3.95
LVs   *Credit* Access, Amex, Diners, Visa

P NCP in Shaftesbury Avenue   **WC**

Head for the ground-floor oyster bar or
basement wine bar for an enjoyable snack or
light meal at this traditional seafood restaurant. At the marble-topped counter it's cold
dishes only, while downstairs the nicely
varied choice ranges from crab bisque and
clam fries to seafood strudel, fresh pasta and
meat dishes like pork brochette with coconut.
Sandwiches and salads make up the evening
choice. *No dogs.* 🥢

La Bersagliera

372 King's Road, SW3
01-352 5993
Map 12 B2

Open 12.30–3 & 7–midnight
Closed some Bank Holidays & two weeks
August

Tagliatelle alla Bersagliera £2.80   Rigatoni all'
amatriciana £2.60
P street meters

Lively, loud and usually busy, this King's
Road trattoria offers a useful range of pizzas
and pasta. The former comes in many
varieties, from basic margherita to four
seasons, with capers, olives, anchovies and
peperoni; the latter is fresh and served with
a choice of sauces. There are also meat and
poultry main courses, moules mariniere,
simple starters and sweets. Minimum charge
£2.50. *No dogs.*

Bill Stickers   `New Entry`

18 Greek Street, W1
01-437-0582
Map 11 B1

Open noon–3am
Closed 1 January & 25 December

Bangers & mash £4.25   Poached salmon
£7.50
Credit Access, Amex, Diners, Visa
P Soho Square   **WC**

Good taste is a term that applies more to the
food than to the gimmicky decor in this late-
closing Soho restaurant. The menu covers
largely familiar ground, with soups, salads
and burgers (including a tasty vegetarian
version), plus Dover sole, bangers and mash
and chilli con carne. On an evening visit the
garlic bread was pretty good, the coffee not
so hot. Eclairs, apple pie and ice creams for
a sweet. Minimum charge of £3.50 except at
teatime. *No dogs.*

Le Bistroquet

273 Camden High Road, NW1
01-485 9607
Map 9 B1

Open noon–6 & 7–11.30 (Sun till 11)
Closed 3 days Christmas

Nouilles fraîches du basilic £2.50   Flétan en
papillote au caviar d'aubergines £5.95
Credit (not bar) Access, Amex, Visa
P meter parking   **WC**

A very popular restaurant with a bustling
French air. The bar menu includes charcuterie, baguette sandwiches, vegetables vi-
naigrette and pasta with basil, plus simple
sweets. Between 3 and 6 the choice is limited
to a few cold dishes. The full restaurant menu
(minimum charge £5) is varied and imaginative, with dishes ranging from delicious
broccoli mousse to halibut en papillote, calf's
liver, steaks and cassis terrine. There are
some excellent cheeses. *No dogs.* 🍵 🍴

Blake's Wine & Food Bar

34 Wellington Street, Covent Garden, WC2
01-836 5298
Map 11 B1

Open 11.45–10.30 (Sun till 10)
Closed 25 & 26 December

Quiche & salad £2.95   Turkey & ham pie with
salad £3.40
LVs   *Credit* Access, Amex, Diners, Visa
P meter parking   ♿   **WC**

The glass-fronted doors open wide in summer on to an attractive outdoor eating area
at this spacious wine bar with a youthful,
animated air. Choose from delicious wholemeal quiches and a speciality savoury pie
like fidget or chicken and mushroom, or tuck
into something hot like chicken casserole or
lasagne in winter weather. Pop in, too, for
tea, coffee and something sweet like gâteau
or cheesecake. *No dogs.* 🍵

Blenheim's

12 Blenheim Terrace, NW8
01-624 5313
Map 9 B1

Open noon–3 & 7–midnight
Closed 1 January & 25 & 26 December

Chicken satay £3.95   Duck à l'orange with
vegetables £4.95
Credit Access, Amex, Diners, Visa
P street parking   **WC**

Posters on the walls, check tablecloths and
parasol-topped pavement tables lend a positively Gallic air to this cheerful wine bar-cum-
restaurant. Check the blackboard for the
day's offerings: creamy soups, baked potatoes, chilli, steak sandwiches and chicken
satay are typical of the simple but appetising
selection. Finish with a nice fruit pie or bread
and butter pudding. Traditional roasts for
Sunday lunch. 🍵

Blooms

130 Golders Green Road, NW11
01-455 1338 Map 9 A1
Open noon–9.30
Closed Fri, Sat, 25 Dec & Jewish hols
90 Whitechapel High Street, E1
01-247 6001 Map 10 C2
Open 11.30–10 (Fri till 2.30)
Closed Sat, 25 Dec & Jewish hols
LVs   *Credit* Access, Visa
P street (NW11) & own car park (E1)   ♿ **(E1)**
WC

Two traditional and much-loved kosher restaurants still in full bloom after more than half
a century's combined trading. Favourite
dishes remain unchanged down the years:
fried or boiled gefilte fish; chopped liver;
kreplach; viennas and frankfurters; the renowned salt beef with potato latkes and
pickled cucumber; weighty lockshen pudding. Quick-serving staff are usually ready
with a quip. *No dogs.*
Viennas £2.90   Salt beef £5.90

Bolton's Wine Bar

198 Fulham Road, SW10
01-352 0251
Map 12 A2

Open 10.30–3 & 5.30–11, Sun noon–2
Closed Sun eve, also all Sun April–October,
some Bank Holidays & 4 days Christmas
Mexican lamb hot pot £3.95   Avocado,
spinach & bacon salad £3.75
Credit Access, Amex, Diners, Visa
P meter parking

French-style baguette sandwiches and croque-monsieur are always available at this
brasserie-style wine bar, where interest fo-
cuses on the blackboard menu of home-
made specials. Start with French onion soup
or a salmon terrine, followed by an exotic
salad featuring ginger-flavoured chicken,
game pie, or a winter casserole – perhaps
boeuf carbonnade. Sorbets or crème brûlée
for afters, and good coffee. No children. ©

Bon Ton Roulet

127 Dulwich Road, Herne Hill, SE24
01-733 8701
Map 10 C3

Open 7pm–10.30pm, Sun 12.30pm–3pm
Closed Sun eve, Bank Holidays, last week
August & 1 week Christmas

Beef Marsala £5.85   Baked stuffed peppers
£5.75
P street parking   **WC**

Colourful company and closely packed tables
make for a carefree, relaxed atmosphere at
Sally Sherratt's tiny restaurant, whose motto
is 'Let the good times roll'. Her tempting
selection of enjoyable dishes ranges from
popular starters like tempura vegetables and
a juicy pear with Stilton and tarragon cream
to beef casserole, kidneys Turbigo, stuffed
peppers and a pork escalope stuffed with
cheese, apple and nuts. Good sweets, too.
Unlicensed. *No dogs.* ©

Bonne Bouche Pâtisserie

2 Thayer Street, W1
01-935 3502
Map 11 A1

Open 8.30–7, Sun 9–6

Welsh rarebit £2.25   Steak & kidney pie from
50p
LVs

P meter parking

A bright, modern pâtisserie, where an excellent range of baking includes chocolate
gâteau, mille-feuille and croissant filled with
ham or garlicky sausage. Lots more, too,
from quiches and toasted sandwiches to
salads, omelettes and daily specials like
cannelloni and beef curry. Breakfast until
11.30, tempting ice cream creations, afternoon set teas. Minimum lunchtime charge
£1.50. Unlicensed. *No dogs.* 🍵

Boos (Wine Bar)

1 Glentworth Street, Marylebone Road, NW1
01-935 3827
Map 9 B2
Open 11.30–3 & 5.30–8
Closed Sat eve, all Sun, also Sat lunch
September–May, Bank Holidays, 3 weeks
September & 2 weeks Christmas
Ham salad £2.95   Vanilla cheesecake £1.35
Credit Access, Amex, Diners
P NCP in Marylebone Road   **WC**

'Simple but delicious' describes the snacks
served in this popular wine bar just off
Marylebone Road. Brown bread sandwiches
include pâté, Bavarian smoked cheese and
excellent home-cooked ham, and there's
quiche, taramasalata, salads and a special
like chicken and ham pie. The only sweet
offered is their delicious cheesecake, vanilla
and a flavour of the week such as maple
walnut. Super choice of wines. No children.
No dogs. ©

Bottlescrue (Wine Bar)

52 Bath House, Holborn Viaduct, EC1
01-248 2157
Map 11 C1

Open 11.30–3 & 5–8.30
Closed Sat, Sun, Bank Holidays & 3 days
Christmas
Roast beef sandwich £1.40   Fresh Scotch
salmon & salad £5.85
Credit Access, Amex, Diners, Visa
P NCP in Snow Hill **WC**

An appetising variety of cold fare is served in
this popular, lively wine bar, where sawdust,
barrel tables and alcove seating contribute
to a pleasantly traditional feel. Cold cuts and
game pie are the basis of simple, fresh
salads, and there are some excellent granary
bread sandwiches – trout with cucumber is
perfect with a good glass of wine. Also a
simple cheese selection, plus berries or apple
pie for sweet. No children. *No dogs.* ✇

Brasserie

11 Bellevue Road, SW17
01-672 7246
Map 9 B3

Open noon–3 & 7–11
Closed 25 & 26 December

Soup of the day 95p   Rack of lamb £3.95
Credit Access, Visa
P street parking & Wandsworth Common
Station car park **WC**

Careful cooking in the modern manner char-
acterises this jolly, informal brasserie overlooking Wandsworth Common. Imaginative
dishes abound, from chilled vegetarian
mousse with saffron sauce and watercress
and spring onion salad topped with hot
Chinese chicken among starters, to colourful
main courses like poached scallops with pink
peppercorns and veal tossed with fresh limes
and sorrel. Home-made raspberry cheesecake to finish. *No dogs.* ✇

La Brasserie

272 Brompton Road, SW3
01-584 1668
Map 12 B1

Open 8am–midnight (Sun from 10am)
Closed 25 & 26 December

Salad niçoise £2.80   Tranche de gigot aux
haricots £6.30
Credit Access, Amex, Diners, Visa
P meter parking ♿ **WC**

It's taped Piaf versus the rest at this bustling
brasserie, where a lively local clientele as-
sembles to enjoy a varied selection of hearty,
well-prepared French dishes. Soupe de pois-
son comes with the usual accessories, and
popular main courses include blanquette de
veau, boeuf bourguignonne, duck with petits
pois and the excellent lamb with garlicky
haricot beans. Interesting daily specials.
Simple sweets. *No dogs.* ✇

Brasserie at L'Escargot   ★

48 Greek Street, W1
01-437 2679
Map 11 B1

Open noon–3 & 5.30–11.15 (Sat from 6)
Closed Sat lunch, all Sun, Bank Holidays & 10
days Christmas
Bayonne ham with fresh figs £3.95   Grilled
poussin with ginger & chillies £5
Credit Access, Amex, Diners, Visa
P NCP in Dean Street & meter parking **WC**

Extremely popular among the young and
fashionable, this wonderfully relaxed Soho
brasserie not only oozes style but serves the
most delicious food, too. Typically imaginative offerings might range from grilled goat's
cheese and salad niçoise made with fresh
tuna to ragout of monkfish, squid and mussels in white wine or spicy chicken with ginger
and chillies. Equally tempting sweets, too.
Late evening cabaret. *No dogs.* ✇

Brown's Hotel Lounge

Dover Street, W1
01-493 6020
Map 11 A2

Open 9am–12.30am

Club sandwich £5.75   Set afternoon tea £7.50
Credit Access, Amex, Diners, Visa

P NCP in Carrington Street   WC

A delightfully English, and highly popular, setting – all oak panelling, moulded ceilings and swift, formal service – in which to enjoy set afternoon tea, served from 3 to 6. Toasted scones, well-filled sandwiches and mouth-watering light pastries go well with an excellent brew. At other times, a stylish snack like blanquette of chicken and asparagus fills that gap admirably. *No dogs.* 🍵

Bubbles Wine Bar

41 North Audley Street, W1
01-499 0600
Map 11 A1

Open 11–3 & 5.30–11
Closed Sat eve, all Sun & Bank Holidays

Roast English lamb £3.75   Vegetable platter
£2.50
LVs   *Credit* Access, Amex, Diners, Visa
P NCP at Marriott Hotel & meters   &   WC

David and Susan Nichol's chic and spacious wine bar on the ground floor offers simple but delicious food. Roast English lamb is a speciality, and there are splendid salads, choice charcoal grills and some irresistible sweets (note chocolate marquise with a crème anglaise sauce). Down in the bistro they serve a two-course meal plus coffee at £12.50. Interesting wines at keen prices, including many by the glass. No children. *No dogs.* 🍵

Café Delancey

3 Delancey Street, NW1
01-387 1985
Map 9 B1

Open 9.30am–midnight
Closed Sun, 1 January & 25 & 26 December

Delancey breakfast £3.20   Poulet poché
Delancey £5.60
Credit Access, Visa
P NCP next door in Arlington Road   WC

Run on Continental lines, with any dish available at any time of day, this friendly café with pavement eating in fine weather also provides the daily papers to accompany your breakfast. Smoked sausages and red cabbage, roast rack of lamb, home-made terrines and croque-monsieur are all popular savoury choices, while smashing sweets include Swiss chocolate cake and beautifully glazed fruit tarts. *No dogs.* 🍵

Café Fish des Amis du Vin

39 Panton Street, SW1
01-839 4880
Map 11 B2

Open 11.30am–11.30pm
Closed Sun

Brill meunière £6.95   Fried plaice fillets £3.95

Credit Access, Amex, Diners, Visa
P Whitcomb Street car park   WC

Fishy pictures and posters adorn this popular place, and the fishy menu is chalked up on huge blackboards. The fruits of the sea come cold, butter-fried, deep-fried, steamed or charcoal-grilled, and the choice spans hake and halibut, turbot and trout, plaice and sole, prawns, crab and lobster. A £1 cover charge includes a little starter of fish pâté. Snackier dishes, plus oysters, in the downstairs wine bar. *No dogs.* 🍵

Le Café du Jardin

28 Wellington Street, WC2
01-836 8769
Map 11 B1

Open noon–2.30 & 6–11.30, Sun noon–10

Emincé de poulet champenoise £6.95   Salade
de poissons fumés £3.80
Credit Access, Amex, Diners, Visa
P meter parking & NCP in Leicester Square
&. **WC**

Described as 'a little corner of France in the
heart of Covent Garden', this popular, brasserie-style restaurant attracts an appreciative clientele for its appetising daily-changing
fare. You can enjoy delicious light bites
including a platter of charcuterie, deep-fried
puff pastry parcels filled with Roquefort and
snails in garlic butter with cream and almonds. Substantial main courses, too. Good
cheeses and coffee. *No dogs.* ⊖

Café Pacifico

5 Langley Street, WC2
01-379 7728
Map 11 B1

Open 11.30–2.45 & 5.30–11.45, Sun noon–
2.45 & 7–10.45
Closed Bank Holidays & lunch Christmas–
New Year
Guacamole £2.35   Tacos £4.85
Credit Access, Visa
P NCP in Drury Lane   **WC**

Very busy, especially at night, this spacious
restaurant is the place to go for some lively
company and enjoyable Mexican food. Try
ceviche (lime-marinated fish) as a change
from the ever-popular guacamole, then one
of the many tortilla-based options, with fillings
ranging from ground beef to pork, cheese or
chicken, their sauces from mild to fiery.
Simple sweets include sorbets and pastries.
No dogs.

Café Pastiche

307 Lillie Road, SW6
01-385 1130
Map 9 A2
Open Wine Bar 11.30–2.45 & 5.30–11;
Restaurant 7.30–11
Closed Sun, 1 Jan, Easter Mon & 25 & 26
December
Coronation chicken £1.75   Fresh pasta from
£1.20 (starter) & £2.35 (main course)
Credit Access, Visa
P street parking   **WC**

A relaxed and friendly wine bar and restaurant where the menu really does tempt the
tastebuds. Fresh linguine and tagliatelle can
be enjoyed as a starter or main course with a
choice of tasty sauces, while alternatives
range from coronation chicken, deep-fried
mushrooms and crudités to juicy steak and
veal in a creamy white wine sauce. Finish
refreshingly with a delicious blackcurrant and
cassis sorbet.

Café Pélican

45 St Martin's Lane, WC2
01-379 0309
Map 11 B2

Open 11am–2 am
Closed 25 & 26 December

Assiette de charcuterie £3.95   Pear & almond
tart £2.95
Credit Access, Amex, Diners, Visa
P NCP in St Martin's Lane   &. **WC**

The nearest thing in the West End to a
Parisian café, with a long, narrow interior and
a few tables set out on the pavement.
Baguette sandwiches, croque monsieur, onion soup and a charcuterie platter are typical
anytime snacks, along with a selection of
pâtisserie to accompany an excellent cup of
coffee. There's also a full lunchtime and
evening menu, and a choice of vegetarian
dishes. *No dogs.* ⊖

Café St Pierre Brasserie

29 Clerkenwell Green, EC1
01-251 6606
Map 11 C1

Open 7.30am–11pm
Closed Sat, Sun, Bank Holidays & 10 days
Christmas
Chicken mousse £1   Breast of chicken with
sage & onion sauce £3.95
Credit Access, Amex, Diners, Visa
P meter parking   **WC**

English and continental breakfasts are
served until 9.30 in this popular modern
brasserie just off Faringdon Road. The menu
offered at mealtimes sticks to quite straightforward dishes, from starters like celery soup
or black pudding to turkeyburgers, grilled
Finnan haddock and good meaty Cumberland sausages (our accompanying apple
sauce was not so good, however). The coffee
is excellent. It's best to book at lunchtime.
No dogs. ♺

Caffe Venezia

15 New Burlington Street, W1
01-439 2378
Map 11 A2

Open noon–3 & 5.30–11.30
Closed Sun & 25 Dec
Tagliatelle venezia £3.50   Mixed fruit flan
£1.50
Credit Access, Amex, Diners, Visa
P NCP in Kingley Street & Savile Row   &
WC

A comfortable, relaxed Italian restaurant,
with good food and particularly pleasant
service. The home-made pasta is an excellent
choice for just-a-biters – our tagliatelle was
served properly al dente with a tasty sauce
of tomatoes, aubergines and a hint of garlic.
There are also some interesting seafood
dishes and a variety of meat and poultry
favourites. *No dogs.*

Camden Brasserie   `New Entry`

216 Camden High Street, NW1
01-482 2114
Map 9 B1

Open noon–3 & 6.30–11.30 (Sun 6–10.30)
Closed 24 December–2 January

Spicy chicken wings £1.75   Steak brochette
teriyaki £5.70

P street   **WC**

Bags of atmosphere at this popular brasserie
with wooden floor, open fire and arty black
and white photographs. Charcoal grills are a
popular choice, and the lamb and steak are
hung on the premises. Excellent pommes
frites accompany, and there's also chicken,
fish and calf's liver. Fresh pasta can be had
as starter or main course, and there's a raw
vegetable salad. To finish, there are daily
desserts and a good cheeseboard. Excellent
espresso. *No dogs.* ♺

Canton

11 Newport Place, WC2
01-437 6220
Map 11 B1

Open dim sum 8–5 (full menu 24 hours)
Closed 3 days Christmas

Dim sum from 90p   Roast duck £2.90

LVs   *Credit* Amex, Diners, Visa
P Cambridge Circus NCP

Twenty-four-hour opening makes this simple
little Chinese restaurant a useful place for
late night feasts. There's a full menu of
starters and main courses, and just-a-biters
in search of a snack must call between 8am
and 5pm to enjoy the dim sum on offer.
Choose from the familiar range, including
wafer-wrapped prawns, char siu buns and
excellent pork and prawn dumplings. Minimum charge £2.50. *No dogs.*

Carriages

43 Buckingham Palace Road, SW1
01-834 8871
Map 12 C1

Open 11.30–2.30 & 5.30–10.30
Closed Sat & Sun in winter & Bank Holidays

Salade niçoise £4.95   Hamburger £4.75
Credit Access, Amex, Diners, Visa

P meter parking   &   **WC**

This smartly contemporary wine bar-cum-restaurant is a popular lunchtime venue for office workers in Victoria. They appreciate the frequently changing menus featuring such imaginative, freshly cooked dishes as deliciously light spinach pâté, flavoursome veal lasagne, Russian fish pie and beef Stroganoff. There are steaks and salads too, and home-made pear tart to finish. Minimum of £4 at lunchtime. No children. *No dogs.*

Charco's Wine Bar

1 Bray Place, off Anderson Street, SW3
01-584 0765
Map 12 B2

Open noon–3 & 5.30–11
Closed Sun, Bank Holidays & 3 days Christmas

Salmon coulibiac £4.20   Crème brûlée £1.50
Credit Access, Amex, Visa
P meter parking   **WC**

Fine wines and appetising food continue to attract an appreciative clientele to this long-established wine bar just off the King's Road. Salads impress by their freshness, colour and variety, while hot dishes might include home-made fish cakes, chilli con carne and the house speciality of beef Wellington. Finish with delicious fruit salad or some fine cheese. Minimum charge of £3 noon–3. *No dogs.*

Chequers

18 Chalk Farm Road, NW1
01-485 1696
Map 9 B1

Open 10am–12.30am
Closed 25 December

Lentil soup with bread £1.35   Cheesecake £1.05

P meters in nearby streets   &   **WC**

Chess players make a beeline for this modest vegetarian café, where games are always in progress. When it's time for refreshment, there's a choice of over a dozen imaginative, freshly prepared salads plus a few hot dishes like thick, nourishing lentil soup and vegetable stew. Finish with a simple sweet such as home-baked cheesecake, apple cake or fresh fruit salad and a good strong cup of coffee. Unlicensed. No smoking. *No dogs.*

Cherry Orchard

241 Globe Road, E2
01-980 6678
Map 10 D1

Open 12–9.30 (Thurs till 2.30)
Closed Sun, Mon, 1 week August & 1 week Christmas
Mushroom moussaka with salad £3.15
Stuffed marrow £1.70
LVs
P street parking   &   **WC**

A walled patio permits outside eating at this thriving vegetarian restaurant run by a Buddhist cooperative. A short but imaginative menu offers wholesome fare like delicious dill-flavoured mushroom soup or a very palatable nut roast containing shredded carrots and beetroot and served with a thick, tangy tomato sauce. Colourful salads; sweets like banana cake. Music and minimum charge of £3.50 alternate Sat eves. Unlicensed. No smoking. *No dogs.*

Chiang Mai

48 Frith Street, W1
01-437 7444
Map 11 B1

Open 12–3 & 6–11.30pm (Sun till 11)
Closed 1 January, 3 days Easter & 2 days
Christmas
Hot & sour beef ball salad £3.50   Omelette
with minced pork £2.95
Credit Access, Amex, Visa
P Soho Square   **WC**

Eat the Thai way at this neat, modern restaurant, choosing a number of small dishes with rice and balancing the mild with the spicy. Satay and tempura make popular appetisers, there's a vast array of soups (including three hot and sour varieties) and main courses range from curries with coconut cream to whole fish with chilli sauce. Noodle and vegetarian dishes are also served. *No dogs.*

Chicago Pizza Pie Factory

17 Hanover Square, W1
01-629 2669
Map 11 A1

Open 11.45–11.30, Sun noon–10.30
Closed 25 & 26 December

Stuffed mushrooms £1.95   Cheese,
mushroom & peperoni pizza (for 2) £6.75
P street parking or NCP in Cavendish Square
WC

Bob Payton's spacious basement restaurant is immensely popular with both Londoners and tourists. The theme is Chicago, from the decor and the football videos to the splendid deep-dish pizzas that are the mainstay of the menu; the regular size feeds two, the large, three or four, and toppings include cheese, mushrooms, olives, anchovies and sausage. Also available: stuffed mushrooms, salads, garlic bread. *No dogs.*

Chicago Rib Shack

1 Raphael Street, Knightsbridge Green, SW7
01-581 5595
Map 12 B1

Open 11.45–11.30, Sun noon–11
Closed 25 & 26 December

Rack of ribs £5.25   Pecan pie £1.85

P NCP in Raphael Street   ♿   **WC**

Don your plastic bib and tuck into the meaty barbecued pork ribs that are the speciality of this cheerful place. Other choices are barbecued beef in a baguette, barbecued chicken and lunchtime burgers, plus a selection of salads and side dishes like onion loaf and stuffed potato skins. For hefty appetites there's cheesecake, pecan pie and ice cream. *No dogs.*

Christys Healthline   **New Entry**

122 Wardour Street, W1
01-434 4468
Map 11 A1

Open 8am–11.30pm (Sat from 10am); Wine
Bar: 11–3 & 5.30–11
Closed Sun & Bank Holidays
Mushroom, nut & beer pâté £1.95   Cream tea
£1.80
LVs   *Credit* Access, Amex, Diners, Visa
P NCP in Wardour Street   ♿   **WC**

A very smart new vegetarian restaurant and bar in the heart of Soho. Breakfast is served until 10 o'clock, when the varied main menu starts to take over with dishes like lentil, tomato and basil pâté, wholemeal pizza and a delicious hot vegetable pie. Salads are fresh and appetising, and there are nice puddings. Vegan dishes are available, and afternoon tea is served 3.30–5.30. Good selection of wines produced by bioagricultural methods. *No dogs.* ♣

Chuen Cheng Ku

17 Wardour Street, W1
01-437 1398
Map 9 B2

Open 11–6 (full menu 11am–midnight, Sun till 11.30)
Closed 25 December
Steamed shrimp dumpling 98p   Mixed seafood noodles £3.40
Credit Access, Amex, Diners, Visa
P Swiss Centre NCP   ♭   **WC**

Daytime snacking is excellent at this vast, traditionally decorated Chinese restaurant. Dim sum are pushed round on heated trolleys (hence some dishes are not warm enough), and the choice includes shrimp or pork dumplings, barbecued pork buns and steamed cuttlefish with satay sauce. There are also some sweet varieties. Other popular snack choices are based on noodles – fried, braised or in soup; chilli-flavoured Singapore noodles are highly recommended. *No dogs.*

City Friends

34 Old Bailey, EC4
01-248 5189
Map 11 C1

Open noon–11.15pm
Closed Sun, Bank Holidays & 3 days Christmas
Prawns in tomato sauce £6   Chicken with cashew nuts £5
LVs *Credit* Access, Amex, Diners, Visa
P meter parking **WC**

Cantonese and Pekinese favourites make up a long menu in this smart basement restaurant, attractively decorated with screens and Chinese harbour scenes. The cooking is careful and consistent, with good crisp vegetables and tender meats. A few typical choices: crabmeat and sweetcorn soup, prawns in tomato sauce, lemon chicken, fried duck with ginger, steamed pork ribs in black bean sauce. *No dogs.*

La Cloche

304 Kilburn High Road, NW6
01-328 0302
Map 9 B1

Open noon–3 & 7–midnight
Closed lunch 1 January & all 25 & 26 December
Deep-fried Emmenthal £1.65   Hot seafood salad £3.85
Credit Visa
P street parking   **WC**

Once a butcher's shop, now a friendly restaurant full of rustic charm. Excellent raw materials are the basis for carefully prepared dishes like crab profiteroles and avocado in filo pastry among starters, duck en croûte, vegetarian pancakes and pork in red wine as typically enterprising main courses. Splendidly fresh salads and vegetables, simple sweets. Traditional Sunday lunches. Sister restaurants: Lantern and Pigeon. *No dogs.* ☞

Le Cochonnet ★   *New Entry*

1 Lauderdale Parade, Maida Vale, W9
01-289 0393
Map 9 B1

Open 12.30–2.45 & 6.30–10.15 (till 11.15 Thurs–Sat), Sun noon–2.45 & 7–10.15

Toulouse sausage lyonnaise £3.95   Veal & pork terrine £2.35
Credit Access, Amex, Diners, Visa
P street parking **WC**

The food here is streets ahead of the average wine bar, so it's not surprising that it's usually busy. Helen Turner produces interesting dishes like spinach and wild mushroom profiteroles; smoked salmon, prawn and cream cheese roulade; Toulouse sausages lyonnaise (the real thing); and corn-fed chicken with a well-judged mustard and Riesling sauce. Mousses, ices, French cheeses. Sunday brunch. Afternoon teas in the summer. *No dogs.* ☞

Colonel Jasper's   *New Entry*

161 Greenwich High Road, SE10
01-853 0585
Map 10 D2

Open 11.30–3 & 5.30–10.30 (Fri & Sat till 11)
Closed Sat lunch, all Sun, Bank Holidays & 4
days Christmas
Beefsteak, kidney & mushroom pie £2.95
Treacle tart with clotted cream £1.65
Credit Access, Amex, Diners, Visa
P own car park   **WC**

Oodles of atmosphere at this cellar bar and
dining room with old photographs on brick
walls, sawdust on the floor and candles in
empty wine bottles. Tasty snacks include
Welsh rarebit, smoked English sausage and
a dish of prawns, and other favourites are
steaks, burgers and steak, kidney and mushroom pie. Also plated salads, English
cheeses and, for sweet, seasonal soft fruits
and treacle tarts. *No dogs.* ☻

Cork & Bottle *(Wine Bar)*

44 Cranbourn Street, WC2
01-734 7807
Map 11 B2

Open 11–3 & 5.30–11, Sun 12–2 & 7–10.30
Closed 1 January & 25 & 26 December

Salmon scallop terrine £2.25   Coq au
Beaujolais with salad & potatoes £5.25
Credit Access, Amex, Diners, Visa
P Swiss Centre NCP   **WC**

Packed at all hours, this marvellously atmospheric cellar wine bar offers a superb selection of imaginative dishes. Oriental pork and
pineapple rice and spicy ham and chicken
salad are just some of the tempting cold
dishes on display, while hot food ranges from
Toulouse sausage casserole to daily specials
like meatloaf with sauce provençal. Super
sweets and cheeses and a carefully chosen
wine list. No children. *No dogs.* ☻

Country Life

1 Heddon Street, W1
01-434 2922
Map 11 A2

Open 11.30–2.30
Closed Sat, Sun, Bank Holidays & 3 days
Christmas
Soup & salad (all you can eat) £2.50
Aubergine Parmesan £1.99
LVs
P meter parking   **WC**

Arrive early for the best choice at this informal
basement restaurant. It's run by Seventh Day
Adventists, who believe in purifying the body
by eating wholefood vegan meals – and
certainly the self-service buffet offers an
appetising way to do just that. Typical choices
might include chick pea and noodle soup,
vegetable pot pie and fresh fruit salad.
Minimum charge of £1.99. Unlicensed. No
smoking. *No dogs.*

Cranks   *New Entry*

17 Great Newport Street, WC2
01-836 5226
Map 11 B1

Open 8–7.30, Sat 10–7.30
Closed Sun & Bank Holidays

Mixed vegetable Stroganoff £1.70   Irish
coffee & hazelnut gâteau £1.30
LVs
P NCP in St Martin's Lane or meters   **WC**

Just a stone's throw from Leicester Square
Underground, this latest Cranks has a simple,
up-to-date appeal. The selection is similar to
that of the other branches – wholemeal baps,
filled jacket potatoes, a well-balanced assortment of salads, soup and a hot dish like
vegetarian cottage pie or spicy chick peas.
Also delicious creamy muesli and nice sweet
things like ginger biscuits or orange and
lemon gâteau. *No dogs.*

Cranks

9 Tottenham Street, W1
01-631 3912
Map 11 A1

Open 8–8 (Sat from 9)
Closed Sun & Bank Holidays

Homity pie £1.25   Mushroom Stroganoff
£2.75
LVs
P meter parking   &   **WC**

Lunchtime queues are a familiar sight at this cool, bright and roomy vegetarian restaurant. Line up at the self-service counter for appetisingly prepared snacks ranging from flavoursome soups, filled wholemeal rolls and crunchy salads to pizzas, quiches and mushroom Stroganoff. Lovely sweet things like rich, moist banana cake and substantial breakfasts of eggs, cereal and scones are served until 10 o'clock. *No dogs.*

Cranks Health Food Restaurant   ★

8 Marshall Street, W1
01-437 9431
Map 11 A1

Open Buffet: 8–7; Dine & Wine: 6.30–11
Closed Sun & Bank Holidays

Split pea & lemon patties £1.25   Leek
croustade £2.75
LVs   *Credit* Access, Amex, Diners, Visa
P NCP at rear   **WC**

Top-quality wholefood and vegetarian fare, available in impressive variety, remains the hallmark of this big daddy of the health-food restaurants. Choose from flavour-packed soups and tasty baps topped with melted cheese, nut roasts, beautifully light wholemeal pastry quiches and crunchy salads displayed in vast bowls. Wonderful breads, cakes and healthy drinks, too – and you can dine and wine by candlelight in the evening. Non-smoking area. ♣

Crêperie

56a South Molton Street, W1
01-629 4794
Map 11 A1

Open 9–8
Closed Sun & 25 December

Savoury pancake £3.10   Lemon pancake
£1.70
LVs   *Credit* Access, Amex, Visa
P Selfridges car park   **WC**

A friendly restaurant on three floors specialising in authentic French crêpes. The savoury versions, made with buckwheat flour, have tempting fillings like cottage cheese and apple, spiced chicken and tuna with mayonnaise, while sweet varieties (white flour) may include seasonal strawberries or perhaps bananas and rum. French onion soup, quiches and salads, plus a few simple sweets, are the only other choices on the menu. *No dogs.*

Criterion Brasserie   **New Entry**

222 Piccadilly, W1
01-839 7133
Map 11 A2

Open noon–3 (Sat 12.30–2.30) & 6–11
Closed Sun & Bank Holidays

Quiche d'aubergines £2.75   Sauerkraut £5.75
LVs   *Credit* Access, Amex, Diners, Visa
P NCP in Denman Street   **WC**

A spectacular brasserie at the hub of the world, with marbled walls, many mirrors and a glittering gold mosaic ceiling. The menu is very French: dishes such as rillettes of pork and goose, soupe au pistou and quail's eggs with salad and mayonnaise start things off, and robust main courses include goujonettes of sole, grilled lamb and a very good Alsatian sauerkraut laden with smoked pork, garlic sausage and frankfurters. *No dogs.*

Cuddeford's Wine Bar

20 Duke Street Hill, SE1
01-403 1681
Map 10 C2

Open 11.30–3
Closed Sat, Sun & Bank Holidays

Plaice florentine with vegetables £4.50
Chocolate fudge cake £1.50
Credit Access, Amex, Diners, Visa
P Snowfields multi-storey NCP   **WC**

Built into a railway arch, this popular wine bar is just as useful if you want a quick snack at the bar – perhaps houmus with pitta bread or a choice from the cheeseboard – or a full meal. Tasty main courses range from cold meat salads to daily hot specials like mild chicken curry, with treacle tart or chocolate fudge cake to finish. No children. *No dogs.* ☕

Da Gianbruno

6 Hammersmith Broadway, W6
01-748 9393
Map 9 A2

Open noon–3 & 6–11.30
Closed 23–28 December

Mushroom risotto £2.50   Scaloppine Marsala £4.50
LVs   *Credit* Access, Amex, Diners, Visa
P car park in Kings Mall shopping centre

Robust, honest flavours are a feature of the cooking at this friendly, family-run trattoria, which stands on the corner of Hammersmith Broadway and Shepherd's Bush Road. The menu covers a wide span of well-prepared Italian dishes, from mushroom risotto and several ways with spaghetti (seafood a speciality) to scaloppine Marsala, chicken valdostana and calf's liver with butter and sage. *No dogs.*

Daly's Wine Bar

46 Essex Street, WC2
01-583 4476
Map 11 B1

Open 8.30–5.30
Closed Sat, Sun & Bank Holidays

Quiche with salad £2.20   Hot dish of the day £2.75
LVs   *Credit* Access, Amex, Diners, Visa
P NCP in Chancery Lane   **WC**

Much appreciated by busy City folk in need of swiftly served and sustaining refreshment, this busy wine bar provides continental breakfasts and afternoon teas as well as tasty lunches. The cold buffet (11.30–3) has cold meats, pies and inventive salads, while flavoursome soups, Dover sole, jacket potatoes and pasta are among typical hot choices. Pleasant sweets, too, and a good selection of cheeses. ☕

Daquise

20 Thurloe Street, SW7
01-589 6117
Map 12 B1

Open 10–11.30
Closed 25 & 26 December

Stuffed cabbage £2.50   Polish kasza £4.50
LVs

P street meter parking   **WC**

New owners, but no other changes at this well-loved if somewhat austere restaurant serving Continental and Polish specialities. Coffee and cakes are the morning rations, and from noon the full menu comes into play with robust fare like stuffed cabbage, meatballs and Hungarian goulash. There are also omelettes, salads, steaks and roasts, plus an occasional fish dish such as boiled or fried trout. *No dogs.*

Davy's Wine Vaults

165 Greenwich High Road, Greenwich, SE10
01-858 7204
Map 10 D2

Open 11.30–3 & 5.30–10.30 (Fri till 11), Sat
noon–3 & 7–11
Closed Sun & Bank Holidays
Ham off the bone & salad £3.60   Avocado
with prawns £2.15
Credit Access, Amex, Diners, Visa
P own car park   **WC**

Candlelight and rustic furniture help create
an atmospheric setting in which to enjoy
generously served portions of traditional
fare. The regular menu includes toasted
fingers of anchovy, sardine or Stilton for a
nibble, cold meat salads, prawns and game
pie, while blackboards list daily specials like
garlic mussels and harvest pie. Finish with
seasonal berries or sherry trifle. Downstairs
to Colonel Jasper's basement bar for a steak
or burger. *No dogs.*

Di's Larder

62 Lavender Hill, SW11
01-223 4618
Map 9 B3

Open 10–6
Closed Sun, Bank Holidays, 3 days Christmas
& 2 weeks August

Tabbouleh 95p   Pasta, nuts & aubergine in
béchamel sauce £1.80
P street parking   **WC**

The blackboard menu changes daily at this
delightful little wholefood and vegetarian
restaurant. Soup (large or small helpings)
could be mushroom and haricot bean or
curried apple vichyssoise, and other dishes
cover a tempting range, from tabbouleh to
quiche, vegetable pizza and pasta with nuts
and aubergines in a béchamel sauce. Apple
crumble is a regular among the sweets.
Unlicensed. No smoking. *No dogs.*

Dining Room

Winchester Walk, off Cathedral Street, SE1
01-407 0337
Map 11 C2

Open 12.30–2.30 & 7–10
Closed Sat–Mon & Bank Holidays

Swiss chard & brown lentil cake £4.50
Mushroom & cheese pancake with salad £4.50

P meter parking at lunchtime   **WC**

Easy to miss, this first-class wholefood
restaurant tucked away behind a vegetable
market offers a short but wonderfully varied
selection of daily-changing dishes, all based
on organically grown produce where possible. Typical delights include steamed cauliflower cake with wine and apple sauce,
buckwheat pancakes filled with pea purée
and beansprout fritters with garlicky tomato
dip. Greek yoghurt and honey makes a
refreshing finale. *No dogs.*

*We neither seek nor accept
hospitality, and we pay for
all food and drinks in full.*

Diwana Bhelpoori House

114 Drummond Street, NW1
01-388 4867
Map 9 B1
Open noon–10
Closed 25 December
P meters in street **WC**

121 Drummond Street, NW1
01-387 5556
Map 9 B1
Open noon–midnight
Closed 25 December
P meters in street

50 Westbourne Grove, W2
01-221 0721
Map 9 B2
Open noon–3 & 6–11, Sat & Sun noon–11
Closed Mon & 25 December
P street **WC**

Three Indian vegetarian restaurants offering consistently enjoyable eating in modest surroundings (Westbourne Grove is the most attractive of the branches). From Bombay come snacks and chat like the popular bhelpoori, a tasty mixture that includes puffed rice, potatoes and green chilli chutney. Crispy vegetable-filled pancakes served with savoury sauce and coconut chutney are the speciality of Madras, while thalis (set meals) originate from Gujarat and are an excellent way of sampling a good range of dishes. To finish, try shrikhand, made with yoghurt, spices, herbs and sugar, or gulab jamun (spongy milk bonbons in syrup). Unlicensed. *No dogs.*

Annapurna thali £3.75 De luxe dosa £2.75
LVs *Credit* Access, Diners, Visa

Dorchester Hotel, Promenade ★

Park Lane, W1
01-629 8888
Map 11 A2

Open 9am–1am

Afternoon tea £8 Sandwiches from £2.60
Credit Access, Amex, Diners, Visa

P NCP in Audley Square ♿ **WC**

Immaculate tail-coated waiters serve dainty, diamond-shaped sandwiches and meltingly delicious scones and pastries while a baby grand plays in the background at this most elegant of settings for afternoon tea. Morning coffee is also popular here, while freshly cut sandwiches, gâteaux and seasonal berries are available all day. Minimum charge of £5 3–6. *No dogs.*

Downs Wine Bar

5 Down Street, W1
01-491 3810
Map 11 A2

Open noon–3 & 5–midnight, Sun noon–2.30 & 7–10.30
Closed 25 December
Chicken roulé with vegetables £4.95 Carré d'agneau à la campagne £4.95
LVs *Credit* Access, Amex, Diners, Visa
P Brick Street garage ♿ **WC**

A busy Mayfair wine bar on two levels connected by a spiral staircase. Excellent plated salads are a permanent feature on the extensive menu, while hot dishes cover a wide span, from moules marinière and scallops mornay to pork Stroganoff and pepper steak. Also an abundance of hors d'oeuvre (deep-fried Camembert, garlic prawns, houmus) and simple sweets. *No dogs.* ☙

Draycott's *(Wine Bar)*

Draycott's (Wine Bar)

114 Draycott Avenue, SW3
01-584 5359
Map 12 B1

Open 12.30–2.45, Sun 11–2.30 & 7–10.30
Closed 1 January & 3 days Christmas
Tarragon burger £4.95   Field & button
mushroom pâté £2.50
Credit Access, Amex, Diners, Visa
P meter parking & NCP in Sloane Avenue   &
WC

A recent facelift has done wonders for this ever-fashionable wine bar, where both decor and cooking now have added zip. Our lunch of warm spinach and chicken liver salad followed by a super seafood brochette with dill cream sauce had immense appeal; other choices include vegetable Stroganoff with noodles and venison steak with chestnut and orange purée. Lovely fresh fruit sorbets to finish. Some fine wines by the glass. Children weekends only. *No dogs.*

Earth Exchange

213 Archway Road, N6
01-340 6407
Map 9 B1

Open noon–3 (Sun till 4) & 6–10.30
Closed Wed, Thurs, some Bank Holidays &
24–31 December

Lasagne with salad £3.20   Fresh fruit flan 95p

P street parking   **WC**

Part of a collective that includes a craft centre and wholefood shop, this pine-furnished basement restaurant offers wholesome vegetarian fare on an efficiently operated self-service basis. Everything is prepared from organically grown produce, and the choice embraces excellent salads, plus hot dishes (always a vegan option) like flavoursome miso soup, aubergine and mushroom chilli, quiches and nut roast. Apple crumble for afters. Non-smoking area. *No dogs.*

East West Restaurant

188 Old Street, EC1
01-608 0300
Map 10 C2

Open 11–10 (Sat & Sun till 3pm)
Closed Bank Holidays & 10 days Christmas

Houmus 75p   Savoury flan £1.10
LVs

P street parking   **WC**

Serious vegetarians should head for this Japanese-influenced restaurant run on strict macrobiotic lines. The daily-changing set meal at £2.95 or £3.95 offers excellent value plus the chance to sample a balanced range of dishes, from scrambled tofu and sea vegetable to pressed Chinese cabbage and boiled greens. Salads, soups and savoury flans are also available, as well as interesting sweets like dandelion mousse. No smoking. *No dogs.*

Ebury Wine Bar

139 Ebury Street, SW1
01-730 5447
Map 12 C1

Open 12–2.245 & 6.30–10.30
Closed 25 & 26 December

Cold salad table £4.59   Rump steak £5.50
Credit Access, Amex, Diners, Visa

P NCP in Semley Place   **WC**

Comfortable surroundings, friendly service and food of consistently excellent quality have made the Ebury a favourite for over 25 years. The prime steaks and cutlets remain as superb as ever, but also worth investigating are tangy soups, terrines and imaginative daily specials like calf's liver with pineapple and mustard sauce. Tempting sweets and cheeses. Book. Minimum charge of £5. Fine wines by the glass from the Cruover machine are a noteworthy feature.

Efes Kebab House

80 Great Titchfield Street, W1
01-636 1953
Map 11 A1

Open noon–11.30
Closed Sun, 1 January & 25 December
Doner kebab £4.30   Special mixed kebab
£5.65
LVs   *Credit* Access, Amex, Visa
P multi-storey car park in Clipstone Street
WC

The tempting aroma of succulent meats cooking over an open charcoal grill is the best advertisement for this bright, comfortable Turkish restaurant. Lamb and chicken kebabs come in a wide range of guises, with fresh herbs and spices for added zest. Don't miss, either, the excellent hors d'oeuvre – delicious houmus, tangy fresh spinach with yoghurt and garlic, pastry parcels filled with cheese. Classic Turkish sweets to finish. Booking advisable at mealtimes. *No dogs.*

El Vino *(Wine Bar)*

47 Fleet Street, EC4
01-353 6786
Map 11 C1

Open 12.15–2.45
Closed Sun & Bank Holidays

Roast beef sandwich £1.25   Smoked salmon
sandwich £2.20
Credit Access, Amex, Visa
P NCP in Shoe Lane   **WC**

Journalists slake their thirst while catching up on gossip at this Fleet Street institution. Food for thought comes in the shape of well-filled sandwiches served in the ground-floor bar, while downstairs in the restaurant (minimum charge £6), salads centre round excellent roast beef and smoked salmon, ham, cheese and game pie. Exceptional wines. Jacket and tie, gentlemen please. No children. *No dogs.*

Equatorial

37 Old Compton Street, W1
01-437 6112
Map 11 B1

Open noon–3 & 6–11.15, Sat noon–11.15 (Sun
till 11)
Closed 24–26 December

Satay £3   Chicken curry £3.10
Credit Access, Amex, Diners, Visa
P NCP Dean Street   **WC**

Splendid flavours and textures distinguish the cooking at this simple little restaurant specialising in South-east Asian dishes. Lamb satay with peanut sauce is a favourite starter, or you could try one of several soups – perhaps fish ball or wun tun. Follow with, say, chilli crab, braised pork in soya sauce or carp in tamarind sauce. At weekends there's a short selection of special dishes. *No dogs.*

L'Express Café

16 Sloane Street, SW1
01-235 9869
Map 12 B1

Open 9.30–6 (Wed till 6.30)
Closed Sun, Bank Holidays & 3 days
Christmas
Crab sandwich £5.95   Cottage cheese &
exotic fruit salad £5.95
Credit Access, Amex, Diners, Visa
P NCP in Cadogan Square   **WC**

Designed on sleek, modern lines, this basement restaurant does a nice line in imaginative lunchtime dishes with a nouvelle touch. Tangy carrot and thyme soup might precede beautifully presented main courses like feuilleté of monkfish with saffron and dill sauce or smoked chicken with mango and avocado. Attractive desserts include lemon charlotte with apricot sauce. Continental breakfasts start the day; tea is served in the afternoon. Minimum of £5.50 noon–3.30.

Falafel House

95 Haverstock Hill, NW3
01-722 6187
Map 9 B1

Open 6pm–11.30pm
Closed Sun & 1st 2 weeks August

Houmus, falafel & oriental salad £2.95
Chicken livers £2.95

P street parking **WC**

The former staff are now the owners of this popular restaurant specialising in Middle Eastern cooking. Avgolemono and gazpacho may be found among the soups, with falafel, tahini and chakchouka other popular starters or snacks. Shaslik and kofta kebabs, tagine and couscous typify the main-course spread, and enjoyable sweets include fruit cheesecake, brandy trifle and Turkish delight. Book for dinner. Minimum charge £3. *No dogs.*

Fallen Angel   New Entry

65 Graham Street, N1
01-253 3996
Map 10 C1

Open 12.30–9

Vegetarian lasagne £2.25   Poppy seed cake 70p
LVs

P meters in street   &. **WC**

The atmosphere is notably relaxed and lively at this vegetarian café-cum-bar tucked away in the back streets of N1. The menu changes daily with mushroom or creamy spinach soup appearing alongside things like avocado bake or cabbage rolls served with a sweet and sour sauce. Poppy seed and banana cakes are delicious. Between 3 and 6 only snacks like tea, coffee and cakes are available. No children.

Fino's Wine Cellar

104 Charing Cross Road, WC2
01-836 1077
Map 11 B1

Open 11.30–3 & 5.30–11
Closed Sun & Bank Holidays

Cannelloni florentina £2.30   Barbecued spare ribs £2.50
LVs *Credit* Access, Amex, Diners, Visa
P meter parking **WC**

Set in the basement of an Edwardian building, this long-established wine bar gets very crowded, so arrive early if you want a table. Hot salt beef sandwiches are a favourite snack, while more substantial offerings range from Lancashire hotpot to cannelloni and moussaka, with perhaps spinach and cheese-stuffed sardines as a piquant starter. Round things off with Amaretto-flavoured gâteau. *No dogs.*

Fino's Wine Cellar

12 North Row, W1
01-491 7261
Map 9 B2

Open 11.30–3 & 5.30–10.30
Closed Sat evening, all Sun & Bank Holidays

Seafood salad £2.30   Fino's pizza £2.15
LVs *Credit* Access, Amex, Diners, Visa

P NCP at Marble Arch **WC**

There's a certain 'smoky dive' appeal about this atmospheric basement wine bar, with its painted brick walls, simple furnishings and assorted bric-à-brac. The short menu offers various salads (including quiche, seafood, chicken and ham pie), pizza, lasagne and spaghetti, plus the day's hot special and a good range of well-filled sandwiches. Informal waitress service. *No dogs.*

Fino's Wine Cellar

19 Swallow Street, W1
01-734 2049
Map 11 A2

Open 11.30–3 & 5.30–11
Closed Sun & Bank Holidays

Lasagne £2.30   Game pie with salad £4.75
LVs   *Credit* Access, Amex, Diners, Visa
P meters in street & NCP in Brewer Street
WC

Hot salt beef and roast beef sandwiches are favourite snacks at this long-established wine bar in the basement of an Edwardian building. More substantial offerings include freshly made pasta (lasagne, spaghetti or cannelloni), burgers with chips, paella and appetising salads based on game pie, seafood or cold meats. Arrive early for a table – it's very popular with the local business community. No children. *No dogs.*

We publish annually so make sure you use the current edition.

First Out

New Entry

52 St Giles High Street, WC2
01-240 8042
Map 11 B1

Open 11am–midnight
Closed Sun & Bank Holidays
Pancakes stuffed with mushrooms & watercress £1.40   Carrot & coriander soup £1.20
LVs
P Central YMCA NCP   **WC**

In the shadow of Centre Point, this lively vegetarian restaurant has quickly built up a regular clientele. Croissants, pastries and small cakes can be enjoyed with tea or coffee throughout opening hours, while hot savoury dishes are available from 12.30 until they run out: typical items could include mushroom bisque, vegetable moussaka and delicious oat-rolled nut rissole with a tasty barbecue sauce. Also a few salads. *No dogs.*

Flamingo *(Wine Bar)*

54 Pimlico Road, SW1
01-730 4484
Map 12 C2

Open noon–2.45 & 6–10.45
Closed Sat lunch, all Sun & Bank Holidays

Prawns mexicana £2.85   Lamb steak in honey sauce with vegetables £6.20
LVs   *Credit* Access, Amex, Visa
P street parking   **WC**

In the heart of bedsit land, this cosy, welcoming wine bar is a useful stop for some appetising fare from a largely Italian menu. As well as excellent minestrone, home-made lasagne and cannelloni, there are more unusual offerings such as halibut meunière, lamb steak in honey sauce and various salads (tuna, turkey, gammon). Delicious gâteaux and pâtisserie from the sweet trolley to finish. Speedy, polite service.

Food for Health

13 Blackfriars Lane, EC4
01-236 7001
Map 11 C1

Open 8–3
Closed Sat, Sun, Bank Holidays & 2 weeks
Christmas
Mushroom omelette £2.20 Orange muesli
55p
LVs
P NCP in Ave Maria Lane & **WC**

Wholesome vegetarian food, well prepared and liberally served; it's a formula that clearly works, and lunchtime in particular brings customers in their droves. What's on offer (the choice changes daily) could be anything from lentil soup to tomato omelette, mushroom Stroganoff and the popular Bircher salad with fresh fruit, fresh vegetables and protein. For sweet, perhaps apple crumble or orange muesli. Unlicensed. *No dogs.*

Food for Thought

31 Neal Street, WC2
01-836 0239
Map 11 B1

Open noon–8
Closed Sat, Sun, Bank Holidays & 22
December–10 January
Spinach & mushroom tagliatelle £1.30 Stir-
fried vegetables with brown rice £1.30
LVs
P NCP in Shelton Street & nearby meters **WC**

Queues of patient office workers are a common lunchtime sight outside this much-loved basement vegetarian restaurant. Hot dishes like stir-fried vegetables, a splendid courgette quiche and cauliflower au gratin are well worth the wait, while sweets like raspberry shortcake and ultra-fresh fruit salad turn your meal into a feast. Snack on sesame flapjacks or carrot and coconut cake at any time. Unlicensed. No smoking. *No dogs.*

Fridays Tex-Mex

24 Russell Street, WC2
01-240 0735
Map 11 B1

Open noon–3 & 5.30–1, Fri & Sat 6.30–3am
Closed Sat lunch, all Sun & Bank Holidays

Southern fried chicken with salad & potatoes
£4.70 Hot fudge sundae £1.40
Credit Access, Visa
P NCP in Drury Lane & nearby meters **WC**

One side of the menu features Mexican food, the other Texan specialities at this roomy, simply decorated basement restaurant. Nachos and tacos, guacamole and enchiladas, chilli and quesadas filled with ground beef, chicken or vegetables all have that authentic fiery Mexican kick, while would-be cowboys will love the ribs, burgers, deep-fried potato skins and crunchy salads on offer. *No dogs.*

Gachon's

269 Creek Road, Greenwich, SE10
01-853 4461
Map 10 D2

Open noon–3, Sat & Sun 11–5.30, also 6.30–
10.30 Wed–Sat
Closed 1st 2 weeks January
Poached eggs in brioche £1.75 Braised lamb
fillet £7
Credit Access, Visa
P Cutty Sark car park **WC**

French posters line the walls of Gachon Dyer's tiny restaurant, a really delightful place where an interesting variety of dishes is prepared with skill and care. Courgette and carrot terrine and grilled sardines in oatmeal are typical starters, while main dishes run from vegetarian pancake mornay to skate, roast pork and pepper steak. Chocolate truffle cake with white chocolate sauce is a delectable dessert. *No dogs.*

Garbanzo Coffee House

411 City Road, EC1
01-833 2888
Map 10 C1

Open 10–6
Closed Sun, Bank Holidays & 2 weeks
Christmas
Cheddar cheese croissant 70p   Quiche of the
day 75p
LVs
P meter parking   **WC**

Whether you take your coffee iced or straight, you're guaranteed an excellent beverage from freshly ground beans at this lively coffee house. Tasty accompaniments include huge, buttery croissants filled with everything from blue cheese to peanut butter and guacamole, and there is also a quiche of the day. Other offerings include granola-topped yoghurt, pecan pie and delicious cheesecake. Unlicensed. *No dogs.*

Geale's   **New Entry**

2 Farmer Street, W8
01-727 7969
Map 9 B2

Open noon–3 & 6–11.30 (Sat till 11)
Closed Sun, Mon, also Tues after Bank
Holiday Mons, 5 days Easter, 3 weeks August
& 2 weeks Christmas
Haddock & chips from £2.20   Fresh shark
£2.80
LVs   *Credit* Access
P street parking   ዼ   **WC**

Close, but not too close, to the bustle of Notting Hill Gate, this traditional fish restaurant has seen many years of success. Fresh fish arrives daily, ready to be coated in a light batter, fried to perfection and served with super golden chips. The choice includes haddock, huss, plaice, sole, skate and sometimes even shark. Check before a Saturday night visit – they close early if they run out of fish! *No dogs.*

Gino's *(Wine Bar)*

70 The Mall, Ealing, W5
01-567 5237
Map 9 A2

Open 12–3, also 7–11.30 (Fri & Sat till
midnight)
Closed Sun lunch & Bank Holidays
Pizza alla Gino £3.40   Scaloppina al limone
£5.80
LVs
P side streets   **WC**

The staff contribute to the merry clamour that pervades this busy, lively Italian wine bar. Dishes are cooked with care, and there's plenty of choice on a menu that includes pasta and pizza, chicken and veal main courses, grills and salads. Daily specials like spicy sausages or monkfish in a delicious garlicky tomato sauce widen the options further. Zuppa inglese (Italian trifle) is a nice sweet. Minimum charge £3.30. *No dogs.* ☕

Goring Hotel Lounge

15 Beeston Place, Grosvenor Gardens, SW1
01-834 8211
Map 12 C1

Open 10–6

Salade niçoise £4   Afternoon tea £4.50
Credit Access, Amex, Diners, Visa

P meters in side streets   ዼ   **WC**

One of London's most civilised settings for afternoon tea, this restful hotel lounge is just the place to indulge in excellent sandwiches, oven-fresh scones and meltingly delicious pastries, all served by friendly, attentive staff. Throughout the day you can also enjoy sandwiches, cold meats and savouries like croque-monsieur. Sorbets and ice cream are popular desserts. *No dogs.* 🍵

Egon Ronay's
CELLNET GUIDE 1987

HOTELS, RESTAURANTS & INNS IN GREAT BRITAIN & IRELAND

Egon Ronay's Cellnet Guide 1987 includes detailed descriptions of over 2500 of the best hotels, inns and restaurants in Great Britain and Ireland.

Restaurants serving outstanding food are awarded stars, and wine comments are included in many entries. There's an extensive section on bargain breaks and lower-priced London restaurants and hotels.

Many new features make the Guide more useful than ever for anyone who travels on business or for pleasure. Among them are

- Town house hotels
- Starred restaurants and high-grade hotels near the motorway network
- Countrywide listing of theatres

Available from AA Centres and booksellers everywhere at £9.95 or £10.95 including postage and packing from:

Mail Order Department
PO Box 51
Basingstoke
Hampshire
RG21 2BR

Govindas

9 Soho Street, W1
01-437 3662
Map 11 A1

Open 11.30–8 (Thurs–Sat till 9), Sun 12.30–3.30
Closed 25 & 26 December
Date & almond cake 95p   Spinach pie with vegetables £3.50
LVs
P meters in streets   **WC**

Cooking at this agreeable vegetarian restaurant follows Hare Krishna principles, with eggs, onions and mushrooms among the ingredients not used. The choice is nonetheless varied and tasty, from jacket potatoes with cottage cheese to carrot soup, vegeburgers, vegetable pie and mixed beans in tomato sauce. Delicious olive bread, simple salads and sweets. Indian-style thali on Sundays. Unlicensed. No smoking. *No dogs.*

Granary

39 Albermarle Street, W1
01-493 2978
Map 11 A2

Open 11.30–8 (Sat till 2.30)
Closed Sun & Bank Holidays

Avocado stuffed with prawns, spinach & cheese £4.20   Beef burgundy £4.20
LVs
P NCP in Burlington Gardens & street   **WC**

The hot counter is particularly tempting and presentation especially attractive at this restaurant just off Piccadilly. Cidery pork, cod with a lemon butter sauce and chicken and shrimp paella are typical choices, and a couple of vegetarian dishes are always available. There's also an interesting selection of salads and some hard-to-resist sweets like tipsy cake or summer pudding. Especially busy at lunchtime. *No dogs.*

Green's Champagne & Oyster Bar

36 Duke Street, SW1
01-930 4566
Map 11 A2

Open 11.30–3 & 5.30–10.45
Closed Sat, Sun & Bank Holidays

Avocado with crab £5   Smoked trout £4
Credit Access, Amex, Diners, Visa

P NCP in Cavendish Hotel & meters   &   **WC**

Just-a-biters should head for the smart, mahogany-panelled wine bar section with snug booth seating and welcoming, club-like air. Here at lunchtime you can indulge in every fishy treat imaginable, from splendid oysters in season, lobster and salmon to kipper pâté and smoked eel, with fruit and good coffee to finish. Steak sandwiches in the evening. No children. *No dogs.*

Green Cottage

9 New College Parade, Finchley Road, NW3
01-722 5305
Map 9 B1

Open noon–11.30
Closed 25 & 26 December

Baked crab with ginger & spring onion £5.50
Roast pork £3.20

P street parking   **WC**

Barbecued meats are the speciality of this unpretentious Chinese restaurant, and an appetising display near the entrance tempts passers-by. The menu is mainly Cantonese, and dishes are carefully prepared and very tasty. Besides the roast duck, belly pork and spare ribs, popular choices include hot and sour soup, baked prawns with spiced salt and fried beef with ginger and pineapple. Friendly staff do their job well. *No dogs.*

Green House

16 Royal Exchange, EC3
01-236 7077
Map 11 C1

Open 11.30–3 & 5–7.30
Closed Sat & Sun

Smoked salmon sandwich £2   Mediterranean
prawns £3.50

P NCP in Broad Street   WC

Set into the very walls of the Royal Exchange building, this tiny little place is a popular spot for a cold snack and a glass of bubbly. The choice varies daily, with pâté, ham, rare roast beef and plump prawns usually available. Quail's eggs and dressed crab were also on the list when we called, along with a very good game pie. No children. *No dogs.* ☕

Grill St Quentin · **New Entry**

136 Brompton Road, SW3
01-581 8377
Map 12 B1

Open noon–3 (Sat & Sun till 4) & 7–midnight
(Sun till 11)

Terrine of salmon £2.80   Grilled veal chop
with pommes allumettes £6.90
Credit Access, Amex, Diners, Visa
P NCP in Montpelier Street   WC

Stairs lead down from the Brompton Road entrance to this stylish new grill. First you come to the wine bar, where baguette sandwiches are made to order; then through to the bright, well-staffed restaurant. The menu here offers two types of main course – excellent charcoal-grilled steaks, cutlets and fish served with pommes allumettes, and hearty French provincial dishes like confit, cassoulet and couscous. Pâtés, salads, good pâtisserie. *No dogs.* ☕

Grosvenor House, Park Lounge

Park Lane, W1
01-499 6363
Map 11 A2

Open 3–5.30

Set afternoon tea £7.50
Credit Access, Amex, Diners, Visa

P Hyde Park NCP   WC

Enjoy the view across Hyde Park from comfortable armchairs at this spacious lounge decorated with huge floral displays. A pianist plays while friendly waitresses serve an enjoyable tea comprising freshly made finger sandwiches, light scones spread with lovely thick cream and some excellent cakes and pastries – including lovely moist orange-flavoured Swiss roll. You can choose from 25 different leaf teas. Minimum charge of £4. *No dogs.* 🍰

Grosvenor House, Pasta, Vino e Fantasia

Park Lane, W1
01-499 6363
Map 11 A2

Open 12.30–2.30 & 7–11.30
Closed Sat lunch, all Sun & Bank Holidays

Ravioli al sugo £4.55   Sardine in carpione
£2.95
Credit Access, Amex, Diners, Visa
P own car park   WC

Tasty pasta dishes like tagliatelle al pesto or spaghetti carbonara are the obvious choice in this cool, crisp restaurant. There's also an extensive self-service buffet with an eye-catching array of charcuterie, seafood, stuffed vegetables and salads. The dessert trolley with its selection of mousses, fresh fruit salads, cheesecakes and gâteaux is equally inviting. Specialities include mussel soup and seafood risotto. *No dogs.*

Grosvenor House, Pavilion Espresso Bar

Park Lane, W1
01-499 6363
Map 11 A2

Open 7am–10pm (Sat & Sun till 10.30)

Smoked turkey sandwich £4.75   Spinach &
ricotta pancake £5.50
Credit Access, Amex, Diners, Visa

P Hyde Park Corner NCP   **WC**

Continental breakfast, with fresh croissants
and brioches, starts the day in this stylish bar
on the lower level of the Pavilion. From mid-
morning the short menu shifts to luxury
sandwiches with fillings like shrimp salad or
ham with Jarlsberg cheese and snacks such
as beef casserole and cold salmon with herb
mayonnaise. There are a few nice sweets,
too. *No dogs.*

Gurkhas Tandoori

23 Warren Street, W1
01-388 1640
Map 11 A1

Open noon–3 & 6–midnight
Closed 25 & 26 December

Murgh nepali £2.95   Vegetable koftas £1.75
LVs   *Credit* Visa

P street parking   **WC**

Gurkha photographs and memorabilia
brighten this little restaurant specialising in
unfailingly delicious Nepalese cooking. The
extensive menu ranges from first-class tandoori meats and breads to biryani and a
particularly good choice of curries, including
mild and creamy chicken masala, the hottest
of vindaloos and delicious vegetable versions
like coriander-spiced aubergine curry. Don't
miss the wonderfully refreshing mango Bulfi
for dessert. *No dogs.*

*We welcome complaints
and bona fide
recommendations on the
tear-out pages for readers'
comments. They are
followed up by our
professional team. Please
also complain to the
management instantly.*

Gyngleboy

27 Spring Street, W2
01-723 3351
Map 9 B2

Open 11–3 & 5.30–9.30
Closed Sat, Sun, Bank Holidays & 3 days
Christmas
Soup & bread £1.50   Poached salmon with
cucumber & cream salad £5.30
Credit Access, Amex, Diners, Visa
P meter parking & **WC**

Close to Paddington Station, this Victorian-
style wine bar with its candlelit tables, glass
partitions and sawdust on the floor is a useful
place for a light bite before a train journey.
There's a small but excellent selection of
cold meats and smoked fish to have with
salad or in a sandwich, plus game pie and
well-kept cheeses. Finish with apple pie or
seasonal berries. *No dogs.*

Hard Rock Café

150 Old Park Lane, W1
01-629 0382
Map 11 A2

Open noon–12.15am (Fri & Sat till 12.45am)
Closed 3 days Christmas

Cheeseburger with salad & French fries £3.75
Club sandwich with French fries £4.45
P meter parking or NCP at Hilton Hotel ♿
WC

Even outside normal mealtimes you're likely to queue at this enormously popular American-style restaurant, now in its mid-teens and as lively as ever. Rock music thumps an accompaniment to generous helpings of transatlantic fare, including giant sandwiches and burgers of all sizes and descriptions. Also T-bone steaks, super salads, excellent French fries and daunting desserts. £3.50 minimum charge lunch and dinner. *No dogs.*

Harrods Dress & Upper Circles

Knightsbridge, SW1
01-730 1234
Map 12 B1

Open 9–4.45 (Sat till 5.45), Wed 9.30–6.45
Closed Sun & Bank Holidays

Vegetarian Provençale quiche £1.10   Apricot, orange & walnut bread 75p
Credit Access, Amex, Diners, Visa
P Pavilion Road NCP ♿   **WC**

The Dress Circle, now with a clean-lined Bauhaus look, is on the first floor, the Upper Circle on the fourth. Both are comfortable, self-service restaurants, with essentially the same menu: Danish open sandwiches, very good quiches, attractively presented salads, stuffed tomatoes, cheeses, goujons of plaice or chicken. There's also a very tempting selection of high-quality pâtisserie and breads. Non-smoking areas. *No dogs.* ♱

Harrods Georgian Restaurant & Terrace

Knightsbridge, SW1
01-730 1234
Map 12 B1

Open 3.30–4.30 (Wed till 6 & Sat till 5.30)
Closed Sun & Bank Holidays

Georgian Restaurant tea £5.75   Terrace tea £6.50
Credit Access, Amex, Diners, Visa
P own car park in Brompton Place ♿   **WC**

Two of Harrods' many catering outlets. In the Georgian Restaurant with its elaborately moulded ceiling, waitresses serve your pot of tea while you move straight to a mouth-watering display that includes éclairs, mille-feuilles, chocolate cakes, tartlets and slices. Go to the adjoining marble-floored terrace for the Terrace tea – waitress service of finger sandwiches and bridge rolls, fresh scones and your run of a trayful of pastries such as chocolate slice and a light sponge. *No dogs.* ♱

Harrods Health Juice Bar

Knightsbridge, SW1
01-730 1234
Map 12 B1

Open 9–4.45 (Sat till 5.45), Wed 9.30–6.45
Closed Sun & Bank Holidays

Sweet & sour salad £1.50   Ravioli with spinach sauce £3.25
Credit Access, Amex, Diners, Visa
P own car park in Brompton Place ♿   **WC**

Salutary salads and juices are served at this spotless corner of the basement grocery department. There are also a few hot dishes. Oranges, apples, carrots and tomatoes produce deliciously refreshing drinks, and salads include fruit, Greek (with feta cheese) and celery with nuts and sultanas. Good breakfast choices are muesli and the morning pick-me-up, a reviving mixture of orange juice, egg, banana, milk and honey. Unlicensed. No smoking. *No dogs.*

Harry Morgan's

31 St John's Wood High Street, NW8
01-722 1869
Map 9 B1

Open 12–3 & 6–10, Sun noon–10
Closed Fri eve, all Mon, 10 days Easter & 3
weeks September

Plate of salt beef £4.95   Lockshen pudding
£1.40
P side streets & street parking in evening   **WC**

An institution in the area for over 20 years,
this much-loved Jewish restaurant offers all
your favourite dishes. Start with chopped
liver or bean and barley soup. Then move on
to the delicious hot salt beef, calf's liver with
onions or stewed meatballs – with lockshen
pudding for the classic finale. A range of
sandwiches is available during the day except
Sunday. Minimum evening charge of £3.50.
No dogs.

Harvey Nichols, Harveys at the Top

Knightsbridge, SW1
01-235 5000
Map 12 B1

Open 9.30–5.30 (Wed till 6.30)
Closed Sun & Bank Holidays

Smoked salmon sandwich £2.99   Set
afternoon tea £2.95
Credit Access, Amex, Diners, Visa
P own car park in Harriet Walk   &   **WC**

Perched atop the fashionable Knightsbridge
store, a pleasantly, airy restaurant with a
colourful sun terrace. English and continental
breakfasts, enjoyable pastries and cut-to-
order sandwiches are served until 11.30,
followed at lunchtime (minimum charge £4)
by more elaborate offerings such as garlicky
deep-fried mushrooms, ragout of aubergine
and tempting sweets from the trolley. Afternoon teas from 3. *No dogs.* 🍵

Hat Shop

11 Goldhawk Road, W12
01-740 6437
Map 9 A2
Open Restaurant: noon–11; Wine Bar: noon–3
& 6–11
Closed 25 & 26 December, also Wine Bar Sat
lunch & all Sun
Smoky bacon pizza (for 2) £5.50   Chilli con
carne £3.35
LVs
P NCP in Shepherd's Bush shopping centre

You'll find this friendly, ground-floor restaurant serving all-American favourites like chilli,
ribs and pizzas behind a milliner's shopfront.
And down in the basement is a busy,
cheerfully informal wine bar offering a daily-
changing selection of interesting dishes that
might include avocado pâté, spinach and
walnut lasagne, cassoulet and filled jacket
potatoes, all carefully prepared. Framed film
posters and church pew seating set the
scene. *No dogs.*

The Heal's Restaurant

196 Tottenham Court Road, W1
01-636 1666, extension 5513
Map 11 A1

Open 10–5.30 (Thurs till 7)
Closed Sun & Bank Holidays
Basque pipérade with basil £2.75   Poached
salmon with watercress mayonnaise £5.75
Credit Access, Amex, Diners, Visa
P meter parking & Central YMCA NCP   &
WC

On the first floor of the department store, this
attractive restaurant has a cool, contemporary look. Lunchtime (12.15–3.30; minimum
charge £5, children £3) brings an imaginative
selection of tasty dishes, from broad bean
soup and grilled ricotta to John Dory garnished with asparagus and Moroccan lamb
stew. Delicious sweets, too, including gooseberry tart and summer pudding. Morning
coffee, afternoon tea. *No dogs.* 🍵

Hiders

755 Fulham Road, SW6
01-736 2331
Map 9 A3

Open 12.30–2.30
Closed Sat, Sun, Bank Holidays, 2 weeks
August & 1 week Christmas
Cheese beignets with gooseberry sauce £2.25
Liver, bacon & onions £6.50
Credit Access, Amex, Visa
P side streets **WC**

Just-a-biters will find much of interest on the lunchtime carte at this immaculate restaurant adorned with huge mirrors, paintings and luxurious drapes. Dishes range from seafood pancakes and toad in the hole to scrambled eggs with smoked salmon and monkfish brochette. Lavish sweets like a trio of white, milk and bitter chocolate mousses to finish. *No dogs.*

Hoults *(Wine Bar)*

20 Bellevue Road, Wandsworth Common,
SW17
01-767 1858
Map 9 B3

Open 12.30–2.45 & 6.30–10.45 (Sun 7–10.30)
Closed 5 days Christmas
½ pint of prawns £2.95   Poached salmon trout
£6.95
Credit Access, Amex, Visa
P street parking **WC**

This civilised wine bar with a simple decor of overhead fans, bare wood floors and potted plants attracts an appreciative clientele for its monthly-changing selection of delicious and imaginative fare. Crab claws sautéed in garlic butter and cheese and spinach parcels make tasty starters, while main courses might include a seafood mélange and roast rack of lamb. Interesting selection of wines by the glass. *No dogs.*

Hung Toa **New Entry**

54 Queensway, W2
01-727 6017
Map 9 B2

Open noon–11
Closed 25 & 26 December

Soup £1   Roast crispy pork £4

P NCP in Queensway   **WC**

A bustling restaurant on cosmopolitan Queensway, open from noon for a good selection of tasty, uncomplicated Cantonese food. The roast duck and pork – see them on display in the window – are among the best in town, and just-a-biters will relish the substantial one-plate rice and noodle dishes. Other choices include mixed meat soup, chicken with nuts and beef with oyster sauce. *No dogs.*

Hyatt Carlton Tower, Chinoiserie

2 Cadogan Place, SW1
01-233 5411
Map 12 B1

Open 8am–1am

Beef sandwich £3.80   Set afternoon tea £6.75
Credit Access, Amex, Diners, Visa

P valet parking & Cadogan Place NCP **WC**

The delightful Oriental decor, wonderful displays of fresh flowers and stunningly lovely china make this luxurious hotel lounge a most elegant setting for a snack or light meal. Continental breakfast starts the day, followed from 11 o'clock by a main menu featuring everything from club sandwiches and salads to omelettes, beef béarnaise and seasonal berries. Afternoon tea is served between 3 and 5.30, and there's a minimum charge of £4.50 from noon–7. *No dogs.*

Hyde Park Hotel, Park Room

65 Knightsbridge, SW†
01-235 2000
Map 12 B1

Open 7am–11pm, Sun 8am–10.30pm

Set afternoon tea £6.75   Roast beef sandwich
£3.25
Credit Access, Amex, Diners, Visa

P Motcomb Street NCP & **WC**

A traditionally elegant room with views across Hyde Park – just the place for a pleasant afternoon tea enhanced by superb service, crisp linen and pretty china. Sandwiches are fresh and tasty, and there are scones, teacakes, light sponges and lovely fruit tartlets. Also breakfasts, morning coffee and all-day light snacks, a luxury lunchtime buffet and a full evening menu. *No dogs.*

Ikeda   **New Entry**

30 Brook Street, W1
01-629 2730
Map 11 A1

Open 12.30–2.30 & 6.30–10.30
Closed Sat, Sun, Bank Holidays & 10 days Christmas
Nigiri sushi from £10   Makimono from £8
Credit Access, Amex, Diners, Visa
P meters in street   **WC**

A modern and very comfortable little Japanese restaurant and sushi bar. Sushi is beautifully presented on a raised wooden platter with wasabi (horseradish) and pickled ginger. The range of fish covers salmon, tuna, sea bass, sea bream, scallops, turbot and mackerel – all zingy-fresh and served with very good vinegared rice. Norimaki, with a wrapping of seaweed, is a delicious variant, and there's also vegetable sushi. *No dogs.*

Ikkyu   **New Entry**

67 Tottenham Court Road, W1
01-636 9280
Map 11 A1

Open 12.30–2.30 & 6–10.30 (Sun from 7)
Closed Sun lunch, all Sat & 8 days Christmas

Five rolled vegetables £6   Assorted sushi £9

Credit Access, Amex, Diners, Visa
P street parking   **WC**

It's usually busy, often hectic, so booking's a must at this basement Japanese restaurant. Prices are reasonable, and there's a very varied selection of raw fish for sushi and sashimi. Yakitori (chicken kebabs) are also popular, and among other dishes we enjoyed are bean curd pancake topped with grated ginger and grilled sea bream. Helpful staff make choosing easier. Try the full-bodied Japanese brown tea as a change from green. *No dogs.*

Inn on the Park Lounge   ★

Hamilton Place, Park Lane, W1
01-499 0888
Map 11 A2

Open 9am–2am (Sun till 1am)

Quiche of the day £3.20   Afternoon tea £7
Credit Access, Amex, Diners Visa

P own car park & **WC**

Elegant and delicious snacks to suit every hour and mood are served – in impeccable style – at this sumptuous panelled lounge decorated with plants and huge fresh flower arrangements. Faultless cakes and pastries accompany morning coffee and afternoon tea, while from noon until the small hours the appetite is tempted by chilled vichyssoise and grilled salmon, club sandwiches and smoked duck breast salad. *No dogs.*

Inter-Continental Hotel, Coffee House ★

1 Hamilton Place, W1
01-409 3131
Map 11 A2

Open 7am–midnight (Sat & Sun till 2am)

Grilled ham & goat cheese baguette £4.30
Sweet selection £3.80

Credit Access, Amex, Diners, Visa
P own car park   **& WC**

Afternoon tea, with finger sandwiches, scones, fabulous French pastries and your choice of six teas, is served in a corner of the lobby between 3 and 6. In the coffee house itself they offer breakfast (buffet and à la carte) and an outstanding range of high-quality dishes, from artichoke bottoms à la florentine to salads and sandwiches, omelettes, pasta and main courses like lobster hot pot or navarin of lamb. *No dogs.* 🍲

Ipphei   *New Entry*

253 Finchley Road, NW3
01-435 8602
Map 9 B1

Open 12.30–3 & 6–10.30
Closed Tues, Bank Holidays & 1 week New Year

Assorted sushi from £5.50   Sukiyaki £8.50
Credit Access
P street parking   **WC**

Helpful staff are ready with advice on what to order in this tiny Japanese restaurant. At lunchtime they offer only set meals that comprise an appetiser, a main course, soya bean soup, pickles and rice. Sushi is available only in the evening, when the set meals, all involving a sashimi course, start at £12. A la carte items include chicken teriyaki, pork with ginger and rice with broiled eel. *No dogs.*

Jade Garden

15 Wardour Street, W1
01-439 7851
Map 11 B2

Open noon–4.30 (full menu noon–11.30, Sun till 10.30)
Closed 25 December
Prawn cheung fun £1.80   Mixed vegetable dumpling £1
Credit Access, Amex, Diners, Visa
P Swiss Centre NCP   **WC**

The red and green decor may not be pristine, but the cooking is as good as ever at this friendly Chinese restaurant. The favourite snack choice is dim sum, which come piping hot from kitchen to table with no trolley ride in between: popular items range from prawn toasts to stuffed bean curd roll, char siu buns and delicious crispy mixed vegetable dumpling. Also super glutinous rice in lotus leaves. *No dogs.*

Jeeves Wine Cellar

139 Whitfield Street, W1
01-387 1952
Map 11 A1

Open 11.30–3.30 & 5.30–midnight
Closed Sun, some Bank Holidays & 1 week Christmas
Chicken Kiev £4.95   Veal Elizabetta £5.25
LVs   *Credit* Access, Amex, Diners, Visa

P meter parking   **WC**

The decor is 1920s at this plush basement wine bar, where the food is attractively and strategically displayed at the foot of the stairs. Choose from home-cooked cold meats and splendid salads, or hot dishes ranging from pasta, steaks and grills to daily specials like chilli and moussaka. Plenty of cheeses, too, and delicious fresh fruit salad, also hot steamed puddings in winter. There is dancing to a resident DJ Wed–Sat evenings. *No dogs.* 🍷

Joe Allen

13 Exeter Street, WC2
01-836 0651
Map 11 B2
Open noon–1am (Sun till midnight)
Closed Christmas

Black bean soup £1.50   Liver with onions
£6.50

P meter parking & street parking   **WC**

As popular and fashionable as ever, so it's essential to book at this lively restaurant specialising in generously served American dishes. The extensive menu ranges from black bean soup and chopped liver through to southern fried chicken, barbecued spare ribs and tasty daily specials like calf's liver with onions. Excellent salads such as spinach and bacon or Waldorf, and classic pecan pie to finish. *No dogs.*

Joy King Lau   ★

3 Leicester Street, WC2
01-437 1132
Map 11 B2

Open dim sum 11–5.30 (full menu 11am–11pm, Sun till 10.30pm)
Closed 24 & 25 December

Dim sum from 95p   Steamed sea bass £6
Credit Amex, Diners
P Swiss Centre NCP & **WC**

A special team of chefs concentrates solely on preparing the delicious dim sum served at this smart, friendly restaurant on four floors. The care and expertise of preparation shine through the two dozen varieties available, including cheung fun filled with shredded chicken, char siu buns, pork and prawn dumplings and turnip paste. Sweet versions come in 10 tempting guises. *No dogs.*

Julie's Bar

137 Portland Road, W11
01-727 7985
Map 9 A2

Open 11am–11.30pm, Sun noon–10.30pm
Closed 3 days Easter & 24–27 December

Pork sausages with potatoes £3.95   Poached
salmon trout with watercress sauce £5.95

P meter parking   **WC**

A delightfully relaxed wine bar, full of character with its labyrinthine rooms, antique furnishings and stained glass. Cakes are served with morning coffee and afternoon tea, while lunchtime brings such stylish offerings as duck liver and ham terrine, poached salmon trout and game and oyster pie. Finish with an appealing sweet like apricot crumble or continental apple flan. Similar evening choice. ✑

Justin de Blank   ★

54 Duke Street, W1
01-629 3174
Map 11 A1

Open 8.30–3.30 (Sat from 9) & 4.30–9
Closed Sat eve, all Sun & Bank Holidays

Lamb & apricot casserole with rice £4.10
Fruit brûlée £1.75
LVs   *Credit* Access, Visa
P Selfridges car park   **WC**

Marvellous food, stunningly presented, is the recipe for success at this counter-service restaurant. There's always an excellent selection of cold meats, quiches and salads, while the hot choice embraces soups, a daily roast and vegetarian specials like crab- and cucumber-filled spinach roulade. Home-baked breads and cakes are first-class, while sweets – from Pavlovas to cheesecakes – rank among London's finest. English and continental breakfasts. *No dogs.* ✑

Justin de Blank at General Trading Company

144 Sloane Street, SW1
01-730 6400
Map 12 B1

Open 9–5.15 (Sat till 2.30)
Closed Sun, Bank Holidays, Sat preceding
Bank Holiday Mons & 1 week Christmas
Ratatouille & salad £4.30   Chocolate roulade
£1.80
LVs
P NCP in Cadogan Place   **WC**

A stylishly civilised basement restaurant whose pretty patio is a favourite meeting place on fine days. Super breakfasts featuring home-made sausages start the day, followed by a tempting array of cakes, flans and biscuits from 11. Summer lunchtimes bring gazpacho, cold meats and poached salmon, while in winter there are hearty hot dishes like goulash and couscous. Sweets include an exquisite cappuccino cheesecake. *No dogs.* ☺

Kitchen Yakitori   **New Entry**

12 Lancashire Court, New Bond Street, W1
01-629 9984
Map 11 A1

Open noon–2.30
Closed Sat eve, all Sun, Bank Holidays & 10
days Christmas

Kabayaki lunch £7.50   Yakitori lunch £3.80
LVs
P NCP in Hanover Square   **WC**

Lunchtime sees the pine tables fill up rapidly at this tiny Japanese restaurant. Assorted set menus offer a starter (we enjoyed wonderfully fresh seaweed and octopus), soya bean soup, rice pickle and fresh fruit to finish, with main course choices ranging from deep-fried breaded pork to chicken teriyaki and the speciality barbecued fillet of eel. Excellent ingredients, artistically presented. Friendly, helpful service. More elaborate evening meals. *No dogs.* 🐾

L.S. Grunts Chicago Pizza Co.

12 Maiden Lane, WC2
01-379 7722
Map 11 B2

Open noon–11.30 (Sun till 9)
Closed 1 Jan, Good Fri, Easter Sun & 25 & 26
December

Salad bar £1.70   Pizza £4.50
Credit Access, Visa
P meters & NCP in Drury Lane ♿ **WC**

Sip a cocktail at the bar while waiting for your made-to order deep-dish pizza at this lively, all-American restaurant. Toppings range from the speciality spicy sausage to peperoni, mushrooms and anchovies – all delicious with garlic bread and salad from the help-yourself bar. Add sizzling stuffed mushrooms to start, sinful ice creams and cheesecake for afters. *No dogs.*

Lantern

23 Malvern Road, NW6
01-624 1796
Map 9 B1

Open noon–3 & 7–midnight
Closed 25 & 26 December

Choux aux crabes £1.55   Salade de fruits de
mer tiède £3.45
Credit Visa
P street parking ♿

In the same ownership as La Cloche and Pigeon, this cheerful, friendly restaurant offers the same interesting choice of enjoyable eating. Profiteroles stuffed with crab and topped with hollandaise make a tasty starter, and main courses include calf's liver with sage, veal casserole and honeyed duck in puff pastry. There's always a dish for vegetarians, plus nice sweets and a roast beef Sunday lunch. *No dogs.* ☺

Laurent

428 Finchley Road, NW2
01-794 3603
Map 9 A1

Open noon–2 & 6–11
Closed Sun eve, Bank Holidays & August
Brique à l'oeuf £1.50   Couscous complet
£5.50
Credit Access, Visa
P side streets, also main road in evening   **WC**

Couscous is the speciality at this friendly little family-run restaurant. The simplest version of this robust, semolina-based North African dish comes with vegetables in stock, the complet adds lamb and spicy sausage, while the royal includes a mixed grill. Steaks and Dover sole are main-course alternatives, while brique à l'oeuf (deep-fried egg parcel) is the classic Tunisian starter. *No dogs.* ☺

Leith's Good Food   `New Entry`

52 Upper Street, N1
01-288 6073
Map 10 C1

Open 8am–8pm
Closed Sat & Sun

Vegetarian Stroganoff £3.40   Stuffed poussin
£5
Credit Access, Amex, Diners, Visa
P Exhibition car park   &   **WC**

On the gallery floor of the Islington Design Centre, this is an excellent snack stop for visitors to the exhibitions. Soup of the day could be carrot and coriander or Stilton and onion, and main dishes (a couple usually available) might include moussaka, lasagne or chicken and leek pie. Cold cuts accompany crisp salads, and there are some delectable sweets like fruit flan or Paris Brest. *No dogs.*

Ley-On's

56 Wardour Street, W1
01-437 6465
Map 11 A1

Open dim sum 11.30–5 (full menu 11.30am–
11.30pm)
Closed 25 & 26 December
Dim sum from 95p   Beef balls with greens
£3.50
Credit Access, Amex, Diners, Visa
P Wardour Street NCP   **WC**

Thirty-eight variations on the dim sum theme provide tasty snacking at this spacious Chinese restaurant. The list runs from paper-wrapped prawns and fried bean curd rolls to beef balls with greens, turnip paste and roast pork in a steamed bun. Several sweet varieties, too, such as sesame sweet croquette. The full menu available throughout opening times offers a wide variety of Hong Kong-style Cantonese dishes. *No dogs.*

Lincoln's Inn Wine Bar

49a Lincoln's Inn Fields, WC2
01-242 0058
Map 11 B1

Open 11.30–3 & 5.30–10.30
Closed Sat, Sun & Bank Holidays
Smoked trout salad £4.95   Stuffed breast of
duck with honey & ginger sauce £6.75
LVs   *Credit* Access, Amex, Diners, Visa
P Russell Square NCP or meters in street
WC

In a corner of Lincoln's Inn Fields, near the shop immortalised by Dickens as The Old Curiosity Shop. It's a pleasant, informal wine bar serving a good selection of well-judged fare, from interesting soups and plated salads to hot dishes such as beef Wellington or stuffed duck breast with honey and ginger sauce. Delicious sweets, too. *No dogs.* ☺

Lindas

4 Fernhead Road, W9
01-969 9387
Map 9 B2

Open noon–2 & 6–10.15
Closed Sat lunch, all Sun, Bank Holidays & 2 weeks annual holiday

Chicken in ginger £1.95   Gâteau 75p
LVs   *Credit* Access, Diners, Visa
P street parking   **WC**

Vietnamese cooking in all its subtle delicacy is the speciality of this cheerful restaurant, where Linda Blaney, her English husband and family share all the duties. Omelettes, prawns in batter and spicy spare ribs are typical dishes, and single-plate meals such as egg-fried rice with mixed vegetables are a real bargain at lunchtime, when three-course meals are also available. Minimum charge of £4 in the evening. *No dogs.*

Lok Ho Fook

4 Gerrard Street, W1
01-437 2001
Map 11 B1

Open dim sum noon–6 (full menu noon–1am, Fri & Sat till 2am)
Closed 25 & 26 December

Dim sum 90p Mixed meats with rice £2.80
LVs   *Credit* Access, Amex, Diners, Visa
P NCP in Cambridge Circus   &   **WC**

Just-a-biters will find plenty of choice at this traditional Chinese restaurant in pedestrianised Gerrard Street. Tasty dim sum include prawn, meat and chicken dumplings, beef balls with greens, spare ribs in soya sauce and dried bean curd rolls; there are also ten sweet varieties. Chow mein and composite rice dishes remain popular one-plate orders. *No dogs.*

London Marriott Hotel, Regent Lounge

Grosvenor Square, W1
01-493 1232
Map 11 A2

Open 24 hours

Calf's liver with vegetables £6.25   Set afternoon tea £6
Credit Access, Amex, Diners, Visa

P NCP under hotel   **WC**

This supremely comfortable hotel lounge, with its gilt mirrors and flowery decor, makes a delightful setting in which to enjoy some elegant light refreshment. Cream cheese-stuffed artichoke hearts, well-filled club sandwiches and seafood brochette are typical of the tempting savoury snacks on offer, while afternoon tea brings such things as delicious pastries, gâteaux and sweets like old English trifle. *No dogs.* 🖑

Loon Fung

37 Gerrard Street, W1
01-437 5429
Map 11 B2

Open dim sum noon–5, Sun 10–5 (full menu noon–12.30am, Sun 10am–11.30pm)

Dim sum from 95p   Dish of prawns £5.50

LVs   *Credit* Access, Amex, Diners, Visa
P Swiss Centre car park   **WC**

Delicious dim sum make ideal daytime snacks at this spacious, long-establishment restaurant in the heart of Soho's Chinatown. Four or five are enough to really satisfy – choose from crunchy mixed-meat yam croquettes, char siu buns, super prawn toast and rice with chicken wrapped in lotus leaves. Friendly, efficient staff take your order on weekdays, but at the busy weekend you make your selection from circulating trolleys. *No dogs.*

Lou Pescadou `New Entry`

241 Old Brompton Road, SW5
01-370 1057
Map 12 A2

Open 12.30–3 & 6.30–midnight
Closed Sun

Pizza from £4   Monkfish £6.80
LVs   *Credit* Access, Amex, Diners, Visa

P meter parking   **WC**

They don't take bookings at this bistro-style restaurant, latest and least formal of the Le Suquet consortium. Omelettes, pizzas and pasta provide tasty snack meals, and there's a good range of seafood, including monkfish, mullet, oysters, clams and langoustines. Also steaks and a few daily specials such as salad of chicken livers, rabbit fricassee or ox tongue florentine. Sound, straightforward cooking with good assertive flavours.

Louis' Pâtisserie

12 Harben Parade, Finchley Road, NW3
01-772 8100
32 Heath Street, NW3
01-435 9908
Map 9 B1

Open Harben Parade: 9–6; Heath Street: 9.30–6 (Mon from 10)
Closed 5–6 days Christmas
Kiwi gâteau 80p   Danish pastry 40p
P street parking   &   Harben Parade   **WC**

Mouthwatering window displays of home-baked cakes and pastries entice the crowds into these two popular little pâtisseries. Chocolate éclairs, mille-feuilles, strawberry slices and cream horns go down beautifully with a refreshing brew, and there are a few specialities from the owner's native Hungary, too, like pishinger – crisp wafers layered with chocolate buttercream and topped with nuts and chocolate. Sausage rolls are the only savoury option. Unlicensed. *No dogs.* 🐾

Macarthurs

147 Church Road, Barnes, SW13
01-748 3630
Map 9 A3

Open 12.30–2.30 & 6–11.30 (Fri till midnight), Sat 12–midnight, Sun 12.30–11.30
Closed Easter Sun & 25 & 26 December
½lb Macarthur burger £3.65   Vegetable lasagne £3.10
LVs   *Credit* Access, Amex, Diners, Visa
P street parking   **WC**

Juicy hamburgers topped with everything from blue cheese to mushrooms in white wine sauce are the real stars of the show at this cheerful, bustling restaurant. Add a tasty baked potato and crisp salad for a real feast, or choose the chilli, a steak or perhaps vegetarian lasagne with spinach and walnuts. Tempting if calorific desserts include chocolate fudge cake and pecan pie. *No dogs.*

Maha Gopal

10 New Cavendish Street, W1
01-580 5607
Map 11 A1

Open noon–3 & 6–midnight, Sun 7pm–11.30pm
Closed Sun lunch

Lamb pasanda £2.50   Banana fritters 85p
LVs   *Credit* Access, Amex, Diners, Visa
P street parking   **WC**

Flavoursome chicken tikka served sizzling in its skillet is typical of the highly enjoyable cooking at this traditionally decorated Indian restaurant. Other good choices on the conventional menu include lamb pasanda, spicy kashmiri vegetable curry, biryanis and dansaks. Accompaniments like nan bread and saffron rice are notably tasty and desserts are rich and honey-sweet. Polite, smiling service. Minimum order of at least a main course when busy. *No dogs.*

Maison Bertaux ★

28 Greek Street, W1
01-437 6007
Map 11 B1

Open 9–6
Closed Sun, Mon, Bank Holidays & following day & 4 weeks July–August
Apple & almond tartlet 85p Fruit tartlet with cream £1
LVs
P NCP in Gerrard Place **WC**

After many successful years this tiny Soho pâtisserie continues to maintain the highest standards. The cakes and pastries cover a wide and colourful range, from tartlets and turnovers to mille-feuilles, éclairs and slices of gâteau. For those wanting something savoury there are croissants and individual quiches. M Vignaud is usually in the bakery, while his charming wife takes excellent care of the shop. No smoking downstairs. Unlicensed. *No dogs.*

Maison Bouquillon, Le Montmartre

45 Moscow Road, W2
01-727 0373
Map 9 B2

Open 8.30am–9.30pm
Closed 25 December

Chicken Kiev £2.50 Raspberry tartlet £1.50
LVs

P meter parking **WC**

Thirteen hours a day, 364 days a year, this neat, unpretentious place just off Queensway provides an excellent variety of high-class baking from the Maison Bouquillon Pâtisserie. Among the mouthwatering array are mille-feuilles, florentines, palmiers and exemplary fruit tartlets. There are savoury items too, from cheese croissants and sausage rolls to more substantial lunchtime dishes like salmon coulibiac and beef Wellington. Friendly service. *No dogs.*

Maison Pechon Pâtisserie Françâise

127 Queensway, W2
01-229 0746
Map 9 B2

Open 8–5 (Sun from 10)
Closed Bank Holidays
Vegetarian moussaka £1.80 Pastries from 65p
LVs
P meter parking in nearby streets & underground car park in Queensway **WC**

Tucked away at the rear of this hugely popular pâtisserie is a friendly, informal little tea shop for the many fans of the goodies on display who can't wait to get them home. Choose from wonderful mille-feuilles, fruit tartlets, macaroons and linzer torten at tea or coffee time. From 11 to 3pm there are more substantial savoury offerings like fluffy omelettes, Welsh rarebit, vegetarian moussaka and ratatouille. *No dogs.*

Maison Sagne

105 Marylebone High Street, W1
01-935 6240
Map 11 A1

Open 9–5 (Sat till 12.30)
Closed Sun & Bank Holidays

Chicken & mushroom vol-au-vent £2.35
Black Forest gâteau 80p

P NCP in Moxon Street ♿ **WC**

A very traditional pastry shop still thriving after 65 years. The window display of marzipan animals is quite magical, and inside there's a tempting array of beautifully made cakes and pastries. Among the many delights are croissants and éclairs, chocolate meringues, Mont Blancs and a delicious rich truffle cake. At lunchtime savoury snacks include chicken and mushroom vol-au-vents, salads and various omelettes. Unlicensed. No smoking. *No dogs.*

Mandeer ★

21 Hanway Place, Tottenham Court Road, W1
01-323 0660
Map 11 B1

Open noon–3 & 6–10.15
Closed Sun & 1 week Christmas

Tofu special (no spices) £3.75   Sev puri £2.50

LVs   *Credit* Access, Amex, Diners, Visa
P NCP under Central YMCA   **WC**

Great skill and care go into the cooking at this Indian vegetarian restaurant, and the evening menu in particular (minimum charge £5) is splendidly varied. Dosas and samosas, vadas and puris feature among the starters, and vegetables can be ordered dry, in a curry sauce or even without spices. There are several appetising set meals. The Ravi Shankar Hall, in the same building, serves good cheap snacks in simple surroundings. No smoking. *No dogs.* 🍵

Manna

4 Erskine Road, NW3
01-722 8028
Map 9 B1

Open 6.30pm–midnight
Closed Bank Holidays

Pumpkin & sweetcorn goulash with rice £3.95
Spinach pancakes with cheese & vegetables £4.10
P street parking   **WC**

Care and imagination shine throughout the wholesome vegetarian fare served at this friendly, simply decorated restaurant. Light dishes might include cucumber yoghurt, Chinese vegetable soup and lots of healthy salads, while for a filling main course there are vegetable bakes, flavoursome bean hot pots and various savoury flans and pancakes (try spinach with cheese). Lovely wholemeal rolls, and homely sweets like apple crumble to finish. Non-smoking section. *No dogs.*

Marine Ices

8 Haverstock Hill, NW3
01-485 8898
Map 9 B1
Open Restaurant: 12–3 & 6–10.15; Ice Cream Parlour: 10.30am–10.45pm, Sun & Bank Hols 11–9 (till 7 October–March)
Closed Restaurant: Sun, Bank Holidays & 3 weeks August; Ice Cream Parlour: Good Fri, Easter Sun & 25 & 26 December
Tortellini Alfredo £3.15 Coppa amaretto £2.60
LVs   **P** street parking   **WC**

They've been making fresh-fruit ices here since 1930, and as well as the simple scoops there's a super selection of cassatas, bombes and sundaes. Pastries and filled rolls are also available in the ice cream parlour, while the restaurant (minimum charge £2.75) serves familiar Italian fare, including very good pizza, pasta with a choice of nine sauces, mushroom risotto, veal, chicken and liver. *No dogs.*

Matono   New Entry

25 Brewer Street, W1
01-734 1859
Map 11 A2

Open noon–2.30 & 6–midnight
Closed Sun lunch

Chirashi sushi from £12   Assorted sushi from £10
Credit Access, Amex, Diners, Visa
P NCP in Brewer Street   **WC**

This newly opened Japanese restaurant in Soho has a particularly good selection to enjoy at the sushi bar. Oshi – based on salmon, sea eel or mackerel – is served in the style of a sandwich, with vinegared rice and seaweed in layers and a topping of thin slivers of fish. Norimaki sushi is rice wrapped in seaweed with fillings like tuna, plum, cucumber and dried melon. *No dogs.*

Maxim *(Wine Bar)*

7 Boston Parade, Boston Road, W7
01-567 9708
Map 9 A2
Open noon–3 & 5.30–11, Sun noon–2 &7–
10.30
Closed some Bank Holiday Mons, 1 January &
25 & 26 December
Crispy duck with pancakes £5   Hot appetisers
in a basket £4
LVs *Credit* Access, Amex, Diners, Visa
P street parking & **WC**

Chinese cooking is the somewhat unexpected speciality of this plush wine bar with its abundance of greenery, marble-topped tables and classical background music. The menu ranges widely, from hot and sour soup, spring rolls and beef satay to griddle-sizzled prawns and chicken in black bean and chilli sauce. Vegetable and noodle dishes are also served, and there are toffee apples or bananas to finish. *No dogs.*

Maxim *(Wine Bar)*   **New Entry**

143 Knightsbridge, SW1
01-225 2553
Map 12 B1

Open 11–3 & 5.30–11, Sun 11.30–2.30 & 6.30–
10.30
Closed 1–2 days Christmas
Crispy duck £5   Szechuan 'sea-spice'
aubergine £2.50
LVs *Credit* Access, Amex, Diners, Visa
P NCP opposite Harrods & **WC**

Soft lighting, intimate alcove seating and an abundance of greenery provide an elegant setting in which to enjoy some delicious Chinese snacks at this stylish wine bar. Try frog's legs in ginger sauce or a basket filled with a variety of starters, followed perhaps by chicken in black bean sauce, crispy shredded beef with chilli or a vegetarian special like fried noodles with bean sprouts. Round it off with toffee apples and bananas. *No dogs.*

Mélange

59 Endell Street, WC2
01-240 8077
Map 11 B1

Open noon–2.30 & 6–11.15
Closed Sun, Bank Holidays & 2 weeks
Christmas
Pear with Stilton mousse £1.80   Chicken with
avocado & bacon £5.20
Credit Access, Amex, Diners, Visa
P Drury Lane NCP **WC**

A delightfully informal, attractive restaurant where the cooking is as delicious as it is innovative. The French menu ranges from excellent appetisers like deep-fried Camembert with redcurrant jelly and feuilleté of mushrooms to such tempting main courses as spinach-filled suprême of chicken and salmon hollandaise. Beautifully cooked vegetables accompany, and to finish there are appealing sweets like rich, creamy chocolate mousse. Book.

Le Meridien Piccadilly   **New Entry**

Piccadilly, W1
01-734 8000
Map 11 A2

Open 8am–2am

Chicken & avocado salad £6.75   Set
afternoon tea £6.75
Credit Access, Amex, Diners, Visa

P valet parking & **WC**

Impeccable service matches the impressive surroundings of this elegant hotel lounge. Between 3 and 5.30 (minimum charge £4) you can enjoy a choice of fine teas with freshly made finger sandwiches, fruity scones spread with thick cream and light cakes and pastries. Tempting snacks are also available all day, with choices like hot buttered muffins, smoked salmon sandwiches and exquisite salads. *No dogs.*

Methuselah's (Wine Bar)

29 Victoria Street, SW1
01-222 0424
Map 10 C2

Open Brasserie: 9am–11pm; Wine Bar: 11.30–3 & 5.30–11
Closed Sat, Sun & Bank Holidays
Ham & cheese pie with vegetables £4.75
Pork and game terrine £2.50
Credit Access, Amex, Diners, Visa
P NCP in Rochester Row **WC**

Handily placed for the Houses of Parliament, this popular estabishment serves a variety of needs. The brasserie at ground-floor level is open all day for morning coffee and croissants, afternoon teas and pastries and mealtime offerings like charcoal-grilled steak, spicy chicken and a daily casserole. The downstairs wine bar (no children) is the place for excellent salads, cold meats and well-kept cheeses. *No dogs.*

Le Metro (Wine Bar)

28 Basil Street, SW3
01-589 6286
Map 12 B1

Open 7.30–3 & 5.30–11
Closed Sun & Bank Holidays
Assiette de viandes sechées £2.40   Escalope de porc Parmesan £5.10
Credit Amex

P NCP in Pavilion Road & meters & **WC**

Softly lit and sophisticated, this basement wine bar (part of the Capital Hotel) is just the place to revive after a shopping expedition at nearby Harrods. Smoked fish pâté, Lyonnaise sausages and blanquette of veal with tomatoes are typical of the tasty French dishes on offer, and the seasonal strawberry tart is notably good. Fine wines available by the glass from the Cruover machine are a plus. *No dogs.*

Millward's

97 Stoke Newington Church Street, N16
01-254 1025
Map 10 C1

Open noon–midnight
Closed 1 week Christmas

Brochette de légumes £4.20   Mushroom Stroganoff with rice £3.85

P street parking **WC**

A friendly and informal vegetarian restaurant with picture windows giving a cool, airy feel. Daily specialities from the blackboard supplement the short regular menu of tasty dishes like cheese and chive mousse, vegetable croquettes with chilli or yoghurt sauce and Tastie Maisie – a selection of first and main courses. Enjoyable sweets; afternoon teas. At mealtimes you are expected to have at least a main course. *No dogs.*

Mother Bunch's

Arches F & G, Old Seacoal Lane, EC4
01-236 5317
Map 11 C1

Open 11.30–3 & 5.30–8.30
Closed Sat, Sun & Bank Holidays

Poached salmon salad £5.75   Smoked chicken salad £4.95
Credit Access, Amex, Diners, Visa
P NCP in Seacoal Lane **WC**

Candlelit tables in glass-enclosed booths create an atmospheric setting for a meal in this busy wine bar nestling in a railway arch. Sandwiches are filled with excellent ham, beef and smoked salmon, or you might opt for a bowl of soup and a cold meat platter. Well-kept cheeses, apple pie. Less evening choice. Fine selection of wines. Best to book for a table at lunchtime. *No dogs.*

Mother Huffs

12 Heath Street, NW3
01-435 3714
Map 9 B1

Open noon–3
Closed Sunday
Home-made soup £1.05   Steak & kidney pie
£3.50
Credit Amex, Visa

P street parking

Simple but appetising food, generously served, is the attraction at this rustic first-floor restaurant tucked away down a court-yard. At lunchtime (minimum charge £2.50) you can follow a flavour-packed soup or colourful salad with robust osso buco, pot roast or popular savoury pie. Sweets are especially good, so finish on a high note with a seasonal summer pudding, cheesecake, or chocolate roulade. More elaborate evening meals. *No dogs.* 🍵

Muffin Man

12 Wright's Lane, W8
01-937 6652
Map 12 A1

Open 8.15–5.45
Closed Sun & Bank Holidays

Original Muffin Man sandwich £1.65   Coffee & walnut cake £1.35
LVs
P meter parking   **WC**

Open throughout the day, this pretty tea room is a popular haven for high-street shoppers. Early birds can pop in for breakfast, and from 11.30 there's a selection of sandwiches with delicious fillings like tuna and tomato, cottage cheese with chopped dates or egg mayonnaise with bacon and green pepper. Much of the baking, including things such as fruit loaf and tea bread, is done on the premises. Unlicensed. *No dogs.* 🍵

Mulford's Wine Bar   ★

127 Shepherd's Bush Road, W6
01-603 2229
Map 9 A2
Open Mon–Fri noon–3 & 5.30–11, Sat 6–11,
Sun 7–10.30
Closed Bank Holidays & 24 December–1 January
Beef & mussel pie £5.25   Chocolate roulade
£1.60
Credit Access, Amex, Diners, Visa
P meter parking   **WC**

The food is full of imagination and interest at this civilised wine bar run by charming owners Peter and Venetia Mulford. Sit at stripped pine tables decorated with fresh flowers and make your choice from the daily-changing menu – perhaps celery and almond soup, parsnip and carrot timbales, oriental meatballs, crab and tomato quiche or aubergine lasagne. Beautifully light chocolate roulade or treacle tart to finish things off nicely. Well-chosen wine list. 🥂

Nakamura   **New Entry**

31 Marylebone Lane, W1
01-935 2931
Map 11 A1

Open noon–2.30 & 6–10.30
Closed Sun lunch, all Sat & Bank Holidays

Sushi lunch £8   Grilled fish lunch £6.50
Credit Access, Amex, Diners, Visa
P NCP behind Debenham's   **WC**

A colourful poster and a helpful chef assist in the choice of sushi at this neat Japanese restaurant. There's quite a wide selection, and the set sushi lunch is a good way to sample the lovely fresh seafood – salmon, tuna, mackerel, scallops and cuttlefish. Also included in the price are an appetiser, pickles and a delicately flavoured soya bean soup. Various other set lunches, plus an extensive à la carte menu. *No dogs.*

Nanten   *New Entry*

6 Blandford Street, W1
01-935 6319
Map 11 A1

Open noon–2 & 6–10
Closed Sat lunch, all Sun, Bank Holidays & 1–3 January

Ramen £3.50   Yakitori lunch £7.20
Credit Access, Amex, Diners, Visa
P meters in street   **WC**

Yakitori is the Japanese equivalent of kebabs, and there are many varieties to enjoy here, including beef, ox heart, asparagus wrapped in sliced pork and different parts of the chicken (flesh, skin, gizzard, heart and liver). Steamed dumplings and sashimi are other appetisers, and main courses include grilled mackerel and beef. A popular evening dish is ramen, Chinese-style noodles served in soup with sliced meat, fish and vegetables. *No dogs.*

National Gallery Restaurant   *New Entry*

Trafalgar Square, WC2
01-930 5210
Map 11 B2

Open 10–5 (Wed till 7.30 July–September), Sun 2–5
Closed 1 January & 25 & 26 December
Spinach & egg roulade £1.65   Lamb & ginger casserole with brown rice £3.25
LVs
P NCP in Orange Street   ♿   **WC**

A roomy self-service restaurant, whose menu features a good range of well-prepared, appetising dishes. Quiches come in Spanish, mushroom and spinach variants, and there's a selection of salads, plus the day's soup and hot special – perhaps vegetable mornay or pork with apple, fennel and brown rice. Sweet tempters include banana bread, fudge cake and vanilla cheesecake. *No dogs.*

Neal's Yard Bakery & Tea Room

6 Neal's Yard, Covent Garden, WC2
01-836 5199
Map 11 B1

Open 10.30–8 (Wed till 3.30, Sat till 4.30)
Closed Sun, Bank Holidays & Christmas–New Year
Vegetarian pizza £1.30   Stuffed pitta bread 90p
LVs
P meter parking or NCP in Drury Lane   **WC**

Healthy wholefood snacks can be enjoyed with an excellent range of teas at this tiny raftered tea room. Only organically grown produce and wholewheat flour are used, so that delights such as pan bagna and pizzas, banana and nut cake and fruit slices not only taste good but are good for you, too. Don't miss the lovely crunchy salads. Unlicensed. No smoking. *No dogs.* ♥

Neal's Yard Bakery at the Ecology Centre

45 Shelton Street, WC2
01-379 4324
Map 11 B1

Open 10–5
Closed Sun & Bank Holidays

Soup with wholewheat roll £1.20   Pizza with mixed salad £2.10
LVs
P NCP in Shelton Street   **WC**

This bright, cheerful little vegetarian café occupies a ground-floor section of the London Ecology Centre. Salads are varied and delicious, and hot options include the day's soup with a wholewheat roll, pizzas, quiches and beanburgers. Scones come in both cheese and fruit varieties, and there are some splendid biscuits and cakes to tempt the sweeter tooth (note the exquisite banana nut cake). Unlicensed. *No dogs.* ♥

New Kam Tong

59 Queensway, W2
01-229 6065
Map 9 B2

Open dim sum noon–5.45 (full menu noon–11.15)

King prawns in spicy sauce £6   Beef with green peppers £4

P NCP in Queensway   **WC**

The whole family can snack on tasty dim sum from noon to 5.45 at this roomy, functional restaurant on bustling Queensway. Savoury choices include braised chicken feet with flavoursome black bean sauce, king prawn dumplings and char siu buns, while for those with a sweet tooth there are egg tarts and light dumplings filled with rich water chestnut paste. Minimum charge of £2.50. *No dogs.*

New Loon Fung

42 Gerrard Street, W1
01-437 6232
Map 11 B1

Open dim sum noon–5, Sun from 11 (full menu noon–11.30, Sun 11–10.30)

Dim sum from 90p   Shrimps with egg fried noodles £3.50
Credit Access, Amex, Visa
P NCP in Cambridge Circus   **WC**

Large and very popular Chinese restaurant in a pedestrianised part of Chinatown. The dim sum here are very good, with mixed meat croquette, turnip paste, prawn dumpling and stuffed bean curd roll among the many tempting varieties available until 5pm. One-plate rice and noodle dishes are other just-a-bite favourites, and there's a full and varied à la carte selection. *No dogs.*

New Shu Shan   `New Entry`

36 Cranbourn Street, WC2
01-836 7501
Map 11 B2

Open noon–midnight

Prawns in garlic & chilli sauce £5.50   Sauté chicken £5
LVs   *Credit* Amex, Diners, Visa

P Swiss Centre car park & meter parking   **WC**

Open twelve hours a day, every day, this welcoming little Chinese restaurant offers good food and attentive service. Spicier dishes such as sliced pork with garlic and chilli sauce are picked out in red on the menu, which ranges from wun tun soup and crispy seaweed to sliced beef with oyster sauce and Hong Kong-style sweet and sour pork. Red bean paste pancakes among the puds. *No dogs.*

No 77 Wine Bar

77 Mill Lane, NW6
01-435 7787
Map 9 B1
Open noon–3 & 6–midnight (Mon–Wed till 11, Sun 7–10.30)
Closed Sun lunch, Bank Holidays & 4 days Christmas
Chicken with artichokes £4.45   Vegetarian lasagne £3.85
Credit Access, Diners, Visa
P street parking   &   **WC**

Dependable home cooking in this attractive wine bar with pine, posters and fresh flowers. The blackboard menu, available both lunchtime and evening, lists such dishes as curried parsnip soup, chicken liver pâté, asparagus quiche and sirloin steak. For pudding, the choice could include frangipane flan, peach vol-au-vent and a very nice pear and apple crumble. Children's portions offered. Outside tables in summer.

Nontas

16 Camden High Street, NW1
01-387 4579
Map 9 B1

Open noon–2.45 & 6–11.30
Closed Sun, Bank Holidays & 2 days
Christmas

Moussaka £3.60   Mezes £5.95
Credit Access, Amex, Diners
P street parking & meter parking   **WC**

The whole Vassilakas family helps out at this
unpretentious little Greek restaurant, where
a favourite snack for two or more is mezes,
offering a bite of various dishes. Alternatively,
light, garlicky taramasalata, egg and lemon
soup and deep-fried squid make tasty starters, while succulent kebabs – try spicy
sausage or lemony fish for a change – are
popular main courses. *No dogs.*

Nosherie

12 Greville Street, Hatton Garden, EC1
01-242 1591
Map 11 C1

Open 8–5
Closed Sat, Sun, Bank Holidays & 10 days
Christmas
Salt beef plate £3.95   Cheese blintz £1.40
LVs
P street parking or NCP in St Cross Street
WC

Old-style standards endure here in the shape
of friendly, personal service and robust,
reliable cooking. The setting couldn't be
simpler, and the menu covers a good spread
of Jewish and Continental fare, headed by
the renowned and excellent salt beef. Other
delights include beetroot soup, gefilte fish,
super fried haddock and braised meatloaf.
For pud, perhaps apple crumble or blissful
blintzes. Minimum charge of £2.25 noon–3.
No dogs.

Nuthouse

26 Kingly Street, W1
01-437 9471
Map 11 A1

Open 10–7, Sat 10.30–5
Closed Sun

Vegetable pancake with tomato sauce £2.25
Cheesy mixed vegetables £1.95
LVs
P NCP in Kingly Street   **WC**

Walk through a little health-food shop to this
recently spruced vegetarian restaurant,
where a blackboard lists what's available
from the service counter. Soup could be lentil
or cauliflower, and hot savouries (more in
winter) could include vegetable risotto or chilli
bean pancake roll served with tomato sauce
and yoghurt. Also quiches, salads, baked
potatoes, nut rissoles and enjoyable sweets.
No dogs.

Odette's Wine Bar

130 Regent's Park Road, NW1
01-586 5486
Map 9 B1

Open 12.30–2.30 & 7–11
Closed Sun, Bank Holidays & 10 days
Christmas

Carrot soup £2   Ragout of lamb £4.50
Credit Access, Amex, Diners, Visa
P street parking   **WC**

By now firmly established in much-improved
and enlarged kitchens, John Armstrong
copes admirably with both restaurant and
wine bar. The latter's menu covers quite an
interesting spread, from delicious hot carrot
soup and deep-fried Camembert to tuna fish
bake, vegetarian moussaka and a really good
ragout of lamb. There are super sweets, too,
like rice pudding or chocolate truffle cake.
No dogs. 🍴

Old Heidelburg Pâtisserie & Pasta & Salad Bar

220 Chiswick High Road, W6
01-994 6621
Map 9 A2

Open Pâtisserie: Mon–Sat 9.30am–5.30pm;
Pasta & Salad Bar: Tues–Sat 7pm–10.30pm
Closed Bank Holidays
Texas bourbon cake £1.10   Penne all'
arrabiata £2.95
Credit Access, Diners, Visa
P street parking   **WC**

High-class pâtisserie by day, splendid pasta restaurant in the evening. The cakes and pastries cover a wide and tempting range that includes some mouthwatering speciality gateaux. Pasta, too, provides abundant variety, from lasagne and ravioli to spaghetti and penne with a choice of a dozen sauces. There are also some very good salads and a chicken dish of the day. Lunchtime savouries also available. Minimum charge £2.50 Sat eve only. *No dogs.* 🐾

Oliver's

10 Russell Gardens, W14
01-603 7645
Map 9 A2

Open noon–10.20, Sun noon–4.20 & 6.15–10.20
Closed 25 & 26 December

Corn on the cob £1   Saddle of lamb forestière £6
P street parking   **WC**

Queues at the door indicate the popularity of the food on offer at this bustling bistro. Daily-changing menus provide ample choice, with starters like curried chicken wings and sautéed mushrooms preceding such hearty main-course offerings as osso buco, saddle of lamb forestière and pepper steak. Finish with a simple sweet like chocolate mousse or home-made trifle. There's a minimum charge of £4.50. Unlicensed so bring your own. *No dogs.* 🐾 ⊝

Ormes Wine Bar & Restaurant

67 Abbeville Road, Clapham, SW4
01-673 2568
Map 9 B3

Open noon–2.30 & 6.30–11
Closed 4 days Christmas

Lancashire hot pot £4.15   Cold seafood platter £4.75
Credit Access, Amex, Diners, Visa
P street parking   **WC**

There's plenty of interesting choice at this relaxed and friendly wine bar-cum-restaurant. Deep-fried mushrooms with garlic mayonnaise and tuna and cucumber mousse are typically tempting light bites, while more substantial offerings might include seafood lasagne, prawn-stuffed chicken breast and pepper steak. Finish with bread and butter pud or popular banoffee pie. *No dogs.* ⊝

Palings Wine Bar

25 Hanover Square, W1
01-408 0935
Map 11 A1

Open 11.30–3 & 5.30–11
Closed Sat lunch, all Sun, Bank Holidays & 3 days Christmas
Coronation chicken with salad £3   Steak bap & salad £4.50
LVs *Credit* Access, Amex, Diners, Visa
P NCP in Cavendish Square   **WC**

Extremely popular with a well-heeled lunchtime set, so you have to arrive early to secure a table at this smart basement wine bar. Crisp salads accompany rare roast beef, French sausages and gravad lax, while the hot choice might include soups and blanquette de veau. Cold buffet only in the evening; no food after 9.30 or at weekends. No children. *No dogs.* ⊝

Pappagalli's Pizza Inc.

7 Swallow Street, W1
01-734 5182
Map 11 A2

Open noon–3 & 5.15–11.15
Closed Sun, Bank Holiday lunches & all 1
January & 25 & 26 December
The 'works' pizza £8.50   Pasta with clam
sauce £3.55
Credit Access, Visa
P street parking & **WC**

'The home of wholemeal pizza' they call
themselves, but you can also get white flour
versions in this comfortable restaurant with
stained-glass windows and carved oak furniture. Pizzas serve two or more and come
loaded with all the usual goodies; Stromboli
is a pie version, pizzarito a parcel for one.
Other items include garlic mushrooms, barbecued chicken wings, salads, pasta and
ices. Minimum charge of £3.25. *No dogs.*

Parsons

311 Fulham Road, SW10
01-352 0651
Map 12 A2

Open noon–12.30am (Sun till midnight)
Closed 25 & 26 December

⅛lb hamburger £2.75 (£2.15 lunchtime)
Vegetarian burritos £3.35 (£2.45 lunchtime)
LVs   *Credit* Access, Amex, Diners, Visa
P meter parking **WC**

A friendly, informal place with ceiling fans
and lots of greenery. The menu covers a wide
spread of familiar fare, from savoury pies
and spaghetti (seconds for the hungry) to
burgers with French fries, charcoal grills,
salads and spicy Tex-Mex dishes. Sandwiches, too, plus snackettes for children and
an assortment of ices and American-style
desserts. *No dogs.*

Pasta Connection

25 Elystan Street, SW3
01-584 5248
Map 12 B2

Open 12.30–2.30 & 7–11.15
Closed Sat lunch, all Sun & Bank Holidays

Lasagne £2.40   Chicken leg pizzaiola £4.95
Credit Access, Visa
P street parking **WC**

On fine days you can eat alfresco at this
attractive Italian restaurant. The menu covers
a simple span of familiar favourites, from
seafood salad and all kinds of pasta to veal
escalopes, chicken sorpresa and grilled
steak. Sweets are equally straightforward –
chocolate mousse, crème brûlée, fruit salad.
Cooking is of a good, reliable standard and
service prompt and friendly. *No dogs.*

Pasta Fino

27 Frith Street, W1
01-439 8900
Map 11 B1

Open noon–11.30
Closed Sun, Bank Holidays & 1 week
Christmas
Soup of the day £1.25   Pasta with baby clams
in tomato sauce £3.75
Credit Access, Visa
P NCP in Dean Street & meter parking **WC**

A cheerful little Italian restaurant where you
can enjoy the freshest of pasta – it's made in
the shop upstairs – that comes plain as well
as prettily coloured red (tomatoes) and green
(spinach). Add a tasty sauce such as bolognese, seasonal vegetables or bacon with
tomatoes and chilli peppers for a really
colourful plateful. Simple starters, ice cream-
based desserts and excellent espresso coffee. *No dogs.*

Pasta Underground

214 Camden High Street, NW1
01-482 0010
Map 9 B1

Open Mon–Fri noon–3 & 6–11, Sat 6–11, Sun
noon–3
Closed Bank Holidays

Chocolate terrine £1.95   Spinach ravioli £3.50

P meters in street   **WC**

Spaghettini with pesto and sliced potatoes is
the unusual and delicious house speciality of
this cheerfully contemporary basement restaurant. Equally appetising pasta alternatives
include fettuccine with tomatoes and spicy
Italian sausage and tagliatelle with cream
cheese and chives – or you can opt for a
meaty main course like pork satay or osso
buco. Tasty starters, also wonderful chocolate terrine with orange sauce among desserts. *No dogs.*

Pasticceria Amalfi

31 Old Compton Steet, W1
01-437 7284
Map 11 B1

Open 10.30am–11pm
Closed 1 January & 25 & 26 December

Strawberry tart 70p   Coffee bun 60p
LVs   *Credit* Access, Amex, Diners, Visa

P NCP in Dean Street   **WC**

This delightful little Soho shop holds a rich
store of splendid pâtisserie to enjoy with a
super cup of coffee. Choose from a mouthwatering window display that includes choux
buns, petits fours, fruit tartlets, éclairs, mille-
feuilles and cannoli siciliani – a pastry horn
filled with sweetened ricotta cheese and
candied fruit, coated in chopped almonds
and dusted with icing sugar. *No dogs.*

Pasticceria Cappuccetto

8 Moor Street, Cambridge Circus, W1
01-437 9472
Map 11 B1

Open 7.30am–8pm
Closed Sun & Bank Holidays

Millefoglie 90p   Strawberry tart £1
LVs

P NCP in Gerrard Street   **WC**

Delicious cakes and pastries, all baked on
the premises, are served with superb espresso coffee in this very popular Italian
pasticceria just off Cambridge Circus. The
choice extends to some 60 items, from sweet
almond tarts and lovely millefoglie to Danish
pastries, palmiers, choux buns and éclairs.
For the savoury palate there are ham or
cheese croissants and slices of quiche.
Unlicensed. *No dogs.*

Pâtisserie Parisienne

2a Phillimore Gardens, W8
01-938 1890
Map 12 A1

Open 8.30–7.30, Sun 10–6
Closed 1 January

Minced beef & vegetable pancake 90p
Asparagus quiche £1.40

P meter parking   **WC**

Shiny glazed strawberry tarts, delicate fruit-
filled cream sponges and the richest, most
velvety of chocolate cakes – just some of the
temptations waiting at this neat, bright pâtisserie off Kensington High Street. Order at the
counter, and if your taste is for the savoury,
there are also fluffy cheese feuilletès, fat
sausage rolls and vol-au-vents to choose
from. Minimum lunchtime charge of £1.50.
Unlicensed. *No dogs.*

126

Pâtisserie Valerie

44 Old Compton Street, W1
01-437 3466
Map 11 B1

Open 8.30–7
Closed Sun & Bank Holidays

Fresh fruit tart £1.40   Vanilla slice 85p
LVs

P NCP in Dean Street   &. **WC**

Delicious cakes and pastries fill the window of this busy little pâtisserie in the heart of Soho. The range is enormous, from pretty plum, peach and cherry pastries, strawberry rum baba and wonderful Black Forest gâteau to spicy apple strudel, croissants and the lightest of mille-feuilles – all accompanied by excellent tea or coffee. Cheerful, informal service. Unlicensed. *No dogs.* 🍵

Pavilion Wine Bar

Finsbury Circus Gardens, EC2
01-628 8224
Map 10 C2

Open 11.30–3 & 5–8
Closed Sat, Sun & Bank Holidays
Smoked chicken & mushroom fettuccine £3.50
Banana cheesecake £1.50
LVs *Credit* Access, Amex, Visa
P NCP in Finsbury Square & meter parking
WC

Overlooking the bowling green at Finsbury Circus Gardens, this airy upstairs wine bar offers an enterprising range of delicious snacks. Salads are particularly imaginative (try tangy herring, apple and celery with sour cream), as are appetising flans like salmon and asparagus, while the cheese selection includes many unusual varieties. Hot specials, too, like lamb tagine, and banana cheesecake to finish. First-class wines, many by the glass. No children. *No dogs.* 🍷

The Peck Provender   `New Entry`

52 Upper Street, N1
01-288 6079
Map 10 C1

Open 8am–11pm, Sun 11–10.30
Closed 25 December

Chicken & chestnut pie £3.90   Bread & butter pudding £1.80
Credit Access, Amex, Diners, Visa
P Exhibition car park   &. **WC**

A cool, smart and spacious restaurant on the first floor of the Islington Design Centre. Breakfast encompasses such diverse choices as croissants and kedgeree, and at other times options range from bar snacks such as jacket potatoes or smoked salmon sandwiches to trout with almonds, sirloin steak and speciality pies like chicken and chestnut or steak and oyster. Bread and butter pudding rounds it off for the really peckish. *No dogs.* 🍷 🍵

Le Petit Prince

5 Holmes Road, NW5
01-267 0752
Map 9 B1

Open noon–2.30 & 7–11.30
Closed lunch Sun & Mon, also lunch June–September & 1 week Christmas

Merguez couscous £4.40   Baked cheese loaf with mayonnaise £1.40
P street parking   &. **WC**

The North African dish couscous is the house speciality at this most relaxed and informal of restaurants. The basic version is a platter of steamed semolina and a bowl of broth with vegetables; to this you can add your choice of meat – braised chicken, meatballs, mutton chop, lamb cutlets or spicy merguez sausages. It's very tasty and very nourishing. Also grills, a few starters, salads, simple sweets. *No dogs.* 🍷

Pigeon

606 Fulham Road, SW6
01-736 4618
Map 9 A2

Open 12–3 & 7–midnight
Closed lunch 1 Jan, also all 25 & 26 December

Smoked chicken pastry £1.55   Steak
d'agneau £3.45
Credit Access, Amex, Visa
P street parking   **WC**

Largest of three sister restaurants, this well-run establishment on two floors offers a regular menu supplemented by daily specials. Portions are generous and quality high – try filo pastry layered with cheese and spinach or crab-stuffed profiteroles to start, then perhaps lamb cutlets with vegetable caviar sauce or market-fresh red mullet. Good salads, simple sweets. Traditional Sunday lunch. Booking advisable in the evenings. *No dogs.* ☺

Pirroni's

116 Tottenham Court Road, W1
01-387 6324
Map 11 A1
Open 8am–10pm
Closed Sun, Bank Holidays, 1 January & 25 &
26 December
Scampi provençale with vegetables £4.95
Tortelloni alla crema £3.50
Credit Access, Amex, Diners, Visa
P NCP at Telecom Tower & nearby meters
WC

For over 20 years the Pirronis have been welcoming customers at their smart and friendly Italian restaurant, whether it's for breakfast, afternoon pâtisserie or a full meal. The savoury choice ranges from tasty soups and antipasti to chicken, veal and fish dishes, pasta, grills and salads. The excellent sweet trolley is typical of the consistently careful cooking. Minimum charge of £3 at lunchtime and after 6. *No dogs.* 🍵

Le Plat du Jour

19 Hampstead Road, NW1
01-387 9644
Map 9 B2

Open 12–3
Closed Sat, Sun & Bank Holidays

Poached eggs with red wine sauce £1.80
Parsleyed best end of lamb £5.10
Credit Access, Diners, Visa
P meter parking   **WC**

Specialities from his native France are offered by charming owner Alain Marcesché and an all-French team in the wine bar section of this bright modern restaurant. Fish soup, garlic snails, perhaps a warm goat's cheese salad make tasty snacks or appetisers, while daily specials range from pepper steak to chicken basquaise and monkfish. Fresh fruit flans and prime French cheeses to finish. ☺

Poons

4 Leicester Street, WC2
01-437 1528
Map 11 B2

Open noon–11.30
Closed Sun & 3 days Christmas

Squid with garlic £3.40   Sweet & sour crispy
wun tun £3

P Swiss Centre NCP   **WC**

Bright modern premises just a stone's throw from Leicester Square provide a friendly venue for the day-long enjoyment of authentic Cantonese cooking. The delights are many and varied, from sweet and sour crispy wun tun and wonderful deep-fried sesame prawns to steamed sea bass, lamb with lettuce leaves and the famous wind-dried duck, pork and sausages. Sweets include almond-flavoured bean curd. Minimum charge of £5 after 6 o'clock. *No dogs.*

Poons

27 Lisle Street, WC2
01-437 4549
Map 11 B2

Open noon–11.30
Closed Mon & 3 days Christmas

Mixed barbecue £2.60   Chinese-style prawns £3.60

P Swiss Centre NCP   **WC**

This simplest and friendliest of Soho restaurants presents a tempting menu of authentic Cantonese dishes. It's perhaps best known for its wind-dried products (duck, pork and sausages), but it offers much more besides, from spicy beef noodle soup to tofu with crispy pork and pungent shrimp paste, quail eggs with crab meat and a number of original dishes which are basically casseroles served in aluminium pots. Minimum charge of £2 after 6 o'clock. Unlicensed. *No dogs.*

Portman Hotel, Portman Corner

22 Portman Square, W1
01-486 5844
Map 9 B2

Open 11am–midnight

Set afternoon tea £6.50   Ploughman's £4.80
Credit Access, Amex, Diners, Visa

P NCP next door   &   **WC**

Dark mahogany and plush seating create a cosy, restful spot for a traditional afternoon tea featuring particularly good home-made pastries. Throughout the long opening hours you can also have anything from a light snack – perhaps chicken and rabbit terrine, a Stilton muffin, quiche or ploughman's – to the day's roast carved to order at the counter. Lunchtime salad bar, too. *No dogs.*

Le Poulbot Pub

45 Cheapside, EC2
01-236 4379
Map 11 C1

Open 8–10.30 & noon–3
Closed Sat, Sun & Bank Holidays

Omelette £2.80   Dish of the day from about £5.50

P NCP in Ave Maria Lane   **WC**

Situated above the Roux brothers' plush basement restaurant, Le Poulbot Pub is a smart brasserie, thoroughly French in decor and cuisine. Morning coffee comes with excellent pâtisserie, and lunchtime brings a well-chosen list of Gallic classics like herby pâté, omelettes and entrecôte béarnaise. The daily special could be poulet fermière or navarin of lamb. Simple sweets – apple tart, peach flan, chocolate gâteau. *No dogs.*

Punters Pie   **New Entry**

183 Lavender Hill, SW11
01-228 2660
Map 11 C1

Open noon–3 & 6–11.30 (Sun from 7)
Closed 25–31 December

Steak & kidney pie £3.95   Cheddar soufflé with salad £3.95
Credit Access, Amex, Diners, Visa
P street parking nearby   **WC**

A colourful, informal restaurant (with tables outside) that specialises in home-made pies with delicious fillings like cod and shellfish, vegetarian, mildly curried chicken, steak and mushroom plus a daily special, chalked up on a blackboard. Starters such as mushroom, garlic and coriander pâté are equally tasty and we noted an excellent Black Forest gâteau. Small select wine list. Friendly staff. *No dogs.*

Raffles

391 Kilburn Road, NW6
01-328 9070
Map 9 A1

Open noon–3 & 6–midnight, Sun noon–midnight
Closed 25 December
Masala dosa £1.75   Chicken tikka masala £2.95
Credit Access, Amex, Diners, Visa
P NCP Kilburn High Road   **WC**

A large palm tree and fans add a colonial touch to this airy, modern restaurant specialising in Indian and Malaysian cuisine. Typically well prepared and judiciously seasoned dishes might include satay or crisply fried bhajis with coconut sauce as your appetiser, with gently spiced lamb pasanda, creamy chicken tandoori and fish Madras among main courses. Appealing accompaniments like citrus-flavoured rice add zest, and vegetables are interesting. *No dogs.*

Raj Bhelpoori House   `New Entry`

19 Camden High Street, NW1
01-388 6663
Map 9 B1

Open noon–11.30

Aloo chana chat £1   Raj thali £3.70
LVs   *Credit* Access, Amex, Diners, Visa

P meter parking & **WC**

The vegetarian cuisine of South India is featured in this neat, friendly restaurant. Fresh herbs and spices are used skilfully in a range of tasty snacks including samosas, vegetable cutlets and delicious idli sambhar – steamed rice sponge cakes in a savoury sauce. Dosas (pancakes made from ground black lentils or semolina) are the basis of most main courses, and there are some very sweet sweets. Unlicensed. *No dogs.*

Rani   `New Entry`

3 Long Lane, N3
01-349 4386
Map 9 B1

Open 12.30–2 & 6–10.30
Closed 25 December

Banana methi & tomato curry £2.20   Special thali £6
Credit Access, Visa
P street parking & **WC**

Delightful staff and a welcoming atmosphere at this brightly decorated Indian vegetarian restaurant. The menu lists and explains a good variety of tasty, well-prepared dishes, among them dosas and samosas, bhajias, breads and steamed rice sponge cakes. Curries include daily specials like stuffed aubergine and potato or dry, spicy vegetables with toasted baps. Thalis are a complete meal. There's a minimum evening charge of £4. *No dogs.*

Raoul's

13 Clifton Road, Maida Vale, W9
01-289 7313
Map 9 B2

Open 8.30–6.30
Closed 25 December

Tuna fish salad £3.95   Rouleau de fromage £2.95
LVs
P street   **WC**

Modest premises stock an impressive variety of cakes and pastries to eat in or take out. Scones, chocolate croissants, fresh cream slices, fruit flans and tartlets are some of the sweet selection, and on the savoury side are cheese rouleaux and ham feuilletés. There's a fairly standard snack menu of sandwiches, quiches, pizzas and omelettes. Friendly, informal service. Minimum lunchtime charge £1.50. Unlicensed. *No dogs.*

130

Ravenscourt Park Tea House **New Entry**

Ravenscourt Park, W6
Map 9 A2

Open 10–5 (Sun till 6)
Closed Good Fri & 9 days Christmas

Vegetarian burger £1   Mushroom slice with
sauce £1.40
LVs

P street parking   **WC**

Located right in the middle of the park, this
unpretentious tea house provides acceptable
snacks prepared on the premises and based
whenever possible on organically grown
produce. Typical dishes – the day's choice is
listed on a blackboard – range from dhal
soup, mushroom slice and courgette and
tomato flan to flapjacks, ginger cake and
chocolate brownies. Also filled wholemeal
rolls. Unlicensed. *No dogs.*

Ravi Shankar

135 Drummond Street, NW1
01-388 6458
Map 9 B1

Open noon–11

Mysore thali £3.95   Daily special £1.90
LVs *Credit* Access, Amex, Diners, Visa

P street parking   **WC**

South Indian vegetarian food is prepared
with care and spicing is sure in this simply
appointed little place just off Euston Road.
The menu takes in starters and snacks
(sausages, pooris, ground black lentil fritters); main course dosas, idli sambhar and
vegetables with paratha; aubergine and okra
bhajees; and rich, milky sweets. There are
also two versions of the traditional set meals
or thali. *No dogs.*

Raw Deal

65 York Street, W1
01-262 4841
Map 9 B2

Open 10–10 (Sat till 11)
Closed Sun, Bank Holidays & 1 week
Christmas
Nutty aubergines £2.50   Courgette & spinach
bake £2.50
LVs
P meter parking   **WC**

Prepare to share a table at mealtimes (minimum £1.75) at this popular corner restaurant,
which has been dispensing wholesome vegetarian fare for more than 20 years. Soup,
crumbles, cakes, tarts and yoghurt are all
made on the premises. There are a couple of
hot savoury dishes like stuffed marrow or
pasta with mushrooms and a tasty tomato
sauce, as well as a dozen crisp, colourful
salads to choose from. Unlicensed. *No dogs.*

*We neither seek nor accept
hospitality, and we pay for
all food and drinks in full.*

Rebato's

169 South Lambeth Road, SW8
01-735 6388
Map 10 C2

Open noon–2.30 & 7–11
Closed Sat lunch, all Sun & Bank Holidays

Champiñones £1.25   Spanish omelette £1.25
Credit Access, Amex, Diners, Visa

P street parking   **WC**

South of Vauxhall on the A203 this richly decorated wine bar makes a comfortable setting in which to enjoy tasty tapas (light snacks) with some fine Spanish wines. Seafood offerings include grilled sardines, octopus, stuffed squid and fresh anchovies, while for carnivores there's Parma ham, pâté and spicy chorizo sausages – plus an authentic Spanish omelette that's certain to please all palates. *No dogs.* 🍵

Richoux

86 Brompton Road, SW3
01-584 8300
Map 12 B1
Open 9–7 (Wed till 8), Sun 10–7
Closed 25 & 26 December
P meters or NCP in Pavilion Road &
Knightsbridge Green   **WC**

72 Piccadilly, W1
01-493 2204
Map 11 A2
Open 8.30am–11.30pm (Fri till 12.30am), Sat
9am–12.30am, Sun 10am–11.30pm
Closed 25 & 26 December
P meters or NCP in Old Burlington Street   **WC**

41a South Audley Street, W1
01-629 5228
Map 11 A2
Open 8.30am–11.30pm, Sat 9am–midnight,
Sun 10am–11.30pm
Closed 25 & 26 December
P NCP in Adams Row   **WC**

Fresh flowers, an abundance of greenery and pretty waitresses in long Laura Ashley-style frocks with lace caps and frilly aprons make a welcome sight at these three smart, civilised havens strategically located to succour the shopper, sightseer and gallery-goer. The extensive menu starts with breakfast and carries on right through to supper time, embracing egg dishes, soups and sandwiches, four varieties of rarebit, burgers, salads and more substantial offerings like bangers and mash, seasonal salmon and steak and kidney pie. After 6pm there are additional dishes like chicken suprême and steak, while afternoon tea brings a feast of warm, fresh scones with jam and cream plus lots of cakes and pastries. High-quality chocolates are on sale in all branches. Chandeliers and a skyscape ceiling make the Mayfair branch a particularly pleasing spot. Minimum charge of £3 at lunchtime, weekends and Bank Holidays. *No dogs.* 🐾

Steak & kidney pie £4.95 Welsh rarebit £3.50
LVs   *Credit* Access, Amex, Diners, Visa

The Ritz, Palm Court

Piccadilly, W1
01-493 8181
Map 11 A2

Open 10–2, 3.30–5.30 & 6–10.30

Set afternoon tea £8.50   Ham sandwich £2.95
Credit Access, Amex, Diners, Visa

P NCP in Arlington Square   ♿   **WC**

With its splendid marble fountain, gilt chandelier and elegant Louis XIV chairs, this is surely London's most opulent setting for afternoon tea (two sittings, booking essential – as are jacket and tie for gentlemen). Dainty finger sandwiches, a light scone with jam and cream, delicious pastries and gâteaux are all served in fine style. Well-filled sandwiches available at other times. Minimum charge of £8.50 3.30–5.30. *No dogs.* 🐾

Rouxl Britannia, Le Café   **New Entry**

Triton Court, 14 Finsbury Square, EC2
01-256 6997
Map 10 C2

Open 7.30am–9pm
Closed Sat, Sun, Bank Holidays, 24–29
December & 31 December–5 January
Poulet pistou aux pâtes fraîches £3.40   Raie
rôtie au persil £2.80
LVs
P NCP in Finsbury Square   **WC**

The Roux Brothers' smart new café is located in an office building on the corner opposite the bowling green. Dishes are cooked sous-vide and reheated, a method which suits some better than others. Main courses include skate with parsley sauce, lamb hot pot with butter beans, chicken with a good basil and saffron sauce, served with fresh noodles. Other things tried were a so-so vegetable terrine and an excellent mulligatawny soup. *No dogs.*

Royal Festival Hall, Riverside Café

South Bank, SE1
01-928 3246
Map 11 B2
Open 10–8 (Fri–Sun till 10)
Closed lunch 26 December & all 25 December

Roast beef & Yorkshire pudding £4.25   Steak
& kidney pie £3.50
LVs

P NCP in Belvedere Road   &   **WC**

Watch the Thames traffic from this spacious, stylish cafeteria offering an immaculately presented array of self-service snacks. As well as sandwiches, cheeses and cakes, there are colourful salads to have with cold meats and pies, while hot lunchtime specials like stuffed aubergines and liver and bacon are accompanied by live music. The cafeteria is on the ground floor, and there are sandwich bars and a buffet upstairs. Non-smoking area. *No dogs.*

Royal Lancaster Hotel Lounge

Lancaster Terrace, W2
01-262 6737
Map 9 B2

Open 11am–11pm

Afternoon tea £5.50   Turkey sandwich £2
Credit Access, Amex, Diners, Visa

P own car park   &   **WC**

Afternoon tea comes with piano accompaniment in the comfortably contemporary surroundings of this relaxing hotel lounge. It's a traditional affair, with freshly cut finger sandwiches, scones with jam and clotted cream and various good-quality pastries and cakes. For the rest of opening time light snacks are available in the shape of pastries and sandwiches (cold meats, smoked salmon, egg, cheese and tomato). *No dogs.*

Sabras

263 High Road, Willesden Green, NW10
01-459 0340
Map 9 A1

Open 12.30–9.15
Closed Mon, 2 weeks August & 2 weeks
Christmas

Kashmiri kofta £1.95   Mini thali £5
LVs   *Credit* Access, Amex, Diners, Visa
P street parking   &   **WC**

A splendid choice of South Indian vegetarian dishes is on offer at this spotless restaurant very ably run by the friendly Desai family. A selection of savoury snacks or Bombay seaside specialities makes a tasty starter, followed perhaps by a curry of spiced vegetable balls in a nutty sauce, with black-eyed beans and fried rice. There are refreshing yoghurt and fruit juice drinks and some delicious sweets. Unlicensed. *No dogs.*

Sagarmatha

Sagarmatha

339 Euston Road, NW1
01-387 6531
Map 11 A1

Open noon–2.45 & 6–11.45
Closed 25 & 26 December

Momo £1.95   Tikka chicken masala £2.95
LVs   *Credit* Visa

P meter parking   **WC**

Gurkha soldiers troop down from their Regent's Park barracks to eat at this excellent little Nepalese restaurant named after Mount Everest. Just-a-biters can feast on tasty little snacks like vegetable samosas and chaola (roast lamb spiced with ginger and garlic) or go for delicious main courses like murgh nepali – chicken cooked with yoghurt in a mild curry sauce. Refreshing mango kulfi to finish. *No dogs.*

The Savoy, Thames Foyer   ★

Strand, WC2
01-836 4343
Map 11 B2

Open 10am–midnight

Set afternoon tea £7.50   Tulipe de sorbets aux fruits exotiques £3.75
Credit Access, Amex, Diners, Visa

P own car park   **WC**

A pianist in an ornamental gazebo accompanies afternoon tea in this splendid room with ornate chandeliers, trompe l'oeil windows and a trio of Art Deco mirrors. Formally attired waiters serve finger sandwiches, excellent scones and meltingly delicious pastries in perfect style, while at other times you can nibble at an elegant salad or sandwich, smoked salmon, omelettes and fruity Danish pastries. *No dogs.* 🍴

Seashell

424 Kingsland Road, E8 01-254 6152
Map 10 C1
Open noon–2 & 5–10, Sat 11.30am–10pm
Closed Sun, Mon, Bank Holidays except Good Fri & 10 days Christmas   **WC**
Cod fillet & chips £3.90   Skate & chips £4.30
49 Lisson Grove, NW1 01-723 8703 Map 9 B2
Open noon–2 & 5.30–10.30
Closed Sun, Mon & 1 week Christmas   **WC**
Cod fillet & chips £4.10   Plaice on the bone & chips £6.50

Two bright, hugely popular sister restaurants serving some of London's best fish and chips. Top-quality, splendidly fresh plaice, cod and haddock are fried to perfection in ground-nut oil and served in generous platefuls with smashing chips made from real potatoes. Splash out with Dover sole and seasonal salmon, adding well-made apple pie for afters. Minimum charge of £2.50/£2.80. *No dogs.*
LVs   *Credit* Access, Visa (Lisson Grove only)

Shampers *(Wine Bar)*

4 Kingly Street, W1
01-437 1692
Map 11 A1

Open 11–3 & 5.30–11
Closed Sat eve, all Sun & Bank Holidays

Hot dish of the day £5.50   Pavlova £1.25
Credit Access, Amex, Diners, Visa

P NCP in Kingly Street   **WC**

With 200 wines by the bottle, 20 by the glass and enjoyable, well-prepared food, it's no wonder that this wine bar is so popular. The dishes, displayed at a glass-fronted counter, include very good salads and pâtés, plus hot specials like steak and kidney casserole or richly sauced Italian baked cod. Nice sweets, too, such as chocolate cheesecake and fruit Pavlova. *No dogs.* 🥂

Sheraton Park Tower Restaurant

Knightsbridge, SW1
01-235 8050
Map 12 B1

Open 6.30am–midnight

Smoked salmon & trout mousse with caviar
£4.75   Afternoon tea £4.75
Credit Access, Amex, Diners, Visa

P NCP in building **&** **WC**

An elegant, conservatory-style restaurant where you can enjoy breakfast until noon and afternoon tea from 3–5.30. Both lunchtime and evening bring an appealing choice of light meals, from sophisticated salads to chopped steak on toasted bread with cheese or macaroni with chicken and mushrooms in a garlic cream sauce. Enjoyable sweets from the trolley. *No dogs.* ☕

Simpson's Wine Bar

Piccadilly, W1
01-734 2002
Map 11 A2

Open 8.45–5.15 (Thurs till 6.15)
Closed Sun & Bank Holidays except 1 January

Open sandwiches from £2.50   Cottage pie
£2.50
Credit Access, Amex, Diners, Visa
P meter parking   **WC**

Meltingly delicious hot croissants filled with ham and cheese are a favourite lunchtime treat at this sophisticated modern café in Simpson's store. Tasty alternatives include wholemeal vegetarian pasties and quiches, pâté and cranberry-topped pork pies. Throughout the day you can enjoy snacks like Danish pastries, chocolate fudge cake and Dutch apple tart with a cup of tea or coffee. *No dogs.* ⊟ ☕

We publish annually so make sure you use the current edition.

Skinkers (Wine Bar)

42 Tooley Street, SE1
01-407 9189
Map 10 C2

Open 11.30–2.45 & 5.30–8
Closed Sat, Sun & Bank Holidays

Poached salmon with salad £5.75   Game pie
£3
Credit Access, Amex, Diners, Visa
P NCP in Stanton Street   **&** **WC**

Lunchtime really buzzes at this atmospheric wine bar underneath the arches at London Bridge Station. City folk cross the bridge to enjoy game pie, a plate of freshly carved ham or a hot special like charcoal-grilled beef and poached halibut with mushroom and seafood sauce. Soup and sandwiches at the bar, cold food only in the evening. *No dogs.* ⊟

Slenders

41 Cathedral Place, Paternoster Square, EC4
01-236 5974
Map 11 C1

Open 7.30–6.15
Closed Sat, Sun, Bank Holidays & 3–4 days Christmas
Celery, brussels sprout & cashew nut bake £2.40   Carrot & raisin cake 65p
LVs
P NCP in Ave Maria Lane   **WC**

Local office workers cross the concrete jungle to enjoy the well-prepared vegetarian snacks provided at this popular little self-service restaurant. What's on offer includes filled baps and rolls, generous hunks of home-baked quiche, a selection of salads and hot specials like vegetable casserole. There are also excellent cakes and pastries and a good range of teas. Minimum lunchtime charge £1.50. Non-smoking area. Unlicensed. *No dogs.* 🐾

Smollensky's Balloon   `New Entry`

1 Dover Street, W1
01-491 1199
Map 11 A2

Open noon–11.45 (Sun till 10.30)
Closed eve 24 & 31 December, all 25 & 26 December & 1 January
Stuffed pasta shells £2.05   Vegetable curry £4.85
Credit Access, Amex, Diners, Visa
P NCP in Arlington Street   **WC**

A trendy operation on two floors, upstairs a bar, downstairs a roomy restaurant. The atmosphere is lively and relaxed, and the eating is nicely varied, from haddock pâté en croute and stuffed pasta shells to vegetable curry and chargrilled steaks. Chocolate mousse and peanut butter cheesecake are among the sweets. A good place to bring the kids, especially for Sunday lunch. Live piano music at mealtimes.

Soho Brasserie   `New Entry`

23 Old Compton Street, W1
01-439 3758
Map 11 B1
Open 10am–11.30pm
Closed Sun, Bank Holidays & 25 & 26 December
Fish soup with croûton, rouille & Gruyère £2.45   Herb sausages with potato purée £4.45
LVs   *Credit* Access, Amex, Diners, Visa
P NCP in Shaftesbury Avenue   **WC**

American chef David Schwartz provides a stylish menu worthy of the fashionable clientele that throngs this lively, popular brasserie. Asparagus in puff pastry with a chive butter sauce, warm chicken liver and celeriac salad and fillet of turbot in a saffron cream sauce with mussels are typical of his light, imaginative touch. Tempting sweets include strawberries with strawberry fool and chocolate truffle cake. Friendly, professional service. 🐾

Solopasta

26 Liverpool Road, N1
01-359 7648
Map 10 C1

Open 12–3 & 6–10.30
Closed Sun, Mon, Bank Holidays & 4 weeks July–August

Spaghetti basilicati alle vongole £3.15   Egg tagliatelle with pesto genovese £3.30
P Parkfield Street & meters   **WC**

Booking is advisable, particularly in the evening, as this tiny, well-kept restaurant is very popular. The menu couldn't be simpler – excellent pasta made on the premises and served with tasty sauces like garlic, tomatoes and chillies or mushrooms, cream and smoked bacon. Antipasto is the only starter (also available as a main course), the garlic bread is a must and coconut syllabub is one of a handful of sweets. *No dogs.*

Spirals Wine Bar & Restaurant

515 Finchley Road, NW3
01-431 2199
Map 9 B1

Open 11–3 & 6–11-30, Sun 12–3 & 7–11
Closed 1 January & 25 & 26 December

Deep-fried Brie with cranberry sauce £2.10
Veal escalope with salad & French fries £6.25
Credit Access, Visa
P street parking **WC**

A lively, atmospheric ground-floor wine bar and comfortable upstairs restaurant linked, naturally, by a spiral staircase. Exuberant owners Arthur and Anesta Atkins offer a wide range of enjoyable dishes, from snacks like taramasalata and garlic- and cheese-stuffed mushrooms to more substantial things such as barbecued spare ribs, chicken in lemon and tarragon sauce and burgers topped with chilli, cheese and bacon. *No dogs.* ☺

Spread Eagle

1 Stockwell Street, Greenwich, SE10
01-853 2333
Map 10 D2

Open noon–2.30 (Sun till 3) & 6.30–10.45
Closed Sun eve, Sat lunch & Bank Holidays

Steamed baby clams £3   Summer pudding £2

Credit Access, Amex, Diners, Visa
P car park in Burney Street   **WC**

An attractive Edwardian-style restaurant where starters from the main menu make excellent snacks to be enjoyed in the elegant little bar. Typically imaginative choices from the daily-changing selection might include avocado with citrus fruit and orange mayonnaise, a Stilton omelette with port and the ever-popular crispy duck salad served hot. There are super sweets like brown bread ice cream with plum sauce. *No dogs.* ☺

Suruchi   **New Entry**

18 Theberton Street, N1
01-359 8033
Map 10 C1

Open noon–3 & 6–10
Closed 25 & 26 December

Bhelpoori £1.30   Thali £3.60
Credit Amex, Visa

P meter parking   **WC**

One of London's newest Indian vegetarian restaurants, this is already quite a success. The ambience is cool and relaxed, the food fresh, tasty and well prepared. Dosas, samosas, idli sambhar and delicious poori make up a fairly standard range, with Gujarati-style thalis for complete meals. There's a larger-than-normal sweet choice, including coconut samosas and finni (rice pudding flavoured with cinnamon and cardamon). Unlicensed. *No dogs.*

Sweetings

39 Queen Victoria Street, EC4
01-248 3062
Map 11 C1

Open 11.30–3
Closed Sat, Sun & Bank Holidays

Welsh rarebit £1.40   Grilled turbot with mustard sauce £7.80
LVs
P NCP in Upper Thames Street   **WC**

Sit up at the mahogany-topped counter and tuck into fresh fish of superb quality at this much-loved City restaurant. Potted shrimps, jellied eels and fried whitebait are among favourite snacks or starters, while main courses range from simple plaice and haddock to Cornish brill, salmon fishcakes and lobster. Finish with a traditional pudding (steamed syrup, bread and butter) or savoury. No children, *No dogs.* ☺

Swiss Centre, Swiss Imbiss

10 Wardour Street, W1
01-734 1291
Map 11 B2

Open 8.30am–11.30pm, Sun & Bank Holidays
11.30am–9pm
Closed 25 December

Quiche £1.70   Mixed salad 75p
LVs   *Credit* Access, Amex, Diners, Visa
P Swiss Centre NCP   **WC**

Right in the heart of the West End, this busy little restaurant (the name means self-service) offers Swiss specialities to an appreciative crowd. Try the classic Bircher muesli, ham or cheese in Swiss bread or perhaps tasty salami topped with cream cheese and gherkins. Hot snacks include soups and savoury flans, and the pâtisserie is rich and irresistibly delicious. *No dogs.* ☺

Tapster *(Wine Bar)*

3 Brewers Green, Buckingham Gate, SW1
01-222 0561
Map 12 C1

Open 11.30–3 & 5.30–8.30
Closed Sat, Sun & Bank Holidays

Salmon salad £5.45   Game pie £3
Credit Access, Amex, Diners, Visa

P meter parking   **WC**

Popular with office workers in Victoria, this pleasant basement wine bar offers an appetising choice of lunchtime fare. Roast beef, game pie, ham and tongue all make delicious salads – and the beef is particularly good in sandwiches, too. There's soup, pâté or prawns to start, apple pie and soft fruits for dessert. Look out for salmon and game in season. No children. *No dogs.* ☺

Tea Time

21 The Pavement, Clapham Common, SW4
01-622 4944
Map 9 B3

Open 9.30–7 (Sun from 10, Bank Holidays from noon)
Closed 1 week Christmas

Turkey & cranberry sandwich £1.95   Famous lemon cake £1
P street parking   **WC**

With its pretty, traditional decor and views over the common, this is a most agreeable little tea shop. Sandwiches are the thing here – on the bread of your choice, plain or toasted with fillings as varied as ham and cucumber, spicy-sauced chicken and mushrooms and peanut butter with honey and banana. Also lots of home baking (nice plain lemon cake), cream teas and anytime continental breakfast. Unlicensed. *No dogs.* 🐾

Le Tire Bouchon

6 Upper James Street, W1
01-437 5348
Map 11 A1

Open 8.30am–9.30pm
Closed Sat, Sun & Bank Holidays

Soupe de poissons £2.35   Gigot d'agneau aux flageolets £5.95
LVs   *Credit* Access, Amex, Visa
P NCP in Brewer Street   **WC**

Breakfast snacks like croissants and scrambled eggs start the day in this smart, split-level restaurant near Carnaby Street. From 11 o'clock the main menu takes over, offering a daily-changing selection of well-prepared dishes ranging from lime-marinated salmon in a flaky pastry case to rib of beef with shallots and herby rack of lamb. French cheeses and a few sweets. Service is prompt and friendly. *No dogs.* ☺

Topkapi

25 Marylebone High Street, W1
01-486 1872
Map 11 A1

Open noon-midnight
Closed 25 & 26 December

Lamb in tomato sauce £5.25   Baklava 75p
Credit Access, Amex, Diners, Visa

P NCP in Moxon Street & WC

A popular and colourful restaurant serving excellent Turkish food for 12 hours every day. Prime raw materials enhanced by fresh herbs and spices are carefully prepared to produce flavoursome dishes like stuffed aubergines, hot cheese pastries and meat-balls among starters, with succulent lamb-based kebabs and grills to follow. Finish with a sticky sweet and aromatic Turkish coffee. Book. Non-smoking area.

Trattoria Imperia

19 Charing Cross Road, WC2
01-930 3044
Map 11 B2

Open noon–2.45 & 6–11.25
Closed Sat lunch, all Sun & Bank Holidays

Lasagne £2.50   Veal siciliana £4.80
LVs *Credit* Access, Amex, Diners, Visa

P NCP in St Martin's Lane WC

A cheerful, bustling trattoria whose menu offers a wide choice of flavoursome dishes, from minestrone, grilled sardines and pâté to pizzas, ravioli, cannelloni and plain or sauced meat and fish main courses. Interesting daily specials might include mussels in a garlicky tomato sauce and baked aubergines with cheese. Simple sweets like zabaglione and cheesecake. Simpatico service. *No dogs.*

Tui   `New Entry`

19 Exhibition Road, SW7
01-584 8359
Map 12 B1

Open noon–2.30 & 6.30–11, Sun 12.30–3 & 6.30–11
Closed Sun, Bank Holiday weekends & 2 days Christmas
Pud se-iew £3.95   Pud woonsen £3.75
Credit Access, Amex, Diners, Visa
P street parking WC

Friendly service adds to the pleasure of a meal in this exceedingly stylish Thai restaurant near the South Kensington museums. Just-a-biters are welcome to order a single dish from the main menu, and at lunchtime there's a special 'noodles & Thai pasta' menu offering tasty one-dish meals like egg noodles with chicken in clear broth or angel's hair pasta topped with Thai-styled beef sauce. *No dogs.* ♥

Tuxedo Junction

190 Broadhurst Gardens, NW6
01-625 5616
Map 9 B1
Open noon–3 & 6–midnight, Sun 12.30–3 & 7–10.30
Closed 1 January lunch & all 25 & 26 December
Barbecued ribs £1.95   Chicken Maryland £5.65
LVs   *Credit* Access, Amex, Diners, Visa
P street parking WC

Great for families, this lively American restaurant offers a huge range of meticulously prepared favourites served up in generous platefuls. There's everything from deep-fried potato skins, guacamole and nachos among appetisers to mainline burgers, steaks, enchiladas and chicken Creole. Lovely crisp salads and classic sweets like pecan pie and chocolate fudge brownies. Minimum charge of £2.50 at lunchtime, £3.50 in the evening.

Egon Ronay's
Minutes
from the Motorway
M25 AROUND
LONDON GUIDE

Newly compiled for 1987, this colourful guide spotlights over 200 carefully selected eating places within easy reach of London's orbital motorway.

Everything from starred restaurants and country pubs to the best tearooms and wine bars.

Special features include detailed area maps.

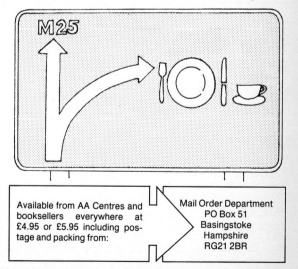

Available from AA Centres and booksellers everywhere at £4.95 or £5.95 including postage and packing from:

Mail Order Department
PO Box 51
Basingstoke
Hampshire
RG21 2BR

Twenty Trinity Gardens   `New Entry`

20 Trinity Gardens, SW9
01-733 8838
Map 10 C3

Open 12.30–2.30
Closed Sat lunch, all Sun, Bank Holidays & 1
week Christmas
Smoked mackerel terrine £2   Pasta with
chicken & prawns £5.25
Credit Visa
P street parking   &   **WC**

Lunchtime snackers can choose just a single dish from the menu at this stylish restaurant, where the cooking is sometimes excellent, sometimes no more than ordinary. The choice is very imaginative, even exotic: salad of salmon trout with lemon and dill mayonnaise, pot-roast poussin, vegetable and bean curd curry, hazelnut meringues with butterscotch sauce. The wine list is also interesting. Full evening meals. No children under eight. *No dogs.*

We welcome complaints and bona fide recommendations on the tear-out pages for readers' comments. They are followed up by our professional team. Please also complain to the management instantly.

---

209 Thai Restaurant   `New Entry`

209 Kensington High Street, W8
01-937 2260
Map 12 A1

Open noon–3 & 6–10.30

Fried rice with beef £3.30   Satay £2.70
Credit Access, Amex, Diners, Visa

P street parking   **WC**

Authentic Thai cooking at very reasonable prices attracts a good following at this dimly lit basement restaurant. The extensive menu offers traditional favourites like satay and fried noodles; various stir-fried meats, perhaps with a fragrant ginger and coriander sauce; seafood soup and steamed fish; chicken and galanga in coconut milk soup; and interesting sweets like dark, syrupy custard pudding. *No dogs.*

Upper Street Fish Shop

324 Upper Street, N1
01-359 1401
Map 10 C1

Open 11.30–2 & 5.30–10
Closed Mon lunch, all Sun, Bank Holidays &
week following & 2 weeks Christmas

Plaice & chips £3.50   Poached halibut with
salad £5
P street parking   **WC**

The atmosphere is friendly and lively at this smart little fish restaurant dominated by the equally diminutive Olga Conway. Tempting daily specials supplement the cod, plaice and halibut on the menu – perhaps native oysters for a start, then sea bream or poached fresh salmon. Traditional sweets like apple pie to finish. Sound cooking, fast and efficient service. Unlicensed. *No dogs.* 🍵

Verbanella

30 Beauchamp Place, SW3
01-584 1107
Map 12 B1

Open noon–3 & 6–11.30
Closed Sun & Bank Holidays

Veal scaloppine £5.20   Tira mi su £1.20
LVs   *Credit* Access, Amex, Diners, Visa

P meter & street parking   **WC**

Wholesome, generously portioned Italian dishes, served in style by flamboyant waiters, have made this cheerful trattoria a firm favourite over the years. The spectacular antipasto misto – perhaps aubergines, squid, mussels, tomato and more – is not to be missed; follow it, if you can, with an appetisingly sauced classic like pollo sorpresa, veal scaloppine or bistecca alla Barolo. Good choice of pasta, too, plus enjoyable vegetables and sweets. *No dogs.*

Verbanella Pasta Bar   *New Entry*

15 Blandford Street, W1
01-935 8896
Map 11 A1

Open noon–10.30, Sat 12.30–3
Closed Sun

Mozzarella salad £2.35   Paglia e fieno £3.25
LVs   *Credit* Access, Amex, Diners, Visa

P street parking   **WC**

Smallish, bright and cheerful premises, decorated with the colours of the Italian flag and some framed modern artwork. Pasta is essentially the main offering, and each variety has its own choice of sauces (bolognese, carbonara and marinara among the six to accompany spaghetti). There are starters like tonno e fagioli or Parma ham, plus a number of daily specials including fish and lamb dishes. *No dogs.*

Victoria & Albert Museum, New Restaurant

Cromwell Road, SW7
01-581 2159
Map 12 B1

Open 10–5, Sun 2.30–5.30
Closed Fri, 1 January, May Day Bank Holiday & 25 & 26 December

Chicken & mushroom pie £1.45   Cherry & walnut slice 55p
P meters in nearby streets   &   **WC**

Use the Exhibition Road entrance to the V & A to get to this stylish basement restaurant. Scones, cakes and croissants accompany morning coffee, and afternoon tea includes some savoury items. In between comes a varied lunchtime menu that offers sandwiches and filled rolls, cold dishes and hot specials such as fisherman's pie or beef and Guinness casserole. There's always some sort of quiche and an attractive array of salads. *No dogs.*

Villa Estense

642 King's Road, SW6
01-731 4247
Map 9 B3

Open 12.30–2.30 & 7–11.30
Closed Sun, Bank Holidays & 4 days Christmas

Pizzas from £1.90   Pasta from £2.50
Credit Amex, Visa
P street parking   &   **WC**

Honest, careful cooking, simpatico service and smart, colourful surroundings make it a real pleasure to eat at this delightful Italian restaurant. Excellent home-made pasta comes in 15 varieties, and there's an even longer list of pizzas – try pescatora with a tasty garlicky topping of tomato, clams, prawns and squid. There are also meaty main courses, salads, standard starters and simple sweets. *No dogs.*

Village Delicatessen & Coffee Shop

61 Blythe Road, W14
01-602 1954
Map 9 A2

Open 9.30–4, Sun 10–2
Closed Bank Holidays

Lasagne al forno £2.25   Aubergine-stuffed
pancakes £2.25
LVs
P street parking   **WC**

Regulars flock for lunch at this charming little basement restaurant beneath a delicatessen, where wholesome home-cooked dishes are generously served. Tasty soups and smoked mackerel pâté, quiches, salads and baked potatoes are all favourite snacks, while hot daily specials might include pasta or a meaty stew. Delicious sweets. Croissants with morning coffee, cakes for afternoon tea. Full English breakfasts at £2 are served Saturday and Sunday. *No dogs.*

Waldorf Hotel, Palm Court Lounge

Aldwych, WC2
01-836 2400
Map 11 B1

Open 10.30–6.30

Set afternoon tea £7.50   Ham & Gruyère
sandwich £3.50
Credit Access, Amex, Diners, Visa

P Drury Lane NCP   & **WC**

The original New York Waldorf salad and its London counterpart lead the elegant savoury snacks now served in the delightful Palm Court Lounge from 10.30 to 3.30. Other treats include goujons of brill, tempting sandwiches (salmon with cucumber and mayonnaise), plus a choice of cakes and pastries. Afternoon tea itself (from 3.30) is an impeccably orchestrated affair involving dainty sandwiches, toasted muffins and scones with jam and cream. *No dogs.*

Westbury Hotel Lounge

New Bond Street, W1
01-629 7755
Map 11 A2

Open 10am–11pm

Quiche with salad £4.75   Set afternoon tea
£5.95
Credit Access, Amex, Diners, Visa

P NCP in Burlington Street   & **WC**

Long known for its afternoon teas, this comfortable pine-panelled lounge certainly performs the ceremony in style, with silver pots and fine china elegant accompaniments to dainty sandwiches, light scones and mouthwatering home-baked pastries. Available throughout opening hours are tempting light snacks including chicken and avocado on rye, quiche and smoked salmon. Smooth service from smartly uniformed staff.

Wholemeal Vegetarian Café

1 Shrubbery Road, SW16
01-769 2423
Map 10 C3

Open noon–10.30pm
Closed 25 & 26 December

Sweet & sour vegetable casserole £2.30
Broccoli & mushroom crumble with rice £2.70

P street parking   **WC**

As popular and as good as ever, this friendly vegetarian restaurant attracts a stream of customers throughout its opening hours. Lunchtime is particularly busy, and you'll probably have to share a table as you enjoy your warming soup, courgette quiche or sustaining vegetable shepherd's pie served with splendid baked haricot beans in tomato sauce. There are also excellent salads and enticing sweets like hazelnut pudding. No smoking. *No dogs.*

Wilkins Natural Foods

61 Marsham Street, SW1
01-222 4038
Map 10 C2

Open 8–5
Closed Sat, Sun & Bank Holidays

Vegetable pie 78p Macaroni & mixed
vegetables in a provençale sauce £1.38
LVs
P NCP in Abingdon Street & meters

Tasty vegetarian fare attracts a good following at this popular little restaurant offering a daily-changing soup, salads and hot savoury. Try barley broth followed by macaroni and courgette casserole, or perhaps mixed vegetables and rice with a white wine and onion sauce. Excellent wholemeal baps and imaginative salads make appetising accompaniments, while sweets include a nice fresh fruit salad and date slice. Unlicensed. No smoking. *No dogs.*

Windmill Wholefood Restaurant

486 Fulham Road,
01-385 1570
Map 9 A2

Open 11–10.45 (Sun from 7pm)
Closed Bank Holidays & 1 week Christmas

Mixed vegetables in cashew nut sauce with
brown rice £2.60 Spinach & feta cheese pie
with salad £2.60
P street parking **WC**

A wide range of well-prepared vegetarian dishes draws the crowds to this busy little restaurant with a nicely laid-back atmosphere. Carrot and orange soup makes a warming starter, with perhaps a Tahitian vegetable curry or mushroom and black-eyed bean Stroganoff to follow. There are colourful salads, and tempting sweets like sherry and sultana cheesecake or a vegan fruit cake. Unlicensed. No smoking. *No dogs.*

Wine Gallery

232 Brompton Road, SW3
01-584 3493
Map 12 B1

Open noon–3 & 7–midnight
Closed Sun & Bank Holidays
Smoked chicken, avocado & melon salad
£3.50 Fish cakes with prawns, lobster sauce
& chips £3.50
Credit Access, Visa
P meter parking **WC**

Contemporary artwork lines the walls of this cosy little wine bar with comfortable banquette seating. Choose just a snack – perhaps prawns with garlic mayonnaise, a club sandwich or baked potato with sour cream and smoked salmon – or make a full meal with gazpacho or potted shrimps followed by, say, mozzarella and turkey croquettes served with ratatouille. Enjoyable sweets include hot toffee cake and cream. ☺

Wine Gallery

49 Hollywood Road, SW10
01-325 7572
Map 12 A2

Open noon–3 & 6–midnight (Sun till 11pm)
Closed 25 & 26 December

Sausages, beans & mash £2.90 Smoked
chicken, avocado & melon salad £3.50
Credit Access, Visa
P meter parking **WC**

Much patronised by the Sloane Ranger set, who appreciate both the excellent food and the fine artwork on display (and for sale) at this delightful wine bar. Dishes such as broccoli soup, moules marinière and deep-fried mushrooms make tasty snacks or starters, while more substantial offerings include kedgeree, monkfish goujons and turkey and mozzarella croquettes with ratatouille. Lovely sweets like treacle tart and fruit crumble to finish. ☺

Wine Gallery

294 Westbourne Grove, W11
01-229 1877
Map 9 A2

Open noon–3 & 6–midnight, Sat noon–
midnight
Closed 25 & 26 December
Sausage, beans & mash £2.90   Smoked
chicken, avocado & melon salad £3.50
Credit Access, Visa
P meters in street   **WC**

All appetites are catered for at this informal
wine bar, whose enterprising menu includes
everything from savoury buckwheat galettes
and sweet pancakes with a variety of fillings
to potted shrimps, cottage pie and barbecued
spare ribs. Salads are full of interest – try
smoked chicken with avocado and melon –
and simple puddings include chocolate
mousse and home-made lemon ice cream. ⊝

Woodlands Restaurant

77 Marylebone Lane, W1 01-486 3862
Map 11 A1
Open 12–3 & 6–11
Closed 25 December
Credit Access, Amex, Diners, Visa
P NCP in Moxon Street   **WC**

37 Panton Street, SW1 01-839 7258
Map 11 B2
Open 12–3 & 6–11
Closed 25 & 26 December
Credit Access, Amex, Diners, Visa
P NCP   **WC**

402a High Road, Wembley 01-902 9869
Map 9 A1
Open 12–3 & 6–11
Closed 25 December
Credit Access, Amex, Diners, Visa
P street parking   **WC**

Three neat modern restaurants serving enjoyable South Indian vegetarian food. The
menu (same for all three) provides an abundant choice of dishes both mild and spicy,
and excellent flavours are enhanced by the
use of fresh herbs, especially coriander. For
those unfamiliar with this cuisine, friendly
staff are ready with advice and guidance.
Snacks/starters include idli (steamed rice
cakes), lentil doughnuts and potato-stuffed
patties. Among the main courses they offer
nine kinds of dosa – rice and lentil or cream
of wheat pancakes served plain or with
fillings like potatoes, onions and nuts; there
are also lentil pizzas, vegetable cutlets and
various rice dishes and vegetable curries.
Good breads, and all the usual milky-sweet
Indian desserts. Fixed meals offer a good
cross-section. There's a minimum charge of
£4. *No dogs.* ⊝

Onion rava masala dosa £3.95   Mango kulfi
£1.95

Yumi   `New Entry`

110 George Street, W1
01-935 8320
Map 9 B2

Open 12–2.30 & 6–10.45
Closed Sat lunch, all Sun, Bank Holidays, 1
week August & 1 week Christmas

Tokujyo nigiri-zushi £10   Kappa-maki £5.50
Credit Access, Amex, Diners, Visa
P NCP in Portman Hotel   **WC**

Run with charm and civility by Yumi Fujii and
her staff, this Japanese restaurant is a
delightful place to visit. Downstairs are private rooms and the little restaurant, upstairs
a lively sushi bar with over 30 different types
of sushi. The first-class sushi comprises
eight kinds of fish, including mackerel, sea
bass and the much-prized salmon roe, served
with vinegared rice, plus a nori roll and an
egg roll. *No dogs.*

Zen W3

83 Hampstead High Street, NW3
01-794 7863
Map 9 B1

Open noon–11.30
Closed 25–27 December

Barbecued seafood £5.50   Crispy duck £5

Credit Access, Amex, Diners, Visa
P street parking & **WC**

Modishly elegant in dove grey and white, this brasserie-style Chinese restaurant offers an equally up-to-date selection of dishes. Fresh mussels in black bean sauce and radiccio-wrapped minced quail are typical of the inventive starters, which could be followed by, say, deep-fried crispy beef, giant prawns steamed with fennel seeds or a salad of green noodles and bean curd. Flavoursome passion fruit sorbet to finish. Shorter menu 3–6pm. *No dogs.*

We neither seek nor accept hospitality, and we pay for all food and drinks in full.

Egon Ronay's
guide to
THE LAKE DISTRICT and YORKSHIRE DALES

This unique guide is a passport to over 200 carefully selected hotels, restaurants, wine bars, inns and tearooms providing exceptionally high standards of cooking and accommodation.

To help memories live on until the beautiful dales and fells can be visited again, Egon Ronay's Guide to the Lake District and Yorkshire Dales also offers some recipes from the top chefs of the area.

Available from AA Centres and booksellers everywhere at £5.95 or £6.95 including postage and packing from:

Mail Order Department
PO Box 51
Basingstoke
Hampshire
RG21 2BR

ENGLAND

Abbots Bromley   *Marsh Farm Tea Room*

Uttoxeter Road
Burton-on-Trent (0283) 840323
Map 4 C4 *Staffordshire*

Open 3–6
Closed Fri & November–Easter

Ham salad £1.80   Sherry trifle 60p

P own car park   **WC**

Marsh Farm itself provides much of the produce used by Mrs Hollins at this wonderfully friendly tea room. Her baking is a treat – light scones with lovely home-made jam, flavoursome sponges, buttered fruit loaf and apple tart – and she also does super sandwiches and salads based on succulent ham, chicken and beef. Bookings only Monday–Thursday. Unlicensed.

Abbotsbury   *Flower Bowl*

3a Market Street
Abbotsbury (0305) 871336
Map 8 D4 *Dorset*

Open 10–12.30 & 2.30–5.30
Closed Sat morning & mid October–week before Easter

Cream tea without cake £1.39   Dorset apple cake 36p
P village car park or street parking   **WC**

Mrs Millar-Smith offers a small but appealing selection of home-baked goodies at this delightfully unpretentious tea room. Light, oven-warm scones with thick clotted cream are a favourite, and equally delicious are treats like the moist and fruity barm brack – thinly sliced and buttered – and excellent cakes such as iced coffee sponge and cherry slice. Unlicensed.

Alfriston   *Drusillas Thatched Barn*

Drusillas Corner
Alfriston (0323) 870234
Map 6 C4 *East Sussex*

Open 10.30–5
Closed November–March

Sussex pie with salad £3.55   Ploughman's platter £2.25
Credit Access, Amex, Visa
P own car park   **WC**

Part of a leisure centre which also includes a zoo, vineyard and bakery, this attractive thatched barn is a popular place for morning coffee and cream teas (do stipulate that that's what you want so as to avoid an entrance fee to the zoo). At lunchtime, enjoy local specialities like Sussex broth, beef and mushroom cobbler and tipsy trifle. Children's menu.

Alfriston   *Singing Kettle*

6 Waterloo Square
Alfriston (0323) 870723
Map 6 C4 *East Sussex*

Open 10–5.30 (till 5 November–Easter)
Closed Mon (except Bank Holidays) & mid December–mid February

Buck rarebit £1.20   Cream tea £1.60

P car park in village centre

Set in a 500-year-old flint cottage, this charming little place with its lace-clothed tables, fresh flowers and pretty china is everybody's perfect tea shop. Betty Carey's excellent home baking is a delight, too – try her oven-warm scones, light sponges and toasted tea cakes, which go well with a good strong brew. At lunchtime there's soup, toasted snacks, pâté and ploughman's to choose from. Attentive service from husband Geoffrey. Unlicensed.

Alnwick   *Hansel Coffee Shop*

5 Bondgate Within
Alnwick (0665) 603235
Map 2 D4 *Northumberland*

Open 10–4.30
Closed Sun & Wed except July & August &
Bank Holidays

Sandwiches from 75p   Chocolate cake 85p
Credit Access, Visa
P street parking   **WC**

Pass through the gift shop to this pleasant little tea room serving simple snacks throughout the day. Home-baked goodies include scones, ginger cake, shortbread and fresh lemon slice, while on the savoury side there are tasty wholemeal sandwiches with fillings like dressed crab or cheese and celery pâté. Home-made soup and rolls are a winter treat. No smoking. *No dogs.*

Alnwick   *Maxine's Kitchen*

1 Dorothy Forster Court, Narrowgate
Alnwick (0665) 604465
Map 2 D4 *Northumberland*

Open 10–5, Fri & Sat 10–2 & 7–11
Closed Sun, Mon, 2 days New Year, 2 days
Christmas & October

Vegetable lasagne £2.70   Raspberry & kiwi
syllabub 90p
P street parking   ♿ **WC**

Maxine and Joe Hepple are your welcoming hosts at this delightful early 18th-century town house. They do a nice line in tasty snacks throughout the day, the choice ranging from sandwiches, salads, omelettes and things on toast to delicious scones, cakes and biscuits. Consult the blackboard for the daily lunchtime special – perhaps a casserole or pasta dish; similar items are available Friday and Saturday evenings. *No dogs.*

Alston   *Brownside Coach House*

Alston (0498) 81263
Map 3 B1 *Cumbria*

Open 10–6
Closed Tues & October–Easter

Smoked trout pâté with salad £2.80
Afternoon tea £1.95

P own car park   ♿ **WC**

A neat little tea room in a converted coach house two miles outside Alston on the A686 to Penrith. Using good local ingredients – and her trusty Aga – Margery Graham offers lovely savoury snacks like bacon and egg pie, brisket of beef and smoked fish quiche salads, plus specials such as pork chops in barbecue sauce on weekends and in high season. Finish with delectable strawberry or peach gâteau. Unlicensed. *No dogs.* ●

Alstonefield   *Old Post Office Tea Room*

Near Ashbourne, Derbyshire
Alstonefield (033 527) 201
Map 4 C4 *Staffordshire*

Open 10–12.30 & 2–5.30, Sun 10–5.30
Closed Wed & mid November–March

Sandwich tea £1.75   Set afternoon tea £1.65
LVs

P street parking   ♿ **WC**

Mrs Allen offers four different sorts of set tea at her charming old tea shop situated right in the heart of the Peak District National Park. Nicely garnished ham and cheese sandwiches or two boiled eggs with bread and butter go down especially well with hungry walkers, and there are lovely light sponges, too, as well as deliciously crumbly scones to have with apple and strawberry jam. Unlicensed. *No dogs.* ●

Altrincham   **New Entry**   *Gander's*

2 Goose Green
061-941 3954
Map 3 B3 *Greater Manchester*
Open noon–3, also 7–10.30 Mon–Wed, 6–
10.30 Thurs, 6–11 Fri & Sat
Closed Sun & some Bank Holidays
Fondue bourguignonne £5.25   Savoury
pancakes £2.75
LVs   *Credit* Access, Amex, Visa
P street parking & Denmark Street car park
WC

Tucked away off a main thoroughfare, this is a comfortable wine bar-cum-bistro. The menu is nicely varied, with starters like hearty vegetable soup, spare ribs or tuna and kidney bean salad preceding savoury pancakes, cidery chicken or sirloin steak. Fondue bourguignonne is an evening speciality. Club sandwiches come in four versions, and there's a good fruit pie to finish. Non-smoking section. *No dogs.* ☕

Altrincham   *Nutcracker Vegetarian Restaurant*

43 Oxford Road
061-928 4399
Map 3 B3 *Greater Manchester*

Open 10–4.45 (Wed till 2)
Closed Sun & Bank Holidays

Hot dish of the day £2.05   Asparagus &
tomato quiche £1.20

P street parking   **WC**

Prettily decorated and furnished with pine, this roomy vegetarian restaurant has long been a local favourite. Help yourself from the counter display to scones, slices (apricot, date, muesli), tiffin and flapjacks at tea or coffee time. From 12–2 there are quiches, salads and hot daily specials like homity pie and cottage cheese and mixed nut bake. Simple sweets like fresh fruit salad. Non-smoking area. Unlicensed. *No dogs.*

Ambleside   *Harvest*

Compston Road
Ambleside (0966) 33151
Map 3 B2 *Cumbria*

Open 10.30–2.30 & 5–8.30
Closed Thurs January–June, also Mon–Wed
January–Easter & all November–27 December

Mexicali bean casserole £3.45   Turkish honey
cake £1.25
P street parking   **WC**

The food is well prepared, wholesome and full of flavour at this attractive vegetarian restaurant near the town centre. Natural fruit juice, marinated mushrooms or an excellent houmus could start your meal, with salads, quiche, vegetable pie or mexicali bean casserole as a main dish. There's always a hot crumble among the sweets, and all the cakes are made with 100% organic wholewheat flour. A children's menu is available. Unlicensed. No smoking.

Ambleside   ★   *Rothay Manor*

Rothay Bridge
Ambleside (053 94) 33605
Map 3 B2 *Cumbria*

Open 12.30–2 & 3–5.30
Closed 4 January–13 February

Soup of the day 85p   Set afternoon tea £3.50
Credit Access, Amex, Diners, Visa

P own car park ⟱ **WC**

The lounges with their antiques, paintings and fresh flowers are pleasant places for a truly delicious snack, and the garden is an equally delightful alternative when the weather permits. Lunchtime brings soup, cold cuts, salads and cheese, and a selection of nice sweets, while teatime delights range from scones with marvellous home-made jam to bara brith, spiced apple cake and old-fashioned treacle tart. *No dogs.* ☕ 🍵

Ambleside ★ *Sheila's Cottage*

The Slack
Ambleside (053 94) 33079
Map 3 B2 *Cumbria*

Open 10.15–5.30
Closed Sun, Bank Holidays & January

Vaudois savoury £3.95   Cumbrian air-dried
ham with pears £5

P King Street municipal car park & **WC**

The Greaveses' marvellous cottage tea shop
is renowned far and wide for its simply
splendid food. Kipper pâté flavoured with dill
and tomato, sugar-baked ham and potted
shrimps are typically tempting savouries,
while sweet treats include rich buttered tea
bread, banana toffee flan and raspberry and
hazelnut roulade. Several interesting Swiss
specialities, too: air-dried meats, raclette,
carrot cake. Lunchtime minimum of £2.50.
No dogs.

Ambleside *Zeffirellis*

Compston Road
Ambleside (053 94) 33845
Map 3 B2 *Cumbria*

Open Garden Room Café: 10–5.30; Pizzeria
12–3 & 5–9.45
Closed Tues & Wed November–March except
Christmas–1 Jan
Pizza funghi £2.50   Lasagne with salad £3.85
Credit Access, Visa
P street parking behind   **WC**

A stylish modern complex that includes a
cinema. In the pizzeria, wheatmeal pizzas
come in three sizes (plus a little one for
children) with a variety of tasty vegetarian
toppings. There's also a fresh pasta dish of
the day, plus omelettes, ratatouille, cold
plates and some good sweets. The Garden
Room Café is open all day for excellent coffee
and delicious home-made cakes and breads.
No smoking. *No dogs.*

Amersham *New Entry* *Fripp's*

29 The Broadway
Map 6 B3 *Buckinghamshire*

Open 9.30–5.30, Sun 1.30–6
Closed 25 & 26 December

Lasagne with salad £2.35   Cream tea £1.15

P street parking   **WC**

Dried flowers, beams and pretty green fabrics
give a cottage air to this neat restaurant
located above a shop on the main road
through Amersham. Snacks available all day
include freshly made sandwiches with fillings
like ham, cheese and tuna, plus ploughman's,
salads and nice pastries. Quiche, lasagne
and jacket potatoes make an appearance at
lunchtime, while the afternoons bring traditional teas with scones and cakes. Unlicensed. *No dogs.*

Amersham *Willow Tree*

1 Market Square
Amersham (024 03) 7242
Map 6 B3 *Buckinghamshire*

Open Sun–Tues 10–5.30, Wed–Sat 10–5 &
7.30–9.30
Closed 1 January & 25 & 26 December
Prawn & spinach roulade £3.10   Chinese-
style chicken £3.50
Credit Access, Amex, Diners, Visa
P town car park & street parking & **WC**

Original beams lend real character to this
delightful restaurant on the market square.
Superb home-baked goodies are available
all day, while lunchtime brings such delicious
dishes as smoked trout mousse, chicken in
mushroom and mustard sauce and traditional
roasts on Sundays. Leave room for a delectable dessert like strawberry meringue. In the
evening more elaborate dishes like pork
medallions with apricots and spinach-
wrapped trout fillets.

Ashbourne   *Ashbourne Gingerbread Shop*

26 St John Street
Ashbourne (0335) 43227
Map 4 C4 *Derbyshire*

Open 8.30–4.30 (Thurs & Fri till 5), Sat 8–5
Closed Sun (except Bank Holiday weekends),
1 January & 25 & 26 December

Cauliflower cheese £1.45   Kiwi fruit
cheesecake 85p
P Shaw Croft car park   **WC**

A delightful old beamed coffee shop run by
the same family of traditional bakers for the
last 100 years. Gingerbread men, plain or
coated in dark chocolate, head a parade of
goodies, which also include éclairs, Danish
pastries and a nicely flavoured kiwi fruit
cheesecake. In addition there's a straightforward savoury selection of things like open
sandwiches, jacket potatoes, salads and a
hot dish of the day. Unlicensed. *No dogs.*

Ashbourne   *Spencers of Ashbourne*

41 Market Place
Ashbourne (0335) 43164
Map 4 C4 *Derbyshire*

Open 9–5.45
Closed Sun, 1 January & 25 & 26 December

Roast pork with apple sauce & stuffing £3.50
Fresh cream & fruit gâteau 75p
Credit Access, Visa
P Market Place car park   &   **WC**

They seem to enjoy life at this bright, well-
run coffee shop, where a smile comes free
with every splendid snack. A slap-up breakfast is served early on, and on either side of
lunch you can get excellent fresh-cut sandwiches, toasted teacakes and some super
cakes like kirsch-flavoured pineapple gâteau.
Lunchtime brings a daily roast and, towards
the weekend, some nice fresh fish. High teas
also. *No dogs.* 🍵

Ashburton   *Ashburton Coffee House*

27 West Street
Ashburton (0364) 52539
Map 8 C4 *Devon*

Open 10–6 (Sun from 12.30)
Closed Mon–Sat October–Easter

Beef lasagne £1.80   Pork chops in mushroom
sauce with potatoes £1.80

P car park off West Street   **WC**

Locals and visitors alike drop in for anything
from a quick snack to a full meal at Brenda
Hale's appealing coffee shop. As well as
ploughman's, salads and omelettes there are
hearty casseroles and pasta dishes from a
daily-changing list, with apricot cheesecake,
strawberry sponge and a positively sinful
devil's food cake among sweet temptations.
Afternoon teas are also served. 🍵 🍵

Ashford   **New Entry**   *Il Cardinale Pasta Parlour*

30 Bank Street
Ashford (0233) 32566
Map 6 D3 *Kent*

Open 11am–11pm
Closed Sun & 2–3 days Christmas

Pasta carbonara £3.25   Gazpacho 95p

LVs   *Credit* Access, Amex, Diners, Visa
P Tufton Centre car park   **WC**

All the pasta is made on the premises at this
newly opened restaurant, an informal setting
with bare floorboards, glass-topped tables
and an open-to-view kitchen. Choose spaghetti, tagliatelle, tortiglioni, fettuccine or
conchiglie with one of nine tasty sauces, or
go for ravioli, lasagne or a daily special like
prawns and mushrooms in a garlic cream
sauce. Simple appetisers, ices, good Italian
cheeses. *No dogs.* 🍵

Ashford-in-the-Water   *Cottage Tea Room*

Fennel Street
Bakewell (062 981) 2488
Map 4 C4 *Derbyshire*

Open 10.30–noon & 2.30–5.30
Closed Tues, 1 January, Good Fri, 25
December & 1 week October

Afternoon tea £2   Toasted teacake with
cheese filling 75p
P Fennel Street car park & **WC**

After a stroll through the picturesque village,
visit this charming tea room for an excellent
brew and some light refreshment. Buttered
currant bread, cheesy herby scones, spicy
farmhouse cake and lovely bread feature in
the choice of set teas, while morning coffee
comes with rich, moist chocolate cake, oat
biscuits or even American pancakes.
Lunches by arrangement. Minimum charge
of £1.50 2.30–5.30. Unlicensed. No smoking.
No dogs. 🍵

Ashstead   **New Entry**   *Bart's*

34 The Street
Ashstead (037 22) 75491
Map 6 B3 *Surrey*

Open 10–2, also 6–10 Thurs–Sat
Closed Sun, Mon, Good Fri & 25 & 26
December

Spiced chick peas with rice £2   Plum crumble
95p
P Peace Memorial Hall car park   **WC**

All the dishes are vegetarian at this coolly
smart restaurant at one end of the main
shopping street. Tomato and lentil soup,
cheese and hazelnut pâté, buckwheat roast,
lasagne with a rich tomato sauce containing
walnuts, sunflower seeds, aubergines and
spinach – these are typical of the tasty,
carefully prepared savouries, and popular
puddings include crumbles and home-made
ice cream. Unlicensed. *No dogs.* 🍵

Atherstone   *Cloisters Wine Bar & Bistro*

66 Long Street
Atherstone (082 77) 67293
Map 5 A1 *Warwickshire*

Open 10–2 & 7–11
Closed 25 December

Lamb & courgette bake with salad £4.65
Mexican chicken £4.95
Credit Access, Visa
P town-centre car parks   **WC**

You'll find a varied selection of enjoyably
prepared food at this informal town-centre
wine bar and bistro. Choose home-made
soup – perhaps French onion or mushroom
– frogs' legs or garlic mushrooms as a starter
or snack, moving on to an appetising main
course like pork in ginger, baked trout or
lamb en croûte if you're hungry. Homely puds
like steamed syrup sponge make a pleasant
finale. *No dogs.* 🅟

Atherstone   **New Entry**   *Muffins Salad Bar*

5 Market Street
Atherstone (082 77) 5638
Map 5 A1 *Warwickshire*

Open 9–5 (Thurs till 2)
Closed Sun, 1 January & 25 & 26 December

Cauliflower & sweetcorn au gratin £1.90
Toasted ham sandwich 80p

P market square   **WC**

Hot and cold snacks are available throughout
opening hours at this friendly, unassuming
place. Toasted sandwiches are popular savoury bites, while fruit-filled pancakes find
favour with the sweeter tooth. There's soup
and pâté, salads, vegetarian dishes and main
courses such as chicken curry, lamb and
potato bake or chilli con carne. There's
always a selection of cakes and pastries and,
in the afternoon, a set cream tea. *No dogs.*

Avebury   *Stones Restaurant*

High Street
Avebury (067 23) 514
Map 6 A3 *Wiltshire*

Open 10–6
Closed end October–mid March

Sweet & sour cashew crumble £2.30   Set
afternoon tea £2.50

P village car park & WC

Dr Hilary Howard's short, wholesome menu
provides plenty of interest at this spacious,
self-service restaurant. Popular midday
choices include mason's lunch (home-baked
bread, farmhouse cheese, chutney salad and
an apple), wholemeal quiches, soups and hot
daily specials like stir-fried vegetables with
cashew nuts. Nice cakes and biscuits such
as tangy lemon sponge and carob fudge cake
go well with fresh fruit juice, tea or coffee.
Non-smoking area. 🍵

Axminster   **New Entry**   *New Commercial Inn*

Trinity Square
Axminster (0297) 33225
Map 8 C3 *Devon*

Open 7.30–4.45 & 6–11, Sun noon–2 & 7–10.30

Chilli con carne with salad £2.85   Baked trout
& vegetables £3.15

Credit Visa
P adjacent & WC

An early morning haven for motorists winding
their way along the A35. Slap-up breakfasts
at £2.85 begin at 7.30 and stay on the menu
all day. Sandwiches are freshly cut to order,
and there's a good range of main meals,
including omelettes and pizzas, spaghetti
bolognese, burgers and grilled gammon.
Salads are based on ham, cheese, prawns
and beef, and they do a set tea with home-
baked scones, strawberry jam and clotted
cream. *No dogs.* 🍵 🍵

Aylesbury   **New Entry**   *Wild Oats*

38 Buckingham Street
Aylesbury (0296) 433055
Map 5 B2 *Buckinghamshire*

Open 9–3
Closed Sat, Sun, Bank Holidays & 1 week
Christmas
Cauliflower in tomato & lentil sauce £1.35
Pork & prawn casserole £1.50
LVs
P Buckingham Street car park &

Primarily a take-away, but you can also enjoy
a snack on the premises. Wholesome eating
is the order of the day, the choice comprising
sandwiches (granary, sesame, wholemeal or
white bread) with interesting fillings like Brie
and pear or lentil pâté, salads, quiches and
hot specials such as liver and bacon or chilli
con carne. Yoghurt and fruit for sweet.
Unlicensed. *No dogs.*

Aysgarth Falls   *Mill-Race Teashop*

Near Leyburn
Aysgarth (096 93) 446
Map 4 C2 *North Yorkshire*

Open 10.30–6.30
Closed Mon–Thurs January & February, also
25 December

Toasted waffles 65p   Cream tea £2.25
P National Park Information Centre car park
& WC

Joyce and Mike Smith run a delightful tea
shop at this converted 18th-century mill,
where everything on the menu is available all
day. Mike does the baking, and his crumbly
scones and featherlight sponges, Danish
pastries and rich fruit cake are delicious with
a strong cuppa. Sandwiches, salads and
filled jacket potatoes are also available, plus
pies and casseroles in winter. Unlicensed.
No dogs. 🍵 🍵

Bakewell

Aitch's Wine Bar & Bistro

4 Buxton Road
Bakewell (062 981) 3895
Map 4 C4 *Derbyshire*

Open 11.30–2.30 & 7–11 (Sun till 10.30)
Closed Sun (October–May), 1 January & 25 December

Fresh swordfish with broccoli £5.95   Tandoori lamb masala £4.50
P town-centre car parks   ₺   **WC**

Good food, carefully chosen wines and a happy atmosphere bring the crowds to this lively, relaxed wine bar. Quiches, attractive salads and good wholemeal bread are pluses, and local fish features strongly: look for daily specials like Mediterranean vegetable soup, grilled swordfish with broccoli, Mexican chicken, garlicky rack of lamb. Chocolate fudge is an indulgent pud, fruit salad for weight-watchers. Children welcome lunchtime and early evening. *No dogs.* ⊖

Bakewell   *New Entry*   ### Green Apple

Diamond Court, Water Street
Bakewell (062 981) 4404
Map 4 C4 *Derbyshire*

Open 12–2, also 7–10 Wed–Sat
Closed Sun, Tues & 25 & 26 December

Chicken & asparagus pie £3.25   Middle Eastern carrot purée £1.95
Credit Access, Diners, Visa
P Granby Road car park   ₺   **WC**

Down a quiet side street off the main square, this pleasant restaurant has a courtyard laid out for summer eating. Owner-chef Roger Green's menu is varied and imaginative, with many dishes of appeal to vegetarians and the health-conscious: spinach and mushroom wholewheat lasagne, nut-studded aubergine pâté, lamb and leek pie, pork and chick pea casserole, an excellent plum brûlée. Whatever your preference, you'll find cooking is careful and flavours are natural.

Bakewell   *New Entry*   ### Marguerite & Stephanie

1 Rutland Square
Bakewell (062 981) 4164
Map 4 C4 *Derbyshire*

Open 9–4.45, Sun 2–5
Closed Sun October–April & 3 days Christmas

Quiche with mixed salad £2.40   Steak & kidney pie with jacket potato £2.70
Credit Access, Visa
P market place car park   **WC**

Snackers can sit at glass-topped tables and look out at life on the square from this well-run rustic-chic coffee shop. The bill of fare is straightforward: good home-baked cakes and biscuits, sandwiches, salads, quiche and lunchtime specials such as cream of mushroom soup, wholewheat lasagne and savoury mince with celery and apple. Children's portions available. Sunday afternoon teas in summer. No smoking. *No dogs.* 🐾

Bamburgh   ★   ### Copper Kettle

21 Front Street
Bamburgh (066 84) 315
Map 2 D4 *Northumberland*

Open 10.30–5.30
Closed early November–early March

Rainbow trout with prawns & almonds £4.10
Local crab salad £5.50

P The Grove   **WC**

Superb home cooking by young owners Richard and Linda Salkeld makes this traditional tea shop a delight to visit. Their magic touch transforms the humblest scone or ham sandwich, and other lovely home-baked treats include rich chocolate tiffin and crumbly almond shortbread slice. Equally wonderful are more substantial dishes such as salads with local crab or freshly smoked trout, as well as Richard's splendid steak and kidney pie. No smoking. *No dogs.*

Banham

Banham Bakehouse

Old Bakery
Quidenham (095 387) 277
Map 5 D2 *Norfolk*

Open 10–4.30 (till 2.30 October–Easter)
Closed Mon (except Bank Hols), Tues, some
Sats, 25 & 26 December, last 2 weeks Sept &
all Jan
Set afternoon tea £1   Crispy seafood
pancakes £5.70
P village green & **WC**

What was once the village bakehouse is now
a stylish restaurant with white walls, polished
pine floorboards and an abundance of greenery. Home baking is still a major attraction,
and at lunchtime Lesley de Boos also prepares enjoyable savoury snacks (soups,
pâté, ploughman's platters) and main
courses like chicken normande or pork
casserole. Nice sweets, too. There's a pretty
garden for summer snacking. *No dogs.* 🐾

Barden

Howgill Lodge

Near Skipton
Burnsall (075 672) 655
Map 4 C2 *North Yorkshire*

Open 10–6.30
Closed Mon (except Bank Holidays), also
Tues–Fri in winter & 1 week Christmas

Ham, egg & chips £4.20   Sherry trifle £1

P own car park

Just off the B6160 between Grassington and
Bolton Abbey, this simple café high up in the
Yorkshire Dales National park offers a warm
welcome and satisfying home-cooked fare.
Lunch and high tea bring hearty platefuls of
ham and eggs, steak or scampi and chips,
while for afternoon tea there are lovely light
scones and rich, moist chocolate gâteau.
Sandwiches and fruit pies are also available.
No dogs. 🐾

Barden ★

Low House Farm

Near Bolton Abbey
Burnsall (075 672) 276
Map 4 C2 *North Yorkshire*

Open 3.30–6.30
Closed Tues, Fri, 25 & 26 Dec, weekdays
March, Nov & Dec & all Jan & Feb

Set tea with cheese, walnut & pineapple salad
£4   Set tea with ham & eggs £4.90
P in farmyard & **WC**

Sensational set teas are served at this
delightful working farm, which lies down a
steep track leading off the B6160. Super
scones, Yorkshire custard pie and a moun-
tain of marvellous cakes and biscuits come
with the main course – perhaps boiled eggs,
ham and eggs, cold meats or a cheese,
walnut and pineapple salad. Minimum charge
£2. Unlicensed. *No dogs.* 🐾

Barnard Castle

Market Place Teashop

29 Market Place
Teesdale (0833) 37049
Map 4 C2 *Co. Durham*

Open 10–5.30 (Sun from 3)
Closed 24 December –2 January

Welsh rarebit £1.10   Steak pie with
vegetables £2.20

P in Market Place **WC**

Sit at a nice old antique table at this
characterful, stone-walled tea shop and enjoy a light snack from the day-long menu.
Toasted teacakes, scones and fresh cream
gâteaux go well with a good brew. Savoury
choices include soup, sandwiches and
salads, which are joined at lunchtime by a
tasty daily special such as home-made
chicken pie and a tasty bake of spinach,
cheese and brown rice. Elaborate ice cream
concoctions to finish. 🐾

Barnard Castle | *New Entry* | *Priors Restaurant*

7 The Bank
Teesdale (0833) 38141
Map 4 C2 *Co. Durham*

Open 10–5 (till 7 June–August)
Closed Sun January–April, 1 January & 25 December
Aubergine lasagne & salads £2.10   Apricot Bakewell tart 75p
Credit Access, Amex, Diners, Visa
P street parking in town centre   **WC**

The Prior family run this attractive restaurant located behind an arts and crafts shop. The food is vegetarian, and some of the vegetables used are organically grown; two soups are offered daily, and other imaginative savouries include stuffed vine leaves, ratatouille roulade and a decent carrot and hazelnut quiche to enjoy with crisp, fresh salads. For sweet, perhaps home-made ices or delicious ginger cake. *No dogs.* ☕

Baslow | *Cavendish Hotel*

Baslow (024 688) 2311
Map 4 C4 *Derbyshire*

Open 12.30–2.00

Wild mushroom soup with herbs £1.50   Iced crème de menthe terrine £3.25
Credit Amex, Diners, Visa

P own car park   **WC**

Saloon luncheons are served with style in this handsome hotel set in the Chatsworth estate. The menu is full of interest, though the results on the plate are somewhat variable. Typical items include cheese and leek tart with hollandaise sauce, baked fillet of monkfish with ratatouille, sirloin steak and a delightful iced crème de menthe terrine with a super chocolate sauce. Children's portions at two-thirds price. *No dogs.* ☕

Bath | *Bath Puppet Theatre*

Riverside Walk, Pulteney Bridge
Town plan *Avon*

Open 10–5.30
Closed 25 & 26 December

Cheese & spinach quiche with salad £1.50
Ploughman's lunch £1.75

P Grove Street   **WC**

A delightfully friendly, very modest little coffee shop that's part of a puppet theatre beneath Pulteney Bridge. Owner Andrew Hume is not only a talented puppeteer but a dab hand, too, at providing wholesome snacks like satisfying soups, toasted sandwiches, quiche, pizzas and garlic bread stuffed with houmous, tomatoes, or cottage cheese. On the sweet side, there are various slices, sponges and flapjacks. Unlicensed. No smoking.

Bath | *New Entry* | *Beaujolais Restaurant*

5 Chapel Row
Bath (0225) 23417
Town plan *Avon*

Open noon–2 & 7–11 (Fri & Sat 7.30–11.30)
Closed Sunday & 4 days Christmas

Coq au vin £4   Bitter chocolate bavarois £1.85
Credit Access, Visa

P Charlotte Street car park   **WC**

A popular restaurant-cum-wine bar with posters and artwork on the walls and a huge collection of corks in the window. French menus offer a small but appealing lunchtime choice (delicious fish soup, skate with caper butter, coq au vin), and a larger variety in the evening, when main courses are priced at around £7 (but no minimum charge). Sweets include a lovely chocolate bavarois.

Bath   *Canary*

3 Queen Street
Bath (0225) 24846
Town plan *Avon*

Open Mon–Fri 10–5.30, Sat 9.30–6, Sun 11–6
Closed 25 & 26 December

Seafood crêpe £2.30   Chicken & coriander pie
£2.50
LVs
P Charlotte Street car park   **WC**

People invariably have to queue for a table at this elegant Georgian tea shop, such is the demand for the day-long selection of scones, Bath buns, and home-made cakes on offer. Lunchtime savouries draw the crowds, too, with choices ranging from croque-monsieur, seafood salad and open sandwiches to daily specials like ratatouille pie, casseroles and crêpes. Tempting sweets and special clotted cream tea. *No dogs.* ⊖ 🍷

Bath   **New Entry**   *Jollys, Circles Restaurant*

13 Milsom Street
Bath (0225) 62811
Town plan *Avon*

Open 9–5
Closed Sun, 1 day Easter & 1 day Christmas

Minced beef & Guinness pie £2.99   Fresh fruit
Pavlova £1.25
Credit Access, Amex, Diners, Visa
P street or Charlotte Street car park   ♿   **WC**

On the first floor of Jollys department store, this smart, self-service restaurant is a good place for a snack. Biscuits, scones and doughnuts, treacle tart and delicious apple-and-raisin-layered shortcake are early morning fare, soon boosted by baps, cold meats, quiches and salads. Lunchtime hot specials could include turkey steaks, Lancashire hot pot and a vegetarian dish like courgette and tomato bake. Cooked breakfast Saturday morning only.

Bath   *Moon & Sixpence*

6a Broad Street
Bath (0225) 60962
Town plan *Avon*

Open noon–2.30 & 5.30–10.30 (Sat till 11), Sun
noon–2 & 7–10.30
Closed 25 & 26 December
Sauté of salmon & scallops £8.50   Terrine of
nougatine £1.60
Credit Access, Amex, Visa
P Broad Street car park   **WC**

An attractive wine bar-cum-restaurant with a delightful fountained courtyard. Lunchtime sees a fine self-service buffet with pâtés, quiches, meats, fish and salads. Upstairs there's a waitress-service lunch, and a similar but more elaborate evening menu of delights such as saffron-sauced chicken quenelles or fillets of beef, veal and pork with Madeira sauce. Also tempting sweets like apricot roulade and lemon tart. *No dogs.* ⊖

Bath   **New Entry**   *Number Five*

5 Argyle Street
Bath (0225) 69282
Town plan *Avon*

Open 11–10 (Sat till 10.30), Sun 11.30–2.30
Closed Sun June–October & 25 & 26
December
Steak & kidney pudding £5.40   Apples in
Calvados £2
Credit Access, Amex, Visa
P Walcot Street car park   **WC**

The doors open at this stylish restaurant with tea, coffee, cakes and croissants. At noon the lunch menu takes over with dishes like walnut and garlic soup, seafood pancakes and chunky chicken pie with a creamy spring onion and parsley sauce; home-made ice cream and hot lemon pudding among the sweets. The choice is the same in the evening, with afternoon tea intervening. Brunch on Sunday. *No dogs.* 🍷

BATH

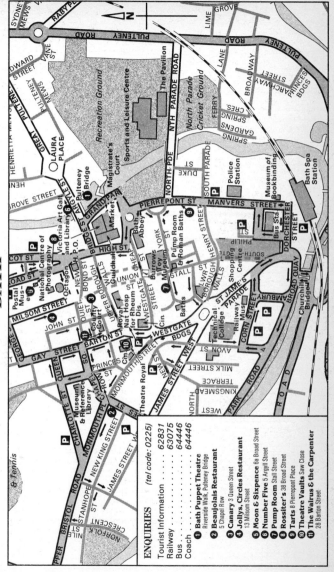

Bath   *Pump Room*

Stall Street
Bath (0225) 66728
Town plan *Avon*

Open 10–5.30
Closed 25 & 26 December

Chicken, bacon & parsley pie £3.95   Bath bun
tea £1.50

P Southgate multi-storey car park & **WC**

The Pump Room Trio provide a musical accompaniment in elegant surroundings, and morning coffee comes with traditional Bath buns, Sally Lunns and Light Wiggs. Afternoon tea brings an extended range of baking, while lunchtime offers a good cold buffet, soup and hot specials such as beef in Guinness and vegetarian shepherd's pie. Sweets might include apricot brandy flan. Minimum lunchtime charge of £4.50. *No dogs.* 🅿 🏮

Bath   *Rossiter's*

38 Broad Street
Bath (0225) 62227
Town plan *Avon*

Open 10–5
Closed Sun & Bank Holidays

Ratatouille terrine £2.95   Seafood pancakes
£3.20
Credit Access, Visa
P Walcot Street multi-storey car park **WC**

On the second floor of Anne Rossiter's household goods store, this stylish little restaurant is a haven for wilting shoppers. Throughout the day croissants, light scones, gâteaux and fruit flans (note the superb apple frangipani) can be enjoyed with a wonderfully reviving cuppa. Then at lunchtime, there's a choice of light bites – soups, filled baps, savoury tarts – or more substantial dishes like old-fashioned fish pie. Non-smoking section. *No dogs.* 🏮

Bath   *Tarts*

8 Pierrepont Place
Bath (0225) 330201
Town plan *Avon*
Open noon–2.30 & 7–10.30
Closed Sun, 1 January & 25 & 26 December
Smoked chicken & avocado pancake £2.30
Pecan-covered chicken breast with mustard
sauce £6.15
Credit Access, Visa
P NCP in Manvers Street & street parking after
6 **WC**

Near the abbey, this cheerfully informal little basement restaurant offers a regularly changing menu of imaginative and capably prepared dishes. Try deep-fried Camembert with an apple and cider relish or mushroom and watercress pâté as your starter, followed by, say, pork escalope cooked in a Madeira and tomato sauce, vegetable moussaka or the day's fresh fish speciality. Enjoyable home-made sweets like lemon cream tart to finish. *No dogs.* 🅿

Bath   *Theatre Vaults*

Sawclose
Bath (0225) 65074
Town plan *Avon*
Open noon–2.30, 6–7.30 & 9–11
Closed Sun, also Mon eve when no
performance & 25 December
Fillet of beef Stroganoff £6.95   Banoffee pie
£1.50
Credit Access, Diners, Visa
P Kingsmead Square or Sawclose car park
WC

The stone vaults of the Theatre Royal make an atmospheric staging for a snack or a full meal. The lunchtime and pre-show menu offers soup, pâté and light meals such as cheesy courgettes or curried lamb samosas, plus main courses like grilled mackerel, creamy-sauced pork or kidneys with chipolatas. Sweets include traditional puddings and lovely light hazelnut meringues. Shorter dinner menu from 9 to 11. *No dogs.* 🅿

Bath   *The Walrus & the Carpenter*

28 Barton Street
Bath (0225) 314864
Town plan *Avon*

Open 6pm–11pm
Closed 25 December

Beefburger with cheese & bacon £3.70
Chestnut casserole £3.75
LVs
P Charlotte Street car park   **WC**

Good cooking and reasonable prices make
this informal, candlelit restaurant a popular
evening rendezvous, so it's best to book.
Beefburgers, kebabs and steaks make up
the choice for meat-eaters, and there's now
a vegetarian menu with things like chestnut
casserole or nut loaf with a mushroom and
red wine sauce. Simple starters like soup or
houmus. Ice creams and home-made gâteaux for afters. *No dogs.*

Beer   *Old Lace Shop*

Fore Street
Seaton (0297) 22056
Map 8 C3 *Devon*

Open 11–5
Closed Mon (except Bank Holidays when
closed Tues) & Mon–Wed in winter

Cottage pie £2.75   Chocolate fudge cake 75p

P town-centre car park   **WC**

Devon cream teas featuring warm scones,
strawberry jam and clotted cream are a
popular line at this friendly little tea shop set
in the cottage where Queen Victoria's bridal
veil was made. There's also a small choice
of home-made cakes, plus made-to-order
sandwiches (wholemeal or white bread),
snacks on toast, ploughman's and salad
platters. Lunchtime brings soups and daily
specials. Children's portions. Non-smoking
area.

Belbroughton   *Coffee Pot*

High Street, Near Stourbridge
Belbroughton (0562) 730929
Map 7 D1 *Hereford & Worcester*

Open 10–5, Sun 12.30–5.30
Closed Mon, Bank Holidays (except Good Fri),
Tues & Wed following Bank Hol Mons & 24–31
December
Chicken with tarragon & orange £1.70
Prawn, asparagus & smoked salmon pie £1.80
P street parking

Splendid home cooking makes this tiny restaurant four miles from junction 4 of the M25
well worth a detour. Appetising lunchtime
choices include nut and wine pâté, marvellous
salads, seafood lasagne and bean and vegetable hot pot – with some super sweets to
follow. Delicious baked goodies include marmalade shortbread, scones, coffee and walnut cake and cherry slice. Minimum charge
50p weekend afternoons. Unlicensed. No
smoking. *No dogs.*

Berkhamsted   ★   *Cook's Delight*

360 High Street
Berkhamsted (044 27) 3584
Map 6 B3 *Hertfordshire*
Open Thurs & Fri 10am–9pm, Sat 10–3, Sun
noon–5
Closed Mon–Wed, Bank Holidays (except
Good Fri), 1 week August & 24–30 December
Vegetarian curry from £3.50   Pumpkin pie
£1.50
LVs   *Credit* Access, Visa
P street parking   **WC**

Tucked behind a healthfood shop, this unassuming little tea room offers superb vegetarian and macrobiotic fare. Choose from
delicious buckwheat quiches with tasty fillings like cod and celery or spicy turkey, bean
casseroles, crunchy salads and wonderfully
wholesome sweets – perhaps rhubarb and
ginger pie or mango and tofu cheesecake.
More elaborate Saturday evening dinner
menu (bookings only). Unlicensed. No smoking. *No dogs.*

Berwick upon Tweed

Kings Arms Hotel, Hideaway

Hide Hill
Berwick upon Tweed (0289) 307454
Map 2 D3 *Northumberland*

Open noon–2.30 & 6–10
Closed eves 1 January & 25 December

Seafood salad £1.50 Farmhouse mixed grill £7.25
Credit Access, Amex, Diners, Visa
P street parking **WC**

Red-brick walls topped with little curtains hanging from brass rails give this smart restaurant its intimate air. You can choose just a starter from the mealtime menu if merely peckish – perhaps mushroom soup, taramasalata and toast, seafood salad – or go for a main course such as chicken, steak or locally caught fish. Simple sweets include spicy apple pie. *No dogs.* ⊖

Berwick upon Tweed

Town House

Marygate
Berwick upon Tweed (0289) 307517
Map 2 D3 *Northumberland*

Open 8.30–5 (till 4.30 in winter), Thurs 8.30–1.30
Closed Sun & Bank Holidays

Omelettes £1 Baked potato with filling 80p

P Parade car park ♿

Expect to fare better than the former occupants of this lively coffee shop in the former dungeons of the Town Hall! Business is fast and furious, so arrive early for a lunchtime table and be warned that the nearest public lavatory is a long way off. Savouries range from home-made soup and sandwiches to omelettes, quiches and baked potatoes, with scones, biscuits and cakes to go with a good strong cup of tea. Unlicensed. *No dogs.* 🍵

Berwick upon Tweed

Wine Bar

1 Sidey Court, off Marygate
Berwick upon Tweed (0289) 302621
Map 2 D3 *Northumberland*

Open 10–3 & 6.30–10.30
Closed Mon eve, all Sun, 1 January & 25 & 26 December

Smoked trout £1.80 Ploughman's lunch £1.65
P Castlegate car park **WC**

Fresh produce is the basis for the tasty, wholesome snacks served in this attractive little wine bar. Filled rolls, Scotch eggs, ploughman's and smoked trout are favourite cold choices, while daily-changing hot dishes could include lasagne, chicken suprême or steak chasseur. There's always a vegetarian special, plus nice sweets like peach pancakes and banoffee pie. Half-portions available for children, mini-portions for babies. *No dogs.* ⊖

Bexhill

Trawlers

60 Sackville Road
Bexhill (0424) 210227
Map 6 C4 *East Sussex*

Open 11.30–1.45 & 5–8.45 (Mon till 7.45)
Closed Sun & 25 & 26 December

Cod & chips £1.90 Plaice & chips £2.20
LVs

P De la Warr Pavilion car park ♿ **WC**

A minute's walk from the seafront, the fish is as fresh as could possibly be at this immaculately kept fish and chip shop. Cod, plaice, huss and skate are all beautifully cooked in exemplary light, crispy batter and served with textbook-perfect golden chips fried to order in small batches. Fishcakes, sausages and savoury pies add variety, and there's locally made apple pie for afters. Minimum charge £1. Children's menu. Unlicensed.

Biddenden

Claris's Tea Shop

3 High Street
Biddenden (0580) 291025
Map 6 C3 *Kent*

Open 10.30–5.30
Closed Mon (except Bank Holidays) & 5 days
Christmas

Creamed mushrooms on toast £1.30   Lemon
Madeira cake 65p
P village car park adjacent &

This charming little tea shop with a patio for
sunny days is just the place to treat yourself
to some delicious homebaking. Sit at pretty
white-clothed tables and tuck into scones,
toasted teacakes, walnut bread and a splendid cream-covered cake flavoured with Coin-
treau. Sandwiches, things on toast (try the
creamed mushrooms), salads and ploughman's are also available all day. Unlicensed.
No smoking. *No dogs.*

Billericay

Webber's Wine Bar

2 Western Road
Billericay (027 74) 56581
Map 6 C3 *Essex*
Open 11–2.30 & 6–10.30 (Mon from 7, Fri & Sat
till 11)
Closed Sun, Bank Holiday lunches, 2 weeks
July–August & 10 days Christmas
Soup of the day £1.95   Shredded smoked
chicken with French beans £4.25
LVs   *Credit* Access, Amex, Diners, Visa
P High Street car park   **WC**

Splendid preparation and presentation distinguish the excellent food at this lively wine
bar. Sit up at the bar or wait for a table and
tuck into cold meats, pâtés and salads from
the display counter, or opt for a blackboard
special such as haunch of venison. Chilli,
quiches and jacket potatoes are regular
stalwarts, and irresistible desserts like banoffee pie and chocolate slice. Minimum
charge of £5 Friday and Saturday evenings.
No dogs. ⏣

Billingshurst   ★

Burdock Provender

59 High Street
Billingshurst (040 381) 2750
Map 6 B4 *West Sussex*

Open 9–5
Closed Mon (except Bank Holidays), Sun mid
September–March, 1 January & 25 & 26
December
Seafood pancakes £2.98   Chicken &
asparagus pie £3.25
P car park opposite   **WC**

Star-quality snacks, friendly service, pretty
table settings – this delightful beamed tea
room in a tile-hung building has the lot. The
baking covers an impressive span, from
chocolate and passion cakes and individual
treacle tarts to little quiches, pizzas and
sausage rolls. Breakfast is served early on,
and noon heralds the arrival of blackboard
specials like chicken and asparagus pie,
gammon salad or macaroni cheese. 🐾

Birmingham   **New Entry**

Bobby Browns in Town

Burlington Passage, New Street
021-643 4464
Town plan *West Midlands*

Open noon–2.15 & 6–11
Closed Sunday lunch & 25 & 26 December

Beefsteak, mushroom & Guinness pie £3.45
Vegetarian special £3.75
Credit Access, Amex, Diners, Visa
P NCP in Stephenson Place   **WC**

Right in the city centre, this attractive basement restaurant pulls in the crowds with its
enjoyably robust cooking. The menu offers a
wide variety of dishes, some simple, others
more elaborate and all at realistic prices.
Spinach soufflé and devilled herring roes are
typical starters, and carefully sauced mains
include pork with apricots, scampi in champagne sauce and mignons of beef with cream
and cucumber. Good sweets. *No dogs.* ⏣

Birmingham · *New Entry* · *Boots Time for a Break*

16 New Street
021-643 7582
Town plan *West Midlands*

Open 9–5 (Thurs till 7, Fri & Sat till 5.30)
Closed Sun, Easter Mon & 25 & 26 December

Jacket potatoes £1.10   Vegetable lasagne
£1.70
LVs   *Credit* Access, Visa
P NCP in Navigation Street   & WC

An attractively laid out coffee shop on the first floor of Boots store. The self-service counter offers an appealing range of snacks, from scones, cakes and pastries to wholemeal quiches (provençale, Stilton and apple, prawn with asparagus) served with an interesting selection of salads. Also tasty sandwiches and a daily-changing lunchtime special like vegetable lasagne, chicken curry or stuffed peppers. Unlicensed. *No dogs.* 🐾

Birmingham · *New Entry* · *Drucker's*

100 Great Western Arcade
021-236 6292
Town plan *West Midlands*

Open 9.30–5.30
Closed Sun & Bank Holidays

Ham, tomato & asparagus sandwich 75p
Strawberry tart 98p
LVs
P NCP in Masshouse

Upstairs at this modest, friendly pâtisserie you can enjoy an excellent cup of tea with your pick of a splendid array of cakes and pastries. The choice is really impressive, from cherry slice, ganache and a nice gooey coffee éclair to rum baba, hazelnut gâteau and apple strudel. There's also an interesting selection of brown-bread sandwiches such as beef and dill cucumber or egg mayonnaise. Unlicensed. *No dogs.* 🐾

Birmingham · *La Galleria Wine Bar*

Paradise Place
021-236 1006
Town plan *West Midlands*

Open noon–2.30 & 5.30–10.30 (Fri & Sat till 11)
Closed Sun & Bank Holidays
Beef Stroganoff with rice £3.95   Lasagne
£2.80
LVs   *Credit* Access, Amex, Diners, Visa
P Cambridge Street multi-storey car park   &
WC

Fresh fish features among the tempting daily specials at this well-liked wine bar, where the cooking shows an Italian slant. Grilled sardines, red mullet and calamari typify the wide choice, and there's also plenty to please meat-eaters. Pasta, pizzas, salads and coarse liver pâté are popular, too, and there are some very nice traditional English puds. No children. *No dogs.*

Birmingham · *New Entry* · *Gingers*

7a High Street, Kings Heath
021-444 0906
Town plan *West Midlands*

Open 6.30pm–9pm
Closed Sun & Bank Holidays except Good Fri

Vegetable pâté 95p   Basque ratatouille £4.80

P street parking & MFI car park   & WC

In a suburb about two miles from the city centre, this attractive little vegetarian restaurant offers a small selection of tasty, well-constructed dishes. Soup, houmous and vegetable pâté are the starters, with Basque ratatouille, Spanish cashew paella and mushroom layer bake among main courses served with fresh, healthy salads. The sweet menu beckons with things like strudel or honey cake. Unlicensed. *No dogs.*

BIRMINGHAM

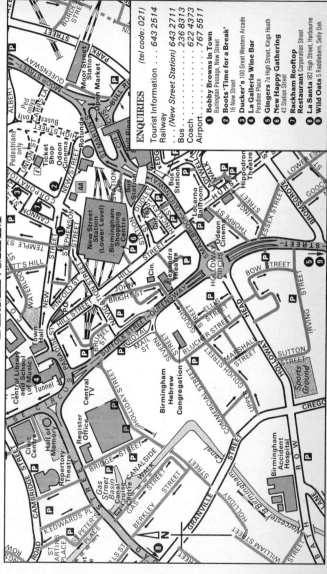

ENQUIRIES   (tel code: 021)

Tourist Information 643 2514
Railway
. . . (New Street Station) 643 2711
Bus 236 8313
Coach. 622 4373
Airport. 767 5511

1 **Bobby Browns in Town**
Burlington Passage, New Street
2 **Boots 'Time for a Break'**
16 New Street
3 **Ducker's** 100 Great Western Arcade
4 **La Galleria Wine Bar**
Paradise Place
5 **Gingers** 7a High Street, Kings Heath
6 **New Happy Gathering**
43 Station Street
7 **Rackham Rooftop**
Restaurant Corporation Street
8 **La Santa** 182 High Street, Harborne
9 **Wild Oats** 5 Raddlebarn Road, Selly Oak

Birmingham | *New Happy Gathering*

43 Station Street
021-643 5247
Town plan *West Midlands*

Open noon–11.45
Closed 3 days Christmas

Beef ball dumpling £1.40   Whole fresh
pineapple with chicken £5
Credit Access, Amex, Diners, Visa
P car park in Smallbrook (Queensway)

A spacious first-floor Chinese restaurant in the heart of the city. Snackers gather happily to enjoy the splendid selection of dim sum, which includes king prawn dumplings, steamed spare ribs with black bean sauce, bean curd rolls and Hong Kong-style deep-fried wun tun. There's also a varied and interesting full menu to tempt you. Friendly service. *No dogs.*

Birmingham | **New Entry** | *Rackhams Rooftop Restaurant*

Corporation Street
021-236 3333
Town plan *West Midlands*

Open Mon–Fri 9-5.30 (Sat till 6)
Closed Sun & 25 & 26 December

Roast beef £4.90   Quiche & salad £2.65
Credit Access, Amex, Diners, Visa

P NCP at New Street Station   &   **WC**

Atop one of the city's busiest department stores, this roomy, self-service restaurant provides a good range of snacks and more substantial dishes. Quiche comes in several varieties to enjoy with a salad, and there are pies and cold cuts. The day's hot roast is a popular choice, and other main courses could include curry or sweet and sour pork served with perfectly cooked rice. Hot and cold sweets. *No dogs.*

Birmingham | **New Entry** | *La Santé*

182 High Street, Harborne
021-426 4133
Town plan *West Midlands*

Open 7pm–10pm
Closed Sun, Mon & Bank Holidays

Fondue savoyarde £3.20   Crepnette farçie à
la niçoise £2.20
Credit Access, Visa
P street parking   **WC**

The decor is quietly elegant at this French vegetarian restaurant on the high street of a Birmingham suburb. The menu, which changes fortnightly, is quite interesting, with starters like spicy lentil soup and garlicky breadcrumbed mushrooms preceding leek pie, raclette or courgettes stuffed with a tasty nut and cheese mixture. Pear and ginger crumble and mango mousse are typical sweets. Some dishes are a touch bland. Unlicensed. *No dogs.*

Birmingham | **New Entry** | *Wild Oats*

5 Raddlebarn Road, Selly Oak
021-471 2459
Town plan *West Midlands*

Open noon–2 & 6–9
Closed Sun, Mon, Bank Holidays & 1 week
Christmas

Mexican bean pot with salad or potato £2.95
Cashew nut roast with salad or potato £2.95
P street parking

First-class ingredients are expertly prepared and full of flavour at this simply appointed vegetarian restaurant. Delicious soups such as green pea, watercress or carrot and coriander make favourite starters, followed, perhaps, by tasty butterbean bake or spinach and cheese flan served with salads. Pleasant sweets like brown bread ice cream or apricot pie round things off nicely. Unlicensed. No smoking. *No dogs.*

Bishop's Castle   *No 7*

7 High Street
Bishop's Castle (0588) 638 152
Map 7 D1 *Shropshire*

Open 10–4 (Wed till 2), Fri 9.30–3.30
Closed Sun & Mon

Leek & mushroom hot pot £1.60   Chocolate
sponge 50p

P street parking & **WC**

An unpretentious little pine-furnished restaurant on the picturesque main street. Kay Townsend has a keen interest in healthy eating, demonstrated by her use of wholemeal flour. The day kicks off with scones and home-made jam, and teacakes and chocolate sponge are other toothsome treats. Soup, cauliflower cheese, meat pie and chick peas with smoked sausage show the lunchtime span. Sweets too, like baked bananas with yoghurt. Full evening menu. *No dogs.*

Bishops's Lydeard   *Rose Cottage*

Near Taunton
Bishop's Lydeard (0823) 432394
Map 8 C3 *Somerset*

Open 12–2 & 7–10
Closed Sun, Mon, Good Fri lunch, first 2
weeks November & 2 weeks Christmas

Fish & prawn mornay with vegetables £4.95
Lamb vol-au-vent with salad £3.45
P own car park **WC**

Find this pink-painted restaurant to the south of the village on the A358. You can make a light meal from one of the starters – perhaps flavour-packed vegetable soup or mushrooms provençale – or add an appetising main course such as local poached trout or stuffed aubergines if you're hungry. Nice puddings, too, like gooseberry fool. More substantial dishes like rack of lamb in the evening. Smoking in bar only. *No dogs.*

Bishop's Waltham   *Casey's*

Corner of Bank & Brook Streets
Bishop's Waltham (048 93) 6352
Map 6 B4 *Hampshire*

Open 10–5
Closed some Bank Holidays

Pâté & toast £1.50   Homity pie & salad £2.25
Credit Access, Visa

P car park opposite & **WC**

Once a granary, now an agreeable restaurant serving wholesome, home-cooked food. A splendid array of cakes, scones and biscuits accompanies morning coffee and afternoon tea, while at lunchtime the simple but appetising selection ranges from soup and home-baked bread, jacket potatoes, quiches and salads to daily specials like cannelloni or courgette gratin. There are tempting sweets, too. More elaborate evening meals Tues–Sat. *No dogs.*

Blanchland   *White Monk Tea Room*

Near Consett
Blanchland (043 475) 276
Map 4 C1 *Northumberland*

Open 2–5
Closed October–Easter, also Mon–Fri Easter–
Spring Bank Holiday

Set afternoon tea £1.55   Tea with scones 90p

P street parking **WC**

Just a short stroll from the bridge that spans the river Derwent, this is a super little spot to pause for a hearty afternoon tea. The full version comprises freshly cut sandwiches, a fruity scone, brown bread with lovely home-made jam, cake and a good pot of tea. Those with less robust appetites can settle for tea and one of the other items. Unlicensed.

Bleasdale   *Bleasdale Post Office Tea Room*

Higher Brock Mill, Near Preston
Chipping (099 56) 349
Map 3 B3 *Lancashire*

Open 9–6 till 5.30 in winter, Sun 9–12.30
Closed 25 & 26 December & 2 weekends
autumn

Set afternoon tea £1.50   Steak pie with chips
& vegetables £2
P car park opposite &

Carole Cox's hearty home cooking draws the customers to this remote little post office and tea room. Juicy gammon steak served with fried eggs, super chips and peas, steak pie and plaice or haddock will satisfy the ravenous, while lighter alternatives include sandwiches, salads and things on toast. She does a nice line in cakes, scones and slices, too, plus simple sweets like fruit pie and meringues. Unlicensed. 🍵

Blewbury   *Lantern Cottage*

South Street
Blewbury (0235) 850378
Map 6 A3 *Oxfordshire*

Open 3–6
Closed Mon–Fri January & February &
Christmas

Afternoon tea £1.10

P street parking   **WC**

Miss Glover provides a delicious set afternoon tea at her quaint little timber-framed cottage that's much admired by visitors to the village. Sit at one of the five tables beneath a beamed ceiling and tuck into hot buttered scones and home-made jam, plus a selection of cakes like coffee and chocolate sponges and dainty iced fairy cakes. Unlicensed. *No dogs.*

Bolton Abbey   ★ *Bolton Abbey Tea Cottage*

Near Skipton
Bolton Abbey (075 671) 495
Map 4 C2 *North Yorkshire*

Open 9.30–6
Closed November–March (except weekends
in fine weather)

Steak & kidney pie £2.95   Afternoon tea £2.45

P car park opposite & **WC**

Part of the Abbey estate, this cosy, welcoming tea room offers splendid breakfasts worth travelling miles for. Later in the day, equally delicious sandwiches, flans and marvellous salads (with fresh salmon in season) make an appearance, as well as popular steak and kidney pie and big fry-ups. Afternoon teas bring an irresistible array of goodies, from plump scones to moist, featherlight sponges. *No dogs.* 🍵

Boot   *Brook House Restaurant*

Holmrook, Eskdale
Eskdale (094 03) 288
Map 3 B2 *Cumbria*

Open 8.30am–8.30pm
Closed November–Easter

Cumberland sausage £2.45   Houmus £1.80

P own parking

A large, creeper-clad house in beautiful Eskdale is the setting for some splendid home cooking and baking. Breakfast goes on until mid-morning, after which there's a really extensive choice, from sandwiches, pâtés and omelettes to oven-baked trout, Cumberland sausage and steak and mushroom pie for the hungriest walker. Set teas offer anything from scones to a fry-up, and puds include meringues, fruit pies and delicious-looking cakes. 🍵 🍵

Borrowdale   ★   *Lodore Swiss Hotel Lounge*

Borrowdale (0596) 84285
Map 3 B2 *Cumbria*

Open 10–7
Closed early November–mid March

Spinach & mushroom salad with garlic
croûtons £2   Set afternoon tea £3.90

Credit Amex
P own car park   &   **WC**

Lovely panoramic views accompany your
impeccably served sweet or savoury snack
at this luxurious picture-windowed lounge.
Swiss dishes like restbrot (cold meat open
sandwich) or a ploughman's with three types
of Swiss cheese, grapes and salad make
elegant light lunches, but the high spot must
be the heavenly pâtisserie – including luscious Swiss apple flan, first-class chocolate
sachertorte and fresh strawberry cheesecake. *No dogs.*

Bournemouth   *Carlton Hotel Lounge*

East Overcliff
Bournemouth (0202) 22011
Map 6 A4 *Dorset*

Open 3.45–5 30

Set afternoon tea £3.45   Ham sandwich £1.75

Credit Access, Amex, Diners, Visa

P own car park   **WC**

The discreetly luxurious lounge of this fine
Edwardian hotel in a splendid cliff-top location makes the perfect setting for a most
civilised afternoon tea. Courteous staff will
serve you dainty cucumber and egg sandwiches, scones accompanied by rich Dorset
clotted cream, and lovely pastries ranging
from chocolate marzipan ring to éclairs and
Vienna whirls. *No dogs.*

Bournemouth   *Coriander*

14 Richmond Hill
Bournemouth (0202) 22202
Map 6 A4 *Dorset*

Open noon–2.30 & 6–11
Closed Sun lunch & 25 & 26 December

Guacamole £1.75   Mixed enchiladas £4.95
LVs   *Credit* Access, Visa

P NCP in Bourne Avenue   **WC**

Vegetarians are well catered for at this
popular Mexican restaurant in the town
centre, with tasty offerings like tostadas,
burritos and cheese and spinach enchilades.
Other diners will find just as much to interest
them in chicken and beef enchiladas, fiery
chilli and barbecued spare ribs, while starters
to suit all tastes include classic guacamole,
fresh coriander soup and deep-fried potato
skins. Simple sweets. *No dogs.*

Bournemouth   *Flossies & Bossies*

73 Seamoor Road, Westbourne
Bournemouth (0202) 764459
Map 6 A4 *Dorset*
Open Flossies: 8–5 (till 10 Fri, Sat & all July–
September); Bossies: noon–2, also 7–10 Fri &
Sat
Closed Sun
Vegetable lasagne £1.50   Lamb with tomato
peppers £1.80
LVs
P Alumhurst Road car park   &   **WC**

A well-run, two-in-one operation offering a
contrast in eating. Meat-eaters should de-
scend to the bistro-style Bossies to tuck into
counter-service dishes like kidneys in sherry
or beef bourguignon; vegetarians remain at
Flossies on ground level for quiches, cheese
and millet rissoles, salads and the like.
There's a selection of cakes and pastries,
and delicious sweets like fruit crumbles or
butterscotch meringue pie. *No dogs.*

171

Bournemouth

Salad Centre

22 Post Office Road
Bournemouth (0202) 21720
Map 6 A4 *Dorset*

Open 9–6 (till 8 July–September)
Closed Sun & 25 & 26 December

Cauliflower, carrot & cheese bake £1.72
Grated apple & honey pie 84p
LVs
P Carrefour multi-storey car park **WC**

The biggest choice of tasty wholefood snacks here starts at noon, and at lunchtime you should expect a small wait at the counter. Salads are fresh and varied, and hot things include soup, quiche and pizza, plus huge trays of mixed vegetable and bean bakes. There's an all-day supply of rolls, sandwiches and good baking, and a tempting range of sweets like spicy bread pudding or cashew and sultana custard to round things off. No smoking. *No dogs.* ☺

Bourton-on-the-Water

Small Talk Tea Room

High Street
Bourton-on-the-Water (0451) 21596
Map 5 A2 *Gloucestershire*

Open 9–5.30 (Fri & Sat in summer till 10)
Closed 25 December

Stilton & walnut flan £2.35   Danish pastries 60p

P street parking & council car park **WC**

Be prepared to share or wait for a table at this popular beamed tea room in a picture-postcard Cotswold village. An attractive variety of home-baked cakes and pastries is available throughout the day, and the meal-time salads, sandwiches, pizzas and pies are supplemented by dishes of the day such as sugar-baked ham or Stilton and walnut flan. Unlicensed. *No dogs.*

Bowdon

Griffin

Stamford Road, Near Altrincham
061-928 1211
Map 3 B3 *Cheshire*

Open noon–2, also 7–10 Tues–Sat
Closed Christmas night

Hot roast beef open sandwich £1.50   Meat & potato pie with granary bread & butter £1.50
Credit Access, Amex, Diners, Visa
P own car park ♿ **WC**

Enjoy a full meal or just a snack at this attractive restaurant with a garden patio at the back of the Griffin Tavern. There are freshly made salads to have with cold meats, savoury flans, pâtés and terrines, plus hot specials like mixed grills, soups and hearty casseroles. Finish with something simple but delicious like rich, moist chocolate fudge cake. Service is efficient and cooking reliable. *No dogs.* ☺

Bowness on Windermere

Hedgerow

Greenbank, Lake Road
Windermere (096 62) 5002
Map 3 B2 *Cumbria*

Open 11–9
Closed Tues & Wed October–April & 2 weeks November
Avocado pâté with salad £1.50   Lasagne with salad £3.40
Credit Access, Diners, Visa
P restricted street parking **WC**

A cheerful, pine-furnished restaurant serving wholesome and imaginative vegetarian fare. Starters include tempting pâtés – avocado with cottage cheese and Brazil nut – which could be followed by a colourful salad or daily hot special like chilli or cheese bake. Finish with a seasonal fruit crumble, dried or fresh fruit salad or perhaps raspberry Pavlova. Cakes and scones are available all day. No smoking. 🍵

Bowness on Windermere
Laurel Cottage

St Martin's Square
Windermere (096 62) 5594
Map 3 B2 *Cumbria*

Open 2.30–5.30 July–mid September, also
Bank Holidays & 1 week Easter
Closed Sat

Open prawn sandwich £2   Cream tea £1.40

P Royrigg Road car park   **WC**

A lesson in good eating goes on at teatime in this former school house, under Cathy and Paul Jewsbury's tutelage. Sandwiches on very fresh white bread, excellent egg mayonnaise, fresh baked scones, home-made cakes, coconut slices and a truly memorable sponge studded with walnuts all add up to an enjoyable spread, not to mention tempting banana loaf and teacakes. Nice cup of tea. *No dogs.* 🍵

Bowness on Windermere
Trattoria Pizzeria Ticino

53 Quarry Rigg, Lake Road
Bowness (096 62) 5786
Map 3 B2 *Cumbria*

Open 10–2 & 6–11.30; 10–3 & 6–11 in summer
Closed Thurs, 1 January & 25 & 26 December

Scaloppine alla Bellinzona £3.95   Frutti di mare alla Sophia £4.25

P Lake Road car park   &   **WC**

Pizzas and pasta dishes are favourite choices at this attractive Italian restaurant with a few outside tables. Pizzas range from basic tomato sauce, mozzarella and oregano to the della casa with a little bit of everything. Pasta lovers can try rigatoni with ratatouille or spaghetti with seafood, as well as more familiar bolognese and carbonara sauces. There's a special light lunchtime menu and a more elaborate choice at night. *No dogs.*

Bradford
Pizza Margherita

Argus Chambers, Hall Ings
Bradford (0274) 724333
Map 4 C3 *West Yorkshire*

Open 10.30am–11.00pm (Fri & Sat till 11.30)
Closed 1 January & 25 & 26 December

Pizza francescana £2.60   Lasagne £2.95
LVs   *Credit* Access, Visa

P Victoria car park & Hall Ings NCP   **WC**

The pizza of your choice will be prepared and baked before your eyes at this bright, modern place in the city centre. Mouthwatering toppings range from the eponymous margherita – just tomato, cheese and oregano – to clementina with sweetcorn, peppers, olives, courgettes, mushrooms and artichoke hearts. There are two folded versions and even one with a potato base. Also simple starters, chilli con carne, lasagne, ice creams. *No dogs.*

Bradford-on-Avon
Corner Stones

32 Silver Street
Bradford-on-Avon (022 16) 5673
Map 8 D3 *Wiltshire*

Open 9–5
Closed Sun & 25 & 26 December

Vegetarian quiche with salad £1.35
Vegetable casserole £1.40

P Market Street car park   **WC**

This spruce little tea shop makes a pleasant place to pause for an excellent cuppa and such delicious home-baked treats as moist apple cake, light scones and spicy gingerbread. Lunchtime savouries often have a vegetarian slant – look out for hearty cauliflower, mushroom and lentil casserole – or you can have cottage pie, a cheesy baked potato and some first-class open sandwiches made with lovely wholemeal bread. 🍵

173

Braintree

Braintree Curry Palace

28 Fairfield Road
Braintree (0376) 20083
Map 5 C2 *Essex*

Open 12–2 & 6–11
Closed 25 & 26 December
Mushroom biryani £3.20   Mixed tandoori
£6.50
LVs (lunchtime)   *Credit* Access, Amex,
Diners, Visa
P street & town car park   &. **WC**

A neat, pleasant Indian restaurant, where
efficient and attentive staff serve you with a
wide range of favourite dishes. Spicy tikkas
and kebabs are popular starters, while main
courses include tandoori specials cooked in
a clay oven, colourful biryanis and curries to
suit every palate – from mild korma and
Kashmir to the heat of vindaloo and Ceylon.
No dogs.

Braithwaite

Book Cottage

Near Keswick
Braithwaite (059 682) 275
Map 3 B2 *Cumbria*

Open 10–12.30 & 2–5.30
Closed Thurs & November–Easter

Ginger cake 50p   Scone with cream & jam 55p

P village parking

Mary Walsh runs this simple little tea room
that's in a converted barn, and in the same
building you'll find her brother's second-hand
book shop featuring over 6,000 volumes for
sale. Her list is rather more limited – traditional
scones and spice buns served with jam and
cream, delicious ginger cake, lovely rich date
and orange slice, oat biscuits and sandwiches, all to be enjoyed with a good cuppa.
Unlicensed. No smoking.

Bricket Wood

Oakwood Tea Room

Oakwood Road
Garston (0923) 674723
Map 6 B3 *Hertfordshire*

Open 9–5, Sat, Sun & Bank Holidays 10–6
Closed 2 weeks Christmas

Ratatouille £1.50   Shepherd's pie £1.50

P own car park   &. **WC**

A mother and daughter team are responsible
for the goodies at this bright, friendly establishment on the A405. As well as a range of
set teas, they offer an impressive display of
home baking, from creamy cheesecake to
light, crumbly scones, coffee and walnut
gâteau and seasonal fruit pies. At lunchtime
come soup and ploughman's plus a more
substantial daily hot special like moussaka,
steak and kidney pie or cauliflower cheese.
Unlicensed. *No dogs.*

Bridgemere   *Bridgemere Garden World Coffee Shop*

Near Nantwich
Bridgemere (093 65) 381
Map 3 B4 *Cheshire*

Open 9–4.30 (till 8 in summer)
Closed 25 & 26 December

Pizza £2   Staffordshire oat cake 75p

P own car park   &. **WC**

In the house plants section of a gigantic
garden centre you'll find this friendly and
usually busy self-service coffee shop. Light
snacks are its perennial stock-in-trade. Pâté,
pork pies, pizzas and pasties are favourite
savoury choices, or you can opt for the cold
buffet, and there's plenty of choice for the
sweeter tooth as well – cream-filled sponges,
a decent apple strudel and the popular
Staffordshire oat cakes. Unlicensed. No
smoking. *No dogs.*

Bridgnorth
Sophie's Tea Rooms

Bank Street
Bridgnorth (074 62) 4085
Map 7 D1 *Shropshire*

Open 10–5.30, Sun 2–6
Closed Sun & Thurs in low season & 4 days
Christmas

Chicken liver pâté with salad £2.15
Ploughman's lunch £1.80
P town-centre car parks & street parking **WC**

Coal fires make the Bennet's pretty Victorian
tea parlour a particularly cosy spot in winter,
when warming soup and a daily hot dish join
the regular menu. Other savouries range
from toasted snacks and salads to vegetarian
specials like cashew paella. The pine dresser
laden with scones, scrumptious chocolate
and coffee cakes, rum and raisin pudding
and much, much more is an inviting prospect
at any time. Unlicensed. *No dogs.*

Bridgwater
Bridge Restaurant

Binfo:d Place
Bridgwater (0278) 451277
Map 8 C3 *Somerset*

Open 9.30–5.30
Closed Sun, Bank Holidays & 1 week
Christmas

Large salad with quiche £3   Fresh fruit salad
£1
P Clare Street car park &

Situated in a row of shops near Bridgwater's
famous old iron bridge, this modest, self-
service restaurant offers an all-day selection
of cakes, pastries and generously filled
granary rolls. The choice expands at lunchtime to include soup, jacket potatoes, pizza
and a hot dish of the day such as cauliflower
cheese or Mexican pork. There's also an
excellent array of interesting fresh salads
like sweet and sour bean shoots. Unlicensed.

Bridgwater
Nutmeg

8 Clare Street
Bridgwater (0278) 457823
Map 8 C3 *Somerset*

Open 8–5.30
Closed Sun & Bank Holidays except by
arrangement

Roast lunch £2.10   Cheese cake 65p
LVs
P Mount Street car park & **WC**

Joyce Forbes' busy day starts at 8 o'clock,
when her smashing cooked breakfasts draw
the early birds to this popular café-cum-
restaurant. From 10, shoppers like to pop in
for a reviving coffee and some tempting
cakes, pastries or biscuits, while at lunchtime
there's a more substantial choice of dishes
such as hot pot and lasagne, curry and the
day's roast. Salads, sandwiches and delicious sweets complete the picture. *No dogs.*

Bridport
Moniques Wine Bar

East Street
Bridport (0308) 25877
Map 8 D3 *Dorset*

Open noon–2 & 7–9.30 (Fri & Sat till 10)
Closed Sun, 1 January & 25 & 26 December

Wholefood cottage pie £2   Fruit crumble
£1.10

P Fine Fare car park **WC**

Background music and posters of local
events add atmosphere to this well-loved
wine bar, where Monique Stephens puts her
considerable culinary skills to good use.
Lunchtime brings things like courgette soup,
quiche, pizzas and a fruit crumble, plus daily
specials such as smoked haddock; the
evening menu often includes a cheese fondue
(for two) and invariably an interesting casserole and a vegetarian dish. Children's portions
available.

Brighton   *Al Duomo*

7 Pavilion Buildings, Castle Square
Brighton (0273) 26741
Town plan *East Sussex*

Open noon–2.30 & 6.30–11.30
Closed Sun, Bank Holidays, Easter & 2 weeks
Christmas

Pizzas from £2   Spaghetti bolognese £2.30
Credit Access, Amex, Visa
P car park in Church Street   &   **WC**

Straightforward, authentic Italian cooking in
a cheerfully informal setting is the formula at
this popular restaurant close to the Royal
Pavilion. Pizzas and pasta come in umpteen
varieties and are the favourite choice; there
are also lots of salads, soup and an antipasto
counter from which you can help yourself.
More substantial meat dishes are announced
on a separate blackboard menu. To finish,
choose from a flamboyant display of home-
made sweets. Children's menu. *No dogs.*

Brighton   *Allanjohn's*

8 Church Street
Brighton (0273) 683087
Town plan *East Sussex*

Open Mon–Thurs 10–5.30, Fri 9.30–6, Sat 9–6,
Sun 10.30–3
Closed 25 & 26 December

Jacket potato filled with crab meat £1.20
Seafood platters from £2.50
P NCP in Church Street

A modest little seafood bar, mainly takeaway
but with four check-clothed tables at the back
for eaters-in. The window display shows
what's on offer: cockles, whelks, shrimps,
prawns, mussels and crab are the mainstay,
and most items are available in bowls, on
platters or as fillings for jacket potatoes or
brown bread sandwiches. Some hot food,
too, including plaice and stuffed oysters.
Unlicensed. *No dogs.*

Brighton (Hove)   *Blossoms*

81 George Street
Brighton (0273) 776776
Town plan *East Sussex*

Open 8.30–4.30, Sun 12–2.15
Closed Bank Holidays (except Good Fri)

Mixed health salad £1.20   Wholemeal lentil
roast £1.30

P Haddington Street car park   **WC**

A self-service restaurant in a busy shopping
street. The menu is mainly vegetarian, with
just the occasional meat dish among the
tasty bean cakes, lentil roasts, wholemeal
quiches and vegetable risottos. Smoked
haddock tagliatelle and seafood pie for fish
fans. Also a selection of cakes and pastries.
Sunday lunch is a three-course set menu at
£5.95. Non-smoking area. *No dogs.* 🍴

Brighton   *Cripes!*

7 Victoria Road
Brighton (0273) 27878
Town plan *East Sussex*

Open noon–2.30 & 6–11.30
Closed 25 & 26 December

Bacon, cheese & corn galette £3.75   Lemon &
honey crêpe £3

P street parking   **WC**

Pancakes are the name of the game at this
pleasant little back-street restaurant. Savoury buckwheat galettes come with a great
range of tasty fillings like cheese and ratatouille, chilli-hot minced beef or chicken
livers, spinach and sour cream. Dessert
crêpes are equally tempting – how about
lemon and honey or banana and rum with
whipped cream? Cider is the traditional drink
with pancakes, and there's a choice of
English or French. *No dogs.*

All the fun of the *FARE*

Party Places

Few words are as capable of striking terror into even the stoutest-hearted parent as: 'When can I have *my* party?' The vision of hordes of small people — for even a few can quickly seem like a crowd — taking over one's house and one's life for the best part of a day can be daunting.

How best to contain their energies? How to be certain of giving them food that they like? How to ensure they're all treated fairly and equally? And how to keep them entertained *without* an army of helpers?

But don't misunderstand: we like children — we're on their side. We welcome the growing trend for eating out en famille, especially if the children are not allowed to disrupt the entire restaurant. And we want them to enjoy themselves. This is why we are particularly pleased to find that more and more eating houses — notably the popular hamburger and pizza chains — are making it their business to cater for family outings in general — and children's parties in particular.

Hats, streamers, games and a special cake often come as part of the deal. In some venues, the establishment is happy to arrange for an entertainer — conjurer, magician, storyteller or Punch and Judy show — to be booked as well. Staff are specially assigned to supervise and play with the children as well as take the necessary orders, and in many places the party area is set apart from the main restaurant so others can eat in relative peace. (It's surprising how often the party atmosphere is contagious, how jolly the afternoon becomes.)

So, deciding that our inspectors deserved a treat, we sent them off to 'come to the aid of the party'. Masquerading as uncles, cousins and family friends, they all entered into the spirit of the thing. Back they came, tired but happy, trailing balloons and party hats, to tell us what they had found.

The establishments visited are, of course, not the only ones that cater for children's parties, but they were chosen as a representative selection. In all cases, it is vital to check with the manager or party organiser at the appropriate restaurant and give details in advance of what you require.

Joy Langridge

SMOLLENSKY'S BALLOON
1 Dover Street, London, W1. Tel: 01-491 1199

In a city where it is notoriously difficult to find anywhere for a decent Sunday lunch with young children, *Smollensky's Balloon* must be a godsend! Every Sunday starting at noon, the family is fed and entertained with fun and magic at the tables, and the parents can enjoy a peaceful half hour between 2.30 and 3pm, when the children are taken to a separate area for a puppet and/or magic show. It's a great way to give the children a lunch party! Everyone gets a balloon on arrival and a lapel badge when leaving. There's a special children's menu (pasta shells, hamburgers ... and smashing desserts), and booster seats (high-chair substitutes) are available. Birthday cakes can be ordered at 48 hours' notice — ours came with candles lit, was huge, colourfully decorated and very tasty.

The service is chaotic and slow, but it doesn't really matter as the children are enjoying themselves, and whilst the food is not of star quality, it's good and plentiful. On our visit — with six adults, four children from three to 12 and a three-month-old baby — the current magician came to our table and performed a few tricks specially for us, then gave a Punch and Judy show to squeals of delights from parents and children alike! (John Styles is a master puppeteer who goes all out for humour and audience participation.) Similar entertainment is offered on weekday afternoons, but there's an extra charge, whereas on Sundays it's all 'for free'.

Our final bill came to around £140 — not cheap, but tremendous value considering that the six adults had steaks and the food was good and plentiful. Most important, the children had a marvellous time — we didn't leave until 4.30 pm. . . .

PIZZALAND

Another inspector took seven children between seven and 11, along with a couple of adults, to *Pizzaland*. The party was welcomed by 'Pizza Pete' and led through to an area away from the main restaurant. Here we found balloons, badges, play mats with games and puzzles for each child (hats were temporarily out of stock), and there was a birthday card for Kevin, whose party it was. All the novelties proved very popular with the children (and are provided at no extra cost). Children choose from a special menu, but 'make sure your guests like pizzas', commented one mother. 'There's no alternative except for spaghetti bolognese.' This was pronounced 'too spicy for me but nice and hot' by ten-year-old Thomas.

Portions were 'aimed at the younger child', said a parent wryly, 'so a ravening horde of older children might expect more. And the garlic bread starter was largely wasted on young palates'. But the pizzas were well received and demolished in record time. Ice cream desserts disappeared equally quickly and the verdict on the exotic-sounding Pizzabocker Glory, 'chocolate sauce at the bottom, mixed fruit in the middle and ice cream on the top' was 'very *nice*'.

After dessert, two 'surprisingly good' sponge cakes were produced and shared out (again, included in the party arrangements). However, the parents commented that the 'party spirit' was left entirely to the adults to organise as, apart from the novelties, nothing else was laid on. The manageress was always on hand, giving out hologram stickers (one for every fizzy orange drink bought) and parried the children's good-humoured jibes with equal good humour. All in all, though, the children enjoyed themelves; they all said they would like to go again!

SWEENEY TODD'S

If you live in — or near — Oxford, Cambridge, Canterbury, Bath or York, you'll probably already know your local *Sweeney Todd's*. This chain of hamburger-style restaurants offers a stylish informality, a joky menu, waitresses with the shortest possible mini-skirts and a Birthday Club for the under-18s. Fill in a form to become a member and three weeks before your birthday you get a personalised letter, an invitation to book a party table, a voucher for a free pizza or hamburger of your choice (which any member of the party can have) and if you go on your actual birthday, there's a free T-shirt as well.

We joined in a party for 13-year-old Nicholas. Children — and children's parties — are more than welcome and we found our table was decorated with streamers, balloons and party hats. One of the staff (all extremely friendly and obliging) took a photograph of the occasion and this was duly presented.

Much fun is had in reading the menu, with its idiosyncratic names and descriptions of dishes. Pizzas are called The Rugged Individualist — your choice of no fewer than 20 different topping ingredients — or The Fast Lane; hamburgers are Pleasure Yodel (mozzarella and mushrooms) or Hot Flash — more peppers and chillies than you'd think possible. There's a small Kiddies Corner on the menu, but most of our party chose the Barbecued Ribs (they come with French fries and a salad). American-style desserts range from Rupture Rapture (six flavours of ice cream, cherries, peaches, nuts . . .) to Philadelphia Cream Cheesecake.

We all enjoyed the quality of the food, the generous portions, the relaxed atmosphere, the friendly staff and not having to clear up afterwards! Wines, beers and cocktails are also featured and if you're over 18, you can join the Old Fogeys Unlimited. On *your* birthday, you get a free bottle of wine. With most dishes around the £4 mark — some cost less — we voted it very good value.

A 'CARE BEAR' party at the PIZZA HUT

This was terrific fun. There were nine children in our party, all aged between three and seven. In a section to the rear of the *Pizza Hut* restaurant, handily placed for the loos (one three-year-old was unable to get out because the handle was too high and the door too heavy . . .), the kids could make plenty of noise without disturbing the other customers too much. We were lucky in having a waitress who loved children and made sure everyone got what they wanted.

Each child received playmats, crayons and a party hat and the walls were festooned with balloons. Everything related to the 'Care Bear' theme; these cuddly characters also love children and appear on both playmats and the special children's menu. While waiting for their food, the kids were supplied with drinks and were soon enjoying themselves. A self-service salad bar with about a dozen well-prepared and presented salads is centrally positioned; the children were soon tucking into these while waiting for their giant pizza. One small six-year-old was heard to remark: 'I don't like pizza. I just come to enjoy myself!' There were ice creams with syrupy toppings, and the birthday cake (it's provided free if there are more than 12 children) was crimson, with candles on it, and shaped like a bear.

The bill, including 'normal fare' for four grown-ups, came to less than £40 and represented *very* good value for money.

'Care Bear'® is a registered trademark.

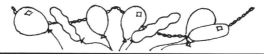

McDONALD'S

Ask any child for his or her idea of culinary heaven, and they will probably plump for *McDonald's*, so it's good to learn that this popular burger chain takes its parties seriously. At every branch — apart from those that are purely takeaways — a party can be organised for 'as many children as the special party area will hold'. This varies, of course; the Wimbledon branch in London will 'cater for up to 20'. And at every branch, there's a specially trained member of staff to run the show, play games with the children and generally see that they enjoy themselves.

McDonald's charge 50p per head for each child (accompanying adults are exempt) plus the cost of the food, and all guests choose from the standard menu: the burgers, fries and popular milkshakes seem to suit most small customers. They'll supply a birthday cake too for under £4; this isn't personalised, but comes with the autograph of the 'Ronald McDonald' clown character whose portrait adorns the wall of the brightly coloured party area. The cake was greeted with cries of glee, as were the party hats, balloons, place mats, glove puppets and crayons given to each child. The birthday girl was given special treatment — a poster, puzzle book and other small novelties. The table was set up in advance and looked extremely festive — appealing to children from 'two to ten', said the manager.

Egon Ronay's

BIRDS EYE *guide to*

HEALTHY EATING OUT

An essential guide containing detailed descriptions of over 500 eating places in Britain serving wholesome and healthy food. Whether you are in the mood for a bistro feast or a sophisticated dinner, this guide leads you there.

Introduction by leading health writer Miriam Polunin and a colour section including recipes from award-winning establishments.

A completely new source of reference for those who care about healthy eating.

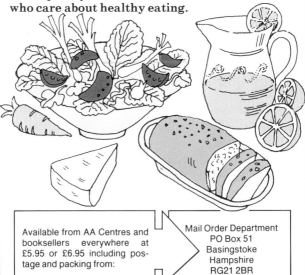

Available from AA Centres and booksellers everywhere at £5.95 or £6.95 including postage and packing from:

Mail Order Department
PO Box 51
Basingstoke
Hampshire
RG21 2BR

Guzzle Puzzle

ACROSS

3 See 8 Across
6 This man's ale was water
7 Drinks in small quantities
8,3 Pain across the Channel
11 Her diet could be men!
14 Bacon and cheese have this
15 Thirsty
16 Roman Goddess of Corn

DOWN

1 Veal producer
2 Head, or something nice with toast
4 Slice of bacon
5 Cider-makers
9 How to make a dish
10 Pasta
12 Good with 4 Down
13 Pudding sounds like start the race

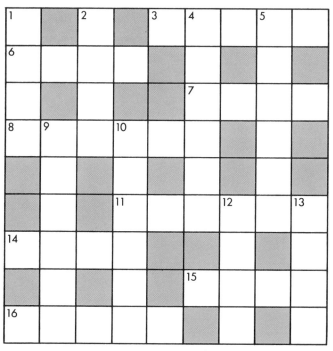

See page 384 for solution.

Junior Inspectors for a Day

We are — all too often — aware that our children are our sternest critics. They have a sturdy common sense. They are not easily fooled. They quickly develop a certain healthy scepticism which cuts straight through much subtle adult subterfuge. They know what they like and what they will not tolerate, appreciate style and distrust humbug. They are not afraid of making their feelings known. They will soon tell you (often quite loudly) when they are not satisfied, and they have a shrewd grasp of what is — to them — value for money. We decided to lay our reputations on the line and invited six children between the ages of 9 and 16 to take on the role of Junior Inspectors.

Theirs was no instant glory. They were sternly bidden to stay anonymous — and they did. All were part of busy families around the country, some living in the inner cities, some in suburban and others in more rural areas. All accepted the challenge, unfazed by the task of making observations and writing up detailed reports. All enjoy food, though for some the opportunities for eating out are limited — usually by their own extraordinarily busy school and social activities.

Armed with *Just a Bite*, they set to work. Brothers and sisters were summoned, family conferences called and parents informed (someone has to organise the transport, after all). There was the usual crop of problems. One restaurant had decided to close on Sundays *and* Mondays, another wasn't open in the evenings, a third had been recently taken over and changed beyond recognition — and only one pizza house was allowed. However, the assignments were completed in record time and none of the restaurants had the slightest idea they were under surveillance.

Here are the reports, with just the occasional adjustment of spelling and the addition of a comma or two. Our regular team had better look to their laurels. . . .

Joy Langridge

SOPHIE JAMES, age 9½, PETERBOROUGH, CAMBS

Sophie James lives in a small village just outside Peterborough. She was delighted that our invitation coincided with her sister Emma's 17th birthday and with her brother Simon's weekend home from London's South Bank Polytechnic. They decided to go out to eat en famille and after due consultation, Sophie chose the George of Stamford. Here is our youngest inspector's report:

GEORGE OF STAMFORD,
St Martin's High Street, Stamford, Lincolnshire

The George hotel in Stamford is about ten miles from our house — and very close to my school. We like going to it for bar meals. They have big log fires and comfortable sofas. The food is very nice, and suitable for children and adults. Daddy and my brother both had lemon sole, my mother had seafood pancake, my sister had lasagne and I chose chicken drumsticks with sweet and sour sauce. For sweet, daddy and mummy had chocolate gâteau, my brother had summer pudding and my sister and I had ice cream. There were lots of different flavours of ice cream and they were very prettily presented. We all enjoyed the meal, although my brother said his pudding was not as nice as mum's. The service was quite good but one portion of chips was a bit late. I recommend the George hotel as a good place for a family meal out.

LUISA PECCHIO, age 12, TIMPERLEY, CHESHIRE

Luisa lives in the pleasant suburban area of Timperley, not far from Wilmslow. She loves 'eating out, especially in Italy', and recently while on holiday with a friend in the Lake District made a special detour to take in tea at Sharrow Bay. The young Cheshire set take their food 'very seriously', and according to Luisa's mother 'can be highly critical of what they eat'. It took some time to decide where to eat. Mother firmly vetoed 'pub-type places'. They would have liked to try the Griffin at Bowdon, but it was closed for redecoration. At one point, they thought they might have to foray as far as Chester, but then they hit upon:

PORTOBELLO, 2 Mellor Road, Cheadle Hulme, Cheshire

The Portobello has a stylish entrance leading to a bright and clean restaurant. I took my two best friends, Melanie and Jane, my gran and my parents. We were greeted cheerfully, then shown into a small bar where we had an apéritif (actually, the young ones had Coca-Cola), whilst we chose from quite an extensive menu. Jane chose mushrooms in garlic sauce and veal cordon bleu. Melanie and I decided on king prawns in garlic sauce and beef Stroganoff — Phew! Too much pepper all round! We then had ice cream with liqueur which was delicious and cooled us down. The service was quick and efficient and the waiters treated us all equally, which was nice (being 12 years of age). My gran (87) thoroughly enjoyed the atmosphere, the food and being able to practise her Italian. The kitchen was practical and spotless. Not suitable for children under 12 — food too spicy — but very good atmosphere.

ANNA and LAURA MURPHY, age 14 and 12, WELLINGTON, SOMERSET

Anna and Laura live a busy and varied life, and both go to Court Fields, the local comprehensive school. Anna is 'keen on cooking', makes an excellent fruit salad and this year has cooked the Christmas puddings. The family don't eat out often, would have gone

to Bow Bar at Taunton — which they all like very much — but 'It's open only at lunchtimes and it's rather far for termtime'. So they decided to try somewhere they hadn't been before, and booked for dinner at:

HENDERSONS, 18 Newport Street, Tiverton, Devon

As we arrived our coats were taken and we sat down in the lounge. Within about five minutes we had been given a menu. It covered a wide variety of foods, but a lot of it was in French, which could have been embarrassing if you could not read it. For starters, we had egg mayonnaise and cheese in choux pastry, both of which were very nice. These were followed by goujons (plaice in breadcrumbs) and chicken italienne (chicken with some kind of sauce and pasta). These came with vegetables in separate dishes. They were all unusual vegetables and there were no 'everday ones', which might have been a problem for some children. For a last course we had chocolate mousse which, although filling, was lovely. We had to wait a long time for the bill, as the proprietor seemed to be involved in a lengthy conversation with other customers! A meal for four cost £50 — this included some wine for the adults. This restaurant is a lovely one to go to but it is not the type of place to take very young children.

JAMIE FLEMING, age 13, REGENT'S PARK, LONDON

Jamie Fleming, who lives in central London, is in his first year at Harrow School. Jamie has been interested in food 'since I was six or seven' and says his school meals are 'not too bad, except for the liver'. He loves soups, most fish (though not shellfish), fruit and all sweets (except cheesecake). The family 'eat out a lot'. On holidays abroad, he has sampled food in Florida (pronounced good), the West Indies, Morocco (though he doesn't like couscous), Cyprus and Spain. He and his mother nipped out to:

THE CHICAGO PIZZA PIE FACTORY, 17 Hanover Square, London, W1

We had to wait a few minutes in the bar before our names were called. A screen above the bar was showing an American football game. The whole place was very crowded but all the waitresses (and

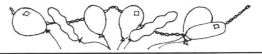

waiters) were doing a good job. As we were only two, we got a table quickly and were lucky we didn't have to share. For starters we had their home-made garlic bread, which is absolutely delicious. The cheese and sausage pizza is their speciality and I recommend it highly: the sausage is very spicy and we also had anchovies and peperoni on it. (My mother scattered dried oregano over hers, but she could have had dried chillies or grated Parmesan.) While you wait for your pizzas, there is plenty to see — loads and loads of pictures all bearing the name 'Chicago'. Lots of bustle, songs by Sinatra ('My Kind of Town') and Elvis. If you go to the toilet, look for a sign saying 'To the johns'. After your pizza you really haven't room for dessert, but if you *do* decide to have it, there's cheesecake, carrot cake or ice cream, which is not like any usual ice cream. Ask your waitress for today's flavours. The service is good and the waitresses friendly. What more do you want from a restaurant?!!

MARK BARLOW, age 13, LIVERPOOL, MERSEYSIDE

Mark Barlow lives in a rambling house right on the edge of the river Mersey, and he attends the Bluecoat School. He generally enjoys food, though he's not terribly keen on fish and his father says he 'makes a great fuss about chops'. Mark likes most European food — so far, and the family are used to eating out. The idea of a French-style restaurant appealed, so he took his parents and brother Justin to:

LA GRANDE BOUFFE, 48a Castle Street, Liverpool, Merseyside

The first thing I noticed was that you could see into the kitchen and hear and (partly) watch your food cooking. We had fun guessing what some of the bangings were for! The price of the meal depends on your main course, varying from £11.25 to £13.25. Main courses include rack of lamb, boeuf en croûte and breast of duck done in a special way. Starters and sweets were included. There was a choice of six starters, but nothing very simple which appealed to me, though my parents and my brother (17) thought it was a *very* good choice. I had a crêpe because I had had them in France, but the courgette and spring onion filling seemed weird. For the main course, I had chicken satay, on a skewer with a separate spicy peanut sauce (too peppery for me), with rice, fresh pineapple and cucumber. The chicken was very tasty. The family's vegetables were all fresh, and my parents liked the fact that they were slightly undercooked. There were many

good puddings, but I chose the Jersey ice cream. This was very soft and distinctly vanilla flavoured. The other puddings were just as good and enjoyed by my family. If you wanted coffee, it was an extra 90p, but you got a lot of coffee served in French cups from a big enamel jug. There was a good selection of drinks for parents and children; soft drinks cost 50 to 60p. The restaurant had a French style with 'Messieurs' and 'Dames' on the toilets. The 'Messieurs' had a mural of typical Paris scenes, which gave me a surprise, but Mum was quite disappointed to find the 'Dames' quite plain. The service was good, with friendly waiters, but we had to wait a long time for the bill. It was fully booked on the Saturday we went.

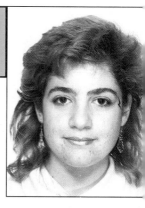

NUALA FRIEDMAN, age almost 16, STONY STRATFORD, MILTON KEYNES

Nuala Friedman goes to Radcliffe Comprehensive School. She is 'mostly vegetarian, could live on avocados and salad'. The family rarely eats out, as 'there are very few places around here of good quality where it's reasonably cheap'. They often compromise by having bar snacks and were absolutely delighted to discover Browns, which everyone agreed was well worth the journey to Oxford.

BROWNS, 7 Woodstock Road, Oxford, Oxfordshire

I really enjoyed my visit here. It was packed (you can't book) and they used an 'auto-call' system for queuing. The waitresses wore black mini-skirts and white blouses, the waiters black trousers and white shirts. As we sat down, I noticed the plants hanging from the ceiling and mirrors on every wall. There was a good choice on the menu and the tasty meal was very filling ('They cater for student appetites', said Mum). There were no starters and the set menu centred round the dishes of the day. The main speciality was spaghetti with a choice of sauces — I had mine with garlic bread, a seafood sauce and an Italian sauce. With it came a mixed salad. My brother Saul chose sirloin steak and chips. For dessert (and the adults couldn't manage one), we had chocolate cake and cheesecake. The staff obviously work really hard to keep Brown's up to scratch. The four of us had a lovely meal for just under £30, which is good value. Overall, I think Browns is a place for people of any age to eat at, with good food at a nice price. I would definitely go again.

191

Fun Fare

Establishments offering children's menus or dishes

LONDON

Le Bistroquet, NW1
Colonel Jaspers, SE10
Davy's Wine Vaults, SE10
Inter-Continental Hotel, Coffee House, W1
Macarthurs, SW13
Parsons, SW10
Richoux, SW3 & W1
Royal Festival Hall, SE1
Smollensky's Balloon, W1
Waldorf Hotel, Palm Court Lounge, WC2

ENGLAND

Alfriston, E. Sussex: Drusillas Thatched Barn
Alstonefield, Staffs: Old Post Office Tea Rooms
Ambleside, Cumb: Harvest
Ambleside, Cumb: Zeffirellis
Axminster, Devon: New Commercial Inn
Bath, Avon: Bath Puppet Theatre
Bath, Avon: Jollys, Circles Restaurant
Bath, Avon: Pump Room
Bexhill, E. Sussex: Trawlers
Bishop's Lydeard, Som: Rose Cottage
Boot, Cumb: Brook House Restaurant
Bournemouth, Dorset: Coriander
Bradford, W. Yorks: Pizza Margherita
Brighton, E. Sussex: Al Duomo
Brighton, E. Sussex: Samsons
Cheam, Surrey: Superfish
Cheddar, Som: Wishing Well Tea Rooms
Chester, Ches: Farmhouse
Chester, Ches: 60s American Restaurant
Dorchester, Dorset: Potter Inn
Dunster, Som: Tea Shoppe
Easingwold, N. Yorks: Truffles
East Molesey, Surrey: Superfish
Elland, W. Yorks: Bertie's Bistro
Ewell, Surrey: Superfish
Gateshead, T & W: Marks & Spencer Garden Restaurant
Great Torrington, Devon: Rebecca's
Great Torrington, Devon: Top of the Town
Guildford, Surrey: Richoux
Harrogate, N. Yorks: Bettys
Ilkley, W. Yorks: Bettys
Ipswich, Suffolk: Tackets

Kendal, Cumb: Farrers Tea & Coffee House
Kew, Surrey: Original Maids of Honour
Leeds, W. Yorks: Ike's Bistro
Leeds, W. Yorks: Salvo's
Louth, Lincs: Mr Chips
Lyme Regis, Dorset: Golden Cap
Magham Down, E. Sussex: Ye Old Forge
Market Harborough, Leics: Taylor's Fish Restaurant
Morden, Surrey: Superfish
Northallerton, N. Yorks: Bettys
Nottingham, Notts: New Orleans Diner
Parkgate, Ches: Chompers
Polperro, Cornwall: Captain's Cabin
Pulborough, W. Sussex: Chequers Hotel
Rottingdean, E. Sussex: Rottingdean Pâtisserie
Salisbury, Wilts: Michael Snell
Salisbury, Wilts: Mo's
Scunthorpe, Humbs: Bees Garden Coffee Lounge
Seaford, E. Sussex: Trawlers
Stockbridge, Hants: Old Dairy Restaurant
Surbiton, Surrey: Fortunes
Swaffham, Norfolk: Red Door
Tewkesbury, Glos: Wintor House
Thames Ditton, Surrey: Skiffers
Tolworth, Surrey: Superfish
Trebarwith Strand, Cornwall: House on the Strand
Tunbridge Wells, Kent: Buster Browns
Warminster, Wilts: Vincent's
Wasdale, Cumb: Greendale Gallery Restaurant
Whitby, N. Yorks: Magpie Café
Winchester, Hants: Wessex Hotel Coffee Shop
Windermere, Cumb: Langdale Chase Hotel
Yeovil, Som: Trugs
York, N. Yorks: Bettys

SCOTLAND
Dirleton, Loth: Open Arms Hotel Lounge
Glasgow, S'clyde: Tom Sawyers
Kincraig, H'land: Boathouse Restaurant
Largs, S'clyde: Green Shutter Tea Room
Newcastleton, Bdrs: Copshaw Kitchen
Selkirk, Bdrs: Philipburn House Hotel
Tomintoul, Gram'n: Glenmulliach Restaurant

WALES
Aberaeron, Dyfed: Hive on the Quay
Aberystwyth, Dyfed: Connexion
Keeston, Dyfed: Keeston Kitchen
Llanycefn, Dyfed: Llain Llogin
Newport, Dyfed: Chapan
Wrexham, Clwyd: Bumble's Coffee Shop

ISLE OF MAN
Castletown, I of M: Castletown Golf Links Hotel

Egon Ronay's
guide to
THE LAKE DISTRICT and YORKSHIRE DALES

This unique guide is a passport to over 200 carefully selected hotels, restaurants, wine bars, inns and tearooms providing exceptionally high standards of cooking and accommodation.

To help memories live on until the beautiful dales and fells can be visited again, Egon Ronay's Guide to the Lake District and Yorkshire Dales also offers some recipes from the top chefs of the area.

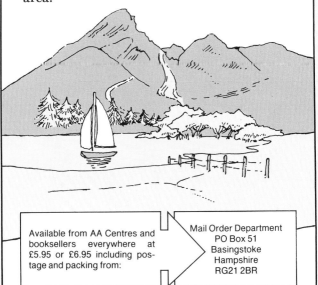

Available from AA Centres and booksellers everywhere at £5.95 or £6.95 including postage and packing from:

Mail Order Department
PO Box 51
Basingstoke
Hampshire
RG21 2BR

TEA. A QUESTION OF QUALITY.

AT WHAT SPEED SHOULD A TEA BUSH GROW
TO ACQUIRE THE RICHEST FLAVOUR?

*HOW MANY TEAS DO YOU NEED TO MAKE
A FINE QUALITY BLEND?*

Brooke Bond

PG tips

As many as twenty eight different teas are used to create PG Tips, because no single tea can produce that unique taste. Crops vary in quality from day to day and country to country and a great deal of skill is required of Brooke Bond blenders to balance the qualities of one leaf against another. Their skill and experience is evident in each day's blend of PG's famous flavour.

WHAT'S THE DIFFERENCE BETWEEN
A FINE QUALITY BLEND AND AN INFERIOR ONE?

Brooke Bond

PG
tips

A fine quality cup such as PG Tips is a skilful blend of many teas. Each leaf adds its own subtle shade of flavour, colour and brightness. Some leaves also infuse, or release their flavour, more

quickly. Brooke Bond blenders sample as many as 500 different teas each week to produce the familiar PG taste. Small wonder that no other blend can boast such a famous flavour. 🍃

Egon Ronay's
Minutes
from the Motorway
M25 AROUND
LONDON GUIDE

Newly compiled for 1987, this colourful guide spotlights over 200 carefully selected eating places within easy reach of London's orbital motorway.

Everything from starred restaurants and country pubs to the best tearooms and wine bars.

Special features include detailed area maps.

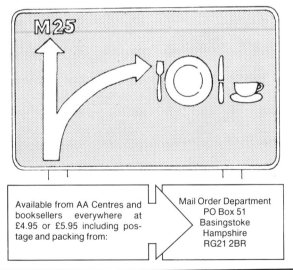

Available from AA Centres and booksellers everywhere at £4.95 or £5.95 including postage and packing from:

Mail Order Department
PO Box 51
Basingstoke
Hampshire
RG21 2BR

Maps

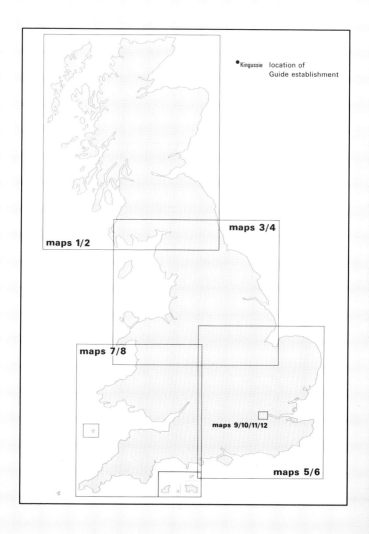

Kingussie location of Guide establishment

maps 1/2

maps 3/4

maps 7/8

maps 9/10/11/12

maps 5/6

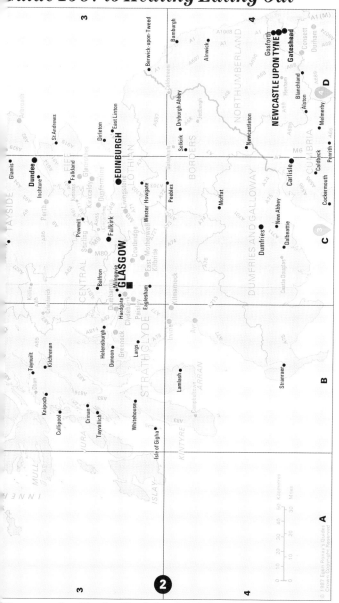

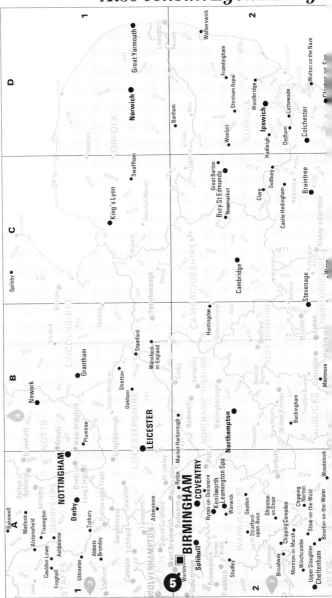

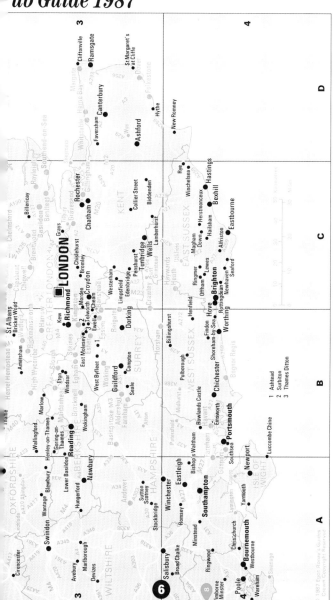

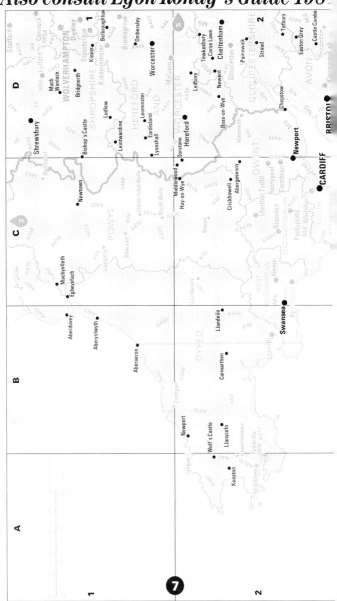

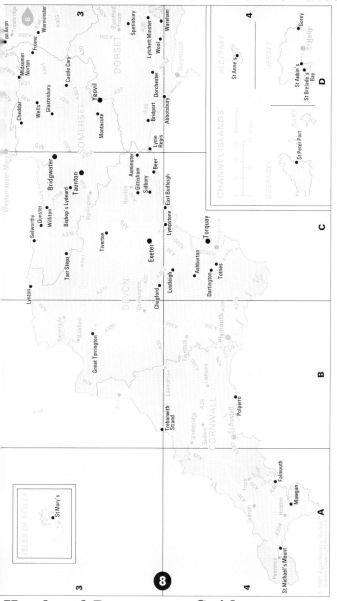

Hotel and Restaurant Guide

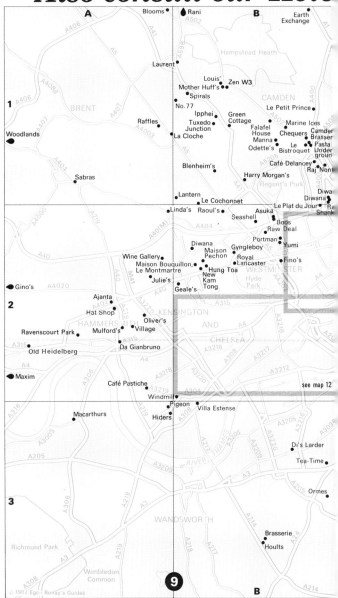

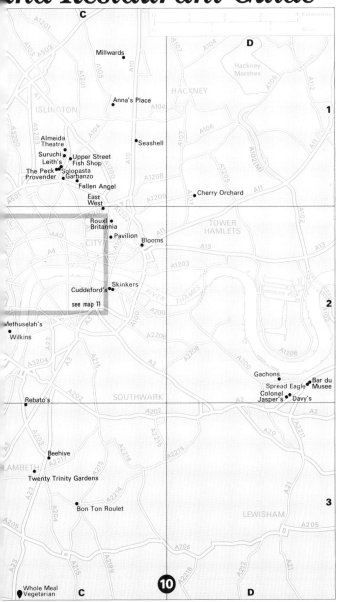

1

- ❶ Le Beaujolais
- ❷ Brasserie at l'Escargot
- ❸ Cafe Fish des Amis du Vin
- ❹ Canton
- ❺ Chuen Cheng Ku
- ❻ Cork & Bottle
- ❼ Criterion
- ❽ Equatorial
- ❾ Jade Garden
- ❿ Joy King Lau
- ⓫ Lok Ho Fook
- ⓬ Loon Fung
- ⓭ Loon Fung
- ⓮ Maison Bertaux
- ⓯ New Loon Fung

- ⓰ Pasta Fino
- ⓱ Pasticceria Amalfi
- ⓲ Patisserie Valerie
- ⓳ Poons
- ⓴ Soho Brasserie
- ㉑ Trattoria Imperia
- ㉒ Woodlands

Hotel and Restaurant Guide

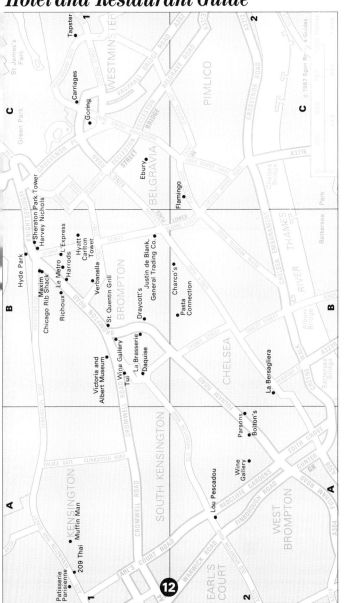

Guide 1987 to Healthy Eating Out

Egon Ronay's
PUB GUIDE 1987

TO BAR FOOD AND ACCOMMODATION
IN BRITISH PUBS AND INNS

- The best British bar snacks and meals
- Highly selective
- Surprising gastronomic finds at low prices
- Pubs that welcome children
- Homely, clean and pleasant bedrooms
- Excellent breakfasts

Plus pubs specially selected for atmosphere and historic interest.

Available from AA Centres and booksellers everywhere at £4.95 or £5.95 including postage and packing from:

Mail Order Department
PO Box 51
Basingstoke
Hampshire
RG21 2BR

Brighton ★ *Food for Friends*

17a Prince Albert Street
Brighton (0273) 202310
Town plan *East Sussex*

Open 9am–10pm (Sun from 11.30)
Closed Christmas–New Year

Broccoli & sweetcorn Washington £1.30
Butter bean & aubergine bourguignon £1.30
LVs
P NCP in Church Street **WC**

Typical decor of plants and pine for this super, self-service vegetarian restaurant in the Lanes. Wholemeal croissants, Danish pastries, muffins and muesli provide breakfast until 11, after which soup and excellent quiches are gradually supplemented by the main savouries such as red bean casserole or butter bean and aubergine bourguignon. Afternoon tea features a great range of baking from their pâtisserie just around the corner. Non-smoking area. *No dogs.* 🍵

Brighton (Hove) *Goodies*

70 Church Road
Brighton (0273) 771739
Town plan *East Sussex*

Open 9–4.30 (Sat till 2.30)
Closed Sun & Bank Holidays

Lasagne verdi £2.75   Cheesecake 75p
LVs

P Hove Town Hall car park **WC**

Neat and bright behind a smart green awning, Goodies serves a varied selection of appetising fare. Breakfast starts the day, and after morning coffee and cakes come things like pizzas and pasta, stuffed marrow, grills and well-seasoned salmon cakes topped with a spicy tomato sauce. For sweet, nice pies and crumbles. No dogs at lunchtime, when there's a minimum charge of £2. 🍵

Brighton ★ *Mock Turtle*

4 Pool Valley
Brighton (0273) 27380
Town plan *East Sussex*

Open 10–6
Closed Sun, Mon, Bank Holidays (except Good Friday), a few days Christmas & 2 weeks autumn
Cream tea £1.50   Plaice with vegetables £2.50
P meter parking **WC**

In the window and on the sideboard, the displays of home baking are equally mouthwatering at this cottage tea shop. Lemon cake, walnut and carrot loaf, gingerbread, meringues oozing fresh cream ... it's all superb, and there's plenty more to savour, from Welsh rarebit and sardines on toast to lunchtime dishes like herb omelette and fillet of plaice served with nice golden chips. Unlicensed. *No dogs.* 🍵

Brighton *Pie in the Sky*

87 St James's Street
Brighton (0273) 692087
Town plan *East Sussex*

Open 12–2.30 & 6.30–11.30
Closed 1 January & 25 & 26 December

Deep-pan pizzas (for two) from £3.85
Chocolate cheesecake £1.25

P meter parking & High Street car park **WC**

Deep-dish pizzas serving two or more are the house speciality at this bright, cheerful place not far from the seafront. Toppings are generous and tasty – tomato, cheese and peperoni is one variety – and at lunchtime one-person wedges are available. Also on the menu are garlic bread, stuffed mushrooms and baked potatoes. Delicious chocolate cheesecake or ice cream for dessert. *No dogs.*

Brighton   *Samsons*

25 St George's Road, Kemp Town
Brighton (0273) 689073
Town plan *East Sussex*

Open 6pm–11.30pm
Closed 4 days Christmas

½lb mushroom burger with chips £3.04
Vegetarian salad £2.80

P street parking **WC**

Hamburgers are what this cheerful restaurant
is all about. Quarter- or half-pounders come
in many tasty varieties (mushroom, chilli
sauce, melted blue cheese), popped into
poppy seed buns and served with a mixed
salad and a baked potato or French fries.
Tuna fish and vegetarian salads are popular
alternatives, and there's always a dish of the
day. Soup, pâté, simple sweets. ☕

Brighton   *Saxons*

48 George Street
Brighton (0273) 680733
Town plan *East Sussex*

Open 11.30–3, also 7.15–10.15 Wed–Sat
Closed Sun, Bank Holidays & 1 week
Christmas

Cheese flan & salad £1.70   Kidney bean
ragout with brown rice £1.50
P Presto supermarket car park & meters

Saxon Howard's neat, simple restaurant
offers a choice of interesting, well-prepared
vegetarian fare. Lunchtime is self-service,
with appetising fare like the very popular hot
cheese flans based on light wholemeal
pastry, supplemented by specials such as
kidney bean ragout with brown rice. Soups
and salads are excellent, and sweet treats
include flapjacks and tipsy pudding. Unlicensed. No smoking before 2. *No dogs.* 🍵

Bristol   *Arnolfini Café Bar*

Narrow Quay, Prince Street
Bristol (0272) 299191
Town plan *Avon*

Open 11–10.30 (Fri & Sat till 11, Sun from
noon)

Seafood pancake £2.50   Chocolate cream pie
80p
LVs   *Credit* Access, Amex, Visa
P NCP in Prince Street or meters   ᗕ   **WC**

Tuck into a freshly prepared salad, lamb
kebab or vegetable curry at this atmospheric
dockland café, part of a popular arts complex
created out of old warehouses. Also on the
menu are quiches, pâtés (including a broad
bean one for vegetarians), cold meats and
gooey sweets like trifle and a fudgy chocolate
cake. *No dogs.* ☕

Bristol   *Edwards*

24 Alma Vale Road
Bristol (0272) 741533
Town plan *Avon*

Open 11.30–2 & 6.30–10.30
Closed Sat lunch, all Sun, Bank Holidays & 2
weeks summer
Pork fillet zurichoise £5.25   Victoria plum
crumble with custard £1.50
LVs   *Credit* Access, Visa
P street parking   ᗕ   **WC**

There's a quiet air of civilised comfort about
the Pitchfords' panelled restaurant, where
honest home cooking is the order of the day.
Perennial favourites such as soup, pâté,
steak and kidney pie and rack of lamb are
supplemented by daily blackboard specials
like seafood lasagne, liver with Dubonnet and
orange and garlicky prawns and scallops. To
finish, perhaps plum crumble or sticky treacle
tart. *No dogs.* ☕

BRIGHTON

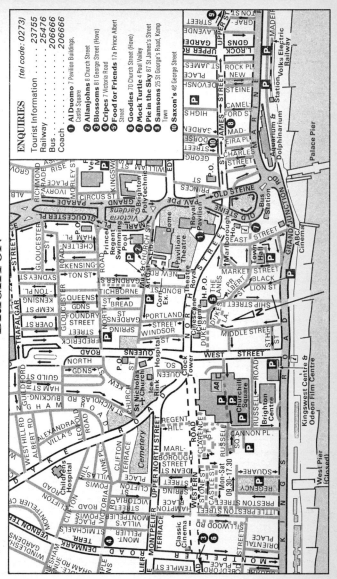

ENQUIRIES *(tel code: 0273)*

Tourist Information	23755
Railway	25476
Bus	206666
Coach	206666

- ① **Al Duomo** 7 Pavilion Buildings, Castle Square
- ② **Allanjohns** 8 Church Street
- ③ **Blossoms** 81 George Street (Hove)
- ④ **Cripes** 7 Victoria Road
- ⑤ **Food for Friends** 17a Prince Albert Street
- ⑥ **Goodies** 70 Church Street (Hove)
- ⑦ **Mock Turtle** 4 Pool Valley
- ⑧ **Pie in the Sky** 87 St James's Street
- ⑨ **Samsons** 25 St George's Road, Kemp Town
- ⑩ **Saxon's** 48 George Street

Bristol   *Guild Café-Restaurant*

68 Park Street
Bristol (0272) 291874
Town plan *Avon*

Open 9.30–5 (Sat till 4.30)
Closed Sun & Bank Holidays

Gratin of cauliflower £2.80   Ginger shortbread
40p

P Park Row multi-storey NCP or meters   **WC**

A leafy outdoor area overlooking a pretty
roof garden is an attractive feature of this
pleasant café-restaurant on the first floor of
a smart little department store. There's a
basic menu of tea, coffee, home-made cakes
and biscuits and cheese rolls. Lunchtime
brings a variety of savoury dishes – spinach
lasagne, aubergine and tomato casserole,
pâté, quiches, salads – and sweets such as
chocolate and brandy mousse. *No dogs.*

Bristol   *Rainbow Café*

10 Waterloo Street, Clifton
Bristol (0272) 738937
Town plan *Avon*
Open 10–5.30
Closed Sun, Bank Holidays & 1 week
Christmas
Salmon & cucumber quiche with mixed salad
£2.60   Gratin of fennel & tomato with green
salad £3.10
LVs
P street parking   **WC**

Their kitchen may be minute, but that doesn't
stop Alison Moore and Tim Ansell from
producing the most delicious goodies
throughout the day. Scrumptious cakes and
biscuits are followed by a lunchtime menu of
flavoursome soups, vegetarian specials like
cashew nut loaf, a hot dish such as casseroled lamb with juniper berries, plus splendid
quiches in tasty combinations like bacon and
spinach. Nice puddings. *No dogs.* 🍵

Bristol   *Wild Oats II*

85 Whiteladies Road, Clifton
Bristol (0272) 734482
Town plan *Avon*

Open 10am–10pm (Mon & Tues till 6, Fri & Sat
till 10.30)
Closed 25 & 26 December
Seitan Stroganoff £6.75   Strawberry tofu whip
95p
LVs
P Clifton Down Shopping Centre NCP   **WC**

Vegetarian, vegans and wholefood buffs are
catered for admirably in this roomy, split-
level restaurant, where chemicals, additives
and preservatives are nowhere to be found.
Wholemeal pizzas and quiches, stir-fried
vegetables and omelettes are favourite light
meals, and there's an eye-catching selection
of inventive salads. Tofu comes in a number
of dishes and delicious home-made cakes
such as ricotta
and rosewater cheesecake. 🍵

Broad Chalke   *Cottage House*

South Street
Salisbury (0722) 780266
Map 6 A4 *Wiltshire*

Open 10.30–12.30 & 2.30–5.30
Closed Sat afternoon (except May–
September), Sun morning, all Mon, 10 days
Christmas & restricted service February &
October
Wiltshire tea bread 40p   Granary cake 50p
P street parking or car park by church   **WC**

Enid and Ian White are prompt to entice
customers into the charming little tea room
at the back of their village stores. Nice oak
furniture sets off the beamed ceiling and
inglenook fireplace, and the cottagy atmosphere is completed by cream teas (with
freshly made scones), Wiltshire tea bread
and delicious home-made cakes such as a
superb jam sponge. There's a pretty patio
for fine weather. *No dogs.* 🍵

BRISTOL

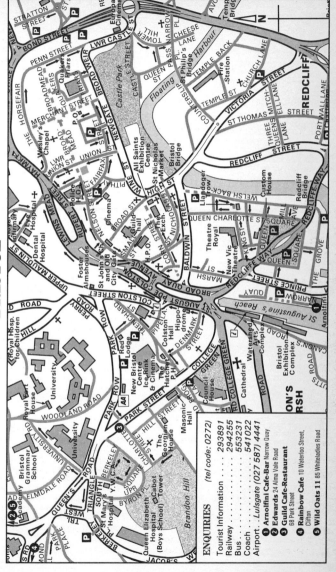

ENQUIRIES *(tel code: 0272)*

Tourist Information	293891
Railway	294255
Bus	553231
Coach	541022
Airport . . Luisgate (027 587)	4441

1. **Arnolfini Cafe-Bar** Narrow Quay
2. **Edwards** 24 Alma Vale Road
3. **Guild Cafe-Restaurant** 68 Park Street
4. **Rainbow Cafe** 10 Waterloo Street, Clifton
5. **Wild Oats 11** 85 Whiteladies Road

Broadway

Coffee Pot

76 High Street
Broadway (0386) 858323
Map 5 A2 *Hereford & Worcester*

Open 10.30–5.30
Closed Wed, also Mon–Thurs November–
December, 25 December, January & February

Cream tea £1.50   Haddock & prawn casserole
£2.90
P street parking   **WC**

Just beyond the turning for Stratford, at the
top end of town, the Taylors' spick-and-span
tea room has many charming features, including a fine display of Staffordshire pottery
figures for sale. On the eating side, a
blackboard announces dishes of the day
such as pizza, bacon and lentil soup or
haddock and prawn casserole. There are
always plain and toasted sandwiches, plus a
tempting array of cakes. Super afternoon
teas are a popular option. 🍵

Broadway   ★

Collin House Hotel

Collin Lane
Broadway (0386) 858354
Map 5 A2 *Hereford & Worcester*

Open noon–1.30pm
Closed 3 days Christmas

Ham & cauliflower bake £3.75   Bread & butter
pudding with brandy cream £1.50
Credit Access, Visa
P own car park   &   **WC**

John and Judith Mills' imaginative cooking
based on prime raw ingredients makes
lunchtimes in the cosy bar of this Cotswold-
stone hotel truly memorable. Wake up those
taste buds with smoked mackerel and cucumber mousse, followed perhaps by curried
chicken with rice or rabbit with a well-judged
mustard sauce. Delightful desserts include
bread and butter pudding, lovely trifle and ice
creams. Enjoy a traditional set lunch on
Sunday. *No dogs.* 🍵

Broadway

Goblets Wine Bar

High Street
Broadway (0386) 852255
Map 5 A2 *Hereford & Worcester*

Open 12–2, 3–5 & 6–9.30 (Sun from 7)
Closed 2 weeks Christmas

Chicken drumsticks with watercress sauce
£2.25   Gingerbread & pear pudding £1.65
Credit Access, Amex, Diners, Visa
P Lygon Arms car park   **WC**

A stylish and very popular wine bar next to
the Lygon Arms. The menu provides a short,
well-balanced selection of dishes both plain
and sauced, from chicken drumsticks with a
fine watercress mayonnaise to rainbow trout,
stuffed marrow, vegetable lasagne and gammon steak with gooseberry sauce. To finish,
perhaps fresh fruit salad or hot gingerbread
and pear pudding. Good wines; cheerful
service. No children. *No dogs.* 🍵

Bromley

Hollywood Bowl

5 Market Parade
01-460 2346
Map 6 C3 *Kent*
Open noon–2.45 & 6–11.15 (Fri & Sat till 11.45,
Sun till 11)
Closed Sun lunch & Bank Holidays (except
Good Fri)
Chilli burger £3.95   Baked Brie with almonds
£1.25   **LVs**
P West Street car park & street parking in eve
WC

Old advertising signs are the chief decorative
feature of this informal American-style restaurant. Hamburgers are the things to order,
cooked how you like and served in a toasted
bun with toppings like chilli or melted cheese.
Potato skins and clam fries appear among
the starters, and non-burger main dishes
include lamb cutlets and lasagne. Also salads
and bumper sandwiches. Service is swift and
friendly. *No dogs.*

Buckingham
Bakery & Austrian Coffee Room

27 West Street
Buckingham (0280) 813124
Map 5 B2 *Buckinghamshire*

Open 9–5 (Sat till 4.30)
Closed Sun, Mon & Bank Holidays

Chicken curry £1.80   Austrian goulash soup
£1.40

P Bridge Street car park   **WC**

Tantalising smells from the bakery below are a great distraction at this spotless little coffee shop with carved booth seating and cow bells for decoration. Everything tastes as good as it looks – and smells – from calorific gâteaux, chocolate éclairs, huge meringues and shortbread men to savoury options like pizzas, pâté, sandwiches and wonderfully satisfying goulash soup. Home-made ice creams, too. Minimum lunchtime charge of 50p. Unlicensed. *No dogs.*

Burnley
Butterfingers

10 St James Row
Burnley (0282) 58788
Map 3 B3 *Lancashire*

Open 9–4 (Tues till 2)
Closed Sun, Bank Holidays & 3 days
Christmas
Beef in cider with herb dumplings £1.75
Banana toffee flan 80p
LVs
P market car park   &

The atmosphere is warm and friendly, the cooking more than capable at this bright little self-service café. Ploughman's and toasties make tasty quick snacks, soups are full of goodness and there are eight tempting fillings for jacket potatoes. Fine flans include a delicious mushroom and cheese version pepped with cayenne. Crisp, fresh salads, and nice sweets such as apple caramel tart. Unlicensed. *No dogs.*

Bury St Edmunds
Beaumonts

6 Brentgovel Street
Bury St Edmunds (0284) 706677
Map 5 C2 *Suffolk*

Open Coffee Shop: 9.30–5; Restaurant: 11–4
Closed Sun & Bank Holidays

Vegan enchiladas with green salad £1.95
Raspberry trifle 95p
LVs   *Credit* Access, Visa
P Old Cattlemarket & street parking   **WC**

Comprising a health-food shop, airily modern coffee shop and restaurant, this is a most attractive place for enjoying healthy, strictly vegetarian fare. Snacks and lunches served in the restaurant include celery and apple soup, goat's cheese flan, baked potatoes and vegetable goulash, with tempting sweets like summer pudding to finish. Upstairs in the coffee shop there's a good choice of cakes and pastries, plus a few savouries. *No dogs.*

Caldbeck
Swaledale Watch

Whelpo, Near Wigton
Caldbeck (069 98) 409
Map 3 B1 *Cumbria*

Open 2.30–6
Closed Mon (except Bank Holidays) &
October–end of May

Cider, nut & honey cake 32p   Cream tea £1.20

P own car park   &   **WC**

In the tiny hamlet of Whelpo, this delightful farmhouse tea room is well worth a visit for Nan Savage's splendid home baking. Cider, nut and honey cake and rich fruit scones are two of the favourite treats, and there are also lovely fruit pies, buttery buns, quiche and baps with the filling of the day. Unlicensed. No smoking. *No dogs.* 🐾

223

Calver Bridge   *Derbyshire Craft Centre Eating House*

Near Baslow
Hope Valley (0433) 31231
Map 4 C3 *Derbyshire*

Open 10–5.30
Closed weekdays January & February

Mushroom quiche £2.50   Fudgy nut pie 75p

P own car park & **WC**

The baking is the main strength of this popular self-service eating house in a craft centre. Quiches include a particularly good mushroom variety, and there's a super array of things to delight the sweet tooth. Filled rolls provide tasty quick bites, and lunchtime brings home-made soup and a short but interesting selection of salads (pasta, beetroot, mushroom). Affable owner Janette Beauchamp leads a happy team. Unlicensed. *No dogs.*

Cambridge   *Nettles*

6 St Edwards Passage, Kings Parade
Town plan *Cambridgeshire*

Open 9–8 (Sat till 3)
Closed Sun & Bank Holidays

Vegetables in white wine & mushroom sauce
£1.20   Ratatouille £1.20

P NCP in Lion Yard   **WC**

Much of the business is take-away, but there are three tables for those wanting to enjoy the excellent wholefood vegetarian fare on the premises. Muesli is very popular, along with flapjacks, oat bars and apple crumble, while savouries run from rolls, quiche and pizza to potato and lentil pie with cheese sauce. Also a couple of salads, one rice-based, the other crisply green. Unlicensed. No smoking. *No dogs.*

Cambridge   *Upstairs*

71 Castle Street
Cambridge (0223) 312569
Town plan *Cambridgeshire*

Open 6.30–11 (Fri & Sat till midnight)
Closed Mon & 1 week Christmas

Gagamp £1.50   Poulet au citron £4.50
Credit Access, Visa

P Shire Hall car park   **WC**

Authentic Middle Eastern dishes are the speciality of this informal little upstairs restaurant decorated with brass lanterns and Moorish arches. Helpful staff will assist with delicious offerings like gagamp (seasoned beef wrapped in cabbage leaves with a tomato and onion sauce), marinated monkfish or salads like sweet pepper rings dressed in lemon, olive oil, honey and mint. Sticky pastries to finish. *No dogs.*

Cambridge   *Waffles*

71 Castle Street
Cambridge (0223) 312569
Town plan *Cambridgeshire*

Open 6.30–11, Sat 12–3 & 6–midnight, Sun
9.30–2.30 & 6–10
Closed Mon, 3 weeks September & 1 week
Christmas
Ham, cheese & mushroom waffle £1.80
Butter, maple syrup & cream waffle £1.45
P Shire Hall car park   **WC**

Waffles are, of course, what you eat at this cheerful, lively restaurant with Victorian-style decor. The rich batter is baked in iron moulds, and each day brings a choice of three savoury and three sweet ones, the former including perhaps tuna suprême, ratatouille and chicken créole (diced chicken with tomatoes, onions and peppers), the latter gooseberries, spiced apple and the classic butter, maple syrup and cream. *No dogs.*

CAMBRIDGE

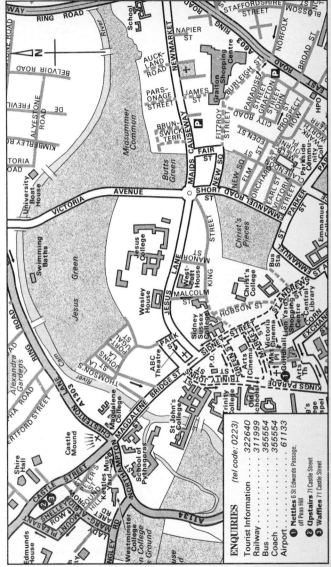

ENQUIRIES	(tel code: 0223)
Tourist Information	322640
Railway	311999
Bus	355554
Coach	355554
Airport	61133

❶ Nettles 6 St Edwards Passage, off Peas Hill
❷ Upstairs 7/ Castle Street
❸ Waffles 7/ Castle Street

Canterbury **New Entry** *Cogan House English Brasserie*

53 St Peter's Street
Canterbury (0227) 472986
Map 6 D3 *Kent*
Open 10.30am–10.30pm (Sun from noon)
Closed 25 & 26 December & 3 weeks early
spring
Whole roast spring chicken £4.75   Puff pastry
with courgettes & almonds in cream sauce
£1.90
Credit Access, Visa
P Marlow car park   **WC**

This delightful restaurant above a shoe shop
is rich in architectural history, the building
itself dating back to 1170. In true brasserie
fashion virtually everything is available
throughout opening hours. Snacks range
from open sandwiches and splendid English
cheeses to marinated smoked haddock with
apple salad. Main dishes could be anything
from grilled trout to spicy sausages and
pepper steak. Super chocolate nut brandy
cake. Non-smoking area. *No dogs.* ⊖

Canterbury *Crotchets* (Wine Bar)

59 Northgate
Canterbury (0227) 45887
Map 6 D3 *Kent*

Open noon–3 & 6.30–midnight, Sun noon–2 &
7–10.30
Tortilla with salad £1.95   Chilli con carne with
rice £2.25
LVs   *Credit* Access, Amex, Diners, Visa
P street parking & St Radigund's car park   ⅏
WC

Joint owner David Rees-Williams plays jazz
piano nightly at this relaxed city-centre wine
bar with a walled garden to the rear. Simple
snacks based on good fresh ingredients
range from taramasalata and ploughman's
to ratatouille and chicken in a cream and
white wine sauce. The garlic bread is highly
recommended, and there are refreshing
sorbets to finish. No children. ⊖

Canterbury *Il Vaticano Pasta Parlour*

35 St Margaret's Street
Canterbury (0227) 65333
Map 6 D3 *Kent*

Open 11am–11pm, Sun noon–10pm
Closed 25 & 26 December
Chicken cacciatore £3.95   Pasta al pesto
£2.60
LVs   *Credit* Access, Amex, Diners, Visa
P multi-storey car park in Rose Lane   ⅏
WC

Pasta fans make a beeline for this bustling,
informal restaurant, where five different
freshly made varieties can be enjoyed with a
choice of eight sauces – from bolognese to
Pernod-flavoured seafood. Ravioli and lasagne are also popular, and there's always a
robust daily special. Start with classic minestrone or tuna with haricot beans and for a
perfect finish, gâteau and an espresso coffee. *No dogs.*

Canterbury *JV's City Brasserie*

4 Church Street, St Pauls
Canterbury (0227) 456655
Map 6 D3 *Kent*

Open noon–2 & 6.30–10.30
Closed Sun & 25–28 December

Lamb cutlets dijonnaise £4.75   Pâté maison
£2.20
LVs   *Credit* Access, Amex, Diners, Visa
P street parking or Roman Wall car park   **WC**

Just outside the city walls but quite close to
the cathedral, this neat wine bar-cum-restaurant offers a varied choice for just-a-biters.
Eggs florentine and tomato salad provençale
are among several vegetarian bar snacks,
and other items include lasagne, lamb cutlets
and seafood pancake. There's also a good
selection of puds. Full à la carte and various
set menus are also available. *No dogs.* ⊖

Canterbury   *Pizza Place*

87 Northgate
Canterbury (0227) 451556
Map 6 D3 *Kent*

Open 10.30am–11.30pm
Closed 25 & 26 December

Pizza toscana £2.35   Chocolate fudge cake
£1.15
LVs
P street parking   &   **WC**

A bright, lively pizza restaurant decorated in the colours of the Italian flag and just as patriotic in its menu selection. Choose a traditional or deep-dish pizza and add a topping like peperoni and spicy sausage, mozzarella and tomato or a medley of seafood. Begin with a tasty starter like garlic mushrooms or tagliatelle and finish with chocolate fudge cake. *No dogs.*

Canterbury   ★   *Sweet Heart Patisserie*

Old Weavers House, St Peters Street
Canterbury (0227) 458626
Map 6 D3 *Kent*

Open 9–6 (till 10.30 in summer)
Closed 2 weeks in winter

Quiche lorraine with salad £2.30   Prawn
sandwich £2.50

P Westgate car park   **WC**

The setting in a 15th-century house is delightful, and the baking is simply magnificent at this splendid pâtisserie. Wickedly rich tortes like the chocolate and cherry brandy confection labelled Falstaff, Canterbury cake (topped with a historic map of the city), spicy apple strudel and Kentish fruit tartlets are all mouthwateringly delicious. Scones and croissants, soups, salads and savoury platters are also served, along with a number of home-made ices. 🐝

Carlisle   *Hudson's Coffee Shop*

Treasury Court, Fisher Street
Carlisle (0228) 47733
Map 3 B1 *Cumbria*

Open 9.30–5 (Thurs till 4)
Closed Sunday & Bank Holidays
Quiche with 4 salads £2.45   Ploughman's
lunch £1.50
LVs
P multi-storey car park in Scotch Street   &
WC

Friendly waitress service ferries cakes and snacks between the pretty dining room and flowery courtyard of this delightful little coffee shop. A light scone, caramel shortbread or delicious chocolate slice goes well with a pot of tea or a cup of coffee. Sandwiches are also available all day, and at lunchtime there are salads, variously filled jacket potatoes and specials like steak and kidney pie. No smoking. Unlicensed. *No dogs.*

Cartmel   *St Mary's Lodge*

Near Grange-over-Sands
Cartmel (044 854) 379
Map 3 B2 *Cumbria*

Open 2.30–5
Closed mid November–end March

Set afternoon tea £2.05   Pavlova 60p

P own car park   **WC**

A friendly welcome and some delicious home baking await visitors to this neatly kept little guest house standing near the priory in picturesque Cartmel. Mrs Gaskins provides lovely lemon and chocolate cakes, cream sponges, scones and several sorts of loaves, including date and walnut, pineapple and moist banana. Raspberry Pavlova provides further temptation. Unlicensed. No smoking. *No dogs.*

Castle Cary   *Old Bakehouse*

High Street
Castle Cary (0963) 50067
Map 8 D3 *Somerset*

Open 9–5.30 (Mon till 1.30)
Closed Sun

Spinach & tomato lasagne £1.50   Toffee date
pudding 75p

P street or town car parks & **WC**

The emphasis is on organically grown produce at this pretty wholefood restaurant with
a delightful courtyard. The daily-changing
menu is headed by soup, followed by things
like prawn and mushroom quiche, vegetable
pie and a slimmer's salad. Carob hazelnut
mousse and spiced fruit compote are typical
sweets. There's also a selection of fine home
baking: super raisin and bran loaf, flapjacks,
shortbread. No smoking.

Castle Cary   *New Entry*   *Tramps Wine Bar*

Woodcock Street
Castle Cary (0963) 51129
Map 8 D3 *Somerset*

Open 11.30–3.30
Closed Sun, Mon, 1 January & 25 & 26
December

King prawns in garlic butter £4.50   Cream tea
£1.60
P museum car park **WC**

Situated above a delicatessen, this village
newcomer has a menu of wide appeal.
Scones and croissants, cakes and pastries
are always available, along with salads,
jacket potatoes and assorted pâtés, cold
meats and salami. King prawns with garlic
mayonnaise is another favourite, along with
fresh fish, vegetarian dishes and excellent
curries like lamb kofta. Treacle tart is a
delicious dessert.

Castle Combe   *Manor House Hotel*

Near Chippenham
Castle Combe (0249) 782206
Map 7 D2 *Wiltshire*

Open 3.30–5.30

Cream tea £2.65   Chef's tea £3.15
LVs *Credit* Access, Amex, Diners, Visa

P own car park **WC**

This creeper-clad 17th-century manor house
is a most pleasant setting for a leisurely
afternoon tea, which may be taken either in
the stylishly redecorated lounge or out on the
lawn. Cream tea comes with freshly made
scones, decent jam and whipped cream,
while chef's tea additionally offers an éclair
or a meringue. Good tea served from a silver
pot. Pleasant staff.

Castle Hedingham   *Colne Valley Railway Restaurant*

Yeldham Road, Near Halstead
Hedingham (0787) 61174
Map 5 C2 *Essex*

Open 10–5 (dusk in winter)
Closed 25 December & January

Stilton quiche £2.75   Steamed lemon sponge
pudding 95p

P own car park **WC**

Visitors to the Colne Valley Railway can
station themselves in a former British Rail
restaurant car to enjoy Mrs Hymas' super
snacks. Lunch gets under way at 12.15, with
tasty soups, savoury pancakes, sugar-roast
gammon and barbecue-sauced burgers as
typical fare. Her home baking is just the ticket
to go with tea and coffee: try tiny scones,
steamed sponge puddings and a marvellous
chocolate cake. Unlicensed. *No dogs.*

Castleton — *Rose Cottage Café*

Hope Valley (0433) 20472
Map 4 C3 *Derbyshire*

Open 10–6
Closed Fri & 3 days Christmas

Hot pot £2.90   Toasted sandwich £1.25

P village car park & **WC**

Hungry hikers often drop in at this delightful rose-covered cottage, so you'll find satisfying soups, grills and omelettes on the menu as well as more traditional tea room fare provided by Mrs Woodsett and her daughter. They bake wonderful cakes (note chocolate and walnut sponge), scones and biscuits – all delicious with a flavoursome brew – and also offer plenty of salads, sandwiches and things on toast. Unlicensed. 🍵

Castleton — *Castleton Tea Rooms*

2 Station Road
Castleton (0287) 60135
Map 4 C2 *North Yorkshire*

Open 10–6.30
Closed Mon–Fri November–March & 25 December

Quiche 95p   Cream tea £1.95

P street parking   **WC**

A tiny corner tea shop run by a thoroughly artistic family – David Aydon draws and paints, while his wife Anne and daughter concentrate their talents on excellent home baking. Delicious cakes and pastries on show include a scrumptious chocolate sponge and featherlight almond tart; there are scones and toasted teacakes, too, plus well-filled sandwiches, quiche and various salads. Unlicensed. *No dogs.* 🍵

Cattawade — *Bucks Wine Bar*

Cattawade Street, Near Manningtree
Colchester (0206) 392571
Map 5 D2 *Essex*

Open 11.30–1.45 & 7–10
Closed Sun eves
Stuffed chicken with walnuts & bacon £5.20
Gravlax of mackerel with sweet mustard sauce £1.90
Credit Access, Amex, Diners, Visa
P own car park   **WC**

Just off the A137 and not far from the river Stour, this pleasant wine bar was formerly a pub. The menu, written on mirrors, reflects the chef's desire to offer not only familiar dishes (seafood pancake, liver and orange pâté) but some more imaginative ones as well – excellent mackerel gravlax, goujons of red bream and saddle of lamb with a blackcurrant glaze. There are some interesting sweets, too, like lemon posset and peaches in chablis. *No dogs.* 🍵

Cauldon Lowe — *Staffordshire Peak Arts Centre*

Near Waterhouses
Waterhouses (053 86) 431
Map 4 C4 *Staffordshire*

Open 10.30–5.30 (Fri till 9 May–September)
Closed Mon–Thurs 1 Nov–31 March

Mushroom burgers £2.20   Homity pie £1.90

Credit Access, Amex, Diners, Visa
P own car park & **WC**

High up in the Staffordshire Peak District, an old schoolhouse now houses an arts centre and a pleasant wholefood vegetarian restaurant. Home baking, including apple cake and lemon curd gâteau, is the morning fare, and at noon tasty hot dishes like lentil and tomato soup, mushroom burgers and courgette-filled oakcakes take the stage, along with nice crisp salads. Good wholesome food, soundly prepared. No smoking.

Chagford   *New Entry*   *Coffee Pot*

High Street
Map 8 C3 *Devon*

Open 8–6
Closed 25 & 26 December & 2 weeks January

Olde English tea £1.50   Filled baked potato
with salad £1.25

P street parking   **WC**

Three rooms with beams and a motley collection of furniture make up this unpretentious tea house opposite the church. The day starts with a cooked breakfast, and tea, coffee and cakes are always available. Lunchtime brings salads, ploughman's and baked potatoes with various fillings – Cheddar cheese and butter, cottage cheese and pineapple, baked beans and sausages. Open after 6 if there are customers. Children's portions. Unlicensed. 🍷

Chatham   *Simson's Wine Bar*

58 High Street
Medway (0634) 42372
Map 6 C3 *Kent*

Open 11.30–2.30 & 7–11
Closed Sun, Mon & 2 weeks January

Lasagne with salad £2.50   Pork in sherry
sauce £4.50
LVs   *Credit* Access, Visa
P Brook car park   **WC**

The first thing you notice about this little high-street wine bar is how friendly and welcoming the staff are. Owner Peter Simson does all the cooking, producing a quite varied range of hearty fare like chicken and vegetable soup, beef and Guinness pie or loin of pork with a tasty mushroom and sherry sauce. Note the interesting photographs of old Chatham on the walls. No children. *No dogs.*

Cheadle Hulme   *Portobello*

2 Mellor Road
061-485 4700
Map 4 C3 *Cheshire*

Open noon–2 & 6.30–11 (Fri & Sat till 11.30)
Closed lunch Bank Holiday Mon, all Sun, 1
January & 25 & 26 December
Pizza napoletana £1.90   Seafood risotto
£2.55
Credit Access, Visa
P street parking   **WC**

A bright, attractive restaurant-cum-pizzeria, in classic style with tiled floor, rough white walls and red waistcoated waiters. The menu spans a good variety of Italian favourites, from a good chunky minestrone and spaghetti with a shellfish sauce to amply topped pizzas, trout with almonds and steak pizzaiola. Nice home-made sweets. *No dogs.*

Cheam   *Superfish*

64 The Broadway
01-643 6906
Map 6 C3 *Surrey*

Open 11.30–2 (Sat till 2.30) & 5.30–11 (Fri &
Sat 5–11.30)
Closed Sun & some Bank Holidays

Cod & chips £2.85   Scampi & chips £3.50
LVs
P Park Road car park   ♿

Aptly named, for the fish is indeed super at this bright, cheerful restaurant in the centre of Cheam. Traditional favourites cod, plaice and haddock are beautifully cooked and served with smashing chips, good pickles and a basket full of lovely hot French bread. Scampi, sole, skate and rock are also available, and there are nice ices to finish. Friendly waiting staff. Unlicensed. *No dogs.* 🍷

Cheddar   *Wishing Well Tea Rooms*

The Cliffs
Cheddar (0934) 742142
Map 8 D3 *Somerset*

Open 10–6
Closed mid Oct–April except Sun in Feb, Mar
& mid Oct–end Nov

Fresh salmon salad £3   Fruit pie & cream 80p

P cheese factory or hamlet car park   **WC**

A mother and daughter team runs this
attractive tea room, where tourists can gorge
themselves on a tempting selection of home-
baked cakes, scones and biscuits, accompanied by a good fresh brew of tea. Freshly
cut sandwiches, salads and snacks on toast
provide a simple savoury choice, augmented
at lunchtime by soup and filled jacket potatoes. Desserts include fruit pie and sherry
trifle. Unlicensed. 🍵

Cheltenham   *New Entry*   *Choirs Tea Rooms*

5 Well Walk
Cheltenham (0242) 510996
Map 7 D2 *Gloucestershire*

Open 10–6
Closed Sun, 1 January & 25 & 26 December

Vegetarian harvest pie with salad £2.35
Farmhouse cider cake 90p

P St James' Square NCP   **WC**

Enormous effort went into restoring these
delightful bow-windowed tea rooms to their
former splendour. Cosy beamed rooms provide the setting for a huge selection of good-
quality baking, with treats like tea loaf,
farmhouse cider cake and apple scones
accompanying a good brew of tea. Savouries
range from bumper sandwiches to jacket
potatoes, vegetable pies and nut loaf with
cheese and herbs. Soup in winter. Unlicensed. *No dogs.* 🐶 🍵

Cheltenham   *Forrest Wine Bar*

Imperial Lane
Cheltenham (0242) 38001
Map 7 D2 *Gloucestershire*

Open 12.30–2.15 & 6.30–10.30
Closed Sun & Bank Holidays (except Mon
eves)
Pork & bacon kebabs with potatoes & salad
£3.50   Three-flavour tortilla with salad £1.95
Credit Access, Visa
P Imperial Square   **WC**

Consistency is the keynote at this cosy
basement wine bar, where excellent snacks
can be enjoyed with a very good selection of
wines, many available by the glass. The daily-
changing menu offers vegetarian dishes and
light meals, plus varied specials spanning
stuffed peppers, seafood pancake and a
first-rate lamb casserole. There's an enticing
display of salads, and sweets include a nice
damson plum fool. *No dogs.* 🐶

Cheltenham   *Langtry Pâtisserie & Tea Rooms*

56 High Street
Cheltenham (0242) 575679
Map 7 D2 *Gloucestershire*

Open 9–5.30 (Sat till 6)
Closed Sun, Bank Holidays & 3 days
Christmas
Chicken & ham vol-au-vent £2.35
Cheesecake £1.05
LVs
P St James car park opposite   ♿   **WC**

Mr Plank's accomplished baking brings both
locals and tourists to this agreeable Victorian
tea shop. From the bakehouse beyond the
garden come all manner of goodies, from
scones and slices to doughnuts and naughty
but delicious cream cakes. There are savoury
snacks, too, including soup, salads, rarebits
and a king-size ploughman's plus daily
specials like cottage pie. Also ice cream
specialities. Unlicensed. *No dogs.*

Cheltenham   *Montpellier Wine Bar & Bistro*

Bayshill Lodge, Montpellier Street
Cheltenham (0242) 527774
Map 7 D2 *Gloucestershire*

Open 12–2.15 & 6–10.15
Closed Sun & Bank Holidays

Roast beef with 5 salads £2.50   Beef &
Guinness casserole with vegetables £2.50
LVs   *Credit* Access, Visa
P street parking   **WC**

Head for the basement bistro and a splendid
cold buffet selection at this immensely popular establishment. There's pâté or smoked
mackerel to start, then zippy salads like
courgette and mint to enjoy with delicious
cold meats, savoury pies or quiches. Check
the blackboard for hot daily specials such as
hearty vegetable soup and navarin of lamb.
Pleasant sweets include various cakes and
sorbets. *No dogs.* 🍵

Cheltenham   *Promenade Pâtisserie*

The Promenade
Cheltenham (0242) 575144
Map 7 D2 *Gloucestershire*

Open 8am–7pm (Sun from 9am)
Closed 1 January & 25 & 26 December

Steak & kidney pie £3.25   Gâteau £1.05
LVs
P street & nearby town car parks   ♿   **WC**

Sister to the Langtry in the High Street, this
modernised tea room provides an equally
tempting selection of super home baking,
including plump scones, Danish pastries,
choux buns and éclairs. Soup, salads and
ploughman's are light savoury snacks, and
other choices include steak and kidney pie,
pizzas and pasties. Ice creams to delight the
kiddies. Unlicensed. *No dogs.* 🍵

Cheltenham   *Retreat* (Wine Bar)

10 Suffolk Parade
Cheltenham (0242) 35436
Map 7 D2 *Gloucestershire*

Open noon–2.15 & 6–9
Closed Sun & Bank Holidays

Lamb portfolio £2.50   Fruit griestorte £1
LVs   *Credit* Access, Amex, Diners, Visa

P street parking   **WC**

Popular with the young and trendy, this
thriving wine bar has an attractive courtyard
garden. A typical day's bill of fare encompasses soup, quiche, taramasalata and hot
dishes such as wholewheat spaghetti, curried crab puffs, chilli with yoghurt or richly
sauced beef stew. Also on the menu are cold
meats, salads and nice sweets like treacle
tart or bread and butter pudding. Can be
noisy in the evening. *No dogs.* 🍵

Chester   *Abbey Green*

2 Abbey Green, off Northgate Street
Chester (0244) 313251
Map 3 B4 *Cheshire*

Open 10–3.30 & 6.30–10.30
Closed Sun, Mon & Bank Holidays except
Good Fri
Mushroom burger with salad £1.95   Cheese,
leek & potato pie with salad £1.80
LVs   *Credit* Access
P city-centre car parks   ♿   **WC**

Close to the cathedral, this listed Georgian
house has three spick-and-span Edwardian-
style rooms in which to enjoy some very good
vegetarian cooking. Stuffed potatoes and
mushroom burgers are popular lunchtime
choices, along with salads and a dish of the
day such as cheese, leek and potato pie.
Cakes and pastries come with morning
coffee and afternoon tea and there's a more
elaborate evening menu. *No dogs.* 🍵

Chester — Chester Grosvenor, Harveys (Wine Bar)

Eastgate Street
Chester (0244) 24024
Map 3 B4 *Cheshire*

Open 12.30–2.30
Closed Sun & 25 & 26 December

Lancashire hot pot £3.75   Home-made soup
95p
Credit Access, Amex, Diners, Visa
P NCP in Newgate Street   **WC**

A smart wine bar in a vaulted cellar beneath the city's showpiece hotel. Lunchtime fare ranges from cold cuts, quiches and attractive salads to a hot dish of the day such as beef Strogonoff or Lancashire hot pot. Puddings include fruit tarts and mousses, and there's a decent selection of well-kept English cheeses. Entrance is from the street or the foyer. No children. *No dogs.* ✆

Chester — Chester Grosvenor Lounge

Eastgate Street
Chester (0244) 24024
Map 3 B4 *Cheshire*

Open 10–5.30
Closed 25 & 26 December

Grosvenor tea £5.25   Platter of smoked fish
£5.25
Credit Access, Amex, Diners, Visa
P NCP in Newgate Street   ♿   **WC**

A tranquil lounge where immaculate waitresses serve you with morning coffee and home-made biscuits, elegant light lunches featuring appealing salads and sandwiches and then splendid afternoon teas. A super pot of tea accompanies fresh sandwiches, oven-warm scones plus cakes and pastries attractively displayed on a central mahogany table. Minimum charge of £3.50 12.30–4.30. *No dogs.* ✆ 🍵

Chester — Farmhouse

Millett's Store, 9 Northgate Street
Chester (0244) 311332
Map 3 B4 *Cheshire*

Open 9.30–5.30
Closed Sun, 1 January, 25 December & some
other Bank Holidays
Chicken in red wine £1.85   Steak &
mushroom pie £1.90
LVs
P city-centre car parks   **WC**

Tasty, wholesome fare is available in good variety at this well-run self-service restaurant located on the first floor of Millett's Store. Pizzas, quiches and soup make pleasant savoury snacks, and chicken in red wine and steak and mushroom pie are typical dishes of the day. There's also a tempting cold display, along with some decent home-made sweets. Vegetarian dishes, too. ✆

Chester — Pierre Griffe Wine Bar

4 Mercia Square
Chester (0244) 312635
Map 3 B4 *Cheshire*

Open 11.30–3 & 5.30–10.30 (Fri & Sat till 11)
Closed Sun & 25 & 26 December
Pâté with salad & bread £2.30   Beef &
mushroom casserole with rice £2.65
LVs
P Cow Lane Bridge car park & street parking
♿   **WC**

Honest, unfussy food wins points from the locals at this simply decorated wine bar with its own large terrace, situated on the upper level of a shopping precinct. Soups and pâtés, cheeses and savoury pies are all popular, and there's good French bread and salad, too. Hot daily dishes might include lamb in white wine and vegetarian lasagne, with delicious home-made desserts like chocolate fudge cake to finish. *No dogs.* ✆

Chester   *60s American Restaurant*

Music Hall Passage, off St Werburgh Street
Chester (0244) 318515
Map 3 B4 *Cheshire*

Open noon–11.15 (Fri & Sat till 11.30)
Closed 25 & 26 December
Burritos £4.50   60s Fantastic Rack (spare ribs, corn on the cob, coleslaw & potato skins) £4.95
Credit Access, Amex, Diners, Visa
P Frosdam Street car park   **WC**

Pop videos and 1960s decor in this agreeable American-style diner located just a minute's walk from the cathedral. Meaty burgers are cooked to order as requested; coleslaw is home-made and crunchy; apple pie and cheesecake are also produced on the premises. Besides the six varieties of burger there are spare ribs, fish dishes, burritos and tostados, plus some calorific sweets. Indifferent chips and coffee. *No dogs.*

Chichester   *Chats Brasserie*

Unit 5, Sharp Garland House, Eastgate
Chichester (0243) 783223
Map 6 B4 *West Sussex*

Open 9.30–4 (Sat till 5.30)
Closed Sun & Bank Holidays

Quiche & salad 95p   Coronation chicken £1.95
LVs
P Priory car park   **WC**

Open sandwiches, topped with tasty combinations like smoked trout and horseradish mayonnaise or cottage cheese with walnuts provide tasty, satisfying snacks at this bright little place. Also on the menu are soup and pâté, salads and quiche, with a blackboard selection of hot and cold specials and good home-baked cakes. Non-smoking section. *No dogs.* ✎

Chichester   ★   *Clinch's Salad House*

14 Southgate
Chichester (0243) 788822
Map 6 B4 *West Sussex*

Open 8–5.30
Closed Sun & Bank Holidays

Celery & onion crêpe £1.55   Dutch apple pie 65p
LVs
P Avenue de Chartres car park   **WC**

Apart from ham and the occasional fish dish, this neat little self-service restaurant is strictly vegetarian, but whatever your inclination, it's a real must for discerning eaters. The food is quite beautifully prepared – a lovely light apple, cheese and onion flan, potato salad with a gentle lift of chives, lentil rissoles with yoghurt sauce and, for sweet tooths, a spot-on summer pudding. The choice is best at lunchtime. Non-smoking area. ✎

Chichester   *Nicodemus*

14 Eastgate Square
Chichester (0243) 787521
Map 6 B4 *West Sussex*

Open 12–2 & 7–10.30 (till 10 in winter)
Closed Mon lunch, all Sun & Bank Holidays

Crespolini con pollo £2.95   Home-made ices 85p

P Cattle Market car park   **WC**

Capable cooking and speedy, smiling service characterise this bustling Italian restaurant near the cattle market. There's plenty to choose from, including pizza and pasta, crespolini with chicken, marinated mushrooms and various meat and fish main courses. Home-made ices and strawberries in red wine among the sweets. Booking is advisable Friday and Saturday evenings, when there's a £5 minimum charge. Carefully chosen wines. *No dogs.*

Chichester   *St Martin's Tea Rooms*

St Martin's Street
Chichester (0243) 786715
Map 6 B4 *West Sussex*

Open 10–6
Closed Sun, Mon, Bank Holidays & 2 weeks
Christmas

Nut roast with salad £2   Fish pie £2

P St Martin's Square car park   &   WC

It's virtually meatless at this traditional but
health-conscious tea room with its own
delightful garden. The menu is quite short
and simple, with a delicious soup to start,
then sandwiches, a first-class Welsh rarebit
and daily specials like prawn salad or nut
roast with Madeira sauce. Scones, shortbread, vegan cake and a few other new-
baked pastries are available. Note freshly
squeezed orange and grapefruit juice. No
smoking. *No dogs.* 🐾

Chichester   *Savourie*

38 Little London
Chichester (0243) 784899
Map 6 B4 *West Sussex*

Open noon–2 & 7–10
Closed Sun, Mon & 25 & 26 December

Cod & prawn au gratin £2.95   Chicken in curry
apricot sauce £3.25
Credit Access, Amex, Diners, Visa
P St Martin's car park opposite   WC

This spacious, attractive establishment
above the more formal Little London restaurant has a comfortable bar and its own patio
for clement days. The frequently changed
menu offers an imaginative selection that
embraces cold choices like mushrooms with
smoked cheese in garlic mayonnaise and
crab and prawn quiche as well as tasty hot
specials such as pork casserole normande.
Simple sweets from the trolley. Book for
after-theatre suppers. *No dogs.*

Chipping Campden   *Bantam Tea Room*

High Street
Evesham (0386) 840386
Map 5 A2 *Gloucestershire*

Open 9.30–5.15 (Sun from 3)
Closed Mon in winter & 25 December

Quiche with salad £2.55   Cream tea £1.50

P The Square   WC

It's hard to resist the window of this pretty
high-street tea shop with its luscious display
of florentines, truffles, shortbreads and fresh
cream gâteaux. Lunchtime brings quiche,
pâté, salads and omelettes, with soup, jacket
potatoes and Welsh rarebit providing winter
warmth. Set teas only after 3.30 (3 in
summer). Charming service deserves a special mention. *No dogs.* 🍵

Chipping Campden   *Kings Arms Hotel, Saddle Room*

The Square
Evesham (0386) 840256
Map 5 A2 *Gloucestershire*

Open 12–2
Closed Sun & 2 weeks January

Black pudding with mustard sauce £2.95
Fruit crumble 95p
Credit Access, Visa
P The Square   WC

The panelled lounge bar and the walled
garden are equally agreeable settings to take
time out for lunch. A home-made soup with
croûtons heads the menu, followed by light
snacks (Welsh rarebit, baked sardines, spinach quiche) and more substantial items such
as guinea fowl casserole, lamb curry or a
massive helping of chunky steak and kidney
pie. Classic puddings to finish. Courteous,
efficient staff. *No dogs.* 🍵

Chipping Norton *New Entry*

Nutters

10 New Street
Chipping Norton (0608) 41995
Map 5 A2 *Oxfordshire*

Open 10–4.30
Closed Sun, Mon & 3 days Christmas

Beef in red wine £1.75   Chocolate fudge cake
with honey yoghurt 85p

P tourist office car park & **WC**

Owned and run by Elizabeth Arnold, this attractive self-service restaurant has a delightful walled garden. The food is fresh and wholesome and the emphasis is on healthy eating: scones made with wholemeal flour, vegan fat-free cake, crisp, colourful salads and lunchtime hot dishes that range from a gentle vegetarian curry with brown rice to beef in red wine. Sweets include a delicious raspberry and apple crumble. Most tables are non-smoking. *No dogs.* 🐾

Chislehurst

Mrs Bridges' Kitchen

49 Chislehurst Road
01-467 2150
Map 6 C3 *Kent*

Open 8–2 (Sat from 9)
Closed Sun, Bank Holidays & 10 days
Christmas

Chicken casserole £1.90   Mixed grill £2.45
LVs *Credit* Access, Visa
P street parking **WC**

An honest and unpretentious little place where the emphasis is on simple, satisfying dishes based on good fresh produce. Farmhouse breakfasts fuel early birds, while lunchtime brings omelettes, grills and bumper toasted sandwiches, plus salads, ploughman's and a caveman's lunch with home-cooked gammon. Chicken casserole served in a tomato sauce is another popular item. *No dogs.*

Christchurch

Salads

8 High Street
Christchurch (0202) 476273
Map 6 A4 *Dorset*

Open 10–3
Closed Sat, Sun, Bank Holidays, 2 weeks
February & 2 weeks Christmas

Cheese flan 70p   Yoghurt lemon sponge 90p
LVs
P Sainsburys car park & **WC**

Miss Cameron and Miss Simmons take justifiable pride in their bright, leafy wholefood restaurant, where eating healthily is a positive pleasure. From well-dressed salads to creamy wholemeal flans, delicious soups to imaginative sandwiches and speciality breads like aniseed with turmeric, everything is freshly made and full of positive flavour. Ginger cake or raspberry and apple flan makes a super finish with an aromatic cuppa. Unlicensed. No smoking. *No dogs.* 🐾

Cirencester

Brewery Coffee Shop

Brewery Court
Cirencester (0285) 4791
Map 6 A3 *Gloucestershire*

Open 10–5.30
Closed Sun, Good Fri & Christmas–New Year

Cheesy leek & pasta bake £2.15   Chicken,
mushroom & vegetable pie £2.45
P Brewery car park **WC**

A tempting counter display rivals the attractions of the artwork displayed on the walls of this busy coffee shop next to a crafts complex. Tuck into home-baked scones, cakes and pastries throughout the day, or drop in for lunch when the menu offers soups, pâtés and quiches, hot dishes like cheesy leek and pasta bake, plus healthy salads. Fresh fruit salad or cheesecake to finish. Minimum lunchtime charge £1.50. *No dogs.*

Cirencester — *Fleece Hotel, Shepherds Wine Bar*

Market Place
Cirencester (0285) 68507
Map 6 A3 *Gloucestershire*

Open 12.15–2.15 & 7–10
Closed 25 December

Gruyère & smoked bacon tart £2.75   Bread & butter pudding £1.25
Credit Access, Amex, Diners, Visa
P own car park   &   **WC**

A town-centre wine bar across the courtyard from the hotel, which was once a coaching inn. A varied menu offers soup of the day and a range of dishes running from Gruyère and smoked bacon tart to prawns with mayonnaise, a platter of smoked salmon trout and chicken, ham and mushroom pie. There's also a noteworthy selection of English cheeses and a fine wine list. The cooking is not quite what it was, and service needs sharpening up. *No dogs.*

Clacton-on-Sea — *Montague Hill China Cup Café*

17 Orwell Road
Clacton-on-Sea (0255) 425463
Map 5 D2 *Essex*

Open 9–4.30 (Wed till 1.30)
Closed Bank Holidays

Toasted cheese & tomato sandwich 88p
Ham salad £1.35

P street parking   &

Mr Wilkinson's charm and his wife's home baking skills are a winning combination at this modest little café. As well as a splendid assortment of gâteaux, there are lovely scones, flapjacks, slices and sponges – all delicious with your choice from the outstanding range of teas and coffees offered. Savouries include soups, salads and simple snacks on toast like perfectly scrambled eggs. Unlicensed.

Clare — *Peppermill Restaurant*

Market Place, Market Hill
Clare (0787) 278148
Map 5 C2 *Suffolk*

Open 11–4.30 May–Oct, 12–2 Oct–May
Closed Sun & Mon

Potato, ham & cheese bake £2.25
Cheesecake 85p
Credit Access, Amex, Diners, Visa
P in square   **WC**

A delightful little restaurant in a corner of the market place. There's a good selection of carefully prepared snacks, including scones, sausage rolls, omelettes, salads and jacket potatoes, and at lunchtime a full menu is offered, with main dishes like beef curry or pork in cider. There's also some enjoyable home baking, and afternoon tea is a summer attraction. Full evening meals by arrangement. *No dogs.*

Clare — *Ship Stores*

22 Callis Street
Clare (0787) 277834
Map 5 C2 *Suffolk*

Open 10–6
Closed 25 December

Ploughman's lunch 90p   Set afternoon tea 75p

P street parking   &   **WC**

The village store at Clare has a tiny tea room, simple and cottagy in style, where Mrs Kies bakes most of the items on offer. Her Irish barm brack is full of fruity flavour, and there are wholemeal cheese or plain fruit scones, lovely tea breads like moist date and walnut and always a super dark, rich chocolate gâteau. A few savouries are also served. Unlicensed. *No dogs.*

237

Cliftonville   *Batchelor's Pâtisserie*

246 Northdown Road, Near Margate
Thanet (0843) 221227
Map 6 D3 *Kent*

Open 8.30–5.30
Closed Sun, Mon, Bank Holidays & 3 weeks
Christmas

Truffle torte 55p   Carrot cake 55p
P street parking & Harold Road car park &

Situated in a parade of shops, this neat
establishment is run in fine, professional
style by Franz and Janet Ottiger. His baking
skills cover a wide range, from really delicious
Danish pastries and Eccles cakes to a classic
Bünder Nuss torte from his native Switzer-
land. On the savoury side, quiche and
coleslaw is a popular snack, along with filled
rolls and toasted sandwiches. Unlicensed.
No dogs. 🍵

Clitheroe   *The Castle*

Station Road
Clitheroe (0200) 24442
Map 3 B3 *Lancashire*

Open noon–2 & 7–10.30 (Fri & Sat till 11, Sun
till 10)
Closed 1 January & 25 & 26 December
Pizza pescatore £2.50   Chicken à la crème
£4.25
LVs   *Credit* Access, Amex, Diners, Visa
P own car park & **WC**

Close to Clitheroe Castle, this is a smartly
contemporary restaurant with decent cooking and very good service led by a first-rate
manageress. Baked egg with sweetcorn and
hot buttered shrimps are typical appetisers,
to be followed by pizza, pasta pancakes or
specialities such as halibut Marie Rose, beef
casserole or chargrilled chicken with a spicy
tomato sauce. Italian ices, various cakes and
cheeses. *No dogs.* ☕

Cockermouth   ★ *New Entry*   *Quince & Medlar*

13 Castlegate
Cockermouth (0900) 823579
Map 3 B1 *Cumbria*

Open 7pm–9.30pm (Fri & Sat till 10)
Closed Sun, Mon & Bank Holidays

Seed & nut bake £4.60   Spinach & cream
cheese nut crumble £3.80
Credit Access, Visa
P street or Market Place car park **WC**

Next to Cockermouth Castle, this well-run
vegetarian restaurant offers wholesome,
high-quality eating in a quiet, candelit setting.
The mouthwatering menus change monthly:
typical dishes include apple and peanut soup,
baked courgettes with rosemary and a Parmesan crumble top, curried mixed vegetables and a super seed and nut bake with
tomato and celery or Stilton and mushroom
sauce. End memorably with a marvellous
lemon cheesecake. No smoking. ☕ 🍵

Cockermouth   *Wythop Mill*

Embleton
Bassenthwaite Lake (059 681) 394
Map 3 B1 *Cumbria*
Open 10.30–5.30, also 6.30–8.30 Thurs; Nov–
Jan Sat & Sun 10.30–4.30, also 7–9 Fri & Sat
Closed Mon & end Oct–Easter except
weekends Nov–Jan
Vegetable lasagne with garlic bread £2.80
Blackcurrant & apple nutty crumble with cream
85p
P own car park **WC**

A mother and daughter team are responsible
for the excellent home cooking at this gleaming tea room in a converted sawmill. Their
super scones and cakes are delicious with
tea or coffee, and at lunchtime you can tuck
into cheesy baked potatoes, pasta, soups
and savoury flans, with lovely nutty crumble
to finish. Bookings only for the evening.
Minimum lunchtime charge £2. No smoking.
No dogs. 🍵

Colchester   *Bistro Nine*

9 North Hill
Colchester (0206) 576466
Map 5 D2 *Essex*

Open 12–2 & 7–10.45
Closed Sun, Mon & 1 week Christmas

Hot dish of the day £2   Entrecôte steak £6
Credit Access, Visa

P NCP off Stockwell St   **WC**

New owners are maintaining good standards at this neat, cosy bistro near the town centre. The downstairs menu offers snacks such as cheddar, Brie or Stilton ploughman's, quiche, honey-baked ham and filled jacket potatoes. Upstairs there's a wider and more expensive choice, with main dishes like poached salmon, pepperpot beef and venison pie. Both menus provide an enjoyable vegetarian special and tempting sweets. *No dogs.* ☺

Collier Street   *Butcher's Mere*

Near Marden
Collier Street (089 273) 495
Map 6 C3 *Kent*

Open 10–7 (Thurs from 2)
Closed Mon-Fri mid November–March

Cream tea £1.75   Meringue & tea £1.75

P own car park   **WC**

An enchanting little place – delightful cottage tea room inside, outside a charming garden beside a reed-bordered duck pond. Louise Holmes is renowned for her excellent teas with well-risen scones accompanied by thick cream and super home-made preserves, chocolate and coffee logs, meringues and lovely light chocolate sponge cake. Lunchtime brings omelettes accompanied by simple fresh salads. Unlicensed. No smoking. *No dogs.* 🍵

Compton   *New Entry*   *Old Congregational Tea Shop*

Near Guildford
Guildford (0483) 810682
Map 6 B3 *Surrey*

Open 10.30–5.30
Closed Mon (except Bank Holidays), Tues, 25 & 26 December & 1 week Christmas

Welsh rarebit 85p   Coffee & walnut cake 55p

P street parking   **WC**

Sally Porter's home and tea shop was once a Congregational Church and stands on the B3000 half a mile from the A3 and just three miles from Guildford. The menu could hardly be simpler: tea, coffee and soft drinks to accompany gorgeous scones served with thick cream and lovely home-made jam (the kind according to what fruits are available); delicious home-baked cakes and cheesecake; soup; Welsh rarebit; toasted sandwiches. Unlicensed. 🍵

Congleton   ★ *Odd Fellows Wine Bar & Bistro*

20 Rood Hill
Congleton (0260) 270243
Map 4 C4 *Cheshire*

Open noon–2 & 6.45–11 (Fri & Sat from 6.30), Sun 7–10.30
Closed Sun lunch, Bank Holiday Mons & 25–27 December
French onion soup £1.65   Beef in garlic £4.85
Credit Amex
P street parking   &. **WC**

The Kirkham brothers really care about food at this splendidly characterful establishment, combining the finest of ingredients with a truly catholic span of dishes. Our mushroom soup and pinkly tender beef au poivre were masterpieces of subtle flavour; other choices range from Mexican pork casserole to fondues and superb salads based on such delights as herrings in Madeira sauce. Marvellously indulgent desserts, too. Children not allowed except in the bistro at lunchtimes. *No dogs.* ☺

Coniston
Bridge House Café

Coniston (0966) 41278
Map 3 B2 *Cumbria*

Open 10–5
Closed end October–March except weekends in February

Ham sandwich with salad garnish £1.10   Fruit cake 50p

P village car park   &   **WC**

The pavement and the courtyard are pleasant for snacking in the sun, and inside it's cheerful and cottagy. Mrs Durston produces an abundance of good baking, including spicy fruit cake, flapjacks, banana bread and king-size gâteaux. Toasted snacks, quiche and ravioli feature among the savoury choice, along with salads, bumper sandwiches and a more substantial daily special such as hot pot with red cabbage. *No dogs.*

Corse Lawn ★
Corse Lawn House

Tirley (045 278) 479
Map 7 D2 *Gloucestershire*

Open noon–2 & 7–10
Closed 25 & 26 December

Grilled queen scallops stuffed with garlic £4.20
Stuffed avocado pear £3.30

Credit Access, Amex, Diners, Visa
P own car park   &   **WC**

Baba Hine is a true artist in the kitchen and the food served in the lounge bar of this lovingly converted coaching inn is nothing short of magnificent. Deceptively simple dishes – Mediterranean fish soup, terrine of vegetables, marvellous shellfish platter, turkey pancake with tarragon and saffron – are feasts of flavour and eye appeal, and Baba's sweets (including blueberry shortcake and rhubarb sorbet) make a superb finale. Splendid service. ✆

Coventry ★ `New Entry`
Trinity House Hotel, Herbs

28 Lower Holyhead Road
Coventry (0203) 555654
Map 5 A2 *West Midlands*

Open 6.30pm–9.30pm
Closed Sun, Bank Holidays & 24 December–5 January

Pine nut loaf £3.95   Vegetable lasagne £3.85

P street parking   **WC**

Robert Jackson takes vegetarian cooking to gourmet heights in the restaurant of a small city-centre hotel. Superbly fresh, high-quality ingredients are used throughout, and the menu changes often enough to keep regulars (even some non-vegetarians) returning. Typical dishes include curried vegetable pâté; herby stuffed pine nut loaf; cracked wheat, pineapple and pepper salad; delicious peach and kiwi fruit fool. No smoking. *No dogs.*

Croydon
Hockneys

98 High Street
01-688 2899
Map 6 C3 *Surrey*

Open noon–10.30
Closed Sun, Mon, Bank Holidays, 2 weeks August & 2 weeks Christmas
Spicy mushroom soup £1 (£1.55 eve)
Lasagne £3.10 (£3.75 eve)
LVs *Credit* Access, Amex, Diners, Visa
P NCP at rear   **WC**

A friendly vegetarian restaurant with counter service till 5.30, then table service and slightly higher prices. The well-chosen menu includes starters such as houmus or gazpacho; quiches, falafels and vegeburgers; salads; and main dishes like spinach lasagne or gado gado. Lots of tempting cakes and sweets, including a superb rum and raisin parfait. Book for dinner. Unlicensed, so bring your own wine (£1.35 corkage per bottle). No smoking. *No dogs.* ✆

Croydon   *Munbhave*

305 London Road, West Croydon
01-689 6331
Map 6 C3 *Surrey*

Open 6pm–11pm (Sat till midnight)
Closed Mon, 1 January, 25 & 26 December & 2 weeks summer

Stuffed aubergine £3.85   Masala dhosa £3.95
Credit Access, Visa
P street parking   &   **WC**

This friendly family-run restaurant specialises in the Gujarati style of Indian vegetarian cooking. Accurate spicing enhances good fresh flavours through a range that includes samosas, bhajias, puris and masala dhosa (pancake filled with mixed vegetables and served with a yoghurt and spice sauce, green chutney and coconut). Whole stuffed aubergine is a speciality, and thalis (set meals) provide a well-balanced selection of dishes. *No dogs.*

Croydon   *Wine Vaults*

122 North End
01-680 2419
Map 6 C3 *Surrey*

Open 11.30–3 & 5.30–10.30 (Fri & Sat till 11)
Closed Sun & Bank Holidays

Dish of prawns £1.55   Charcoal-grilled rib of beef £5.20
Credit Access, Amex, Diners, Visa
P Whitgift Centre car park   **WC**

Atmospheric cellar wine bar with sawdust, candles and huge casks of port and sherry on show. You can nibble at shell-on prawns or a plate of toasted anchovy fingers or tuck into a generous charcoal-grilled steak; there's also excellent ham, tongue or beef to enjoy with salad or in a sandwich. Finish with prime Stilton or perhaps apple pie with cream. *No dogs.*

Dartington   ★ *Cranks Health Food Restaurant*

Shinners Bridge, Near Totnes
Totnes (0803) 862388
Map 8 C4 *Devon*

Open 10–5
Closed Sun (except in summer), 1 January, Good Fri & 2–3 days Christmas

Vegetable crumble £2.75   Apricot slice 60p
LVs
P own parking   **WC**

Part of the Dartington Cider Mill complex, this self-service restaurant is stocked with the vegetarian goodies for which Cranks is renowned. The savoury selection is particularly light and appetising, from pepper quiche and lentil-based salads to a delicious vegetable crumble. Wholesome sweet treats include carob slice and fresh fruit trifle. Minimum lunchtime charge £2. There's a patio for summer snacking in the sun. Non-smoking area. *No dogs.*

Dedham   *Essex Rose Tea House*

Royal Square
Colchester (0206) 323101
Map 5 D2 *Essex*

Open 9–6
Closed 3 days Christmas

Crab salad £3.50   Cream tea £1.80

P street parking   &   **WC**

With its old beams and lattice windows, this is the very model of a traditional village tea house. It's a convivial place that really pulls in the crowds, especially for the delicious afternoon teas with scones and a selection of fresh cream gâteaux. Lunchtime fare comprises made-to-order sandwiches and cold cuts served with fresh salad. Service is friendly and willing. *No dogs.*

Dent   *Dent Crafts Centre*

Helmside, Near Sedbergh
Dent (058 75) 400
Map 3 B2 *Cumbria*

Open 10.30–5.30
Closed Mon & Christmas–Easter

Pizza 89p   Wholemeal scone with jam &
cream 45p

P own car park   **WC**

An old barn, set in lovely countryside, has
been turned into a really delightful crafts
centre. In a flagstoned area surrounded by
country craft work are a counter and a few
tables, where snackers can enjoy an excellent cup of tea and something to eat. Date
slice, walnut cake and wholemeal scones are
part of a small pastry selection, and for
savoury tastes there's a generously topped
pizza, with perhaps an appetising soup at
weekends. No smoking. 🖤

Derby   *Lettuce Leaf*

21 Friar Gate
Derby (0332) 40307
Map 4 C4 *Derbyshire*

Open 10–7.30
Closed Sun & Bank Holidays

Vegetables provençale £1.80   Cream tea
£1.20
LVs
P Friar Gate car park   **WC**

An unpretentious little wholefood restaurant
where a blackboard lists daily specialities
like celery hot pot and marrow provençale. In
addition, the standard menu offers a variety
of savoury snacks such as omelettes, flans
and grills, salads, toasties and open sandwiches. Choose your cakes, scones and
biscuits from the tempting counter display –
and don't miss the delicious individual lemon
meringue pies. *No dogs.*

Devizes   ★   **New Entry**   *Wiltshire Kitchen*

11 St John's Street
Devizes (0380) 4840
Map 6 A3 *Wiltshire*

Open 9.30–5.30
Closed Sunday, Bank Holidays & 1 week
Christmas

Chicken in orange sauce £3   Walnut & lemon
meringue gâteau 75p
P station car park & street parking   **WC**

Everything is home produced and of superb
quality at Ann Blunden's neat restaurant in
an old tile-hung building near the town hall.
Roulades are something of a speciality (super
seafood, chocolate, raspberry and lemon),
and other temptations – the choice changes
constantly – range from cheese scones and
monster meringues to spinach and mushroom lasagne and chicken in orange sauce.
No smoking. *No dogs.* 🖤

Dodd Wood   *Old Sawmill*

Underskiddaw, Near Keswick
Keswick (0596) 74317
Map 3 B1 *Cumbria*

Open 10.30–5.30
Closed end October–2 weeks before Easter

Cumberland ham salad £2.70   Toasted
sandwiches £1

P own car park   ♿

The food may be simple, but what they do
they do very well at this tea room, a former
sawmill with views of Bassenthwaite Lake.
Woodman's lunch – cheddar and Cheshire
cheese with French bread and pickles – is a
popular order, and there are good sandwiches (plain or toasted), soup and salads.
On the sweet half of the menu are home-
baked scones, cakes and apple pie. Unlicensed. No smoking. *No dogs.* 🍵

Dorchester   *Potter In*

19 Durngate Street
Dorchester (0305) 68649
Map 8 D3 *Dorset*

Open 10–5
Closed Sun & Bank Holidays

Pork in cider £2.50   Carob brownie 40p

Credit Access, Visa
P Ackland Road car park   **WC**

Those who know about this friendly little self-service restaurant don't so much potter as flock in. From opening time a selection of baking, including splendid cider cake, can be had with a good cup of tea, while the savoury of tooth can tuck into pizza, seafood quiche or the hot lunchtime special – usually a hearty casserole. There's a fine array of interesting salads such as pickled cabbage with ginger and mushrooms with coriander, plus some tempting sweets. ☕ 🍵

Dorking   *Burford Bridge Hotel Lounge*

Box Hill
Dorking (0306) 884561
Map 6 B3 *Surrey*

Open noon–10.30

Set afternoon tea £6.25   Roast beef & horseradish sandwich £2

LVs   *Credit* Access, Amex, Diners, Visa
P own car park   **WC**

A comfortably elegant lounge in a rambling hotel at the foot of Box Hill. Home-made cakes, scones and biscuits are delicious at any time of day, while well-filled sandwiches (smoked salmon, roast beef, turkey) and a three-cheese platter with pickles and apple provide tasty savoury snacks. There's a particularly wide range of herbal teas, and set teas are served every afternoon. ☕ 🍵

Dorstone   *Pump House Tea Room*

Golden Valley
Peterchurch (098 16) 438
Map 7 D2 *Hereford & Worcester*

Open 10–12.30 & 2.30–5.30
Closed Wed & Christmas–mid February

Cream horn with jam 55p   Hot Welsh cake with butter 30p

P own car park   ♿ **WC**

Tea room and crafts shop combine in the nicest possible way in this delightful country setting, where an excellent brew accompanies a good selection of super home baking. Fruit scones and wholemeal honey scones, shortbread biscuits and sliced loaf cake are among the favourites, and the lovely apple pies use home-grown fruit. The room features comfortable pine furnishings and old oak beams, and there's a pleasant cottage garden. Unlicensed. No smoking. 🍵

Dunster   *Tea Shoppe*

3 High Street
Dunster (0643) 821304
Map 8 C3 *Somerset*

Open 9–6
Closed 3 January–14 March, also weekdays 14 March–4 April & 1 November–18 December & 25 December
Fisherman's casserole £1.85   Local sausages with jacket potato £2.40
P street parking   ♿ **WC**

A red-brick facade hides a 500-year history at this delightful village tea shop, where the Bradshaws regale customers with a splendid selection of home-cooked fare. The cake table groans under its mouthwatering display, while from the kitchen come treacle tart, hot bread pudding and many other sweet treats. Tasty lunchtime savouries include quiche, vegetable casserole and herb or garlic pork sausages. 🍵

243

Eardisland — *Elms*

Leominster
Pembridge (05447) 405
Map 7 D1 *Hereford & Worcester*

Open 2.30–5.30 (July & August till 6)
Closed Sun in June & September–Spring Bank Holiday except Easter

Cream tea £1.26   Farmhouse tea £1.90

P own car park   **WC**

Mary Johnson not only runs the farm and the guest house, but turns her hand to some good, old-fashioned home baking for this spotless little tea room. The formula is simple – a cream tea with plain scones, home-made jam and whipped cream, or the farmhouse version with bread and butter, wholemeal fruit scones, moist, dark fruit cake and nice light Victorian sandwich. Unlicensed. No smoking. *No dogs.*

Easingwold — *Truffles*

Snowdon House, Spring Street
Easingwold (0347) 22342
Map 4 C2 *North Yorkshire*

Open 9–5.30 (Sat till 5)
Closed Sun & Mon (except some Bank Holiday weekends), 1 January & 25 & 26 December

Vegetarian pancake £1.75   Cream tea 95p
P street parking   ♿   **WC**

A warm welcome is guaranteed at this attractive, pine-furnished coffee shop, and you can also bank on some enjoyable eating. Appetising snacks of brown or white bread sandwiches and toasties, salads, cakes and sweets are available all day, and there are set afternoon teas (cream or full). Lunchtime brings a wider savoury choice, with hot dishes ranging from omelettes and stir-fry vegetables to curried prawns and minute steak Rossini. *No dogs.*

East Budleigh — *Grasshoppers*

16 High Street
Budleigh Salterton (039 54) 2774
Map 8 C4 *Devon*

Open 10–5.30
Closed Mon (except Bank Holidays), 25 & 26 December, 1 week May Day Bank Holiday & 2 weeks mid October
Budleigh fish pie £2.15   Treacle tart with clotted cream £1.10
P car park in side street opposite   **WC**

Festooned with flowers, this delightful little gift and tea shop is a lovely place to pause for a snack. Home-baked cakes and pastries slip down a treat with a good cup of tea, and lunchtime savouries include jacket potatoes, devilled kidneys and fish pie. Salads all day; super sweets like treacle tart, apricot sponge pudding and steamed jam roly poly. Unlicensed. No smoking.

East Molesey — **New Entry** — *Langan's Bar & Grill*

3 Palace Gate Parade, Hampton Court
01-979 7891
Map 6 B3 *Surrey*
Open noon–2.30 & 7–11 (Fri & Sat till 11.30, Sun till 10.30)
Closed 25 & 26 December
Scallops wrapped in bacon with béarnaise sauce £3.20   Rosettes of pork with apple & Calvados £5.75
Credit Access, Amex, Diners, Visa
P in Palace Gate Parade   **WC**

Located just a stone's throw from the Thames at Hampton Court Bridge, this smart bar and grill will serve anything from a single course to a full meal. The menu's an interesting one, running from baked eggs with sherried chicken livers to T-bone steak béarnaise, Cumberland sausages with onion sauce and poached salmon with a lovely sauce of morels. Super fresh vegetables; delicious sweets; cheeseboard. *No dogs.*

East Molesey
Superfish

90 Walton Road
01-979 2432
Map 6 B3 *Surrey*

Open 11.30–2 (Sat till 2.30) & 5.30–11 (Fri &
Sat 5–11.30)
Closed Sun

Cod & chips £2.85   Scampi & chips £3.50
LVs
P public car park to rear   &   **WC**

Aptly named, for the fish is indeed super at
this bright, cheerful restaurant in a parade of
shops. Traditional favourites like cod, plaice
and haddock are beautifully cooked and
served with smashing chips, good pickles
and a basket full of lovely hot French bread.
Scampi, sole, skate and rock are also available, and there are nice ices to finish. Friendly
waiting staff. *No dogs.* 🐶

Eastbourne
★
Byrons

6 Crown Street, Old Town
Eastbourne (0323) 20171
Map 6 C4 *East Sussex*
Open 12.30pm–1.30pm
Closed Sat lunch, all Sun, Bank Holidays & 1
week Christmas

Chicken & herb terrine £2.25   Pot au feu £3.60
Credit Amex, Diners, Visa

P street parking   **WC**

Strong-willed regulars often opt for one dish
only at this tiny bohemian bistro, but Simon
Scrutton's French-inspired menu is so tempting that it's difficult to stop at the duck rillettes
and ratatouille. Dishes like pot au feu, an-
chovy-stuffed beef parcels and lamb's kidneys in mustard sauce are all delicious, and
there are some faultless sweets, too. Booking essential. More elaborate evening meals.
No children under eight. *No dogs.* 🍴

Eastbourne
Ceres Health Food Restaurant

38a Ashford Road
Eastbourne (0323) 28482
Map 6 C4 *East Sussex*

Open 9.30–5
Closed Sun & Bank Holidays

Cheese, tomato & mushroom savoury £1.26
Dutch apple cake 75p
LVs
P Junction Road multi-storey car park   **WC**

This light, spacious healthfood restaurant is
located above a garage next to the railway
station. The new owner plans to add some
fish dishes and perhaps white meat to a
vegetarian menu that offers items such as
cheese, pepper and tomato flan, Scotch eggs
and a good nut roast served with mushroom
sauce. Sweet things include various slices
and a nice banana and raspberry crumble.
Self-service. Unlicensed. Non-smoking area.
No dogs. 🍴 🐶

Eastbourne
★
Nature's Way

196 Terminus Road
Eastbourne (0323) 643211
Map 6 C4 *East Sussex*

Open 9.30–5
Closed Sun, Mon, Bank Holidays (except
Good Fri), 1 week March–April, 1 week
November & 1 week Christmas
Leek & macaroni bake £1.60   Nutty log 40p
LVs
P Trinity Trees multi-storey car park   **WC**

Pine, plants, self-service counter, blackboard
menu – the surroundings are pretty typical of
a vegetarian restaurant, but the food is way
above average. Mr and Mrs Fossitt share the
cooking, ringing the changes daily among
hot pots, nut loaves and rissoles, pizza pie
and quiches. A range of salads accompanies
these, and for sweet there are nice things
like sherry trifle and nutty log. Unlicensed.
No smoking. *No dogs.* 🍴 🐶

Eastleigh   *Piccolo Mondo*

1 High Street
Eastleigh (0703) 613180
Map 6 A4 *Hampshire*
Open noon–2.30 & 6.30–11 (Thurs–Sat till
midnight)
Closed Sun & Bank Holidays
Vitello all'ucelletto £5.65   Tonno e fagioli
£2.50
LVs   *Credit* Access, Amex, Diners, Visa
P multi-storey car park in Southampton Road
♿ **WC**

Authentic Italian cooking in spacious, comfortable surroundings is the appealing formula at this popular trattoria. An appetising
range of pizzas, pasta, veal and chicken
dishes is supplemented by deliciously different specialities like herby home-made sausages, served with tasty tomato sauce.
Worthy of investigation, too, is the splendid
club-sandwich with mortadella, mozzarella
and anchovies. Super ice creams and espresso to finish. *No dogs.*

Easton Grey   *Easton Grey Garden Restaurant*

Easton Grey House, Near Malmesbury
Malmesbury (0666) 840345
Map 7 D2 *Wiltshire*

Open 10.30–5.30
Closed Sun, Good Fri & 10 days Christmas

Toasted sandwich £2.50   Lasagne with salad
£2.75

P own car park ♿ **WC**

Teas, coffees and lunches are served
throughout the day at this stylish boutique-
cum-restaurant in the grounds of Easton
Grey House. The home-baked cakes, scones
and shortbread are a delight, and there are
sandwiches (regular, open or toasted),
salads and hot dishes such as chicken à la
crème or ravioli topped with melted cheese.
Tempting sweets, too, including sherry trifle
and waffles. *No dogs.* ☃ ❤

Edenbridge   *Buffin's Restaurant*

95 High Street
Edenbridge (0732) 863938
Map 6 C3 *Kent*

Open 10–2
Closed Sun, Mon, 1 January & 25 & 26
December
Escalope of veal £2.50   Banana & rum gâteau
90p
Credit Access, Amex, Diners, Visa
P Church Street car park **WC**

Located on the main street, this black-
beamed restaurant has a warm, homely feel.
In the morning you can tuck into a traditional
English breakfast or enjoy a teacake, a
Danish pastry or Black Forest gâteau. Omelettes are also available, and from noon there
are main courses such as grilled plaice, lamb
cutlets, a salad or the day's roast. There are
more elaborate evening meals and a traditional Sunday lunch. Half-portions available.
No dogs. ☃

Edensor   *Stables Tea Rooms*

Edensor Post Office
Baslow (024 688) 2283
Map 4 C4 *Derbyshire*

Open 10.30–5.30 (till 4 in winter)
Closed Tues (except Easter, spring & summer
school holidays), 1 January, 25 & 26
December, also Sat December–end February

Cream tea £1.60   Full afternoon tea £2.25
P own car park ♿

The Walkers are delightful hosts at this neat
little tea room that is part of the village post
office and shop (the church spire is your
marker for the location). The main offerings
are a Derbyshire cream tea, with lovely
scones, jam and cream, and a full afternoon
tea, with the addition of sandwiches and a
cake. Individual tea items also available, plus
soup, cheese and biscuits, fresh cream trifle.
Unlicensed.

Elland ★ *Bertie's Bistro*

7 Town Hall Buildings
Halifax (0422) 71724
Map 4 C3 *West Yorkshire*

Open 7pm–11pm, Sun 5–9.30
Closed Mon, 1 January & 25 & 26 December

Stilton & bacon croquettes £1.45   Poached salmon with watercress & scampi sauce £5.95

P Town Hall car park & WC

A very well-run bistro decorated in Victorian style, with cooking by Michael Swallows that is both skilled and imaginative. A tempting choice of starters might include chicken and spinach terrine or delicious mushroom and walnut soup, while among the main dishes could be moussaka, goulash, vegetarian lasagne or poached salmon with a lovely watercress and scampi sauce. Sweets are equally enticing – try Bertie's bombe or white wine syllabub. *No dogs.* ☺

Emsworth `New Entry` *Cloisters*

40 North Street
Emsworth (0243) 373390
Map 6 B4 *Hampshire*

Open 10–5
Closed Sun & 25 & 26 December

Fish cakes with tomato sauce £1.95   Scones, jam & cream 60p

P street parking & North Street car park WC

Anna Warburton, sometime English teacher, runs this charmingly informal restaurant, a cottage room with a little conservatory that leads to a peaceful, pretty garden. Home-prepared snacks, available throughout the day, span a wide range, from sandwiches and toasties to soup, omelettes, filled baked potatoes, lamb chops and a tasty fish pie. Also scones and a few cakes; sweets include cheesecake and pancakes. Unlicensed.

Eton *Eton Wine Bar*

82 High Street
Windsor (0753) 854921
Map 6 B3 *Berkshire*

Open noon–2.30 & 6–11, Sun noon–2 & 7–10
Closed Easter Sun & 3–4 days Christmas

Chicken, ham & pepper cocotte £4.25   Veal & almond casserole with turmeric rice £4.75
Credit Access, Visa
P high street car park & WC

The blackboard menu in this neat, pine-furnished wine bar shows a short selection of imaginative, well-prepared dishes. Cauliflower and cress soup and smoked salmon and spinach mousse are typical starters, preceding main courses like chicken, ham and pepper cocotte. Nice sweets, too, including a pleasantly tart summer pudding. Note the especially good house wine. No smoking. *No dogs.* ☺

Ewell *Superfish*

9 Castle Parade, By-pass Road
01-393 3674
Map 6 B3 *Surrey*

Open 11.30–2 (Sat till 2.30) & 5.30–11 (Fri & Sat 5–11.30)
Closed Sun & some Bank Holidays

Cod & chips £2.85   Scampi & chips £3.50
LVs
P street parking & WC

Aptly named, for the fish is indeed super at this bright, cheerful restaurant in a parade of shops. Traditional favourites like cod, plaice and haddock are beautifully cooked and served with smashing chips, good pickles and a basket full of lovely hot French bread. Scampi, sole, skate and rock are also available, and there are nice ices to finish. Friendly waiting staff. *No dogs.*

Exeter   **New Entry**   *Clare's Restaurant*

13 Princessay
Exeter (0392) 55155
Map 8 C3 *Devon*

Open 8–5.30
Closed Sun & Bank Holidays

Country-style chicken £2.75   Cheese &
courgette quiche 88p
LVs
P Princessay multi-storey car park   **WC**

In a town-centre pedestrian precinct, this
friendly, self-service restaurant offers a day-
long selection of enjoyable snacks. Sandwiches, pizza, quiches and salads are the
savoury choice, added to at lunchtime by hot
specials like pork and apple casserole or
lasagne. On the sweet side there are Bakewell tarts, a well-flavoured carob cake and a
very good bread and butter pudding. Children's portions available. *No dogs.*

Exeter   *Cooling's Wine Bar*

11 Gandy Street
Exeter (0392) 34183
Map 8 C3 *Devon*
Open 11–2.15 & 5.30–10.15 (till 10.45 in
summer)
Closed Sun, Bank Holiday lunches, 1 January
& 25 & 26 December
Chicken Waldorf £1.95   Quiche with salad
£1.65
LVs
P Paul Street multi-storey car park   **WC**

Come early or risk queuing for table space at
this popular wine bar in the city centre. The
hot and cold dishes on offer certainly make
an attractive display, the choice ranging from
warming lentil soup, macaroni cheese and
cottage pie with red cabbage to sugar-baked
ham, quiche and smoked mackerel served
with crisp, colourful salads. Be sure to leave
room for a tempting sweet like Belgian fudge
cake. *No dogs.* ☺

Falmouth   *Secrets*

6 Arwenack Street
Falmouth (0326) 318585
Map 8 A4 *Cornwall*

Open 10–4.30 & 7–10; winter 11–2.30, also 7–
10 Fri & Sat
Closed Sun in winter & 25 & 26 December
Seafood pie £3.95   Jacket potato with garlic &
mushroom £1.95
Credit Access, Visa
P Well Street car park   **WC**

This pleasant, informal restaurant with harbour views and a sizeable terrace is a firm
favourite with both locals and tourists. Morning sandwiches and cakes are supplemented
by the main daytime menu of stuffed pancakes, jacket potatoes, quiche, salads and
specials like chilli con carne. Cream teas,
and a long list of puds, from tipsy trifle to
banana split. More hot main dishes such as
seafood lasagne and chicken Kiev in the
evening. Non-smoking area. *No dogs.* 🐾

Faversham   ★   *Recreation Tavern*

16 East Street
Faversham (0795) 536033
Map 6 D3 *Kent*

Open noon–2 & 7–10
Closed eve 25 December–3 January

Chicken in curry mayonnaise £3   Chocolate
rum & raisin cream £1.25
Credit Access, Visa
P street parking

Finesse and refinement are hallmarks of the
cooking at this pleasant self-service restaurant with an attractive patio. Imaginative
starters like crab mousse and lamb satay
with peanut sauce might be followed by
salmon en croûte, guinea fowl with a peach
and brandy sauce or sausages casseroled in
red wine. Vegetables are delicious and the
rich, tipsy sweets a must. Minimum charge
£4 at lunchtime. *No dogs.* ☺ 🐾

Findon — *Tea House*

1 The Parade, High Street, Near Worthing
Findon (090 671) 3365
Map 6 B4 *West Sussex*

Open 10.30–5.30
Closed Mon except Bank Holidays when
closed Tues

Roast beef & Yorkshire pudding £2.80   Baked
apricot sponge 70p
P own car park   **WC**

Joan Ralph's splendid scones, cakes and
pastries take pride of place at this modest
little tea room just off the A24. Those who
like savoury things are catered for, too:
freshly cut sandwiches are always available,
and lunchtime brings traditional delights like
steak and kidney pie and a daily roast.
Spotted dick is a typical nice, old-fashioned
pudding. Derick Ralph is a thoughtful host.
Unlicensed. *No dogs.* 🍵

Framlingham — *Tiffins*

14 Fore Street
Framlingham (0728) 723015
Map 5 D2 *Suffolk*

Open 10–noon & 2.30–6
Closed Fri (except Good Fri) & Christmas–mid
March

Chocolate sponge 65p   Walnut gâteau 75p

P street parking

Tiffins is a tiny tea room occupying part of a
crammed antiques shop. It's a charming,
homely place, and owner Pat Macgregor not
only mans the kitchen but serves both
snackers and shoppers. A small side table
displays some nice home baking, including
almond fingers, scones, ginger crunch, old-
fashioned fruit cake and a good light chocolate cake. Best choice in mid-summer. Minimum charge of £1.25. Unlicensed. No
smoking. *No dogs.* 🍵

Froghall   *New Entry* — *The Wharf Eating House*

Foxt Road, Near Cheadle
Ipstones (053 871) 486
Map 4 C4 *Staffordshire*
Open 11–6 Spring Bank Holiday–end
September; 11–5 in winter
Closed Mon, also Tues & Wed in winter & all
October–mid March
Set afternoon tea £1.80   Cheese & onion pie
with rice salad £1.60
Credit Access, Diners
P own car park   ♿ **WC**

Whether you eat in the lovingly converted
200-year-old warehouse alongside the Cal-
don Canal or afloat on the Froghall Wharf
Passenger Service barge, the menu is the
same and the surroundings delightful. Buffet
lunches bring a particularly good choice of
vegetarian dishes, including pâtés, pizzas
and savoury pies, while for afternoon tea
there are scones with jam and cream plus a
range of home-made cakes, pastries and
biscuits. *No dogs.* 🍵

Frome — *Old Bath Arms*

1 Palmer Street
Frome (0373) 65045
Map 8 D3 *Somerset*

Open noon–1.45
Closed Sun, Bank Holidays & 25 December–4
January
Roast beef & Yorkshire pudding £2.30   Steak
& kidney pie £2.10
Credit Access, Visa
P own car park at rear   **WC**

Buffet-style lunches are a popular feature of
this pleasant establishment in an old stone
building. There's always a roast, casserole
and a hot pie (perhaps steak and kidney),
plus lighter options such as quiche, cold
meat salads, smoked mackerel and seafood.
Nice home-made sweets like apple and
raspberry pie, with steamed sponge pudding
a winter favourite. Minimum charge £2.10.
Full evening meals. *No dogs.* ⊘ 🍵

Frome

Settle

15 Cheap Street
Frome (0373) 65975
Map 8 D3 *Somerset*

Open 9–5, Thurs 9–2 (till 4 in summer), Sun &
Bank Holidays 2.30–6.30
Closed Sun October–April, 1 January & 25 &
26 December
Priddy oggies £2.50 Set afternoon tea £1.85
Credit Access, Visa
P market car park **WC**

Cheap Street is an attractive pedestrian way,
with many interesting buildings including this
cosy, rustic tea shop. Home cooking's the
name of the game, and favourites range from
traditional breakfast to cottage pie, kedgeree
and Somerset cream teas. Margaret Vaugh-
an's famous bobbins (cider-soaked fruits in
pastry whirls) now come in a version with
vegetables and cheese. Also many other
scrumptious cakes and pastries and an
English cheeseboard. 🍵 🫖

Gateshead

New Entry

Garden Restaurant

Unit 46, Metro Centre
Tyneside (091) 493 2222
Map 4 C1 *Tyne & Wear*

Open 10–8 (Thurs till 9), Sat 9–6
Closed Sun, 25 & 26 December

Haddock, chips & peas £2.50 Bacon roll 75p

P Metro Centre car park ♿ **WC**

Marks & Spencer's in-store restaurant is a
light, airy place with pink decor and an
Italianate garden mural. It's self-service and
very busy, and the day divides into three:
cakes, croissants, bacon rolls, salads and
sandwiches till 11.30; very good lunchtime
dishes like chilli beef or chicken chasseur
(minimum charge £1.50); and a reversion to
light snacks (plus something hot) for afternoon tea. No smoking. *No dogs.*

Gaydon

New Entry

Gaydon Lodge

Kineton (0926) 640414
Map 5 A2 *Warwickshire*

Open 9.30–6
Closed Mon (except Bank Holidays), 26
December, 1 January & 1 week January

Traditional tea £1.75 Sunday lunch £4.95

P own car park ♿ **WC**

Pleasant owners Christine and Roy Hatten
greet, cook and serve at this neat tea room-
cum-restaurant on the A41. Toasted snacks,
wheatmeal sandwiches and jacket potatoes
are available throughout the day, along with
some very enjoyable home baking. Lunchtime brings more substantial items like pizza,
mixed grill and trout with herb butter, with a
set lunch on Sunday. Excellent classic set
teas. *No dogs.* 🫖

Gittisham

Combe House Hotel

Near Honiton
Honiton (0404) 2756
Map 8 C3 *Devon*

Open noon–2 & 2.30–5.30
Closed 12 January–26 February

Afternoon tea £2.50 Ploughman's £2.25
Credit Access, Amex, Diners, Visa

P own car park ♿ **WC**

A treat awaits those who follow the long drive
that leads to this rambling Elizabethan mansion. A splendid refectory table is laid for old-
fashioned tea in the imposing entrance hall.
Choose from dainty sandwiches, scones and
home-made cakes (the tipsy fruit cake is
superb) and retire to one of the elegant
lounges to await a tray of freshly brewed tea.
Lunchtime visitors will find light snacks like
Danish open sandwiches in the bar. 🫖

Glastonbury   *Rainbow's End Café*

17a High Street
Glastonbury (0458) 33896
Map 8 D3 *Somerset*

Open 10–4.30 (Tues from 9.30)
Closed Sun, Wed, Bank Holidays & 2 weeks
Christmas

Vegetable lasagne £1.40   Yoghurt & banana
flan £1
P Market Place car park   **WC**

A rustic café with a friendly air and a good
array of wholefood and vegetarian snacks.
Throughout the day cheese scones, muesli,
fruit crumble and wholesome cakes and
biscuits may be enjoyed with a good cup of
tea or home-made lemonade. The choice
widens at lunchtime to include hearty soups,
quiches, pizza and salads, plus daily-changing hot specials and sweets like fresh fruit
salad. Outside eating. *No dogs.* 🍵 🍵

Goring-on-Thames   *Coffee Pot*

3 The Arcade
Goring-on-Thames (0491) 872485
Map 6 B3 *Oxfordshire*

Open 9–5.30
Closed 1 week Christmas

Lasagne with salad £2.25   Smoked haddock
flan £1.50

P village car park   ♿

Smartly revamped by its new owners, this
agreeable coffee shop serves dishes to suit
most tastes. Cooked breakfasts, soup, pâté
and pizza are offered throughout opening
hours, and daily-changing lunchtime specials
range from sherry-sauced pork fillet to
salmon and yoghurt flan. Sweet things include currant-studded scones and a fine
lemon meringue pie. More elaborate evening
meals. Unlicensed. *No dogs.*

Gosforth   `New Entry`   *Girl on a Swing*

1 Lansdowne Place
Tyneside (091) 2859672
Map 4 C1 *Tyne & Wear*

Open 6.30pm–11.30pm
Closed Sun & Bank Holidays

French onion soup £1.50   Boreks £3.50

P street parking   ♿   **WC**

The decor is about the only thing that hasn't
changed since this was the Chatterbox.
Wholefood vegetarian dishes from all points
of the globe make up the menu, with French
onion or beetroot soup, nut pâté and stuffed
vine leaves among the starters, and main
dishes like aubergines with tomato, onion
and cheese, filo parcels filled with spinach
and feta, or spicy stewed okra served with
tabbouleh. Nice sweets, too. Booking advisable. *No dogs.*

Grange-in-Borrowdale   *Grange Bridge Cottage*

Keswick
Keswick (0596) 84201
Map 3 B2 *Cumbria*

Open 10–5.30
Closed Mon (except Bank Holidays & July–
September), also November–Easter except
occasional weekends
Ploughman's lunch £1.75   Cottage pie with
salad £1.75
P village car park   ♿

Next to a stone bridge across the Derwent,
this charming, cottagey tea room is a popular
spot with summer visitors. A fine dresser
displays a tempting assortment of scones
and cakes – rich fruit, lemon and orange –
which you can enjoy at any time of day.
Savoury alternatives range from home-made
soup to pizzas, houmus and the daily hot
special such as pasta bake. Unlicensed. No
smoking. *No dogs.* 🍵 🍵

Grange-over-Sands   *At Home*

Danum House, Main Street
Grange-over-Sands (044 84) 4400
Map 3 B2 *Cumbria*

Open 10–2
Closed Sun, Mon, 25 December–1 January,
February & November
Asparagus & ham quiche £2.60   Italian trifle
£1.05
Credit Access
P car park behind post office   **WC**

Very much a family business, with Howard
Johns the genial host and his wife Jean and
their daughter in the kitchen. Morning coffee
gives way at noon to soup, salads, omelettes
and open sandwiches, plus daily specials like
smoked mackerel pâté or a very good chicken
and ham pie. Nice puds, too, such as
chocolate fudge cake or a toothsome gooseberry and strawberry pie – an unusual
combination that works well. More elaborate
evening menu. ☺

Grantham   `New Entry`   *Knightingales*

Guildhall Court, Guildhall Street
Grantham (0476) 79243
Map 5 B1 *Lincolnshire*

Open 9.30–4.30
Closed Sun & Bank Holidays (except Good
Fri)
Celery & cashew nut soup 65p   Lasagne verdi
£1.85
P Morrisons car park off Guildhall Street   ♿
WC

Decor is attractive and up to date at Anne
Knight's spacious wholefood and vegetarian
restaurant. A blackboard lists the daily-
changing choice of dishes, many of which
are set out on a display counter: smoked
mackerel and chicken liver pâtés, wholemeal
leek and cheese flan, mushroom and tomato
cheesy bake, an assortment of salads. Sweet
items include brown sugar meringues, superb carob slice and a really delicious
nectarine Pavlova. *No dogs.*

Grasmere   *Baldry's*

Red Lion Square
Grasmere (096 65) 301
Map 3 B2 *Cumbria*

Open 10–6 (till 7.30 July–September)
Closed Fri (except July–September) & Mon–
Fri early November–mid March

Roast ham salad £3.75   Chestnut &
mushroom roast £2.95
P municipal car park near garden centre   **WC**

Paul and Elaine Nelson offer a most appetising selection of daily-changing lunchtime
dishes at their counter-service restaurant.
Typical dishes include home-baked ham,
quiche, ploughman's and vegetarian lasagne, with traditional sweets like bread and
butter pudding and seasonal fruit crumble to
finish. Throughout the day there are tempting
goodies like rich chocolate cake and sticky
gingerbread. No smoking. *No dogs.*

Grasmere   *Coffee Bean*

Red Lion Square
Grasmere (096 65) 234
Map 3 B2 *Cumbria*

Open 9–5.30 (10–4 Sat & Sun November–mid
March)
Closed Mon–Fri November–mid March

Home-made soup & roll 75p   Custard tart 40p

P municipal car park near garden centre

The upstairs bakery provides all the goodies
to enjoy with tea or coffee at this simple little
tea room in the heart of Grasmere. Chocolate
cake, scones and toasted teacakes, Bakewell tarts and flapjacks are all popular, while
savoury items include soup, quiches, flans
and Cornish pasties. Everything on the menu
is available all day. Unlicensed.

Grasmere — *Rowan Tree*

Grasmere (096 65) 528
Map 3 B2 *Cumbria*

Open 10.30–7.30
Closed Mon–Thurs November–March

Lasagne with baked potato & salad £2.95
Cheese & asparagus quiche with baked potato & salad garnish £2.65

P village car park ♿ **WC**

Drink in the beauty of the lake before retiring to this chic yet delightfully cottagy restaurant for a refreshing brew and some delicious home-baked goodies. Choose from fruity wholemeal scones, crisp almond slice, tea-bread and splendidly moist date slice. Savoury snacks include quiches and jacket potatoes, while at mealtimes there are tasty offerings like cheese and broccoli bake and beef casserole. *No dogs.*

Grays — *R. Mumford & Son*

6 Cromwell Road
Grays Thurrock (0375) 374153
Map 6 C3 *Essex*

Open 11.45–2.15 & 5.30–11
Closed Sun, Bank Holidays (except Good Fri) & 10 days Christmas

Skate & chips £3.50 Chicken salad £2.70
LVs
P street or car park opposite ♿ **WC**

Watch the blackboard for seasonal daily specials like crab, lobster and salmon at this bright, modern fish restaurant. Other equally tasty choices include market-fresh cod, plaice, halibut and skate, lightly battered and served with jumbo chips or a crisp salad. Steak and chicken are also available, plus simple starters and creamy sweets. Minimum charge £2.50. *No dogs.*

Great Barton — *Craft at the Suffolk Barn*

Fornham Road, Near Bury St Edmunds
Great Barton (028 487) 317
Map 5 C2 *Suffolk*

Open 10–6
Closed Mon (except Bank Holidays), Tues & Christmas–mid March

Cheese platter with salad £1.30 Coffee sponge 35p
P own car park ♿ **WC**

Step back in time at this ancient, lofty barn in a quiet, rural setting. Today it's both gift shop and tea room, where Margaret Ellis provides a daily-changing selection of home-baked treats to enjoy with tea or coffee. Typical choices include Somerset cider cake, raspberry slice and iced gingerbread – plus a few savouries like toasted sandwiches and quiche. Enjoy it all outside in the well-tended garden in good weather. Unlicensed. *No dogs.*

Great Torrington — *Rebecca's*

8 Potacre Street
Torrington (0805) 22113
Map 8 B3 *Devon*

Open 9am–10pm
Closed Sun & 3 days Christmas

Crempog las (Welsh pancake) £1.75 Breast of chicken with ham & scallions £5.50
LVs *Credit* Access, Amex, Visa
P School Lane car park **WC**

Paul & Jill Lilly share the cooking at this friendly restaurant, where you can drop in throughout the day for anything from a quick bite to a full meal. The menu has plenty to tempt, from Welsh mushroom pancakes and hot cheese scones to trout, cidery pork chops and homity pie. Vegetarian dishes, puds and various set teas (including Paddington with a marmalade sandwich). Ask about the children's menu. *No dogs.*

Great Torrington

Top of the Town

37 South Street
Torrington (0805) 22900
Map 8 B3 *Devon*

Open 10–5
Closed Sun, 1 January & 25 & 26 December

Steak & kidney pie with vegetables £2.60
Chocolate cake 55p
Credit Access, Amex, Visa
P South Street car park **WC**

The owners prepare and cook all the food in this neat little restaurant with white plaster walls and mock rustic beams. Buttered toast, scones and teacakes, blackberry pie and chocolate cake go down well with morning coffee or afternoon tea, and lunchtime produces a good choice of savouries, from flans, omelettes and pork with beans to grilled lamb chop and chicken in a mushroom and cream sauce. Children's dishes. *No dogs.* ☺ 🍴

Great Yarmouth

Friends Bistro

55 Deneside
Great Yarmouth (0493) 852538
Map 5 D1 *Norfolk*

Open 10–4 & 7–10
Closed Mon eve, all Sun & Bank Holidays

Chicken mozzarella with vegetables £2.95
Prawn & mushroom roulade with salad £2.95
LVs *Credit* Access, Visa
P King Street car park ♿ **WC**

Call into this friendly, prettily decorated restaurant throughout the day for cheese or fruit scones, Bakewell tarts and sausage rolls. From about noon there are tasty hot dishes like Wiltshire ham bake, delicious quiches and chicken and vegetable pie, plus a daily vegetarian special. Book for dinner, when skate with black butter is a typical main course. *No dogs.* ☺

Guildford

Richoux

17 The Friary
Guildford (0483) 502998
Map 6 B3 *Surrey*

Open 9–6
Closed Sun & Bank Holidays except 1 January & Good Fri

Chicken & ham pie £3.25 Afternoon tea £1.95
LVs *Credit* Access, Amex, Diners, Visa
P Bedford Road multi-storey car park **WC**

Brass chandeliers, mirrors and plants provide a smart setting for light refreshments at this Richoux establishment on the top floor of the Friary shopping centre. Waitresses in long aprons and frilly caps will serve you everything from breakfasts, club sandwiches, burgers, steak and kidney pie or salad to cream cakes, pastries and gâteaux from the trolley. Ice creams and a children's menu also available. *No dogs.* 🍴

Hadleigh

Weaver's Bistro

23 High Street
Hadleigh (0473) 827247
Map 5 D2 *Suffolk*

Open 7pm–9.30pm
Closed Sat–Mon, Bank Holidays except Good Fri, 2 weeks July & 1 week Christmas
Avocado prawns £2 Baked trout with almonds £4.35
Credit Access, Visa
P street parking ♿ **WC**

Sally and Roy Ghijben have created a wonderfully friendly atmosphere at this popular beamed bistro set aside from the main restaurant. Their menu is brief but full of interest and everything is most enjoyably prepared, from garlicky mushroom hot pot to lamb's kidneys in a white wine and mustard sauce or the day's fresh fish special. Don't miss the excellent garlic bread and the delicious home-made desserts. Minimum charge £1.30. *No dogs.* ☺

Hailsham   *Homely Maid*

2 High Street
Hailsham (0323) 841650
Map 6 C4 *East Sussex*

Open 9.30–4.30 (Sat till 1.30)
Closed Sun, Bank Holidays & 2 weeks from 24
December

Cheese, spinach & almond flan 90p   Toasted
teacake 40p
P town-centre car park   **WC**

This friendly little tea shop is a deservedly
popular stop for morning coffee and afternoon tea. Lovely cakes and pastries, scones,
hot sausage rolls, flans and pastries from its
own cake shop go beautifully with the good
choice of leaf teas, while at lunchtime there's
a varied choice of hot dishes, with fruit pie
and custard for afters. Unlicensed. No smoking. *No dogs.*

Hailsham   *Waldernheath Country Restaurant*

Amberstone Corner
Hailsham (0323) 840143
Map 6 C4 *East Sussex*

Open noon–2
Closed Sun, Mon, 25 December & 1 week
autumn
Omelette paysanne £2.75   Hors d'oeuvre
variés £5.75
Credit Access, Amex, Diners, Visa
P own parking   **WC**

On the A271 just north of Hailsham, this is a
charming restaurant in a 15th-century country house. A lunchtime just-a-bite menu offers
a short list of tasty items such as stuffed
savoury pancakes, Mediterranean prawns
with aïoli and succulent steak with chips. The
still-hungry can switch to the sweets menu
and things like delicious gooseberry pie
served with lashings of thick cream. Minimum
charge £3.50. Patio. *No dogs.*

Harrogate   *Bettys*

1 Parliament Street
Harrogate (0423) 64659
Map 4 C2 *North Yorkshire*

Open 9–5.30, Sun 10–6
Closed 1 January & 25 & 26 December

Yorkshire rarebit & ham £3.35   Selection of
fruit cakes £1.40
LVs
P Union Street multi-storey car park   **WC**

The Harrogate branch was the first Bettys
coffee shop (opened in 1919) and, like the
Ilkley, Northallerton and York outlets, serves
a vast range of really good, wholesome
snacks. Rarebits are a speciality, and other
savouries include sandwiches, toasties and
omelettes, plus grills and fish. Scones, tea
breads and a fine range of cakes and pastries
accompany excellent tea or coffee. There are
special children's and healthy eating menus.
No dogs.

Harrogate   *New Entry*   *Chimes Tea Room*

Unit 9 Westminster Arcade, Parliament Street
Harrogate (0423) 506 663
Map 4 C2 *North Yorkshire*

Open 9.30–5
Closed Sun & Bank Holidays

Double decker sandwich £1.15   Cream tea
£1.40

P Union Street multi-storey car park

Fresh, appetising snacks are served in this
attractive tea room, which stands on the first
floor of an old-fashioned arcade with some
fine wrought-iron work. Granary rolls are
filled with things like egg mayonnaise, tuna,
cottage cheese and peppers or chicken with
sweetcorn, and there are double-decker
sandwiches combining brown and white
bread. Salads, too, plus a good choice of
baking that includes coconut tart, date slice
and cream cakes. Unlicensed. *No dogs.*

Harrogate   **New Entry**   *Vani's Pizzeria*

15 Parliament Street
Harrogate (0423) 501 313
Map 4 C2 *North Yorkshire*

Open noon–2.30 & 6–11.30 (Sun till 11)
Closed 25 & 26 December

Spaghetti carbonara £2.95   Pizza americana
£3
Credit Access, Amex, Visa
P Union Street multi-storey car park   **WC**

The pizzas are particularly large and satisfying at this leafy Italian restaurant on the main
street. Crisp, well-baked bases have generous toppings that include seafood, minced
meat and vegetarian (spinach, artichokes,
peppers and onions). Besides the pizzas,
there's plenty of pasta, plus burgers, shish
kebabs, steaks and creamy-sauced savoury
pancakes. Straightforward starters and
sweets. Service is friendly without being
obtrusive. *No dogs.*

Harrogate   *William & Victoria Downstairs*

6 Cold Bath Road
Harrogate (0423) 506883
Map 4 C2 *North Yorkshire*

Open noon–3 & 5.30–11
Closed Sat lunch, all Sun & Bank Holidays

Country terrine £1.90   Poached salmon with
cucumber sauce £4.95
Credit Access
P street parking   **WC**

A basement wine bar with plenty of character
and atmosphere and a blackboard menu full
of interest and variety. Seafood pâté, moules
marinière and garlic mushrooms make tasty
snacks or starters, and main courses could
include pork spare rib chops, braised beef or
poached salmon with a really good cucumber
sauce. Sweets are also very tempting – try
gooey banana and caramel pie. *No dogs.* ⊖

Harrogate   *William & Victoria Restaurant*

6 Cold Bath Road
Harrogate (0423) 521510
Map 4 C2 *North Yorkshire*

Open 6.30pm–10pm
Closed Sun & Christmas night

Roast half duckling with Yorkshire sauce
£5.95   Treacle tart £1.35
Credit Access
P street parking   **WC**

Not to be confused with the William & Victoria
Downstairs, this smart, ground-floor restaurant offers a good range of brasserie-style
dishes. Eat as much or as little as you fancy
– from smoked salmon mousse and a glass
of wine to a well-prepared main course such
as roast topside of veal, sea trout, beef
casserole or roast duckling, followed by a
delicious seasonal dessert. Excellent wine
list. No children under 14. *No dogs.* ⊖

Hastings   *Brant's*

45 High Street, Old Town
Hastings (0424) 431896
Map 6 C4 *East Sussex*

Open 10–5 (Wed till 2) summer; 10–4 winter
Closed Sun, Bank Holidays, Wed in winter, 2
weeks April & 2 weeks autumn

Nut savoury 95p   Apricot slice 45p
LVs
P street parking & seafront car park   **WC**

Pictures by local artists are displayed on one
wall of this pleasant little vegetarian restaurant, where Mr Stevens cooks and his wife
serves at the counter. The choice, though not
extensive, is very appetising, spanning savoury and fruit flans, an interesting choice of
salads and cakes like coconut slice or carob
brownies. Lunchtime produces a couple of
hot dishes such as chick pea curry or
succulent nut savoury. No smoking. 🍵

Hastings   *Judge's*

51 High Street, Old Town
Hastings (0424) 427097
Map 6 C4 *East Sussex*

Open 10–5 (Wed till 2)
Closed Sun, Mon, also Wed January–May,
last 2 weeks May & 1st 2 weeks October
Roast beef & Yorkshire pudding £2.45
Chicken & mushroom pie £2.45
LVs
P street parking & seafront car park   ♿   **WC**

A mother and son team are behind the success of this cosily traditional restaurant. Eileen Inwood prepares the satisfying lunches featuring home-made soup, savoury pies, a daily roast and fish dish, while her son (working from the bakery next door) is responsible for the fine window display of lovely light scones, gooey meringues, florentines, Eccles cakes and much, much more. No smoking. *No dogs.* 🦃

Hastings   *Town House*

3 Marine Parade
Hastings (0424) 438487
Map 6 C4 *East Sussex*

Open 7.30–11pm.
Closed Tues.

Beef casserole £2.30   Treacle sponge 70p

P street parking & seafront car park   **WC**

In a terrace of seafront shops, this unassuming place provides good snacking from early morning to late evening. Breakfast makes way at noon for tasty lunchtime fare like cheese-topped smoked cod ramekin, fish and potato pie or beef casserole. They're proud of their chocolate mousse and have a good range of fruit pies and crumbles. Afternoon tea with home baking and a slightly more elaborate evening menu. ☕ 🦃

Hathersage   *Country Fayre Tea Room*

Main Road, Near Sheffield
Hope Valley (0433) 50858
Map 4 C3 *Derbyshire*

Open 10–5.30
Closed Mon–Fri October–June

Cheese & tomato omelette £1.85   Apple, almond & apricot tart 75p

P street parking & village car park

An attractive tea room above a village crafts shop. The tiny kitchen supplies a good range of fine baking, including scones, fruit pies, super coffee sponge and the splendid lemon Wensleydale tart. Breadcakes (baps) and open sandwiches make very good savoury snacks, and there are salads, omelettes and Welsh rarebit, with warming winter specials like cottage pie or a casserole. Excellent loose-leaf tea. Unlicensed. Non-smoking area. *No dogs.* 🦃

Hawes   *Cockett's Hotel*

Market Place
Hawes (096 97) 312
Map 4 C2 *North Yorkshire*

Open 10.30–noon & 3–5
Closed end October–beginning April

Cream tea £1.60   Date & walnut cake 50p

P in Market Place   ♿   **WC**

Morning coffee and afternoon tea can be enjoyed either in the courtyard or in the pleasantly traditional restaurant of this market-place hotel. Sound baking is exemplified by lovely light scones (ours came with delicious home-made gooseberry jam), flapjacks, lemon and chocolate sponges and the always popular date and walnut loaf. The biscuits are delicious, too. Friendly service is another plus. *No dogs.*

Hawkshead

Minstrel's Gallery

The Square
Hawkshead (096 66) 423
Map 3 B2 *Cumbria*

Open 10.30–5.30
Closed Fri & mid December–mid February

Chicken & mushroom pie with baked potato
£2.75   Mushroom omelette with salad or
baked potato £2.70
P municipal car park   &

Teatime is the busiest part of the day at the
Russells' charming flagstoned tea room, as
William Russell's home-baked goodies come
into their own. Sticky gingerbread, scones
spread with good jam and cream and delicious meringue glacé with fresh strawberries
all go down well with a refreshing brew. At
lunchtime, there are a few light savoury
dishes such as chicken and mushroom pie.
Unlicensed. No smoking. 🫖

Helmsley

Crown Hotel

Market Square
Helmsley (0439) 70297
Map 4 C2 *North Yorkshire*

Open 3.30–5.45
Closed 25 & 26 December

Grilled ham & egg tea £3.80   Light afternoon
tea £1.50
Credit Access, Visa
P own & Market Square   &   **WC**

Afternoon appetites are well catered for at
this attractive, 16th-century inn on the Market
Square. Set teas offer good home-baked
scones and cakes, farm eggs, ham sandwiches or creamed mushrooms on toast; the
very hungry can opt for one of the high teas,
which centre round things like fillet of haddock, pork sausages and various cold meats.
Half-portions available. *No dogs.* 🐱

Henfield

Norton House

High Street
Brighton (0273) 492064
Map 6 C4 *West Sussex*

Open 9.30–5.30, Sun 10–12.30 & 3–5.30
Closed Tues & 3 days Christmas

Chocolate gâteau 50p   Shortbread 30p

P at rear or public car park opposite   **WC**

The Georgian facade of this delightful tea
house hides an older building, dating from
the late 17th century – a charming setting in
which to enjoy Jean Sinclair Young's excellent baking. Featherlight meringues, buttery
shortbread, chocolate or tangy lemon gâteau
and spicy ginger cake are all delicious with a
good cuppa. There are plenty of wrought-
iron tables and chairs in the well-tended
gardens to the front and rear. Unlicensed.
No dogs. 🫖

Henley-on-Thames

Barnaby's Brasserie

2 New Street
Henley-on-Thames (0491) 572421
Map 6 B3 *Oxfordshire*

Open noon–2 & 7–10.30
Closed lunch Sun & 1 Jan, all 25 & 26
December
Barbecued spare ribs £4.75   Chilli con carne
with rice £3.35
LVs
P King's Road car park   **WC**

Set in a timbered 14th-century building, this
friendly, low-beamed restaurant scores high
on atmosphere, while a versatile menu en-
ables you to enjoy just a bite or a full meal.
Home-made soup or garlic mushrooms
makes a tasty snack, while more substantial
offerings range from roast lamb to pasta and
barbecued steaks and kebabs. Finish with a
homely pud like treacle roly-poly. *No dogs.*

Henley-on-Thames　**New Entry**　　*Copper Kettle*

18 Thameside
Henley-on-Thames (0491) 575262
Map 6 B3 *Oxfordshire*

Open 10–6 (till 5 November–March)

Steak & mushroom pie £3.25　Hot chocolate
fudge cake £1.10

P town-centre car parks　&　**WC**

Cosy, quaint surroundings for a snack. There
are ornaments everywhere, and a splendid
Victorian carriage lives in the wrought-iron-
furnished conservatory. The bill of fare comprises a soup of the day and a main lunchtime
dish such as lamb curry or chicken and
mushroom pie, plus ploughman's, pâté and
filled jacket potatoes. Baking includes date
slice, meringues, florentines and the popular
hot chocolate fudge cake. *No dogs.* ⊖

Henley-on-Thames　　　　*Henley Tea Shop*

26 Hart Street
Henley (0491) 576536
Map 6 B3 *Oxfordshire*

Open 10–5.30, Sun 10.30–6
Closed some Wed & 25 & 26 December

Cream tea £2.40　Toasted sandwich & tea
£2.50

P street parking　**WC**

The results of Margaret Hallsworth's excellent home baking are grouped in the bow
window of this traditional tea shop and draw
the crowds in like a magnet. Lovely Austrian
coffee cake, buttered fruit loaf, scones and
Bakewell tarts all go beautifully with a refreshing brew – and taste even better eaten from
dainty Minton china. Minimum afternoon
charge £1.70, £2.20 weekends. Unlicensed.
No smoking. *No dogs.* 🌶

Hereford　　　　　　　　　*Effy's*

96 East Street
Hereford (0432) 59754
Map 7 D2 *Hereford & Worcester*

Open noon–3 & 6–10
Closed Mon eve, all Sun & 1 week Christmas

Spinach & walnut loaf £2.40　Pigeon breast
with honey & figs £5.45
Credit Access, Amex, Diners, Visa
P Widemarsh NCP　**WC**

New owners Carole and William Chichester
have taken over this bright, attractive restaurant near the Town Hall. They offer a set
lunch at £6.95, from which just-a-biters can
order only a main course. Typical dishes
include cream of broccoli soup with almonds,
chicken with tarragon, sautéed king prawns
and for dessert perhaps caramel-topped
apple ice. Evening meals are a little more
elaborate. *No dogs.* ⊖ 🌶

Hereford　　　　**New Entry**　　　*Fodder*

2 Capucin Yard, Church Street
Hereford (0432) 58171
Map 7 D2 *Hereford & Worcester*

Open 10–4.30
Closed Sun & Bank Holidays

Vegetable bake £1.20　Provençale quiche
with salad selection £1.50
P street parking (limited) & pay & display at
Tesco　&　**WC**

Additive-free foods and organic vegetables
are the order of the day at this little vegetarian
restaurant in a courtyard where a potter, a
watch repairer and a violin maker are among
the other traders. Nut loaf, savoury slices
and samosas are typical fare, along with
soups, vegetable bake and regularly replen-
ished salad bowls. Also on display are
cheesecake, treacle tart, sesame cake and
various other baked goodies. No smoking.
No dogs. 🌶

Hereford   *Marches*

24 Union Street
Hereford (0432) 55712
Map 7 D2 *Hereford & Worcester*

Open 8.30–5.30
Closed Sun, Bank Holidays & 2–3 days
Christmas

Nut roast 65p   Cheese & tomato quiche 65p
LVs *Credit* Access, Amex, Visa
P Gaol Street car park   **WC**

Mrs Vale's inviting wholefood restaurant
shares its premises with a health-food shop
and gift gallery. She rises early to prepare at
least 12 different salads each day, along with
beautifully light wholemeal flans, warming
soups, a daily hot special and a selection of
vegetarian main courses. What is more, she
does all manner of baking: fruit pies, flapjacks, gâteaux and a most tempting lemon
meringue pie. Non-smoking area. 🍵 🍴

Herstmonceux   *Cleavers Lyng*

Church Road
Herstmonceux (0323) 833131
Map 6 C4 *East Sussex*

Open 10–11.45, 12.30–1.30 & 3–5
Closed afternoon tea Mon–Fri in winter & all
Christmas–1 February

Steak & kidney pie £2.60   Trifle 80p

P own car park   **WC**

Summer tea finds a peaceful and picturesque
setting in the lovely garden of a tile-clad
house dating from the 16th century. Inside is
pleasant, too, with beams, brasses and
wheelback chairs. The set tea – bread and
butter, drop scones and various cakes – is
available for all three sessions, and at
lunchtime there are other things like soup,
lemon sole, steak and kidney pie and omelettes, plus ices and home-made sweets. 🍴

Herstmonceux   **New Entry**   *Praise the Lord*

Gardener Street
Herstmonceux (0323) 833219
Map 6 C4 *East Sussex*

Open 9–5.30 (closed 1–2 November–Spring
Bank Holiday)
Closed Sun, 1 January, 25 & 26 December,
also Good Fri from noon
Sussex mushroom pastie with salad £1.85
Cream meringue 65p
P street parking

An appealing tea shop in the middle of the
village, with pretty tablecloths and some nice
antiques. Excellent French bread is baked on
the premises, and it features in the set teas
along with wholemeal bread, scones, fruit
loaf and some nice cakes. Other offerings
include quiche, pasties and sausage rolls,
and at lunchtime there are a few simple
salads. Good selection of speciality teas –
and cosies for the teapots. Unlicensed. 🍴

High Lorton   *White Ash Barn*

Near Cockermouth
Lorton (090 085) 236
Map 3 B1 *Cumbria*

Open 10.30–5
Closed end October–1 week before Easter

Chicken liver pâté £1.50   Chocolate gâteau
90p

P own car park & street parking   **WC**

The Georges offer a warm welcome at their
Lakeland tea room and gift shop housed in a
converted 18th-century barn. Throughout the
day you can enjoy Mrs George's excellent
home baking – flavoursome wholemeal
scones, moist apple cake, popular lemon
fridge cake – with a fragrant cuppa served in
pretty china. Light lunches (available summer
only) feature pâté and quiche, home-baked
gammon and colourful salads. Unlicensed.
No smoking. *No dogs.* 🍴

Holmfirth

New Entry

Wrinkled Stocking

30 Huddersfield Road, Upperbridge
Huddersfield (0484) 681408
Map 4 C3 *West Yorkshire*

Open 9.30–7 (till 5.30 in winter)
Closed 25 December

Cream tea £1.30   Salad-filled wholemeal pitta
bread £1.10
Credit Access, Visa
P Crown Bottom car park 🚻 **WC**

The BBC TV series 'Last of the Summer Wine' was filmed in Holmfirth, and this attractive tea room stands next to Nora Batty's cottage (hence the curious name). Simple, appetising snacks are its forte: sandwiches cut to order, pâté, quiche, wholemeal pitta bread filled with salad. Among the baked goodies are fruit pie and super light scones, and sherry trifle appears at weekends. Unlicensed. 🍵

Hope

Hopechest

Near Sheffield
Hope Valley (0433) 20072
Map 4 C3 *Derbyshire*

Open 9.15–5
Closed Sun, also Mon except August &
December & 25 December

Quiche & roll £1.25   Bakewell tart 60p
Credit Access, Diners, Visa
P village car park 🚻 **WC**

Three retired schoolteachers run this pin-bright tea room at the back of a shop. Taking it in turns to bake and serve, they produce a small but delicious selection of daily-changing goodies, and the range is from soup, quiche and cheese scones on the savoury side to toasted teacakes, exemplary Bakewell tarts and a sensational chocolate brandy cake. Excellent tea and coffee accompany. Unlicensed. No smoking. *No dogs.* 🍵

Horsforth

Stuarts Wine Bar

166 Town Street, Near Leeds
Leeds (0532) 582 661
Map 4 C3 *West Yorkshire*

Open noon–2 & 7–10
Closed Mon eve, all Sun, Bank Holidays & last
2 weeks August

Mixed meat salad £4.95   Garlic prawns £1.40

P street parking **WC**

The cold buffet is a popular draw at this friendly wine bar, with perfectly cooked, carved-to-order joints being accompanied by a large variety of salads. Starters include soup, smoked trout and garlic snails, while hot main courses range from prawn omelette and scampi to entrecôte steak and medallions of pork with a splendid champagne sauce. Tempting sweets, too, like strawberry crumble or chocolate and brandy mousse, and excellent cheeses. *No dogs.* 🍷

Hungerford

Bear, Kennet Room

41 Charnham Street
Hungerford (0488) 92512
Map 6 A3 *Berkshire*

Open 12.15–2 & 7.30–9.30 (Fri & Sat till 10)
Closed 25 December
Stuffed aubergine with cheese sauce £3.95
Terrine of summer fruit with raspberry coulis
£1.95
Credit Access, Amex, Diners, Visa
P own car park 🚻 **WC**

Local trout baked with vegetables, ham with melon, lasagne and beef in a cream and paprika sauce are some of the main courses on the menu at this pleasant pub. You can choose just one dish, or go for a meal and start with Stilton and walnut pâté or a saffron-flavoured fish soup served with superb French bread, and end with a sweet like iced nougat with raspberry sauce or a wedge of farmhouse cheese. *No dogs.* 🍷

Huntingdon

Old Bridge Hotel Lounge

1 High Street
Huntingdon (0480) 52681
Map 5 B2 *Cambridgeshire*

Open 10am–10.30pm
Closed eve 25 December

Grilled sardines with lemon butter £3.95   Cold
buffet from £6
Credit Access, Amex, Diners, Visa
P own car park   **WC**

A sunny terrace overlooking the river Ouse
makes an attractive summer spot for coffee
or afternoon tea at this comfortably elegant
hotel lounge. At lunchtime there's a tempting
cold buffet featuring cold meats or salmon
with serve-yourself salads, as well as appetising hot dishes ranging from fresh pasta to
grilled sardines. Tea, coffee and sandwiches,
plus some sweets, are available throughout
the day. *No dogs.* ☕

Hurst Green

Whitehall

Near Stonyhurst
Stonyhurst (025 486) 456
Map 3 B3 *Lancashire*

Open 11–6
Closed Mon (except Bank Holidays), Tues,
January, September & 25 December

Beef in wine with vegetables £2.50
Sandwiches from 90p
P street parking   ♿   **WC**

Built on modern lines but of traditional stone
and slate, this delightful craft centre also
houses a charming tea room offering snacks
and meals throughout the day. Savoury
choices include soup and toasted sandwiches plus daily-changing specials like cottage pie, a roast or lasagne, all served with
salad or vegetables. Nice home-made cakes
and scones, too, plus traditional sweets like
fruit pies and crumbles. Unlicensed. ☕ 🍵

Hythe

New Entry

Natural Break

115 High Street
Hythe (0303) 67573
Map 6 D3 *Kent*

Open 9–5
Closed Sun & Bank Holidays

Lentil lasagne £1.60   Sugar-free Dundee cake
40p

P car park opposite police station

A simple, quiet small vegetarian restaurant
linked to a wholefood shop in the High Street.
It's run by two charming girls, who share the
cooking: a self-service counter displays
cakes and pastries, and from about 11.30
until closing time there's a short selection of
tasty hot dishes such as lentil lasagne,
mushroom quiche and leek gratin. Also soup
of the day and jacket potatoes. Unlicensed.
No smoking. *No dogs.*

Ilkley

Bettys

32 The Grove
Ilkley (0943) 608029
Map 4 C3 *West Yorkshire*

Open 9.30 (Sat from 9)–5.30 (Sun till 7)
Closed 25 December

Yorkshire rarebit £3.35   Selection of fruit
cakes £1.40

P town-centre car park   **WC**

The menu provides for almost endlessly
varied eating at this attractive, well-run coffee
shop, and at all times you can get anything
from a tiny bit to a slap-up meal. Freshly cut
sandwiches, bacon and eggs, rarebits and
deep-fried mushrooms are just a few of the
savoury items, and there's a vast array of
fine baking on the trolley. Special healthy
eating and children's menus along with an
excellent selection of teas and coffees.
Noteworthy service. *No dogs.* ☕ 🍵

Ipswich   *Belstead Brook Hotel Lounge*

Belstead Road
Ipswich (0473) 684241
Map 5 D2 *Suffolk*

Open 12.30–2.30 & 7.30–9.30

Hot creamed shrimps £2.25   Spaghetti
carbonara £2.75
Credit Access, Amex, Diners, Visa

P own car park   ♧   **WC**

Ask for the bar snack menu in the very attractively decorated lounge bar of this fine hotel on the outskirts of Ipswich. The choice is simple but enjoyable, with things like pâté, spaghetti carbonara, soup of the day (perhaps the unusual vegetable and walnut), sandwiches and a cold meat salad. Sorbets and a few other sweets. There are tables on the lawn for use in fine weather. *No dogs.*

Ipswich   *Marno's Restaurant*

14 St Nicholas Street
Ipswich (0473) 53106
Map 5 D2 *Suffolk*

Open 10.30–2.15 (Thurs–Sat till 10)
Closed Sun & Bank Holidays

Nut roast £1.50   Vegetable compote £1.50
LVs

P St Nicholas Street car park   ♧   **WC**

Lunchtimes are particularly popular at this unpretentious vegetarian restaurant owned by three sisters. Typical choices range from a flavoursome daily soup to wholewheat pasta and mushroom bake, sweet and sour pancakes and a hearty vegetable casserole. Fruit tarts and crumbles for afters, cakes and flapjacks at other times. More elaborate evening meals are served Thursday–Saturday. *No dogs.*

Ipswich   ★   *New Entry*   *Orwell House*

4a Orwell Place
Ipswich (0473) 230254
Map 5 D2 *Suffolk*

Open noon–2.30, also 7–10 Wed–Sat
Closed 24 December

Seafood soufflé omelette with mornay sauce £3.50   Tagliatelle with mussels £1.80
Credit Access, Amex, Diners, Visa
P Cox Lane car park   **WC**

Super cooking by John Gear in this stylish establishment near the town centre. Just-a-biters should stay at ground level and order from the short café menu. Tagliatelle with mussels and authentic eggs bénédictine are typical starters, while main dishes include grilled sole, peppery pork cutlet and barbecued chicken with a classic sauce smitane. Particularly tempting desserts like apple and Calvados mille-feuille. More formal restaurant upstairs. *No dogs.* 🍵

Ipswich   *New Entry*   *Tackets*

2 Tacket Street
Ipswich (0473) 50548
Map 5 D2 *Suffolk*

Open 10–9.30 (Mon & Tues till 4.30)
Closed Sun & Bank Holidays

Tuna salad granary bap £1.47   Chocolate nut
sundae £1.30
LVs   *Credit* Access, Amex, Diners, Visa
P Tacket Street car park   **WC**

A town-centre restaurant with waitress service and a pleasant atmosphere. The daytime menu includes granary baps, jacket potatoes, salads and wholemeal or plain waffles with a variety of toppings both sweet and savoury. In the evening the emphasis moves to Italian dishes like pollo cacciatora, lasagne and a number of other sauced pasta dishes. Sweets include ice cream specialities, passion cake and a morish hot toffee cake. Non-smoking area. *No dogs.* 🕭

Kendal   *Corner Spot Eating House*

Branthwaite Brow
Kendal (0539) 20115
Map 3 B2 *Cumbria*

Open 8.30–4.45
Closed Sun, Thurs & Bank Holidays

Quiche lorraine 85p   Haddock & prawn flan 85p
LVs
P Blackhall Road multi-storey car park   **WC**

On the lower corner of a little cobbled hill stands this unpretentious eating house known for its good baking and friendly, homely atmosphere. Scones, biscuits, apple slices and lemon meringue pie are just a small selection from the tempting range, and lunchtime brings a variety of wholesome quiches. Salads and jacket potatoes are other popular snacks, along with sandwiches cut freshly to order. 🍴

Kendal   **New Entry**   *Eat Fit*

3 Stramongate
Kendal (0539) 20341
Map 3 B2 *Cumbria*

Open 9–5
Closed Sun & Bank Holidays

Mushrooms Stroganoff £1.40   French bread pizza 55p

P riverside car park   **WC**

The menu is largely vegetarian at this pleasant self-service restaurant, though fish and chicken sometimes appear. Crunchy nut tagliatelle, mushrooms Stroganoff and lentil loaf are typical dishes, and on our visit there was a really good chicken and leek pie, its wholemeal pastry top sprinkled with sunflower seeds. Also jacket potatoes, French bread pizzas, cakes and pastries (very good gingerbread, nice light scones). Unlicensed. Non-smoking area. *No dogs.* 🍴

Kendal   **New Entry**   *Farrers Tea & Coffee House*

13 Stricklandgate
Kendal (0539) 31707
Map 3 B2 *Cumbria*

Open 9.30–4.45
Closed Sun & Bank Holidays

Jacket potatoes with Waldorf salad £1.80
Cinnamon & apricot finger 65p

P Stricklandgate car park   **WC**

Farrers Tea and Coffee House goes back to 1819 and is full of period charm. In the cellar (and in an upstairs room for smokers) well-prepared snacks may be enjoyed with an excellent beverage: jacket potatoes are a popular lunchtime choice, and there's good home-made soup, generously filled sandwiches, steak and kidney pie and chilli with salad. Tempting pastries and desserts, too. Unlicensed. *No dogs.* 🍴

Kendal   *The Moon*

129 Highgate
Kendal (0539) 29254
Map 3 B2 *Cumbria*

Open 6pm–10pm (Fri & Sat till 11, Sun from 7)
Closed 3 days at Christmas

Broccoli, cheese & mushroom pie £3.05
Meatloaf £3.60
Credit Access, Visa
P Peppercorn car park   ♿   **WC**

Warmth and character are all around in this delightful and popular restaurant. The blackboard dinner menu changes daily and offers a good choice for both carnivores and vegetarians: delicious houmus, asparagus mousse, Italian lamb casserole, a lovely braised meatloaf served with a super lettuce and nut salad. Pure, positive flavours abound, and the high standards are sustained by delicious sweets like Irish whiskey and orange syllabub. *No dogs.*

Kendal   *Nutters*

Yard 11, Stramongate
Kendal (0539) 25135
Map 3 B2 *Cumbria*

Open 9.30–7
Closed Sun & Bank Holidays

Beef and tomato cobbler £2.45   Sticky toffee
pudding 85p

P New Road car park   **WC**

The building dates back to 1670, and there's
a wealth of old beams in this friendly, relaxed
coffee shop. Savoury snacks on the blackboard menu could include smoked cod
quiche, tasty beef and tomato cobbler and
baked potatoes with fillings like bolognese
or bean goulash. For the sweeter tooth,
perhaps lemon meringue pie, coffee cake or
sticky toffee pudding. Tea comes in a huge
brown pot. Non-smoking area. *No dogs.*

Kendal   *Waterside Wholefoods*

Kent View
Kendal (0539) 29743
Map 3 B2 *Cumbria*

Open 9–4
Closed Sun, 1 January & 25 & 26 December

Vegetable lasagne £1.75   Paradise tart 60p

P riverside car park   **WC**

Right next to the river Kent, this little vegetar-
ian-cum-wholefood restaurant is a pleasant
place to pause for a healthy bite. Our
wholemeal pancake filled with tomato and
chilli sauce was a very tasty snack, and
practically all the salads, soups and quiches
use organically grown vegetables. To go with
morning coffee there's some nice cakes,
including carrot, walnut and delicious sticky
fig. Unlicensed. No smoking. *No dogs.*

Kenilworth   **New Entry**   *Castle Green Tea Shop*

2a Castle Green
Kenilworth (0926) 512676
Map 5 A2 *Warwickshire*

Open 10–6
Closed Christmas–March

Cream tea £1.25   Toasted cheese & tomato
sandwich 85p
Credit Access, Amex, Diners, Visa
P Castle car park   **WC**

Paintings hang on the walls of this friendly
little tea shop, as a gallery occupies the same
premises on the green opposite the 12th-
century castle. The bill of fare offers a simple
choice of home-produced goods, from large,
light scones and various cakes and pastries
(very good bran teabread) to savoury snacks
such as sandwiches, quiche and variously
filled jacket potatoes. Unlicensed. Non-
smoking section. *No dogs.*

Kenilworth   **New Entry**   *George Rafters*

42 Castle Hill
Kenilworth (0926) 52074
Map 5 A2 *Warwickshire*

Open noon–2 & 7–10.30
Closed 25 & 26 December

Guacamole £1.85   Pork dijonnaise £4.95
Credit Access, Amex, Diners, Visa

P street parking   **WC**

In a quiet part of town hard by the castle, this
pleasantly appointed restaurant presents a
menu of interest and variety. Familiar dishes
like guacamole, veal cordon bleu and brochettes of beef stand beside dishes that are
just that little bit different, like pineapple with
prawns and a creamy coconut dressing or
breast of chicken with a super sauce of port,
apples, cream and hazelnuts. *No dogs.*

Kents Bank

Abbot Hall Coffee Shop

Near Grange-over-Sands
Grange-over-Sands (044 84) 2896
Map 3 B2 *Cumbria*

Open 10–4.30, Sun 2.30–4.30

Coconut fudge cake 45p   Peanut & raisin
shortbread 45p

P own car park   &   **WC**

The warm welcome and commendably high
standards of baking make this attractive little
coffee shop within a Victorian guest house a
popular local meeting place. Choose from a
display counter featuring sweet treats like
superb caramel shortcake, chewy florentines
and chocolate and mint squares. Soup,
salads and quiches make tasty lunchtime
treats, and freshly cut sandwiches accompany afternoon tea. Unlicensed. No smoking.
No dogs.

Keswick

Bryson's Tea Rooms

42 Main Street
Keswick (076 87) 72257
Map 3 B2 *Cumbria*

Open 9–5.30
Closed Sun, 1 January, 25 & 26 December & 1
week November–week before Easter

Quiche & salad £2.40   Fresh cream cake 45p

P car park at rear   **WC**

Above a busy baker's shop, this cottage tea
room offers an enjoyable range of cakes and
pastries. Strudel, fruit cake and creamy,
featherlight roulade are typical of the choice
from the trolley, and there are set teas – the
Cumberland farmhouse and the lavish Lakeland, a feast of scones, apple pie, fruit cake
and plum pie! Savoury snacks include
omelettes, salads and Cumberland sausage
with egg and pineapple. Unlicensed. *No dogs.*

Keswick

Mayson's

33 Lake Road
Keswick (076 87) 74104
Map 3 B2 *Cumbria*

Open 9.30–5 & 6.30–10
Closed Mon eve

Lasagne £1.95   Sweet & sour barbecued fish
£4.80
Credit Access, Amex, Visa
P Bell Close car park   &   **WC**

A lofty, modern restaurant with a tiled floor
and climbing greenery. The daytime self-
service buffet offers an appetising choice
ranging from Stilton and broccoli quiche to
beef or chicken served curried, casseroled
or stir fried. Salads are fresh and imaginative,
and there are some delicious home-made
cakes and sweets. The evening menu, in
contrast, is quite cosmopolitan, with a distinctly Eastern slant, and includes a number
of vegan dishes. *No dogs.*

Keswick

Squire's

31 Lake Road
Keswick (076 87) 73969
Map 3 B2 *Cumbria*

Open 10–5
Closed Tues, 1st Mon January–mid February,
also weekdays November–2 weeks before
Easter
Toast Hawaii £2.30   Shish kebab £4.60
Credit Access, Amex, Visa
P Central car park

Call in throughout the day for a snack at this
bright, appealing restaurant. Toast specialities are always popular ('For Him' combines
sirloin steak with anchovies and olives), and
there are lots of sandwiches plus soup and
ice cream concoctions. Bigger appetites will
go for shish kebabs or perhaps grilled
Borrowdale trout. Set teas are served starting
at 2.30. There's a more elaborate evening
menu. *No dogs.*

266

Keswick   *Underscar Hotel*

Applethwaite
Keswick (076 87) 72469
Map 3 B2 *Cumbria*

Open 10–6
Closed mid December–mid February

Elizabethan pork casserole £3.50   Salmon in pastry £3.75
Credit Access, Amex, Diners
P own car park   &   **WC**

An imposing Victorian mansion where exquisite light lunches can be enjoyed in the lounge in a setting of great elegance. From delicious soups like brown onion and cider, salads and attractive open sandwiches to game liver pâté with Cumberland sauce or trout in herb butter, everything is prepared with skill and attention to detail. There are also lovely cakes and biscuits to have with tea or coffee. More elaborate evening meals. No smoking. *No dogs.*

Kew   ★   *Original Maids of Honour*

288 Kew Road
01-940 2752
Map 6 B3 *Surrey*

Open 10–5.30 (Mon till 1)
Closed Sun & Bank Holidays

Maid of Honour 60p   Set afternoon tea £2.25

P street parking   &   **WC**

In the Newens family for well over 100 years, this renowned temple of traditional baking has a reputation that is almost worldwide. The range and quality of the produce are quite outstanding, and nothing will leave you indifferent, from the legendary Maids of Honour to cream slices, crunchy brandy snaps and marvellous mille-feuilles. Equally impressive are savoury delights like sausage rolls and steak pies. *No dogs.*

Kew   *Pissarro's (Wine Bar)*

1 Kew Green
01-940 3987
Map 6 B3 *Surrey*

Open 11.30–2.30 & 7–10.30, Sun noon–2 & 7–10
Closed Easter Sun & Mon & 25 & 26 December
Salmon mousse £1.70   Calf's liver with sage £5
P street parking   **WC**

The day's bill of fare is chalked up on a blackboard at this attractively rustic wine bar. Thick, well-flavoured minestrone or smoked mackerel mousse could be your choice for a starter, with something like beef bourguignon or lobster-sauced seafood with rice to follow. The cold buffet is a popular alternative, and there's a good variety of sweets both bought-in and home-made, such as chocolate mousse. No children.

Kew   *Wine & Mousaka*

12 Kew Green
01-940 5696
Map 6 B3 *Surrey*

Open noon–2.30 & 6–11.30
Closed Sun, Bank Holidays & 3 days Christmas

Moussaka £3.75   Mezes £6.85
LVs   *Credit* Access, Amex, Diners, Visa
P street parking   **WC**

Many dishes are charcoal-grilled at this friendly Greek restaurant overlooking Kew Green, and the distinctive, oregano-tinged aroma of the cooking certainly attracts the crowds (booking advisable). Try the cumin-flavoured lamb sausages, poussin or pork kebabs prepared this way, or opt for oven-baked moussaka, red wine sausages or dolmades. Taramasalata, calamari and tsatsiki (minty cucumber and yoghurt dip) among starters. *No dogs.*

King's Lynn

Antonio's Wine Bar

Baxter's Plain
King's Lynn (0553) 772324
Map 5 C1 *Norfolk*

Open noon–2 & 7–10.30
Closed Sun, Mon, Bank Holidays & 2 weeks mid August

Minestrone 98p   Pasta dishes from £2.80

P Blackfriars Street car park at rear   **WC**

Ebullient Antonio dominates this lively wine bar, where the most popular dishes are minestrone and lasagne. Also on the menu are a full range of Italian favourites, from Parma ham and tuna fish with beans to pizzas (including one with fresh mackerel) and freshly made ravioli and tortellini. Sandwiches and rolls provide lighter bites, with Italian ice creams or delicious trifle for afters. *No dogs.*

Kinver

Berkley's Bistro

Unit 5, High Street
Kinver (0384) 873679
Map 7 D1 *Staffordshire*

Open noon–2 & 7–10
Closed Sat lunch & all Sun

Seafood pancake £1.80   Pork fillet with cider & apricot sauce £4.95
Credit Access, Amex, Diners, Visa
P car park opposite   &   **WC**

Smart yet informal, this friendly bistro in a row of shops offers an enjoyable selection of robust dishes. Flavour-packed soup, garlic mushrooms and deep-fried potato skins are favourite starters; there are also pasta and vegetarian dishes, along with steaks, fish and appetising daily specials. Nice sweets like meringue gâteau and Norwegian cream from the trolley to finish. *No dogs.*

Knaresborough

Crumpets Coffee Shoppe

25 Castlegate
Map 4 C2 *North Yorkshire*

Open 10–5.30 (till 5 in winter)
Closed Mon (except Bank Holidays), 1 January & 25 & 26 December

Buck rarebit £1.30   Plaice, chips & peas £1.80

P Castle Yard car park

Adrian Bartaby takes as much trouble with his customers as with the simple but delicious food served at this popular little coffee shop. Market day Wednesdays are especially popular, when a tasty offering like beef pie joins the regular menu of sandwiches, toasted snacks, omelettes and pizzas. Winter brings crumpets and muffins, and there are always oven-fresh scones (and teacakes), sponges and fruit pies. Unlicensed.

Lamberhurst

The Down

Lamberhurst (0892) 890237
Map 6 C3 *Kent*

Open 9.30–5.30
Closed Mon (except Bank Holidays) & 25 December–2 January

Speciality ploughman's £3   Lardy cake tea £1.90

P on green opposite   **WC**

A pair of tile-hung cottages now houses this tiny village shop and tea room with a pretty garden for summer eating. Morning scones and cakes, spicy apple strudel and lardy cake all feature again in the delicious set afternoon teas, while lunchtime brings soup, salads based on cheese, ham and quiche, toasted snacks and a lovely ploughman's with apples, grapes, walnuts and wholemeal bread. Unlicensed. No smoking. *No dogs.*

Lancaster — *Dukes Playhouse Restaurant*

Moor Lane
Lancaster (0524) 67461
Map 3 B2 *Lancashire*

Open 10–4 & 5.30–9 (till first interval)
Closed Mon eve, all Sun & Bank Holidays

Golden pea soup 75p   Algerian-style
aubergine £1.70
P St Leonard's Gate car park at rear   &
WC

An informal theatre restaurant that is popular with actors, audience and public. Vegetarian dishes play a leading role – asparagus flan, houmus, stuffed tomatoes, cauliflower and walnut paella – but there are meaty things, too, like liver and onions, lamb Madras or stir-fry chicken. Also good home-made soups, filled baked potatoes, sandwiches and a variety of cakes, pastries and puddings. *No dogs.*

Lancaster — *Libra*

19 Brock Street
Lancaster (0524) 61551
Map 3 B2 *Lancashire*

Open 9–6
Closed Sun, Bank Holidays & 1 Week
Christmas

Leek & mushroom pie £1.90   Samosa 45p

P Dalton Square & street parking   &   **WC**

A pleasant vegetarian restaurant, with literature and decor reflecting the alternative society. Most of the food is made on the premises, including good wholemeal bread and yoghurt. Salads are attractively displayed, and they do an excellent houmus. Leek and mushroom soup, bean and cheese bake and harvest pie filled with swedes and greens typify the hot specials, and there's always a selection of vegan cakes. Non-smoking area. *No dogs.*

Lancaster — *Marinada's*

27 North Road
Lancaster (0524) 381181
Map 3 B2 *Lancashire*

Open noon–2 & 6.30–11
Closed Sun, 1 January & 25 & 26 December

Calzone nostrano £2.90   Vegetable rissoles
£3.90
Credit Access, Amex, Diners, Visa
P car park opposite   &   **WC**

Still very much the 'in' local place, this smart, spacious and extremely well run restaurant offers an excellent choice of Italian dishes prepared to consistently good standards. Pizzas and pasta always please, and if a full meal appeals, try garlic snails or fried whitebait followed by a steak, appetisingly sauced veal or chicken special or one of the several vegetarian main courses. Nice home-made sweets. *No dogs.*

Lancaster — *Potters Coffee House*

Brewery Arcade, Brock Street
Lancaster (0524) 39847
Map 3 B2 *Lancashire*

Open 9–5
Closed Sun, Wed & Bank Holidays

Prawn & haddock flan £1.40   Meat & potato
pie £1.20
LVs
P Dalton Square & street parking   **WC**

It's self-service at this pleasant little coffee house in a small shopping arcade near the city centre. Goodies on display range from home-made soup and savoury flans to filled jacket potatoes, salads and open sandwiches, with home-made fruit pie for afters. The various cakes include éclairs, chocolate crisp and an enjoyable biscuit and fruit loaf. Charming service. *No dogs.*

269

Leamington Spa ★ *Mallory Court*

Harbury Lane, Bishop's Tachbrook
Leamington Spa (0926) 30214
Map 5 A2 *Warwickshire*

Open 3.30–5
Closed 26 December–2 January

Set afternoon tea £5   Smoked salmon
sandwich £4.50
Credit Access, Amex, Visa
P own car park   **WC**

Enjoy your afternoon tea in the elegant
drawing room, peaceful lounge or out on the
terrace of this superb country house hotel.
And what a feast it is – generously filled and
exquisitely presented sandwiches, light,
crumbly scones served with excellent jam
and cream, marzipan-topped fruit cake and
featherlight sponges, all accompanied by a
fine speciality brew. Minimum charge of £5.
No children under 12. *No dogs.*

Leamington Spa   **New Entry**   *Piccolino's*

9 Spencer Street
Leamington Spa (0926) 22988
Map 5 A2 *Warwickshire*

Open noon–2.30 & 5.30–11 (Sun till 10.30, Fri
till 11.30), Sat noon–11.30
Closed 1 January & 25 & 26 December

Tagliatelle misto carbonara £2.95   Piccolino's
special pizza £3.10
P Chapel Street car park   **WC**

Bright colours and simple furnishings set the
scene in this friendly Italian restaurant, where
customers can see their pizzas being baked
to order. Good crisp bases carry generous
toppings in many combinations, including the
special with mozzarella, tomato, ham, mushrooms, smoked provalone and asparagus.
There's also plenty of pasta, plus appetisers
like pâté or whitebait, main-course salads
and some conventional sweets. *No dogs.*

Leamington Spa   **New Entry**   *Regency Fare*

72 Regent Street
Leamington (0926) 25570
Map 5 A2 *Warwickshire*

Open 9–6
Closed Sun & 26 December

Steak & kidney pie £4.35   Toasted teacake
42p
LVs   *Credit* Access, Visa
P Park Street multi-storey car park   **WC**

Open all day for coffee, this busy, town-
centre restaurant comes into its own at noon
with a wide variety of tasty fare to please
most palates and appetites. Omelettes,
salads and a variety of sandwiches make
good light meals. If you're really peckish, you
could start with soup, go on to one of the
many fish and meat main courses and finish
up with apple pie. Children's meals 25% off.
No dogs. ✐

Leamington Spa   **New Entry**   *Ropers*

1a Clarendon Avenue
Leamington Spa (0926) 316719
Map 5 A2 *Warwickshire*

Open 8am–10.30pm (Sun from 10am)
Closed 1 January & 25 December
Prawn granary sandwich £1.50   Stuffed
aubergine £3.45
Credit Access, Amex, Visa
P multi-storey car park in Russell Street   &
WC

Excellent eating all day long at this very smart
conservatory-style brasserie. A splendid
choice of breakfasts is served early on, and
the snack menu includes super granary
sandwiches and pastries. The main menu,
available from 10 o'clock, offers a dazzling
diversity of dishes, from chilled watercress
soup and grilled black pudding to salade
niçoise, Mexican-style pork and custard
treacle tart. £2 minimum lunchtime charge.
No dogs. 🖤

Ledbury   *Applejack Wine Bar*

44 The Homend
Ledbury (0531) 4181
Map 7 D2 *Hereford & Worcester*
Open 11–2.30 (Sun noon–2) & 7–10.30
Closed Sun eve, 1 January & 25 & 26
December
Chicken pâté with wholemeal toast £1.50
Meatballs with apricot & yoghurt sauce £1.95
Credit Access, Diners, Visa
P street parking & St Katherine's car park   ⓖ
WC

Interesting lunchtime and evening snacks are served in this popular wine bar that's simply furnished in pine. Vegetarians are well catered for with dishes like mushroom gougère, fried avocado in a nut and cream sauce and hot pitta bread stuffed with salad. Burgers can be meaty or meatless, and there are spicy meatballs, grilled sardines and some good home-made sweets. Full restaurant meals upstairs. *No dogs.* ⓔ

Ledbury   *Feathers Hotel*

High Street
Ledbury (0531) 5266
Map 7 D2 *Hereford & Worcester*

Open noon–2
Closed 25 December

Steak, kidney & mushroom pie with Guinness
£3.15   Quiche with salads £2.10
Credit Access, Amex, Diners
P own car park   ⓖ   **WC**

A fine selection of savoury pies dominates the lunchtime choice at this lovely old half-timbered hotel. Try the spicy Ledbury sausage flavoured with cider, the curried chicken or perhaps minty lamb with butter beans. Tasty alternatives include jumbo club sandwiches, soup and smoked mackerel, while the cold buffet features invitingly fresh salads and excellent meats. Eat in the bar, in the restaurant or by the lounge fire. ⓔ

Ledbury   *Verzons Country Hotel Bistro*

Trumpet
Trumpet (053 183) 381
Map 7 D2 *Hereford & Worcester*

Open noon–2 & 7–9.30 (Fri & Sat till 10)
Closed Sun lunch

French mustard chicken £4   Beef burgundy
£3.60
Credit Access, Amex, Diners, Visa
P own car park   ⓖ   **WC**

An intimate area leading off the bar forms this convivial bistro, part of a fine Georgian hotel on the A438 Hereford road. Attractively presented dishes range from nicely seasoned soups served with garlic bread to popular favourites like chicken Kiev, steaks and chilli. Blackboard specials, too, plus pleasant sweets to finish such as chocolate nut crunch or treacle tart. ⓔ 🍵

Leeds   *Flying Pizza*

60 Street Lane
Leeds (0532) 666501
Town plan *West Yorkshire*

Open noon–2.30 & 6–11.30, Sun 12.30–3 &
6–11
Closed 1 Jan, Easter Sun & 25 & 26 December

Pasta dishes £2.75   Pizza funghi £2.40
Credit Access, Amex, Visa
P street parking   **WC**

Pizzas are just part of the attraction at this cheerful, spotlessly clean Italian restaurant near Roundhay Park. There's also a fine variety of pasta, from cannelloni and spaghetti bolognese to tagliolini with smoked salmon, plus many meat and chicken main courses. Lots of starters, typical Italian sweets, including ice cream and very good fresh fruit salad. Meals served open air on fine days. *No dogs.*

Leeds · New Entry · *Ike's Bistro*

1 Cross Belgrave Street
Leeds (0532) 433391
Town plan *West Yorkshire*

Open noon–2 & 5.30–11
Closed lunch Bank Holiday Mons & all 1
January & 26 December

Pizza quatro stagione £2.90   Moussaka £3.95
LVs   *Credit* Access, Amex, Diners, Visa
P Merrion Centre NCP   **WC**

A lively modern bistro with a menu to suit most appetites and palates. Crudités, spare ribs and mushrooms à la crème are typical starters, and mains include pizza, pasta, burgers and bistro dishes like chicken Kiev, chilli con carne or lamb noisettes grand veneur. Also vegetarian and low-calorie meals, a kiddies' menu and desserts mainly of the calorific kind. Service is very friendly and cheerful. *No dogs.*

Leeds · *Reed's Café*

64 Albion Street
Leeds (0532) 440398
Town plan *West Yorkshire*

Open 9–5
Closed Sun & Bank Holidays

Cheese and onion toasted sandwich £1.35
Tuna quiche £1.55
LVs
P Schofields or Albion Street NCP   **WC**

A simple, cosy little tea room above a chocolate shop. The menu features a selection of freshly made sandwiches – plain, open or toasted – plus salads and a fisherman's lunch with pilchards and cheese. The cream tea offers buttered scones with whipped cream and strawberry preserve, and a good choice of baking includes éclairs, fruit cake and Danish pastry. Very good tea, and a fine range of coffees. Unlicensed. *No dogs.* 🖐

Leeds · *Salvo's*

115 Otley Road, Headingley
Leeds (0532) 755017
Town plan *West Yorkshire*

Open noon–2 & 6–11.30
Closed Sun, 1 January & 25 & 26 December

Pizza francescana £2.95   Penne arrabiata
con salame £2.95

P street parking   **WC**

It's busy, it's delightful, it's Italian and it's on the A660 about three miles from the city centre. The menu is outstanding in its variety: pizzas come with toppings both traditional and less familiar (prawns and mushrooms; bolognese sauce), and the range of pasta is equally appealing. Starters and the main courses include a long list of daily specials, and the sweets (all home-made) also change daily. *No dogs.*

Leeds · New Entry · *Strawberryfields Bistro*

159 Woodhouse Lane
Leeds (0532) 431515
Town plan *West Yorkshire*

Open 11.45–2.30 & 6–11
Closed lunch Sat & Bank Holidays, all Sun &
25 & 26 December
Red bean moussaka £3.25   Cumin chicken
£5.50
LVs   *Credit* Access, Visa
P NCP in Woodhouse Lane   **WC**

The menu has a wide appeal at this simply appointed bistro just out of the city centre. Pizzas and burgers are popular snack meals, and there are salads, vegetarian dishes and meaty main courses such as chicken espagnole, Hungarian goulash or sirloin steak with a choice of sauces. Extra lunchtime items include ploughman's, savoury flans and filled baked potatoes. There's apricot muesli crumble, plus heftier sweets like Mississippi mud pie. *No dogs.*

LEEDS

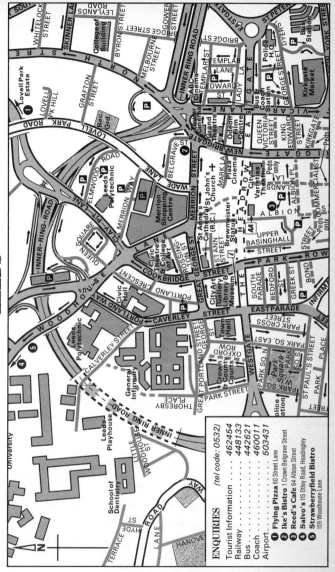

ENQUIRIES (tel code: 0532)

Tourist Information	462454
Railway	448133
Bus	442621
Coach	460011
Airport	503431

1. **Flying Pizza** 60 Street Lane
2. **Ike's Bistro** 1 Crown Belgrave Street
3. **Reed's Cafe** 64 Albion Street
4. **Salvo's** 115 Otley Road, Headingley
5. **Strawberryfield Bistro** 159 Woodhouse Lane

Leicester   *New Entry*   *Blossoms*

17b Cank Street
Leicester (0533) 539535
Map 5 B1 *Leicestershire*

Open 9.30–4
Closed Sun & Bank Holidays except Good Fri

Courgette & red bean bake £1.40   Mixed
vegetable hot pot £1.40
LVs
P St Peters Lane car park   **WC**

The food is displayed and served at a counter in this simply appointed upstairs restaurant. It's all vegetarian, and the lunchtime selection, which changes daily, spans baked potatoes, bhajias and samosas, nice fresh salads and hot dishes such as pasta with mixed vegetables or courgette and red bean bake. Good baking to go with coffee or tea includes banana and walnut loaf, cherry slice and fruit cobbler. Quick, friendly service. Unlicensed. Non-smoking area. *No dogs.*

Leicester   *New Entry*   *Joe Rigatoni*

3 St Martins Square
Leicester (0533) 533977
Map 5 B1 *Leicestershire*

Open noon–2.30 (Sat till 3) & 6.30–11
Closed 1 January & 25 & 26 December

Spaghetti bolognese £2.85   Vitello al Marsala
£5.25

Credit Access, Visa
P Holiday Inn NCP   **WC**

Located on two floors in a modern shopping arcade, this light, airy Italian restaurant is a good place to break for a quick snack or to linger over a full meal. Starters include spare ribs, hot potted shrimps and corn on the cob with cumin butter. There's pasta and pizza, omelettes, pancakes and a good choice of scampi, chicken and meat main dishes. Italian cakes and ices. *No dogs.*

Leicester   *New Entry*   *Peacock Alley*

64 High Street
Leicester (0533) 538155
Map 5 B1 *Leicestershire*

Open 9.30–6
Closed Sun & Bank Holidays except Good Fri

Florentine 55p   Poacher's pie £1.65

LVs
P St Peters Lane car park   **WC**

One of the partners, Susan Bishop, designed this attractive tea room, with an all-day menu that covers a fair selection of tasty snacks. Rolls, sandwiches, cakes and pastries are available for light bites, and there's soup and salads, hot pots and savoury pies (poacher's contains rabbit, pork and turkey). Also vegetarian dishes like mushroom and onion roll. Excellent choice of leaf and exotic teas. Unlicensed. *No dogs.* 🍃 🐾

Leintwardine   ★   *Selda Coffee Shop*

Bridge Street
Leintwardine (054 73) 604
Map 7 D1 *Hereford & Worcester*

Open Nov–March 11–3.30, April–June 9.30–
5.30, July–August 9–6, Sept–Oct 10–5.30
Closed Sun & Mon Nov–end Feb

Bacon bravonium £1.35   Border tart 75p
LVs
P street parking   ♿   **WC**

Patricia Longley runs this delightful little place by the village green. Home-baked goodies particularly impress, with lovely fruit loaves, almond slices and wickedly rich cakes like coffee and chocolate to choose from. Tasty savouries showing judicious use of fresh herbs range from Welsh rarebit to hot cheese and onion puffs, with imaginative salads like celery, apple and cheese with yoghurt and lemon sauce, too. Unlicensed. No smoking. *No dogs.* 🐾

Leominster — *Granary Coffee House*

6 South Street
Map 7 D1 *Hereford & Worcester*

Open 7am–4.30pm (Thurs & Sat till 2)
Closed Sun, Bank Holiday Mons, 1 January &
25 & 26 December

Lasagne £1.40   Cherry meringue pie 45p

P Saveright car park   **WC**

Be prepared to share a table at this cheerful coffee house, whose counter display offers numerous simple, tasty snacks. Sandwiches and wholewheat rolls, quiches and thick slices of pizza are popular savoury items, along with a selection of cold meats such as ham and chicken to enjoy with inventive salads. Lunchtime brings a hot special like chilli or jacket potatoes. Date and walnut slice, flapjacks and gâteaux for the sweeter tooth. Unlicensed. *No dogs.* ⊖

Lewes — *Lunch Counter*

7 Station Street
Lewes (0273) 477447
Map 6 C4 *East Sussex*

Open 10–3
Closed Sun, Bank Holidays & 2 weeks
Christmas

Spring chicken kebabs £2.80   Trifle £1
LVs
P station car park

A popular self-service restaurant where good, sound cooking has long been a feature. Lunch could start with a bowl of excellent soup, and there are usually a couple of hot main dishes like spicy chicken kebabs or a bean bake, in addition to quiche and jacket potatoes. Cold cuts (chicken, ham, salami) are accompanied by a good variety of salads, and puds include trifle and a particularly tasty banoffee pie. Non-smoking section. ⊖

Lewes — *Mike's Wine Bar*

197 High Street
Lewes (0273) 477879
Map 6 C4 *East Sussex*

Open 10–2 & 6–10.30, Sun 11–2 & 7–10
Closed 25 & 26 December

Vegetable roulade with tropical salad £2.75
Lasagne verdi £3.25
Credit Amex, Diners, Visa
P street parking   **WC**

Book at weekends to be sure of a seat in this popular high-street wine bar, especially if you fancy Sunday brunch. Cooking is enthusiastic, and the monthly-changing menu includes home-made lasagne, burgers, jacket potatoes and grills, as well as the more imaginative sweet and sour butter bean hot pot and a courgette and mushroom tagliatelle. Try the hot fudge cake or Fiona's sherry-soaked trifle for afters. ⊖

Lewes — *Pattisson's Coffee Shop*

200 High Street
Lewes (0273) 473364
Map 6 C4 *East Sussex*

Open 9.45–5.30
Closed Sun & Bank Holidays

Mushroom pie £1.70   Apple cobbler £1
LVs

P town-centre car park   **WC**

Everything is home-made at the Pattissons' delightful coffee shop, and you can feast all day on Janet's freshly baked scones, shortbread, fruit loaf and featherlight sponges. Lunchtime brings soup, salads, savoury flans and a hot special such as lasagne or chicken and bacon pie, with jacket potatoes topping the local pops. Friendly, informal service. Non-smoking room. Unlicensed. ⊖ 🐾

Egon Ronay's
guide to
THE LAKE DISTRICT and YORKSHIRE DALES

This unique guide is a passport to over 200 carefully selected hotels, restaurants, wine bars, inns and tearooms providing exceptionally high standards of cooking and accommodation.

To help memories live on until the beautiful dales and fells can be visited again, Egon Ronay's Guide to the Lake District and Yorkshire Dales also offers some recipes from the top chefs of the area.

Available from AA Centres and booksellers everywhere at £5.95 or £6.95 including postage and packing from:

Mail Order Department
PO Box 51
Basingstoke
Hampshire
RG21 2BR

Limpsfield

Limpsfield Brasserie

High Street
Oxted (0883) 717385
Map 6 C3 *Surrey*

Open 11–3 & 6–11
Closed lunch Mon & Sat, all Sun, 1 January,
Good Fri & 25 & 26 December
Steak & kidney pie £4.50   Prawn & pineapple
salad £2.50
Credit Access, Visa
P own car park   **WC**

The bar snacks have really caught on at the
Old Lodge, and the cooking is organised
separately from the main restaurant. The
menu is straightforward, with starters like
pâté, lasagne or outstanding individual
quiche lorraine and main dishes such as fish
pie, steak and kidney pie or chicken kebabs
served with potatoes and salad. Enjoyable
apple crumble, strawberry cheesecake or
banana split to finish. *No dogs.* ☻ 🐾

Lincoln

Harveys Cathedral Restaurant

1 Exchequergate
Lincoln (0522) 21886
Map 4 D4 *Lincolnshire*

Open noon–2 & 7–9.30

Brie tart with salad £1.95   Seychelles chicken
ribbons £6.50
Credit Access, Visa

P castle square car park   **WC**

Near the west front of the cathedral, this
smart yet informal restaurant offers a very
imaginative selection of tasty, well-prepared
dishes. Marbled fish mousse and chicken
liver parfait are typical starters, while main
courses span vegetarian stuffed peppers,
lamb curry and pot-roast beef with an unexpected but enjoyable raspberry sauce. For
afters, perhaps chocolate pot, cheese or a
baked apple. *No dogs.* ☻

Lincoln

Wig & Mitre

29 Steep Hill
Lincoln (0522) 35190
Map 4 D4 *Lincolnshire*

Open 8am–midnight
Closed 25 December

Fresh asparagus & mushrooms on toast £1.95
Coq au vin £3.25
LVs   *Credit* Access, Amex, Diners, Visa
P Castle Square car park   🚻   **WC**

On a steep hill in the medieval part of Lincoln,
this bustling pub restaurant serves the whole
range of its excellent food throughout the
long opening hours. And what a range it is,
from cakes and sandwiches to eggs and
bacon, seafood pie, chicken lasagne and
beef bourguignon. There are also vegetarian
dishes and nice sweets such as plum crumble
and orange roulade. *No dogs.* ☻

Liverpool

Armadillo Restaurant

20 Mathew Street
051-236 4123
Town plan *Merseyside*

Open 10.30–3 & 5–7
Closed Sun, Bank Holidays & 1 week
Christmas
Beef in beer with herb dumplings £2.95
Celery & apple soup 80p
LVs   *Credit* Access, Visa
P NCP in Paradise Street   **WC**

Set opposite the 'Cavern', where the Beatles
made their name, this smart, self-service
restaurant tempts with a fine array of snacks.
Baking ranges from caramel slice and sticky
tea bread to very good quiches like courgette
and bacon; sustaining soups and fresh
salads are supplemented at lunchtime (minimum charge £1.75) by a daily-changing hot
dish such as beef in beer with herb dumplings.
Full evening menu. *No dogs.* ☻ 🐾

Liverpool   *Everyman Bistro*

Hope Street
051-708 9545
Town plan *Merseyside*

Open noon–11.30
Closed Sun & Bank Holidays

Quiche 80p   Meatballs with tomato sauce &
rice £2.60
LVs
P street parking   **WC**

Beneath the Everyman Theatre, this informal
basement bistro attacts its own fans for the
robust, wholesome food on offer. Queue up
at the self-service counter for light snacks –
flavoursome pâtés and pizza, jacket potatoes
and quiche – or opt for a tasty main course
like coriander pork with rice or vegetarian
broccoli and sour cream bake. Appealing
puddings and fruit slices to finish. ©

Liverpool   *La Grande Bouffe*

48a Castle Street
051-236 3375
Town plan *Merseyside*

Open noon–6
Closed Sun, Bank Holidays & 24–26
December
Fresh salmon fishcakes with watercress
butter £3.10   Apricot-glazed apple tart £1.10
LVs   *Credit* Access, Amex, Visa
P Brunswick Street car park   **WC**

The good foods and the warm-hearted ambience bring customers on return visits to
this friendly basement restaurant. The busy
lunchtime period brings all sorts of tasty
things, from vegetable soup and salmon
fishcakes to courgette and mushroom lasagne, navarin of lamb and a super damson
pie. There are plenty of cakes to go with
afternoon tea. *No dogs.* ©

Liverpool   *Mandarin*

40 Victoria Street
051-236 8899
Town plan *Merseyside*

Open noon–11.30 (Sun from 5.30)
Closed 1 January & 25 & 26 December
Crab & sweetcorn soup £1   Sweet & sour
chicken £3.50
LVs   *Credit* Access, Amex, Diners, Visa

P NCP in Victoria Street   **WC**

A large and loyal following gives top marks
to this centrally located Chinese restaurant
in a converted warehouse. Dim sum served
throughout the long opening hours make
ideal snacks – choices include steamed spare
ribs, paper-wrapped prawns and delicious
pork dumplings with a fiery chilli sauce – and
there are lots of seafood, meat and poultry
main courses, too. Finish with a toffee fruit
dessert. *No dogs.*

Liverpool   *Streets*

4 Baltimore Street
051-709 2121
Town plan *Merseyside*

Open noon–11 (Sat, Sun & Bank Holidays from
7pm)
Closed 25 December

Barbecued beef with rice & salad £3
Cheesecake 95p
P street parking   **WC**

Friendly waiters create a cheerful atmosphere at this heavily beamed restaurant-
cum-wine bar that's popular with students.
Soup, pizzas and burgers are the main fare
upstairs, while downstairs a blackboard
menu supplements various ways with steaks
– pepper, Diane, pizzaiola, grilled – and some
chicken, veal and fish dishes. Cooking is
generally capable, and sweets include
cheesecake and fresh fruit pies. ©

LIVERPOOL

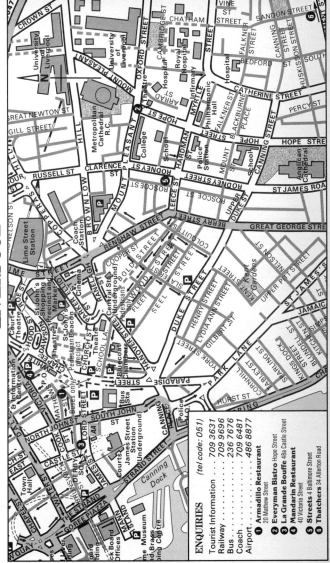

ENQUIRIES

(tel code: 051)

Tourist Information	709 3631
Railway	709 9696
Bus	236 7676
Coach	709 6481
Airport	486 8877

1. **Armadillo Restaurant** 20 Mathew Street
2. **Everyman Bistro** Hope Street
3. **La Grande Bouffe** 48a Castle Street
4. **Mandarin Restaurant** 40 Victoria Street
5. **Streets** 4 Baltimore Street
6. **Thatchers** 34 Allerton Road

Liverpool

Thatcher's

34 Allerton Road
051-734 0542
Town plan *Merseyside*

Open 10–4.30 (Wed till 4)
Closed Sun & Bank Holidays

Seafood pancakes £1.10   Hot pot with
cabbage £1.75
Credit Visa
P street parking   **WC**

Run by staunch Tory ladies, this friendly
coffee shop specialises in honest home
cooking. The menu is simple, including fruit
cake (regularly dispatched to Mrs T. herself)
and there are lots of other sweet items, too,
like almond slice, walnut loaf and Bakewell
tart. Popular savoury snacks include sandwiches and things on toast, while pancakes,
pies and substantial salads make nice light
lunches. Unlicensed. *No dogs.*

Louth

Mr Chips

17 Aswell Street
Louth (0507) 603756
Map 4 D3 *Lincolnshire*

Open 11am–11pm
Closed Sun

Haddock, chips, peas & tea £2.50   Dover
sole, peas, chips & tea £3.85

P Queen Street car park   &   **WC**

One generation of Hagans has said goodbye,
Mr Chips, and another has taken over this
large cafeteria-style fish and chippery in the
centre of town. Cod, plaice, haddock and
sole, all admirably fresh, are carefully cooked
in a good light batter and come with super
chips and either mushy peas or baked beans,
plus bread and butter and a decent cuppa.
Children's menu. *No dogs.*

Lower Basildon

Cottage Restaurant & Tea Rooms

Reading Road
Upper Basildon (0491) 671780
Map 6 A3 *Berkshire*

Open 9–6
Closed Mon, also Tues in winter & 3 days
Christmas

Soup of the day 90p   Fish & chips £2.90

P own car park   **WC**

Throughout the day you can pull into this
charming cottage by the A329 for a tasty bite
to eat. Breakfast is served early on, and the
lunchtime selection includes sandwiches and
salads, baked potatoes, omelettes and gammon steaks. Good home-produced cakes,
pastries and sweets always available. Also a
more elaborate menu lunchtime plus Friday
and Saturday evenings. *No dogs.*

Luccombe Chine

Dunnose Cottage

Near Shanklin
Isle of Wight (0983) 862585
Map 6 B4 *Isle of Wight*

Open 10.30–7
Closed Mon & weekdays November–Easter

Chocolate cake 50p   Fried plaice with chips
£2.90

P own car park   **WC**

Ideally placed on a clifftop walk between
Shanklin and Ventnor, this delightful old
thatched cottage – with a pretty garden –
offers a day-long menu of salads, sandwiches and snacks, topped up with fried fish,
chops and chips at lunch and suppertime.
Tea is one of the highlights of the day, with
lovely home-made scones and cakes and a
really nice pot of tea. Book for the popular
traditional Sunday lunch at £5.25.

Ludlow ★ *Hardwicks*

Quality Square
Map 7 D1 *Shropshire*

Open 10–5
Closed Sun & 25 & 26 December

Vegetable lasagne £2.10   Spinach provençale £2

P castle car park & WC

There's a light, summery air about this spotless restaurant tucked away in a picturesque courtyard. Patricia Hardwick is a simply marvellous cook and can turn her hand to everything from mouthwatering baked goodies – scones, petits fours, super coffee or chocolate and bilberry cake – to super hot specials like spinach au gratin, chicken tandoori and warming winter soups. Savoury snacks include quality flans and granary rolls.

Ludlow *Olive Branch*

2 Old Street
Ludlow (0584) 4314
Map 7 D1 *Shropshire*

Open October–May 10–3 (Fri till 2.30), Sun 12.30–5.30; June–September 10–5 (Thurs–Sat till 8), Sun 12.30–5.30
Closed 2 weeks Christmas
Soup of the day 85p   Spinach lasagne with salads £2.25
P town-centre parking   WC

On a busy corner in the town centre, this bright, informal vegetarian restaurant offers a daily-changing selection of simple but enjoyable fare. Consult the blackboard for tasty snacks served at mealtimes – pizzas, baked potatoes, colourful salads, plus more substantial items like leeks au gratin. In the morning and afternoon you can enjoy freshly baked scones, rich, dark chocolate cake and buttered fruit loaf. *No dogs.*

Ludlow *Penny Anthony Restaurant*

5 Church Street
Ludlow (0584) 3282
Map 7 D1 *Shropshire*

Open 10.30–2 & 7–10
Closed Sun

Lamb's kidneys Dubonnet £3.50   Vegetable pancake £4.50
Credit Amex, Diners, Visa
P car park adjacent & WC

Choose just one course or a full meal at this smart town-centre restaurant with a wide choice of menus. Seafood pancake, cheese and herb pâté or terrine of scallops makes an appealing snack or starter, while more substantial offerings include lamb's liver with pepper sauce, trout meunière, best end of lamb and excellent lasagne. A crisp salad or vegetables accompany. There are some nice cakes and scones to go with morning coffee. *No dogs.*

Lustleigh ★ *Primrose Cottage*

Near Newton Abbot
Lustleigh (064 77) 365
Map 8 C4 *Devon*

Open 10–5.30 (till 5 in winter)
Closed 25 & 26 December, also Mon–Fri December–February & 4 weekends around Christmas
Hazelnut meringue with apricots 95p   Hot honey-roast ham with orange sauce £3.40
P street parking   WC

Roger and Miranda Olver prepare the scrumptious fare that puts this yellow-painted Dartmoor cottage firmly among the stars. The chief attraction is a marvellous array of baking that includes éclairs, fruit sponges, perfect scones and a quite wonderful apple strudel. The same quality comes out clearly in lunchtime snacks like pizza, pastries and a thoroughly satisfying daily special such as savoury mince or chicken and ham pie. Unlicensed.

Lyme Regis   **New Entry**   *Golden Cap*

65 Broad Street
Lyme Regis (029 74) 2049
Map 8 C3 *Dorset*

Open 10–8.30
Closed November–March

Cottage pie £1.95   Lyme Bay plaice with
vegetables £4.50

P alongside   ♿   **WC**

Through the windows of this seaside restaurant you can watch the fishermen catching the plaice and sole that feature on the menu. Owner Peter Froom is a Lyme Regis man and cooks the fish with appropriate care and pride, while his wife Anneliese contributes a subtly spiced schnitzel. A speciality sweet combines ice cream, advocaat, meringue and chocolate sauce. Also light meals, children's dishes and afternoon snacks. ☘ 🍵

Lympstone   ★   *River House*

The Strand
Exmouth (0395) 265147
Map 8 C4 *Devon*

Open noon–1.30
Closed Mon, Bank Holidays (except Good Fri),
2 January & 27 December
Seafood temptation £5.75   Tagliatelle salad
£5.75
Credit Access, Amex, Visa
P village car park   **WC**

Light lunches of outstanding quality are served in this delightful waterfront restaurant. Fish is a prominent feature in Shirley Wilkes' menus, with salmon kedgeree, seafood pancakes and seven different fish in a wine and cheese sauce among the tasty treats. Garlicky stuffed mushrooms, moussaka and a hot tagliatelle salad are other possibilities. All dishes are priced at £5.75. No children under five. *No dogs.* ☘

Lynton   ★   *Lee Cottage*

Lee Abbey
Lynton (059 85) 2621
Map 8 C3 *Devon*

Open 11–12 & 1–5
Closed Sun & early September–early May

Cream tea £1.20   Filled roll with salad garnish
60p

P own car park   **WC**

Run by the Lee Abbey Christian Community, this delightful little tea room enjoys a tranquil, breathtakingly beautiful setting reached by a winding clifftop road. Enjoy a delicious cream tea in the lovely garden – freshly baked scones with jam and thick clotted cream, lovely light sponges – or a lunchtime snack of filled rolls and ploughman's with Stilton or Double Gloucester. Unlicensed. ☘

Lyonshall   ★   *Church House*

Kington
Lyonshall (054 48) 350
Map 7 D1 *Hereford & Worcester*

Open 3–5.30
Closed 25 & 26 December

Cream tea 95p   Cakes from 40p

P own car park   ♿   **WC**

The setting is delightfully old-fashioned, with Edwardian books and bric-à-brac and fine bone china. But the biggest delight at this guest-house tea room is the marvellous baking by local girls: fruit scones light, warm and crusty; lemon spicy cake with a wonderful balance of fragrance and zing; fruit cake that's rich, dark and faintly tipsy. Advance notice required for the full set tea with finger sandwiches. Unlicensed. *No dogs.* 🍵

Lytchett Minster

Slepe Cottage Tea Rooms

Dorchester Road, Poole
Morden (092 945) 281
Map 8 D3 *Dorset*

Open 10.15–5.45 (Sun from 2)
Closed Mon (except Bank Holidays) & end
October–1 March

Mushroom omelette £1.40   Dorset cream tea
£1.70
P own car park & **WC**

Two miles outside the village on the A35
Dorchester road stands this cosy tea room
with its delightful garden. It's the ideal setting
in which to enjoy some good simple snacks.
Set teas, available throughout the day, include one with cucumber sandwiches and a
choice of delicious cakes. Lunchtime brings
a small savoury selection comprising sandwiches, salads, toasted snacks and omelettes. Unlicensed. No smoking. *No dogs.*

Lytham

Lytham Kitchen

9 Market Square
Lytham (0253) 736492
Map 3 B3 *Lancashire*

Open 10–4.30
Closed Sun, Mon, 25 & 26 December & last
two weeks February
Salmon coulibiac £2.55   Spaghetti bolognese
£1.95
LVs
P street parking &

Marble-topped tables are set in booth-style
seating at this agreeable restaurant, where
the cooking is reliable and the choice for
snackers wide. Sandwiches, toasties, omelettes and grills satisfy savoury appetites
throughout the day, and lunchtime brings
extra things like chicken vol-au-vent or beef
bourguignon. There are also decent salads,
and lots of cakes, pastries and sponges.
Non-smoking section. *No dogs.*

Magham Down

Ye Old Forge

Near Hailsham
Hailsham (0323) 842893
Map 6 C4 *East Sussex*

Open 9–5.30 (till 2.30 November–Spring Bank
Holiday)

Cream tea £2   Steak & kidney pie with chips
£2.50
Credit Access, Visa
P own car park & **WC**

The hard-working Thomases welcome customers every day of the year to their cosy
beamed restaurant. They offer everything
from generous fried breakfasts to ploughman's lunches and dainty cucumber sandwiches to set cream teas (available spring to
October). Full midday meals might start with
home-made soup, then perhaps spaghetti
bolognese followed by apple pie. More
elaborate evening carte. *No dogs.*

Manchester

Pizzeria Bella Napoli

1 Kennedy Street
061-236 1537
Town plan *Greater Manchester*

Open 12.15–11.30pm (Sun from 6.30)
Closed Bank Holidays

Pizza calabresi £2.50   Spaghetti carbonara
£3

P car park in Deansgate **WC**

This popular Italian restaurant in well-main-
tained basement premises specialises in
pasta and pizzas. Spaghetti, tagliatelle, cannelloni and lasagne are served nicely al dente
with a variety of tasty sauces, and the pizzas
come in a range that includes margherita,
veneziana and the speciality quattro stagioni.
Also good antipasto and minestrone, home-
made pâtisserie and ice creams. Pleasant,
speedy service. *No dogs.*

Manchester

Pizzeria Italia

40 Deansgate
061-834 1541
Town plan *Greater Manchester*

Open noon–11.30 (Sun from 6.30)
Closed 1 January & 25 & 26 December

Pizza Italia £2.60   Paglia e fieno £2.30

P car park in Deansgate   &   **WC**

Ideal for pre- and after-theatre meals, this large modern restaurant (under the same ownership as the Bella Napoli) offers some favourite Italian dishes. Pizzas come sizzling hot from the oven, spaghetti has a choice of five sauces, there are two-toned noodles, barbecued chicken or a burger. Finish with a gâteau or ice cream. *No dogs.*

Manchester

Venezia Trattoria

2 Mount Street, off Albert Square
061-834 5330
Town plan *Greater Manchester*

Open noon–3 & 6–midnight
Closed lunch Sun & Bank Holiday Mon, all 1 January & 25 & 26 December

Pizza peperoni £3   Risotto marinara £3
Credit Access, Amex, Diners, Visa
P city-centre multi-storey car parks   **WC**

Calzone veneziana – folded pizza filled with mushrooms, mozzarella, ham and anchovies – is a house speciality at this Italian basement restaurant in the city centre. There are flat pizzas, too, plus antipasti and pasta (both available as either starter or main course), and a range of fish and meat dishes. Decent home-made sweets from the trolley. *No dogs.*

Manchester

Woo Sang

19 George Street
061-236 3697
Town plan *Greater Manchester*

Open noon–11.45
Closed 25 & 26 December

Dim sum from 90p   King prawns £6.40
LVs   *Credit* Access, Amex, Diners, Visa

P NCP in Faulkner Street   **WC**

Right in the heart of Manchester's Chinatown, this comfortable first-floor restaurant remains a popular rendezvous, especially at lunchtime. The best just-a-bite choice (available throughout opening times) is the wide range of expertly prepared dim sum, from steamed beef balls and roast pork rice roll to spare ribs with soya beans and lotus leaves wrapped round glutinous rice with assorted meats. *No dogs.*

Manchester

Yang Sing

34 Princess Street
061-236 2200
Town plan *Greater Manchester*

Open noon–11.30
Closed 25 December

Dim sum £1   Sweet & sour chicken £4
LVs   *Credit* Access, Amex

P NCP in Portland Street   **WC**

Despite new larger premises, you still need to book to be sure of a table at the Yeung family's ever-popular Chinese restaurant. Ask Gerry Yeung to help you find your way around his vast menu: he may recommend featherlight prawn dumplings, superb goujons of sole with asparagus and a Cantonese steak cooked before you. Good choice of dim sum for budget-eaters, and generous portions of delicious rice. *No dogs.*

MANCHESTER

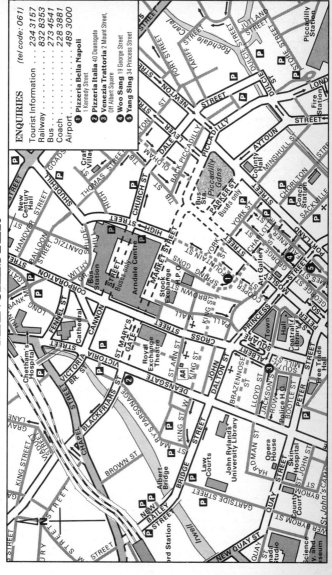

Market Harborough

Taylor's Fish Restaurant

10 Adam & Eve Street
Market Harborough (0858) 63043
Map 5 B2 *Leicestershire*

Open 11.45–2 & 4.45–10
Closed Sun, lunch Bank Holidays, 1 January &
25 & 26 December
Cod & chips £1.60   Halibut steak & chips
£3.10
LVs
P St Mary's Road car park   &   **WC**

Upstairs is smarter and roomier than the self-service cafeteria, but both offer the same range of fish and chip dishes that make this such a popular restaurant. The choice includes cod, haddock, plaice and dog fish, along with sole, skate and scampi, and occasionally you'll find seasonal specials like crab or mussels. Children's menu offered. Half the seating is reserved for non-smokers. *No dogs.*

Marlborough ★

Polly

26 High Street
Marlborough (0672) 52146
Map 6 A3 *Wiltshire*

Open 8.30–6, Sat 8–7, Sun 9–7
Closed 1 Jan, 1st two Fri & Sat in October & 3
days Christmas

Set afternoon tea £1.95   Gâteau £1.30
Credit Access, Amex, Diners, Visa
P street parking   **WC**

A marvellous traditional tea room on Marlborough's main street. The delights that wait within are manifold: full breakfast or morning coffee; lunchtime dishes like fish mousse and pâté, quiche and honey-baked gammon; speciality ices; set teas and a wonderful kaleidoscope of cakes and pastries, including macaroon fingers, Viennese whirls, lemon cream shortbread and an unusual Piña Colada gâteau. Minimum charge £1.95 after 3 o'clock. *No dogs.* 🍵

Marlow

Burgers

The Causeway
Marlow (062 84) 3389
Map 6 B3 *Buckinghamshire*

Open 8.30–5.30
Closed Sun, Bank Holidays & 25 & 26
December

Steak & kidney pie £2.85   Welsh rarebit &
bacon £2.30
P Pound Lane car park   &   **WC**

Fresh cream cakes, Viennese whirls, florentines and other fancy pastries continue to attract customers to the Burger family's long-established corner shop-cum-restaurant. Their Welsh rarebit remains a favourite, and they also do sandwiches, toasties and omelettes as well as cream teas. Come early for a croissant and coffee or full English breakfast. Unlicensed. *No dogs.* 🍽️🍵

Matlock

Strand Restaurant

43 Dale Road
Matlock (0629) 4444
Map 4 C4 *Derbyshire*

Open 10–2, also 7–10 Fri & Sat
Closed Sun, Mon, Bank Holidays & 1 week
Christmas

Cottage pie £1.55   Bakewell tart 95p

P Matlock Bridge car park   &   **WC**

Originally a Victorian draper's shop, this agreeable restaurant has a lot of period charm. Coffee and pastries are the morning fare, replaced at noon by enjoyable dishes like leek and courgette soup, a savoury flan and a superior steak and kidney pie. A vegetarian dish is also offered, plus steaks, a few salads and some calorific sweets (nice Bakewell tart). Similar evening menu Friday and Saturday. Children's portions available. *No dogs.* 🍽️

Mawgan   *Yard Bistro*

Trelowarren Estate, Near Helston
Mawgan (032 622) 595
Map 8 A4 *Cornwall*

Open 11–2
Closed Sun eve, Mon (except Bank Holidays)
& mid December–early March

Cauliflower & courgette gratinée £2.95   Fresh
crab salad £4.50
P own parking & **WC**

This bright, cheerful bistro is situated in the old coach house of a country mansion. Coffee is the only offering until noon, after which you can choose from tasty snacks like mushroom soup, filled jacket potatoes, crab or beef salads and a dish of the day such as our very good courgette and cauliflower gratinée. For pud, there might be rhubarb crumble or chocolate brownies. More elaborate evening meals. *No dogs.*

Melmerby   ★   *Village Bakery*

Near Penrith
Langwathby (076 881) 515
Map 3 B1 *Cumbria*

Open 8.30–5 (Sun & Bank Holidays from 9.30)
Closed Mon (except Bank Holidays) &
Christmas–Easter

Creamy vegetable pie £3.50   Trout pâté £1.05

P own car park   **WC**

A lovingly converted old barn houses this marvellous bakery and tea room, run by the dedicated Whitleys, who provide all the organically grown vegetables, fruit, milk and meat from their own smallholding. The imaginative menu extends from super breakfasts to lunchtime offerings of, say, broccoli and lemon quiche, cottage cheese-filled spinach roulade and gooseberry pie to finish. Delicious home-baked cakes and scones, too. No smoking. *No dogs.*

Mentmore   *Stable Yard Craft Gallery & Tea Room*

Near Leighton Buzzard
Cheddington (0296) 668660
Map 5 B2 *Bedfordshire*

Open 10–6
Closed Mon (except Bank Holidays), Tues &
25 & 26 December

Cream scones 80p   Quiche & salad £1.65

P own parking & **WC**

A 150-year-old stable block has been renovated and turned into a most attractive craft shop and little tea room. The original partitions and horse troughs survive, making an unusual setting in which to scoff sausage rolls and quiches, home-made scones, apple pie and splendid chocolate cake. A friendly, welcoming place, with alfresco eating when the sun shines. Unlicensed. *No dogs.*

Middlewich   *Tempters*

11 Wheelock Street
Middlewich (060 684) 5175
Map 3 B4 *Cheshire*

Open 7pm–10.30pm (Fri & Sat till 11pm)
Closed Sun, Mon, 1 January, Good Fri, 25 &
26 December & 2 weeks October
Prawn & mushroom ramekin £1.60
Butterscotch cream crunch £1.20
Credit Access, Visa
P street parking   **WC**

Pam and Allan Diamond continue to tempt customers at their pleasantly relaxed restaurant with a frequently changing menu of carefully prepared dishes that taste as good as they look. Main courses include beef provençale, pork Stroganoff, venison pie and a poacher's pot of salmon with ginger, currants, wine and cream. Garlic mushrooms, spiced prawns and wholesome soup make tasty starters, and there are rich home-made sweets like treacle pudding.

287

Middlewood   *Burnt House Barn*

Near Clifford
Clifford (049 73) 472
Map 7 C2 *Hereford & Worcester*

Open 10–6 (Thurs till noon), also Fri 7–11
Closed 25 December

Afternoon tea £1.50   Omelette, chips & peas
£1.50

P own car park   **WC**

The Middlewood sign on the B4352 points the way to this converted barn with all the delightful atmosphere of a farmhouse kitchen. The hospitable Stutzes will tempt you to a feast of home baking, much of it straight from the oven, and there are also salads, sandwiches and fry-ups. Friday nights are devoted to fish and chips, and you need to book for the marvellous-value Sunday lunch. Advance warning needed for more elaborate meals. 🍵

Midsomer Norton   *Mrs Pickwick*

70 High Street, Near Bath
Midsomer Norton (0761) 414589
Map 8 D3 *Avon*

Open 9–6
Closed Sun & Bank Holidays

Cottage pie £1.50   Cream tea £1.25
LVs

P street parking

Friendly little tea rooms behind and above a high-street cake shop. All through the day there's a good selection of pastries and confectionery, including custard slices, Bath buns, scones and cheesecakes. Sandwiches, rolls and toasted snacks provide tasty savoury bites, and lunchtime brings soup, pâté, omelettes and daily specials like macaroni cheese or cottage pie. Unlicensed. *No dogs.* 🍵

Minstead   `New Entry`   *Honey Pot*

Near Lyndhurst
Southampton (0703) 813122
Map 6 A4 *Hampshire*

Open 10.30–5.30
Closed Nov–Mothering Sunday

Cottage pie £3.25   Chocolate cake 85p
Credit Access, Visa

P own car park   **WC**

Plain or wholesome scones, excellent jam and super clotted cream make up the popular Queen Bee tea served at this neat little building behind a lovely thatched cottage. Savoury snacks are also available, including rolls and sandwiches, salads, a very good quiche and a hot dish of the day such as cottage pie. Moist, light chocolate cake is tempting, as are ice cream sundaes. There's a quiet, pretty garden. 🍵

Montacute   *Montacute House Restaurant*

Martock (0935) 824575
Map 8 D3 *Somerset*

Open 12.30–5
Closed Tues & end October–1 April

Cream tea £1.65   Ploughman's £1.85
Credit Access, Diners, Visa

P National Trust car park   ♿

After visiting the house and gardens of this 16th-century National Trust property, call in at this brightly decorated coffee shop for an excellent cup of tea and a bite to eat. Lunchtime brings sandwiches, ploughman's, quiche and mackerel salad, along with hot dishes (except July and August) like soup, sausage plait and shepherd's pie. From 2.30 cakes, sponges and cream teas are served. *No dogs.* 🍵

Morden   *Superfish*

20 London Road
01-648 6908
Map 6 C3 *Surrey*

Open 11.30–2 (Fri & Sat till 2.30) & 5.30–11 (Fri & Sat 5–11.30)
Closed Sun & Bank Holidays

Cod & chips £2.85   Skate & chips £3.40
LVs
P Presto supermarket car park & **WC**

Aptly named, for the fish is indeed super at this bright, cheerful restaurant. Traditional favourites like cod, plaice and haddock are beautifully cooked and served with smashing chips, good pickles and a basket full of lovely hot French bread. Scampi, sole, skate and rock are also available, and there are nice ices to finish. Friendly waiting staff. *No dogs.*

Moreton-in-Marsh   *Market House*

4 High Street
Moreton-in-Marsh (0608) 50767
Map 5 A2 *Gloucestershire*

Open 9am–10pm in summer, 10–6 in winter
Closed 25 & 26 December & 2 weeks February

Chicken Kiev £5.25   Market House grill £3.95

P street parking & **WC**

The Dickensian bow window of this well-run tea shop reveals an enticing display of home-made goodies. You can feast on lovely light fruit scones, yummy coffee and hazelnut cake, rich chocolate cake, flapjacks and teacakes all day. Lunchtime brings a few hot dishes – fish or steak and kidney pie – plus sandwiches and salads. Efficient, thoughtful service. *No dogs.*

Much Wenlock   *Scott's Coffee & Wholefood Shop*

High Street
Much Wenlock (0952) 727596
Map 7 D1 *Shropshire*

Open 10–5
Closed Wed, also Sun–Tues January & 1 week Christmas

Home-made soup 65p   Bean lasagne £2.90

P town-centre car park &

Sit surrounded by shelves of wholefood products in this simple coffee shop on the High Street. The menu is mainly, though not exclusively, vegetarian, and runs from vege-table soup and quiche to bean lasagne, grilled fish and a good macaroni cheese. There's a limited selection of salads, and various cakes, including yoghurt (light but bland), cherry and ginger. Nancy Welsh runs the place with precision. 🍷

New Romney   *Country Kitchen*

18 High Street
New Romney (0679) 64642
Map 6 D4 *Kent*

Open 7.30–5 (Mon till 1, Sat till 3)
Closed Sun, Bank Holidays & 25 December–1 January
Chicken & ham pie with vegetables £2.75
Walnut sundae 99p
Credit Access, Visa
P street parking & car parks & **WC**

Baking starts betimes at this charming beamed restaurant, where morning coffee and afternoon tea are accompanied by a wide range of sweet and savoury snacks. Lunchtime brings more substantial choices like omelettes with chips, cheese and onion quiche, fillet of plaice and the very popular chicken and ham pie. Cold things, too, plus ices and a fruit pie. *No dogs.* 🍷

Newark

Gannets

35 Castlegate
Newark (0636) 702066
Map 4 D4 *Nottinghamshire*

Open 10–4.30
Closed Sun, Bank Holidays & 1 week
Christmas

Bobotie £2.25   Aubergine bake £2.15

P street parking   **WC**

Capable, unfussy cooking is the key to excellent snacking at Hilary Bower's smart, friendly restaurant furnished in pine. With morning coffee and afternoon tea comes a fine selection of baking, including date and hazelnut cake, banana loaf and wholemeal scones served with scrumptious home-made jam. Lunchtime brings things like pâté, quiche and lasagne, plus daily specials such as bobotie or cauliflower and mushroom au gratin. Nice sweets, too. *No dogs.* ⊝

Newbury

Crafty Cat

5 Inch's Yard, Market Street
Newbury (0635) 35491
Map 6 A3 *Berkshire*

Open 9.30–4.45 (Mon till 4)
Closed Sun, Bank Holidays & 4 days
Christmas
Italian fish stew £2.70   Cauliflower & broccoli
cheese £2.65
Credit Access
P Market Street multi-storey car park   **WC**

An attractive, well-run coffee shop situated above a gift shop on the upper floor of a barn-like building. Nice scones and short-bread, moist banana cake and caramel square go well with tea or coffee, while at lunchtime, wholemeal baps, quiches, salads and baked potatoes are supplemented by hot daily specials like pasta and leeks au gratin. *No dogs.* ⊝ 🫖

Newcastle upon Tyne

Blackgate Restaurant

The Side
Tyneside (091) 2617356
Town plan *Tyne & Wear*

Open noon–3
Closed Sat, Sun & Bank Holidays

Pastrami sandwich £1.95   Smoked salmon &
cream cheese bagel £3
Credit Access, Amex, Diners, Visa
P Dean Street car park   ё   **WC**

Tucked away in a cobbled back street, this popular German restaurant offers appetising lunchtime snacks in its lounge bar. Open sandwiches served on rye or caraway seed bread are a favourite choice, while the blackboard features specials like robust potato and turnip soup, beef and tomato with spätzle and poached fillet of sole. Sweets like apple strudel to finish. Full meals are available in the restaurant. *No dogs.*

Newcastle upon Tyne   **New Entry**

Madeleine's

134 Heaton Road, Heaton
Tyneside (091) 2765277
Town plan *Tyne & Wear*

Open noon–1.30 & 7–9.30
Closed Sun & 1 week Christmas

Walnut & cottage cheese pâté 90p   Burgundy
casserole £3.20
Credit Access, Visa
P street parking   **WC**

The menu at this well-run little restaurant in a row of shops features a daily-changing selection of vegetarian and vegan dishes. The choice could include anything from a simple vegetable broth to walnut and cottage cheese pâté, soya-based burgundy casserole and hazelnut roast with sweet and sour sauce. Delicious garlic bread, and tempting sweets like lemon cheesecake or brown bread ice cream. *No dogs.*

NEWCASTLE-UPON-TYNE

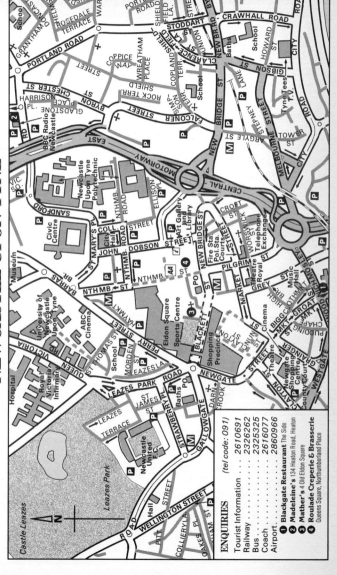

ENQUIRIES

(tel code: 091)

Tourist Information	2610691
Railway	2326262
Bus	2325325
Coach	2616077
Airport	2860966

❶ **Blackgate Restaurant** The Side
❷ **Madeleine's** 134 Heaton Road, Heaton
❸ **Mather's** 4 Old Eldon Square
❹ **Roulade Creperie & Brasserie**
  Queens Square, Northumberland Place

Newcastle upon Tyne · *Mather's*

4 Old Eldon Square
Tyneside (091) 232 4020
Town plan *Tyne & Wear*

Open 9.30am–10pm
Closed Sun & Bank Holidays
Moussaka with salad £3.45   Nut loaf with
salad £2.35
LVs
P NCP in Newgate Street; street parking in eve
WC

A varied choice of enjoyable home cooking is on offer throughout the long opening hours at this informal basement restaurant. Omelettes, moussaka, quiche lorraine and spaghetti bolognese are typical dishes, and there's a nut loaf for vegetarians. Sweet things include cheesecake, apple pie and a very good chocolate gâteau. Half portions available for children. 🛇 🦃

Newcastle upon Tyne · *Roulade Crêperie & Brasserie*

Queens Square, Northumberland Place
Tyneside (091) 261 4811
Town plan *Tyne & Wear*

Open 10am–10pm (Mon till 6.30)
Closed Sun, 1 January, Easter Mon & 25 & 26 December
Brittany crêpe £2.10   Chicken suprême crêpe £2.25
LVs *Credit* Access, Amex, Diners, Visa
P NCP in New Bridge Street   **WC**

A smartly contemporary restaurant in a little shopping precinct specialising in made-to-order crêpes. Tasty fillings range from chicken with mushrooms and pimentoes to vegetarian specials and sweet versions like peach Melba. Imaginative starters like baked Brie with cranberry sauce are appealing, and there are brasserie-style dishes such as venison with black cherries and chicken breast with tarragon butter. *No dogs.*

Newent · *Good News Centre Coffee House*

High Street
Newent (0531) 821456
Map 7 D2 *Gloucestershire*

Open 9–5
Closed Sun, Bank Holidays & 1 week Christmas
Italian tagliatelle £1.20   Chicken à la king £1.20
Credit Access
P own car park   ♿ **WC**

The atmosphere is friendly, relaxed and informal at this simply appointed coffee house behind a religious bookshop and Third World crafts shop. Cakes and all sorts of biscuits are served throughout the day, and at lunchtime there are savoury snacks – baked potato, salad, quiche – plus a daily special such as macaroni cheese or chicken à la king. Unlicensed. No smoking. *No dogs.*

Newhaven · *Kenya Coffee House*

7 Bridge Street
Newhaven (0273) 515050
Map 6 C4 *East Sussex*

Open 9–5
Closed Sun, Bank Holiday & several days Christmas & New Year

Seafood au gratin £1.80   Fruit pie 80p

P town-centre car parks   ♿ **WC**

A friendly welcome and charming service are part of the appeal of this cheerful little coffee shop, which now boasts a capacious tea garden. Sweet and savoury snacks – cakes and gâteaux, freshly cut sandwiches, pizzas, sausage rolls – are always on the bill of fare, and lunchtime brings more substantial dishes like chicken risotto, chilli con carne and seafood au gratin. Good range of teas and coffees. Unlicensed. 🦃

Newmarket

Jane's Wine Bar

29 High Street
Newmarket (0638) 668031
Map 5 C2 *Suffolk*

Open 9–4.30
Closed Sun & Bank Holidays

Savoury filled crêpe & salad £2.60   Banana & walnut slice 40p
LVs   *Credit* Access, Amex, Diners, Visa
P town-centre car parks   **WC**

Hot food is served from 11.30 till about 3 in this agreeable basement restaurant. Mushroom pancakes and cider-sauced pork are typical tasty main dishes, and in winter there are baked potatoes with a variety of tempting fillings. Sandwiches, soup and omelettes are popular light snacks, and they bake their own bread and cakes (fruit and nut loaf, plum tart, raisin and banana gâteau). *No dogs.* ℰ 🍵

Newport

God's Providence House

12 St Thomas Square
Isle of Wight (0983) 522085
Map 6 A4 *Isle of Wight*

Open Restaurant: 10–5; Upstairs Parlour: 11–3
Closed Sun & Bank Holidays

Steak pudding £2.65   Lemon meringue pie 75p
P multi-storey car park in Pyle Street   **WC**

A fine old town house whose interesting features include Georgian bow windows. Sandwiches, pastries and light bites accompany tea and coffee in the restaurant, and from noon till 2 there's a menu of things like steak pudding, quiche and the day's roast. In the upstairs parlour a mainly vegetarian snack selection is on offer – open sandwiches, jacket potatoes, wholemeal cheese and onion pie. There's a non-smoking area. *No dogs.* 🍵

Northallerton

Bettys

188 High Street
Northallerton (0609) 5154
Map 4 C2 *North Yorkshire*

Open 9–6 (Sun from 10)
Closed 1 January, Easter Sun & 25 & 26 December

Yorkshire rarebit £3.30   Chocolate mousse & cream £1.20
P disc parking in town centre   **WC**

The smallest of a little chain of reliable, well-run coffee shops offering the same appetising all-day menu. Snackers can pop in for a toasted tea cake, a freshly made sandwich or maybe one of the speciality rarebits. Bacon and eggs, omelettes and fried fillet of plaice are among the main dish choices, and there's always a splendid selection on the cake trolley. Children's menu. Non-smoking area. *No dogs.* ℰ 🍵

Northampton

Lawrence's Coffee House

35 St Giles Street
Northampton (0604) 37939
Map 5 B2 *Northamptonshire*

Open 7.45–5.30 (Sat till 4.30)
Closed Sun & Bank Holidays

Quiche 65p   Lemon meringue pie 65p
LVs
P The Riding car park   **WC**

A colourful window display of appetising snacks pulls the crowds into this popular self-service shop in the heart of town. Crusty rolls filled with cheese and tomato, ham or succulent turkey with stuffing, sausage rolls and slices of quiche make tasty savoury bites, while the range of sweet items includes éclairs, Danish pastries, lemon meringue pie and a very good chocolate sponge slice. Unlicensed. *No dogs.*

Northenden | *Nut 'n' Meg*

444 Palatine Road
061-998 4589
Map 3 B3 *Greater Manchester*

Open 10–4
Closed Sun & Bank Holidays

Mushroom quiche 75p   Date & walnut slice
45p

P street parking   &   **WC**

Just three tables in this tiny vegetarian café
at the front of a wholefood shop in a parade
of shops. The best things are the cakes,
made with vegan margarine – try delicious
coconut slice, chocolate and peppermint
biscuits or date and walnut slice. Among the
short selection of savoury snacks you'll find
things like spring rolls, tofu burgers and
wholemeal mushroom quiche. Unlicensed.
No smoking. *No dogs.*

Norwich | *Britons Arms Coffee House*

9 Elm Hill
Norwich (0603) 623367
Map 5 D1 *Norfolk*

Open 10–5
Closed Sun & Bank Holidays

Soup of the day 60p   Mushroom gratin with
salad £2.40

P Monastery car park   &   **WC**

Two tiny rooms in an ancient timbered
cottage near the cathedral are the setting for
some simple but appetising light refreshments. Toasted sandwiches, sausage rolls,
home-made cakes, scones and biscuits are
available all day, while at lunchtime (minimum
charge £1.50) you can tuck into Scotch egg
and salad, Swedish herrings, open sandwiches and some fine truckled cheddar.
Exotic ices or yoghurt and honey to finish.
No dogs.

Norwich | *Café La Tienda*

10 St Gregory's Alley
Norwich (0603) 629122
Map 5 D1 *Norfolk*

Open 10.30–5
Closed Sun & Bank Holidays
Spinach & aubergine layer with tomato & nut
sauce £2.20   Fresh crab pâté with pitta bread
£1.95
P St Andrew's Street multi-storey car park
WC

Health-conscious new owners use organically grown produce from their market garden
in this friendly restaurant. The meatless menu
offers a daily-changing selection of wholesome snacks, from potato and onion soup to
taramasalata in granary bread and crumble-
topped fish, tomato and mushroom bake.
Sweet items include fresh fruit salad, lemon
sponge and a very good carob and fruit cake.
Full meals Fri & Sat eves. *No dogs.* 🐾

Norwich | *Mange-Tout Bistro & Coffee Shop*

24 White Lion Street
Norwich (0603) 617879
Map 5 D1 *Norfolk*

Open 8am–10.30pm, Sun 10.30–4.30
Closed 25 & 26 December

Salade niçoise £3.30   Plat du jour £2.90
Credit Access, Amex, Diners, Visa

P Castle Hill car park   **WC**

The kitchen's open-plan, so customers can
see their food being prepared at this friendly
first-floor bistro. There's ample variety, from
quick snacks like filled rolls and croissants to
seasonal salads, sirloin steak and a very
tasty vegetable roulade with a good thick
tomato and celery sauce. For the sweet-
toothed, gâteaux, cheesecakes, chocolate
mousse, ices. Minimum charge of £2 noon–
2pm. *No dogs.* 🌱

Norwich — *Waffle House*

39 St Giles Street
Norwich (0603) 612790
Map 5 D1 *Norfolk*

Open 11am–10pm (Fri & Sat till 11)
Closed Sun & Bank Holidays
Waffle with bolognese & cheese sauce £2.70
Waffle with banana & fresh orange sauce from £1.10
LVs
P St Giles Street multi-storey car park   **WC**

A delicious selection of sweet and savoury waffles, available with hot or cold toppings, are served at this popular restaurant. Combinations can be as varied as you fancy – try creamy tuna, sweetcorn and mayonnaise or chilli with cheese sauce, followed by, say, fresh peaches and cream or chocolate mousse with chopped nuts. Good salads, too, and thick milkshakes to drink. Unlicensed (bring your own). Non-smoking section. *No dogs.*

Nottingham — *Alice's Restaurant*

2b High Street
Nottingham (0602) 584753
Map 4 C4 *Nottinghamshire*

Open 9–5
Closed Sun & Bank Holidays

Lasagne £1.50   Egg & bacon quiche with salad £1.55
LVs
P Victoria Centre car park   **WC**

On the first floor of Spoils household goods store, this neat modern restaurant uses Lewis Carroll's Alice for much of its decorative inspiration. Scones, cakes and pastries are available throughout the day, and savoury snacks include sandwiches, jacket potatoes and very good quiches served with a choice of salads. Lunchtime brings extra items such as soups, lasagne or a curry. Sound, straightforward cooking. Unlicensed. *No dogs.*

Nottingham   *New Entry* — *Brasserie St Marie*

30 High Pavement
Nottingham (0602) 581616
Map 4 C4 *Nottinghamshire*

Open 10.30–2 & 6–10
Closed 1 January & 25 & 26 December

Merguez with salad £1.90   Calf's liver & vegetables £5.80
Credit Access, Visa
P Fletcher Gate car park   ♿   **WC**

Good food and a lively atmosphere make it fun to visit this bright modern brasserie just out of the city centre. Omelettes (including an unusual variety with smoked mackerel and horseradish) are a favourite snack meal, and other typical dishes include chicken liver pâté, pigeon fricassee and mussels with an excellent cream, tomato and herb sauce. Other main dishes might be calf's liver or poached salmon, and there are simple sweets. *No dogs.*

Nottingham — *Café Punchinello*

35 Forman Street
Nottingham (0602) 411965
Map 4 C4 *Nottinghamshire*

Open 8.30am–10pm (Sat till 10.30)
Closed Sun & Bank Holidays

Cottage pie 95p   Kidney & mushroom casserole £1.95
LVs
P Trinity Square car park   **WC**

An excellent place, this, popular for its good cooking, good prices, jolly staff and long opening hours. Breakfast starts things off; then scones and simple snacks precede nourishing lunchtime fare like beef Stroganoff, shepherd's pie and lasagne. There's always a choice for vegetarians, as well a selection of salads, and sweets like cherry and almond flan or oranges in raisin syrup present quite a temptation. *No dogs.*

Nottingham — *New Entry* — *Café Royal Brasserie*

27 Market Street
Nottingham (0602) 413444
Map 4 C4 *Nottinghamshire*

Open 10.30am–10.30pm, Sun noon–7
Closed 1 January & 25 & 26 December

Coq au vin £3.50   Croque monsieur £1.75
Credit Access, Amex, Visa

P Woolaton Street car park   &   WC

This stylish modern brasserie stands opposite the Theatre Royal in a complex that also includes a bar and restaurant. Food is available all day: croissants, croque monsieur and charcuterie in the morning; pâtisserie for afternoon tea; and at lunchtime things like omelettes, salads, goujons of plaice and a tasty carbonnade of beef. Separate vegetarian menu. Lighter choice at night. Capable cooking, helpful service. No children. *No dogs.*

Nottingham — *New Entry* — *New Orleans Diner*

3 Charlton Street, Hockley
Nottingham (0602) 473041
Map 4 C4 *Nottinghamshire*

Open 11am–11pm (Sun from 6pm)
Closed Bank Holidays

New Orleans ribs £3.95   Cotton Club
sandwich £2.95
LVs   *Credit* Access, Diners, Visa
P Fletcher Gate car park   WC

American in mood and menu, with videos belting out a day-long accompaniment to some very good eating. Begin perhaps with garlic mushrooms or crisp-fried potato skins and go on to a burger, barbecued spare ribs, sirloin steak or chicken breast with a sweet and sour sauce. Sandwiches and salads provide further choice, and, to finish, there's cheesecake, pies and various ice cream concoctions. Children's menu. *No dogs.*

Nottingham — *Pagoda*

31 Greyfriar Gate
Nottingham (0602) 501105
Map 4 C4 *Nottinghamshire*

Open dim sum noon–4.30 (full menu noon–midnight)
Closed 25 December
Cantonese-style fillet steak £8   Paper-wrapped prawns £1.40
LVs   *Credit* Access, Amex, Diners, Visa
P Astoria car park or street parking   WC

Portions are generous at this modest Chinese restaurant with a varied menu of attractively presented Cantonese dishes. Dim sum snacks like prawns wrapped in rice paper are served until 4.30pm, while main course dishes include such favourites as sweet and sour pork and roast Peking duck, along with the more exotic pork ribs in champagne, stuffed squid and baked silver pomfret. *No dogs.*

Nottingham — *New Entry* — *The Q in the Corner at Ziggi's*

3 Victoria Street
Nottingham (0602) 506956
Map 4 C4 *Nottinghamshire*

Open 9.30–5
Closed Sun & Bank Holidays except Good Fri

Courgette bake £1.50   Lasagne & salad £1.75
Credit Access, Visa

P Fletcher Gate   WC

Entrance to this welcoming little restaurant is through a ladies' fashion shop. Customers just wanting coffee and a pastry will find a good range of baking, including lemon and coconut cake, date shortbread and almond slice. Wholemeal quiches are served with a choice of salads, and typical hot dishes of the day are lasagne, courgette bake and chilli con carne. Dependable cooking, friendly service. Unlicensed. *No dogs.*

Nottingham   *New Entry*   *Ten*

10 Commerce Square, off High Pavement
Nottingham (0602) 585211
Map 4 C4 *Nottinghamshire*

Open noon–11 (Mon till 3, Fri & Sat till 11.30)
Closed Sun & Bank Holidays except Good Fri
& lunch 25 December
Nut rissoles with sweet herb sauce £2.85
Bean & sweet pepper pâté 75p
Credit Access
P Commerce Square   **WC**

In a basement, but there's no lack of space or light at this informal vegetarian restaurant. There's also no lack of variety on the menu, with daytime choices ranging from bean and sweet pepper pâté to riceburgers, nutburgers, buckwheat flans and savoury herb waffles. Also specials like our very tasty mushroom and cauliflower pie, and cakes and sweets. More elaborate evening choices such as shell pasta mexicane and fennel, blackcurrant and hazelnut roast. *No dogs.*

Oakham   *Oakham Gallery*

17 Mill Street
Oakham (0572) 55094
Map 5 B1 *Leicestershire*

Open 9.30–5 (Sun from 2)
Closed Mon & 25 & 26 December

Vegetarian shepherd's pie £1.75   Date, apple & honey pancake 80p

P Burley Road car park   **WC**

Mrs Lant produces some really good snacks to enjoy in this attractive tea room above an art gallery. Lovely light scones, cherry cake and caramel slice go well with an excellent cup of tea, and freshly cut sandwiches (including open ones) are a popular savoury bite. Lunchtime brings things like pizza, fish pie and spaghetti bake, plus nice fresh salads and several wholefood dishes such as curried nut loaf. *No dogs.* 🐾

Offham   *Old Post House*

Near Lewes
Lewes (0273) 477358
Map 6 C4 *East Sussex*

Open 2–5.30, also 10–12.30 Sat & Sun
Closed Tues, also Mon–Fri October–March, 1
January & 25 & 26 December

Sussex cream tea £1.75   Gâteau tea £1.60

P own car park   **WC**

Joyce Standley does the baking while husband Peter looks after the many customers who flock for tea to this charming old brick and flint cottage. Lovely wholemeal scones spread with thick cream and jam, super cakes, pastries and meringues sandwiched with ice cream are a delicious indulgence – and taste even better in the garden when it's fine. Set teas only at weekends. Unlicensed. No smoking. *No dogs.* 🐾

Ombersley   *Ombersley Gallery Tea Room*

Church Terrace, Near Worcester
Worcester (0905) 620655
Map 7 D1 *Hereford & Worcester*

Open 10.30–5
Closed Sun, Mon, 25 & 26 December &
January

Moussaka & salad £2.15   Salmon pâté with
toast & salad £1.30
P street parking   ♿   **WC**

Opposite the church, this olde-worlde tea room shares a half-timbered house with a quaint antique and picture gallery. Miss Munday cooks from home, so the choice depends on what she sends in. Biscuits and scones, Genoa sponge, coffee and walnut gâteau and rhubarb flan are typical toothsome goodies, and savouries could include pâtés, quiches and a hot special such as chicken casserole or moussaka. Unlicensed. *No dogs.* 🍵 🐾

Oswestry

Good Companion (Wine Bar)

10 Beatrice Street
Oswestry (0691) 655768
Map 3 B4 *Shropshire*
Open 12–2.30 & 7.30–11
Closed Mon lunch, all Sun, 1 January & 25 & 26 December
Home-made soup with bread from 85p
Cashewnut lasagne, salad & garlic bread £3.50
Credit Amex, Diners
P Bailey Head market   ♿   **WC**

An informal and unpretentious little establishment offering very good home cooking. Seafood lasagne is served with garlic bread, while pitta is a good companion for houmous, kofta kebabs and chilli con carne. Soups, salads and vegetarian specials are other favourite choices, and puddings include ice creams and fudgy banana pie. *No dogs.*

Otley   *New Entry*   *Chatters Tea Shoppe*

3 Bayhorse Court
Otley (0294) 466691
Map 4 C3 *West Yorkshire*

Open 10–4.30 (till 5 Sat & daily in summer), Sun 2–5.30
Closed Sun October–April, August Bank Holiday & 24 December–2 January

Gammon & eggs £2.20   Quiche lorraine £1.75
P Lix car park   **WC**

Set in an attractive courtyard just off the main road through town, this welcoming tea shop done up in Victorian style offers a simple but appealing bill of fare. The local cured ham is a great favourite, as the basis of a salad or in a sandwich, omelette or jacket potato. There's also soup, pâté and a selection of baking including scones, Eccles cake, fruit cake and gâteaux. Cream teas. Unlicensed. *No dogs.*

Oxford

Browns

7 Woodstock Road
Oxford (0865) 511995
Town plan *Oxfordshire*

Open 11am–11.30pm, Sun noon–11.30pm
Closed 24–28 December

Club sandwich £3.45   Fisherman's pie £4.25

P meter parking in St Giles   ♿   **WC**

Oxford students love this leafy, informal restaurant, where pretty waitresses serve fresh croissants until noon and scones for afternoon tea. At other times there are super snacks like spaghetti, hot salt beef sandwiches and salad in such delicious combinations as avocado, bacon and spinach, along with substantial dishes like fresh fish, savoury pie, barbecued ribs and sirloin steak. Non-smoking area. ☯

Oxford

Go Dutch

18 Park End Street
Oxford (0865) 240686
Town plan *Oxfordshire*

Open 6–11 (Sat, Sun & Bank Holiday Mons from noon)
Closed 1 week Christmas
Smoked bacon & apple pancake £2.50
Cherry pancake £3.25
LVs
P railway station car park   ♿   **WC**

People often queue to get into this excellent restaurant, whose speciality is Dutch pancakes, made of the lightest possible batter and absolutely delicious. Fillings are savoury – smoked bacon and apple, cheese and salami, ham with corn and green pepper – or sweet, including blackcurrants with cream and ice cream. Other sweets, too, like Dutch apple pie and nut-stuffed chocolate biscuit cake. Full meals only at peak hours. *No dogs.*

OXFORD

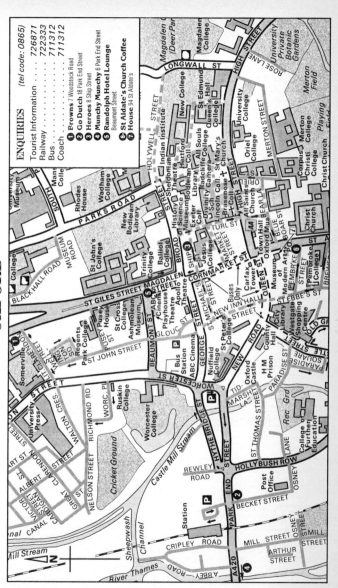

ENQUIRIES *(tel code: 0865)*

Tourist Information	726871
Railway	722333
Bus	711312
Coach	711312

❶ **Browns** 7 Woodstock Road
❷ **Go Dutch** 18 Park End Street
❸ **Heroes** 8 Ship Street
❹ **Munchy Munchy** 6 Park End Street
❺ **Randolph Hotel Lounge** Beaumont Street
❻ **St Aldate's Church Coffee House** 94 St Aldate's

Oxford ★ *Heroes*

8 Ship Street
Oxford (0865) 723459
Town plan *Oxfordshire*

Open 9–5
Closed Sun, Bank Holidays, 10 days Easter &
10 days Christmas

Chicken mayonnaise with pitta bread £1
Caramel chocolate slice 40p
P Broad Street car park & **WC**

Sandwiches don't come much better than
those produced in this modest little place in
the heart of the City. Brown, white, French
and pitta bread are crammed with super
fillings like chicken mayonnaise, rare roast
beef and home-cooked ham. Fine home-
made soup to start, delectable banana bread
or apple slice for sweet. Toasted snacks and
hot croissants are served between 9 and 11.
Unlicensed. Non-smoking area.

Oxford ★ *Munchy Munchy*

6 Park End Street
Oxford (0865) 245710
Town plan *Oxfordshire*

Open noon–2.10 & 5.30–9.40
Closed Sun, Mon, Bank Holidays, 3 weeks
August–September & 3 weeks December–
January
Lamb with spicy passion fruit sauce £3.85
Papaya £1.20
P Worcester car park **WC**

Indonesian and Malaysian dishes are given
the special Ethel Ow treatment in this simply
appointed food bar near the station. She
uses herbs, spices and fresh fruit to great
effect in super dishes like lamb in papaya
sauce or beef slices with sweet basil, Szechuan pepper, fennel seeds, ground peanuts
and coconut milk. Ice cream and tropical fruit
for sweet. Unlicensed (bring your own). No
children Fri & Sat eves. *No dogs.*

Oxford **New Entry** *Randolph Hotel Lounge*

Beaumont Street
Oxford (0865) 247481
Town plan *Oxfordshire*

Open 3–6

Set afternoon tea £4.50

Credit Access, Amex, Diners, Visa

P own car park & **WC**

Enjoy a full afternoon tea in the elegant and
comfortable lounge of Oxford's premier hotel. Fresh finger sandwiches, wholemeal
currant scones, moist madeira cake and
pineapple-topped cream pastries all slip
down nicely with an excellent cup of tea. Two
nice features: a range of complimentary
newspapers and a pianist who picks his way
completely through Cole Porter and Irving
Berlin. *No dogs.*

Oxford **New Entry** *St Aldate's Church Coffee House*

94 St Aldate's
Oxford (0865) 245952
Town plan *Oxfordshire*

Open 10–5
Closed Sun, Bank Holidays & 4 days
Christmas
Lamb, fruit & nut risotto £1.65   Chocolate slab
cake 40p
LVs
P Westgate car park **WC**

On a corner site opposite Christ Church, this
bookshop and self-service coffee house
were opened in 1963 by the then Archbishop
of Canterbury. Cakes, scones and biscuits
are served morning and afternoon, flanking
lunchtime dishes like vegetable soup, green
noodles with cream and ham sauce and beef
casserole with ginger. Crisp, fresh salads;
nice fruit flans and sherry trifle. Unlicensed.
No smoking. *No dogs.*

Painswick   *Cup House*

Bisley Street
Painswick (0452) 812322
Map 7 D2 *Gloucestershire*

Open 10–1.45 & 2.45–5
Closed Sun morning, all Wed (except August)
& 25 & 26 December

Scampi & salad £2.95   Cream tea £1.50

P street parking & town-centre car park   ♿

A pleasant sheltered patio is an added attraction when the sun shines on this cottagy little tea room. Home-made scones, slices, flapjacks, teacakes and fresh cream cakes (weekends only) go down a treat at tea or coffee time, while for lunch there's a simple choice of sandwiches, salads and things on toast. In winter, hot specials like soup, steak and kidney pie and lasagne join the range. Unlicensed. *No dogs.* 🖤

Painswick   *Painswick Hotel*

Kemps Lane
Painswick (0452) 812160
Map 7 D2 *Gloucestershire*

Open noon–2
Closed Sun

Summer cold buffet £3.50   Home-made
gâteaux 90p
Credit Access, Amex, Diners, Visa
P own car park   **WC**

The new owners of this elegant and civilised hotel have retained the popular summer buffet, which includes cold meats, salads, jacket potatoes and a hot dish of the day such as blanquette of lamb or beef bourguignon. Also simple sweets like fresh salad or various gâteaux. Enjoy it all on the terrace when the weather's kind. In winter the choice is restricted to a hearty soup, a sandwich, ploughman's or pâté. ✉

Parkgate   *Chompers*

The Parade
051-336 1567
Map 3 B3 *Cheshire*

Open 5.30–11.30, Sat noon–midnight, Sun
noon–11.30
Closed 25 & 26 December
Sardines à la portugaise £2.50   Chicken tikka
£5.20
LVs   *Credit* Access, Amex, Diners, Visa
P car park at rear   **WC**

Overlooking the Dee estuary (crayons for capturing the scene and binoculars provided), this smartly informal restaurant offers a most imaginative range of dishes. Look for choices like deep-fried mushrooms stuffed with Brie and almonds, vegetable chilli served with potato skins and sour cream and fresh sardines in a garlicky tomato sauce. Delicious home-made desserts too. Sunday brunch from noon–5 is very popular. *No dogs.* ✉

Pateley Bridge   *Willow*

Park Road
Pateley Bridge (0423) 711689
Map 4 C2 *North Yorkshire*
Open noon–2 & 6.30–9.30
Closed Sun eve, all Mon, Tues, Bank Holidays
(except Good Fri & 25 December) & 2 weeks
February
Grouse in red wine & herb sauce £7.25
Smoked oyster & bacon kebabs £2.25
Credit Access, Amex, Visa
P Park Road car park   **WC**

New owners the Naylors are retaining the same style menu as in previous years at this neat, beamed restaurant. Dishes like choux pastry filled with prawns in garlic mayonnaise or smoked oyster and bacon kebabs make deliciously different snacks or starters, while main courses such as chicken in a creamy lemon sauce or pork fillet with apple stuffing in puff pastry provide plenty of interest. Tempting sweets include well-made Danish apple pie. *No dogs.* 🖤

Penrith — Bluebell Tearoom

Three Crowns Yard
Penrith (0768) 66660
Map 3 B1 *Cumbria*

Open 9.30–4.30
Closed Sun, Bank Holidays & 1 week
Christmas

Cider fruit slice 45p   Honey & sesame cake
50p
P Bluebell Lane car park   **WC**

In a tiny bookshop overflowing with volumes, this homely place is ideal for browsers in search of both a bargain book and some light refreshment. First-class tea and coffee go beautifully with home-made goodies like Lancashire lemon tart, walnut and wheat-germ squares, cider fruit slice and good sticky gingerbread – all baked from stone-ground wholewheat flour and other unprocessed ingredients. Unlicensed. No smoking. *No dogs.* 🍵

Penshurst — Fir Tree House Tea Rooms

Near Tonbridge
Penshurst (0892) 870382
Map 6 C3 *Kent*

Open 3–6
Closed Mon in season (except Bank Holidays
when closed Tues), Mon–Fri January–Easter &
all November & December

Tea & scones £1.50   Strawberry tea £2.20
P street parking

Caroline Fuller-Rowell serves her delicious teas in a charming tea room with Tudor windows and Victorian pews made of pitch pine. The building is overlooked by fir trees, and there's a pretty garden at the rear for sunshine snacking. Lovely light scones come with whipped cream and home-made jam, and other goodies include coffee and walnut sponge, chocolate cake and nut-studded tea bread. Unlicensed. No smoking. 🍵

Piercebridge — George Wine Bar

Near Darlington
Piercebridge (032 574) 576
Map 4 C2 *Co. Durham*

Open 7pm–10pm, Sun noon–2

Seafood vol-au-vent £4   Steak & mushroom
pie £4.20
Credit Access, Visa

P own car park   **WC**

An attractive wine bar within a pleasant riverside pub offering enjoyable food to please all the family. Spit-roast chicken is a popular choice and there's always fish on the menu, or you can have steak, a burger, bacon chop or savoury pie. Deep-fried mushrooms with garlic mayonnaise makes a tasty starter, and the long list of desserts includes apple pie and bramble syllabub. *No dogs.* ⊖

Plumtree ★ Perkins Bar Bistro

Station Road
Plumtree (060 77) 3695
Map 5 B1 *Nottinghamshire*

Open noon–2 & 7–10
Closed Sun, Mon, Bank Holidays (except
Good Fri) & 3 days Christmas
Avocado with seafood £1.95   Calf's liver in
herb butter £4.95
Credit Access, Amex
P own car park   **WC**

Built by the Midland Railway Company in 1880, old Plumtree Station is now a lovingly converted bistro, where Tony and Wendy Perkins delight with their splendid seasonal food served in a delightfully informal setting. A cold counter displays pâtés, terrines and gravad lax, while the hot choice ranges from super soups to skate in black butter with capers and wood pigeon casseroled in red wine. Delectable sweets like apricot French tart. *No dogs.* ⊖

Polperro · *Captain's Cabin*

Lansallos Street
Polperro (0503) 72292
Map 8 B4 *Cornwall*

Open 11.30–2.30
Closed Sun, also Sat early & late season & all
December–January
Fried fillets of lemon sole £3.20   Fresh cream
meringues 80p
Credit Access, Amex, Diners, Visa
P village car park   **WC**

Seafood forms a major part of the menu at this old-world quayside restaurant, and Eddy Jacobs is a dab hand at obtaining the pick of the local catch. Crab, prawns, sole and whiting are among the favourites, and there are also some meat dishes. Sandwiches and salads provide lighter snacks, and home-made sweets include cheesecake, apple pie and fresh cream meringues. More elaborate evening meals. 🍵 🍴

Poole · *Inn à Nutshell*

27 Arndale Centre
Poole (0202) 673888
Map 6 A4 *Dorset*

Open 9.30–5
Closed Sun & Bank Holidays
Mushroom Stroganoff £1.45   African pilaff
£1.50
LVs   *Credit* Access, Amex, Diners, Visa
P Kingland multi-storey car park adjacent
WC

This busy, self-service restaurant to the rear of a modern shopping centre attracts a good following for its appetising vegetarian snacks. Imaginative salads accompany hot dishes like cheese and oatmeal roast, broccoli mornay and wholemeal pastries, and there are well-filled sandwiches and lots of home-baked goodies – including barm brack, marmalade cake and treacle tart. Friendly, efficient staff. No smoking. *No dogs.* 🍴

Portsmouth (Southsea)   **New Entry** · *Country Kitchen*

59 Marmion Road
Portsmouth (0705) 811425
Map 6 B4 *Hampshire*

Open 10–6
Closed Sun, 1 Jan, Good Fri & 25 & 26
December
Stuffed cabbage with tomato & onion sauce
£1.95   Ginger & peach crumble 75p
LVs
P car park opposite

Bright, clean and cheerful, this vegetarian restaurant is found just off Southsea's main shopping street. Many of the goodies are displayed at a self-service counter, including wholemeal sandwiches and rolls, baked potatoes, salads, quiches, cakes and slices. Lunchtime brings a tasty soup and black-board specials like vegetable bake with mushroom sauce. There's a wide choice of teas. Unlicensed. No smoking. *No dogs.* 🍴

Portsmouth (Southsea) · *Rosie's Vineyard* (Wine Bar)

87 Elm Grove
Portsmouth (0705) 755944
Map 6 B4 *Hampshire*
Open 7pm–10.30pm (11 in summer) also Sun
noon–2
Closed 1 January & 22 December–27
December
Houmus with hot pitta bread £1.50   Pork
paprika with tagliatelle £3.60
Credit Access, Visa
P street parking   **WC**

This former greengrocer's – note the mahogany fruit bins and floral stained glass – makes a lively, unpretentious wine bar. The daily blackboard menu offers tasty hot dishes like moussaka, vegetarian chilli, stuffed trout and tender pork and tagliatelle in a paprika sauce, while light bites include soup, pâté and taramasalata with hot pitta bread. Twosomes can share a luscious meringue and fruit sweet. *No dogs.* 🍵

Poulton-le-Fylde

Anna's Bistro

15 Breck Road
Poulton-le-Fylde (0253) 882336
Map 3 B3 *Lancashire*

Open 8.30–3.30 & 7–10.30, Sun 10.30–2 & 6–9
Closed Mon & Tues eves, all Wed, Bank
Holidays & 10 days Christmas

Chicken salad £1.95   Steak & kidney pie
£3.50
P town-centre car parks

Cheerful owner Anna Pawson turns out a
good variety of daytime snacks in this
agreeable little restaurant near the centre of
town. Bacon barmcakes, burgers, pizzas and
omelettes are typical items, along with sandwiches, salads and a selection of cakes,
pastries and fresh cream gâteaux. The
evening meal is more formal, featuring dishes
like prawn curry, chicken à la crème and
carbonnade of beef. Unlicensed.

Preston

Angelo's

31 Avenham Street
Preston (0772) 57133
Map 3 B3 *Lancashire*

Open noon–2 & 7–11.30 (Fri & Sat till midnight)
Closed Sun lunch, Mon & Bank Holidays

Pizzas from £2.50   Risotto £3
Credit Access, Visa

P Avenham Street car park   **WC**

Arches and an ornamental fountain combine
with white walls, pine tables and red chairs
to give this piazza-style Italian restaurant a
bright, fresh appeal. Baked oysters and
chicken livers sautéed with onions and chillis
are among the more unusual starters, while
main courses range from perennially popular
pizzas and pasta to chicken sorpresa and
veal cooked in a white wine and mustard
sauce. *No dogs.*

*We publish annually so
make sure you use the
current edition.*

Pulborough

Chequers Hotel

Church Place
Pulborough (079 82) 2486
Map 6 B4 *West Sussex*

Open noon–2 & 3.45–5.30

Home-made soup 80p   Sussex cream tea
£1.85
Credit Access, Amex, Diners, Visa

P own car park   **WC**

Eat in one of the cosy lounges or out in the
pretty garden of this welcoming hotel overlooking the Sussex downs. Charming hosts
the Searanckes offer a lunchtime snack menu
of liberally filled sandwiches (plain or
toasted), salads with cold meats, pies or pâté
and ice cream desserts. Teatime brings
sandwiches along with excellent cakes such
as sponge or Dundee and scones with home-
made jam. 🍵

Ramsgate   *Sands Wine Bar*

12 Cliff Street
Thanet (0843) 586911
Map 6 D3 *Kent*

Open noon–2.30 & 7–11
Closed Sun & 25 & 26 December
Prawns in garlic £1.85   Chicken Elizabeth
£3.25
Credit Access, Amex, Diners, Visa
P street parking & multi-storey car park nearby
WC

Good food served in a friendly atmosphere
is on offer at this pleasant wine bar down a
side street near the city centre. Unusual
dishes like Bombay baskets and Camembert
samosas in cranberry sauce are among the
imaginative savouries on the blackboard
menu, which also includes Welsh rarebit,
lasagne, chilli con carne and a delicious
chicken Elizabeth served with savoury apple
rice. *No dogs.*

Reading   *Mama Mia*

11 St Mary's Butts
Reading (0734) 581357
Map 6 B3 *Berkshire*

Open noon–2 & 6–10 (Fri till 10.30), Sat noon–
10.30
Closed Sun & Bank Holidays

Fettuccine vongole £3.15   Veal romano £5.95
Credit Access, Amex, Diners, Visa
P Butts Centre multi-storey car park   **WC**

A combination of sound, reliable cooking and
good service makes this town-centre Italian
restaurant a very popular and lively place.
The menu offers a really good choice, from
all sorts of pasta (starter or main course) to
pizzas and various preparations of chicken
and meat such as the popular veal romano
with a wine, cream, sage and mushroom
sauce and a topping of avocado. Traditional
sweets. *No dogs.*

Reading   *Wine Butts*

61 St Mary's Butts
Reading (0734) 509363
Map 6 B3 *Berkshire*

Open noon–2.30 & 6–10 (Fri & Sat till 10.30)
Closed Sun, Mon & Bank Holidays

Chicken liver pâté with brandy £1.35   Steak,
kidney & Guinness pie £3.35
LVs   *Credit* Access, Visa
P Butt Centre car park   **WC**

Attractive modern premises in a shopping
centre in middle of Reading, with a large
glass frontage extending up to the first-floor
wine bar. The cooking's very good, the menu
reasonably varied: soup, pâtés and ploughman's can be had for starters or snacks, and
there are various pasta dishes, specialities
like goujons of cod or chicken and mushroom
pie and dishes of the day such as sauté of
pork. *No dogs.* ✆

Richmond   *Mrs Beeton*

58 Hill Rise
01-940 9561
Map 6 B3 *Surrey*

Open 10–5 (Sun from 11), also 6.30–11 (Wed–
Sat)
Closed 1 week Christmas

Courgette roulade £2.70   Mexican gâteau 85p

P Paradise Road multi-storey car park   **WC**

Every day brings something new in this
popular restaurant, where pairs of local ladies
work in rotation. A recent visit found the
kitchen in the capable hands of Maureen
Slaven and Jo Pettman, whose menu ranged
from pork and thyme pâté to tasty tuna gratin,
courgette roulade and blanquette of lamb.
Cakes and sweets included lemon tart and a
lovely brown sugar meringue of chocolate,
coffee and cream. Unlicensed. *No dogs.* ✆

Richmond   *New Entry*   *Refectory*

6 Church Walk
01-940 6264
Map 6 B3 *Surrey*

Open 10–2, Sun noon–2.15
Closed Mon, Bank Holidays & 8 days
Christmas

Lamb casserole £2.75   Chocolate cream
pudding £1.45
P Paradise Road NCP   **WC**

Old church rooms with a nice little courtyard for summer eating. Morning coffee makes way for a lunchtime menu (minimum charge £1.50) of dishes such as granary bread with potted meats, smoked mackerel pâté and savoury flans, plus specials like cheese-topped cottage pie, nut loaf and a tasty lamb casserole. Interesting vegetables, and pleasant sweets such as apricot fool or chocolate cream pudding. 🐚

Richmond   *Richmond Harvest*

5 Dome Buildings, The Quadrant
01-940 1138
Map 6 B3 *Surrey*

Open 11.30–11 (Sun till 10.30)
Closed 25 December–1 January

Mediterranean courgette casserole £3.15
Cheese & vegetable pie £1.85
LVs
P Lichfield Terrace   **WC**

A tiny vegetarian restaurant in mid-town, with close-packed tables, cheery staff and an ever-changing selection of home-prepared vegetarian fare. Everything is commendably fresh and wholesome, from piping hot barley and vegetable soup to crunchy salads and main courses such as courgette casserole with olives, tomatoes, black-eyed beans and plenty of garlic. Hot fruit crumble's a super sweet, and there are cakes for afternoon coffee. Minimum charge £1.95. *No dogs.*

Richmond   *New Entry*   *Wildefoods Wholefood Café*

98 Kew Road
01-940 0733
Map 6 B3 *Surrey*

Open 9–7, Sun noon–5
Closed Sun in winter, 1 January, Good Fri, 25
& 26 December & 1 week summer

Cheese & lentil bake 40p   Date slice 25p

P street parking

A few tables in a vegetarian wholefood shop and take-away. Items available to eat in include samosas, a couple of quiches, Gruyère and watercress pie and lentils in the form of balls and burgers. There are also decent salads, plus baps, sandwiches, jacket potatoes and all sorts of cakes, pastries and slices. Organically grown vegetables are used as much as possible. Unlicensed. No smoking. *No dogs.* 🍵

Ringmer   *Coffee House*

72 Springett Avenue
Ringmer (0273) 812855
Map 6 C4 *East Sussex*

Open 9–5 (Wed till 2), Sun noon–2
Closed Mon, Bank Holidays & 2 weeks
autumn

Cream tea £1.50   Two-course lunch £2.50

P street parking   ♿   **WC**

A tempting variety of excellent snacking brings an appreciative clientele to this neat little establishment in a parade of shops. Scones and flapjacks, mincemeat slices and chocolate gâteau are just a few of the home-baked goodies, and lunchtime (minimum charge £2.50) brings a fine-value set meal centred on favourites like roast pork, liver and bacon or fried plaice. There are children's portions available. Unlicensed. No smoking. *No dogs.* 🍵 🐚

Ringwood　　　　*New Entry*　　　　*Old Brown House*

10 High Street
Ringwood (042 54) 5075
Map 6 A4 *Hampshire*

Open 10–5
Closed 26 December & 2 weeks November

Crêpe normande £1.10　Savoury croissant
75p
Credit Access, Amex, Visa
P main town car park　**WC**

An old timbered building with a pleasantly
cottage interior. Scones and teacakes, made-
to-order sandwiches, quiche and sweet pancakes appear on the morning coffee and
afternoon tea menu, along with croissants
and an excellent French apple tart. At lunchtime there's pâté, quiche, jacket potatoes
and other hot dishes like omelettes, grilled
plaice and chicken curry. More elaborate
evening meals. 🍵

Ripon　　　　　　　　　　　　　*Warehouse*

Court Terrace, Kirkgate
Ripon (0765) 4665
Map 4 C2 *North Yorkshire*

Open 9.30–5.15
Closed Sun, 1 January, 1 May & 25 & 26
December

Minted lamb with potatoes & vegetables £2.95
Strawberry meringue gâteau 95p
P Morrison's or market square car parks　**WC**

A bewildering selection of enticing dishes is
laid out at this friendly, stylish restaurant
above a craft shop. Help yourself to tasty
wholemeal flans, crisp salads and gorgeous
cakes – from caramel shortbread to walnut
and chocolate sponges. Lunchtime brings
hearty home-made soups along with delicious hot dishes like minted cucumber and
lamb and chicken with peaches. Non-smoking areas. *No dogs.* 🥗 🍵

Rochdale　　　　　　　　　　　*Casa Capri*

19 Baillie Street
Rochdale (0706) 46214
Map 4 C3 *Greater Manchester*

Open noon–2.30 & 6.30–10.30 (Fri & Sat till 11)
Closed Mon & Bank Holidays

Lasagne £2.80　Chicken Kiev £4.85
Credit Access, Diners, Visa

P multi-storey car park at bus station　**WC**

Right by the main bus station, this stylish little
Italian restaurant offers enjoyably prepared
dishes served by smart, attentive waiters.
Classic favourites like minestrone, pizzas
and pasta (note the nicely sauced spaghetti
alla carbonara) are supplemented by such
appetising blackboard specials as seafood
salad and garlic mushrooms. There are
plenty of meat and fish main courses, too,
along with pleasant sweets from the trolley.
No dogs.

Rochester　　　　　　　　　　　*Casa Lina*

146 High Street
Medway (0634) 44993
Map 6 C3 *Kent*

Open 9.30am–10pm
Closed Sun, Mon, Bank Holidays, 2 weeks
late September & 1 week Christmas

Pizza de Casa Lina £3.70　Cheesecake 80p
Credit Access, Visa
P Blue Boar Lane car park　♿　**WC**

Enterprise and zip are much in evidence at
this little high-street pizzeria. From noon till
closing you can take your pick from some 17
pizzas, ranging from a simple sora (mozzarella and tomato) to the glories of a casa
nostra with a dozen ingredients. Also on the
menu from 9–5 are pastas, grills, fish and
omelettes, as well as salads and sandwiches.
No dogs.

Romsey   *Cobweb Tea Rooms*

49 The Hundred
Romsey (0794) 516434
Map 6 A4 *Hampshire*

Open 10–5.30 (Bank Holiday Sun from 2.30)
Closed Sun (except if open Bank Holiday
Mon), Mon (except some Bank Holidays), last
week Sept, first week Oct & 1 week Christmas
Chicken & asparagus casserole £2.25
Chocolate hazelnut torte 80p
P Love Lane car park   **WC**

Angela Webley's home baking attracts both
locals and tourists to this neat little tea room.
Scones, flapjacks, coffee cake and nice
sticky Danish pastries are a few among many
temptations, and if you want something
savoury there are toasted sandwiches, country platters and lunchtime specials like
chicken and asparagus casserole. Non-
smoking tables. *No dogs.*

Romsey   *Latimer Coffee House*

11 Latimer Street
Romsey (0794) 513832
Map 6 A4 *Hampshire*

Open 9.15–5.15
Closed Sun & 25 & 26 December

Savoury flan with salad £2.50   Filled jacket
potatoes £1.50
P own car park & public car park opposite
  WC

Tourists make a beeline for this friendly little
coffee house with a pretty garden and cottagy
interior. Baskets of scones and tempting
cakes (coconut and cherry slices, lemon
drizzle cake, spicy carrot cake) make way at
lunchtime for home-made soups and flans
(tuna, mushroom, sweetcorn and onion),
salads, and daily specials like jacket potatoes. *No dogs.*

Ross-on-Wye   *Meader's*

1 Copse Cross Street
Ross-on-Wye (0989) 62803
Map 7 D2 *Hereford & Worcester*

Open 10–3
Closed Sun, 1 January & 25 & 26 December

Hungarian layered cabbage £2   Lasagne
£1.90

P street parking   **WC**

A Hungarian owner means the bonus of
robust lunchtime dishes like beef or pork
goulash and braised cabbage with minced
meat and spicy smoked sausage at this
friendly restaurant. Other tasty choices include vegetarian and vegan dishes, along
with grills and fry-ups, and there are simple
sweets like tangy lemon cheesecake. Flapjacks and slices are served with morning
coffee. Set menus in the evening, including
one for vegetarians.

Ross-on-Wye   *Walford House Hotel*

Walford Road
Ross-on-Wye (0989) 63829
Map 7 D2 *Hereford & Worcester*

Open 11–2.30 & 3.30–4.45

Omelette with creamed prawns £3.50   Set tea
£5.50
Credit Access, Amex, Diners, Visa

P own car park   **WC**

Raymond and Joyce Zarb run this characterful hotel, which stands in splendid gardens
about three miles from Ross-on-Wye. Coffee
and biscuits are served until noon, then a fine
selection of tasty bar snacks ranging from
soup and pâté to sandwiches, croque monsieur, omelettes and a superb cheeseboard.
For afternoon tea, a refreshing brew comes
with finger sandwiches, scones and luscious
gâteaux. Enjoy it all in the bar, sun lounge or
sitting room.

Rottingdean   *Old Cottage Tea Rooms*

62 High Street
Brighton (0273) 33426
Map 6 C4 *East Sussex*

Open 10–5 (till 6 weekends)
Closed Tues

Quiche with jacket potato & salad £2.40   Set
afternoon tea £1.50
Credit Access
P public car park opposite   **WC**

You can eat in either of the two cottagy tea
rooms or in the garden of this charming, old-
fashioned tea shop. As well as a set afternoon
tea, Rosaleen Cleghorn offers enjoyable
home-baked items like cherry pie and Madeira cake, scones and shortbread. At lunchtime, there are ploughman's, omelettes and
toasted snacks, too. Unlicensed. Non-smoking room. *No dogs.*

Rottingdean   *Rottingdean Pâtisserie*

32 High Street
Brighton (0273) 32180
Map 6 C4 *East Sussex*

Open 10–5 (till 4.30 in winter)
Closed Mon (except Bank Holidays) & January

Welsh rarebit with side salad £1.75   Quiche
with salad £2

P car park opposite   **WC**

Just a few yards from the seafront, this quaint
tea shop draws the crowds with an amazing
array of home baking by the talented Theo
Walz. Gâteaux and roulades, creamy cakes
and fruit tarts, scones and strudels are just
part of the truly mouthwatering selection, and
light lunches from noon–2 offer soups and
salads, quiches, flans and toasted sandwiches. Unlicensed.

Rowlands Castle   **New Entry**   *Coffee Pot*

14 The Green
Rowlands Castle (0705) 412538
Map 6 B4 *Hampshire*

Open 8.30–5 (Sun & Bank Holidays from 2.30)
Closed 1 January & 25 & 26 December

Steak pie 60p   Millionaire's shortbread 35p

P street parking   **WC**

Four little pine tables in a modest, cheerful
tea shop on the village green. Nearly all the
snacks are home made, the individual steak
pies being a particularly popular line; there
are also delicious sausage rolls, quiches and
many treats for the sweet tooth – raspberry
tartlets, coffee cake, Bakewell tarts, a rich,
many-layered chocolate cake. Outside eating. Unlicensed. No smoking. *No dogs.* 🫖

Rye   *Swiss Pâtisserie & Tea Room*

50 Cinque Ports Street
Rye (0797) 222830
Map 6 C4 *East Sussex*

Open 8–4.30 (Tues till 12.30pm)
Closed Sun

Pâté with French bread £1   Set afternoon tea
£1.40

P street parking   **WC**

Locals and visitors alike appreciate the good
things on offer at this splendid little tea room.
An alluring display of home baking includes
scones, shortbreads, fruit cake and fruit
tarts, along with éclairs, mille-feuilles and
Sachertorte. Savoury snacks, too, from pies
and pasties to soup, sandwiches, giant
sausages and ravioli. Home-made ice
creams; set afternoon tea. Unlicensed. No
smoking. *No dogs.*

Ryton   *New Entry*   *Ryton Bridge Hotel Bistro*

Near Coventry
Coventry (0203) 301585
Map 5 A2 *Warwickshire*

Open 11.30–2.30 & 6–11, Sun noon–2 & 7–10.30

Chicken breast baked with avocado £4.95
Lamb kebabs £4.95
Credit Access, Visa
P own car park & **WC**

The cooking is consistently enjoyable in this attractive country-style bistro, part of a hotel alongside the A45. The menu provides plenty of interest, with dishes like mushrooms with bacon and garlic, vegetarian lasagne, stuffed grilled trout and succulent breast of chicken baked with avocado. Burgers and steaks come in various guises, and hot fruit kebabs are an unusual and appealing sweet. Friendly service. *No dogs.*

Ryton   *New Entry*   *Ryton Gardens Café*

Warwick Road
Coventry (0203) 303517
Map 5 A2 *Warwickshire*

Open 9–4 October–March; 9–6 April–September
Closed 25 & 26 December

Vegetable curry £1.20 Vegetarian cottage pie £1.50
P own car park & **WC**

All the food is made from organically grown produce at this cosy café. Daily-changing hot dishes are available throughout opening hours and might include well-seasoned vegetarian cottage pie, quiche, onion soup and mushroom or curried vegetable roll. Salads are always available, and you can finish with carrot cake or a tasty wholemeal apple bun. Preparation is careful and service is friendly. Unlicensed. No smoking. *No dogs.*

St Albans   *Kingsbury Mill Waffle House*

St Michael's Street
St Albans (0727) 53502
Map 6 B3 *Hertfordshire*

Open 11–6 (Sun from noon); in winter 11–5 (Sun from noon)
Closed Mon, Tues & 10 days Christmas

Ham, cheese & mushroom waffle £2.50
Banana waffle £1
P own car park **WC**

Freshly baked waffles are the only choice at this ancient mill that stands on the banks of the river Ver. Sit on church pews beneath the original beams and enjoy your waffle (plain or wholewheat) topped with anything from cream cheese with herbs and garlic or ratatouille to black cherries, coconut or chocolate mousse. Minimum charge £1 weekends and Bank Holidays. Unlicensed. No smoking. *No dogs.* 🫖

St Margaret's at Cliffe   *Roses*

Near Dover
Dover (0304) 852126
Map 6 D3 *Kent*

Open 10–1 & 2.30–5.30 (Sun till 5)
Closed Sun morning, Mon (except Bank Holidays), Sun October–June, 1 January, 25 & 26 December, 2 weeks spring & 1 week autumn
Carrot cake 60p Cream meringue 70p
P car park adjacent

A pretty little craft shop (formerly Country Fayre), where you can sit at one of the four tables and enjoy Joyce Grimer's excellent home baking accompanied by a flavoursome brew. Light scones arrive in a little basket and taste delicious with Joyce's plum jam, there are lovely cakes (try the Kentish apple) and her meringue gâteau laden with cream and fruit is an indulgent delight. Garden. Unlicensed. No smoking. *No dogs.* 🫖

St Mary's

Isles of Scilly
Scillonia (0720) 22540
Map 8 A3 *Cornwall*

Open 12.30pm–1.45pm
Closed end October–March

Open crab sandwich £1.60   Hot smoked
mackerel £1.95
Credit Access, Amex, Diners, Visa
P street parking   **WC**

Tregarthens Hotel

Hot smoked mackerel with parsley butter and
horseradish sauce is one of the tasty lunchtime snacks served in the lounge or bar or
out on the sun terrace of this pleasant hotel
overlooking the harbour. Locally caught crab
and lobster are popular choices, and there's
soup, pâté and baked potatoes with a choice
of tasty fillings. Salads are crisp and simple,
and sweets include a good apple pie. Minimum charge £1.10. *No dogs.* 🍵

St Michael's Mount

The Harbour, Near Marazion
Penzance (0736) 710748
Map 8 A4 *Cornwall*

Open 10.30–5.30 (weather & tide permitting)
Closed end October–April

Seafood pancake £3.50   Cream tea £1.65
Credit Access, Amex, Visa

P in Marazion   **WC**

Sail Loft

Reached by foot or ferry across the causeway, this converted boathouse is owned by
the National Trust. Morning coffee makes
way at 12.30 for an appealing light lunch
menu with soup, pâté, flans, salads and
seafood pancakes (there's a three-course
roast lunch on Sundays). Afternoon teas
feature excellent home baking, including
lovely Cornish splits served with clotted
cream. Local fish a speciality. No smoking.
No dogs. 🍵 🍴

Salisbury

18 Fisherton Street
Salisbury (0722) 22134
Map 6 A4 *Wiltshire*

Open 10–5
Closed Sun, Bank Holidays & 1 week
September

Cossack pie £1.10   Pineapple Pavlova 78p
LVs
P central car park   **WC**

Mainly Salads

There's a fresh, bright look about this vegetarian restaurant near the city centre. Ron
and June Ceresa prepare some very enjoyable fare, including imaginative composite
salads. Lunchtime (£1.50 minimum charge)
brings hot things like cheese and onion pie
and a tasty curried nut loaf. For pud, perhaps
chocolate rum cream or Dutch apple pie and
there are nice home-baked cakes to go with
tea and coffee. Unlicensed. No smoking.
No dogs. 🍴

Salisbury

8 St Thomas's Square
Salisbury (0722) 336037
Map 6 A4 *Wiltshire*

Open 9–5
Closed Sun & Bank Holidays

Mushroom flan with salad £2.95   Strawberry
gâteau £1.30

P central car park   **WC**

Michael Snell

A busy place right in the heart of the city that
tempts the customers with a wide range of
tasty fare. Savoury flans (asparagus, cheese
and prawn, quiche lorraine) are popular all-
day snacks, and at lunchtime they are served
with salads as main courses, along with
things like deep-fried chicken breast or beef
curry. Gâteaux and pâtisserie come in great
variety, and home-made ices and sorbets are
firm favourites. Unlicensed. *No dogs.* 🍵 🍴

Salisbury   *Mo's*

62 Milford Street
Salisbury (0722) 331377
Map 6 A4 *Wiltshire*
Open noon–2.30 & 5.30–11.15 (Fri & Sat till
midnight, Sun 6–10.30)
Closed Sun lunch, 1 January & 25 & 26
December
Pizza burger £2.55   Mushroom croustade
£3.40
LVs
P Culver Street multi-storey car park   **WC**

Carefully cooked hamburgers, dressed with
everything from garlic mayonnaise to mozzarella and spicy tomato and served up in
sesame buns, are the mainstay of the menu
at this delightfully friendly, informal restaurant. Other tasty choices include steaks,
barbecued spare ribs and chilli, and there's
always a daily vegetarian special like courgette croustade. Finish with the decadent
chocolate crumb made with cream and
sherry. Children's menu. *No dogs.*

Scunthorpe   *Bees Garden Coffee Lounge*

4 Cole Street
Scunthorpe (0724) 848751
Map 4 D3 *Humberside*

Open 9–5
Closed Sun & Bank Holidays
Quiche lorraine with baked potato & coleslaw
£2.75   Roast ham & pineapple toasted
sandwich £1.15

P Cole Street car park   **WC**

There's a summery feel about this bright city-
centre coffee lounge that's popular with
peckish shoppers and office workers alike.
Sandwiches a-plenty please – in French
bread, open and toasted – or choose a salad
based on cold meats, quiche, pâté or cheese.
Enjoyable hot meals include lemon poached
plaice and vegetarian lasagne, while sweet
items range from scones and teacakes to
apple pie. Unlicensed. *No dogs.* ⊝ 🍵

Seaford   *Trawlers*

32 Church Street
Seaford (0323) 892520
Map 6 C4 *East Sussex*

Open 10.30–2 & 5–9
Closed Sun, 1 January & 25 & 26 December

Cod with chips or salad £1.95   Pineapple
fritter 65p
LVs
P street parking ♿ **WC**

Pam Dunn looks after customers while husband Alan takes charge of the frying at this
bright, modern fish and chip shop. He uses a
light batter for his beautifully fresh cod,
plaice, huss and scampi, all served with crisp,
golden chips or salad. Imaginative alternatives include vegeburgers and buckwheat
crêpes (sweet ones, too), and there are also
pies and sausages. Morning coffee served
until 11.30. Children's menu. 🍵

Seale   *Herbs*

Manor Farm, Wood Lane
Runfold (025 18) 3333
Map 6 B3 *Surrey*

Open 10–5 (till 4.30 in winter), Sun 2–5.30
(October–March from 1)
Closed Mon & 24 December–1 February

Spinach roulade with mushroom sauce £2.85
Chocolate fudge cake with cream £1.20
P own car park ♿ **WC**

Mrs Hine and her helpers offer tasty home
cooking in this neat, stone-walled tea shop
that's part of a farm and crafts complex.
Soup could be courgette and tomato or
pumpkin with basil; then there's beery rarebit,
pâté, filled jacket potatoes and a vegetarian
dish of the day. A nice selection of cakes and
pastries like fruit crumble and raspberry
cheesecake is displayed on a central table.
Sunday roast lunch October–March (book).
No dogs. 🍵

Selworthy   ★   *Periwinkle Cottage Tea Rooms*

Selworthy Green, Near Porlock
Porlock (0643) 862769
Map 8 C3 *Somerset*

Open 11–6 (Wed from 1)
Closed Sat & end September–Easter

Set afternoon tea from £1.55   Oak-smoked turkey breast with salad £3.20

P church car park   **WC**

In this picture-postcard cottage with its flower-filled garden, the Woods cook like angels. Try oven-warm scones, superlative grapefruit, raisin and almond loaf or passion cake filled with fromage blanc. From 11–2 lunchtime savouries are served: choose from glazed ham, curried chicken mayonnaise or a cheddar ploughman's platter, and do leave room for one of the wonderful desserts – perhaps coffee and cream cheese mousse pie. Unlicensed. *No dogs.* ☕ 🍰

Settle   *Car & Kitchen*

Market Place
Settle (072 92) 3638
Map 3 B2 *North Yorkshire*

Open 9.30–5 (Sun from 11)
Closed 1 January & 25 & 26 December

Aubergine Parmesan £2.25   Curried chicken mayonnaise £2.20

P Market Place   **WC**

This pleasant little upstairs coffee shop is a convivial spot for enjoying a snack. Morning coffee and afternoon tea come with some fine baking, from scones and flapjacks to lemon bread or date and walnut loaf. Lunchtime (no smoking) heralds an interesting savoury choice that could include quiche, meatloaf and aubergine Parmesan. Filled jacket potatoes are popular, and you might finish with a nice fruit crumble. Unlicensed. *No dogs.* ☕ 🍵

Sheffield   ★   *Just Cooking*

16 Carver Street
Sheffield (0742) 27869
Map 4 C3 *South Yorkshire*

Open 11–3.30 (Sat from 10)
Closed Sun, Mon, Bank Holidays except Good Fri & 1 week Christmas

Lamb & apricot casserole £3.65   Vegetarian lasagne with salad £2.90
P meters & NCP in Carver Street   ♿   **WC**

A really excellent spot for just-a-biters, with outstanding food dispensed from the central service counter. The lunchtime selection includes super dishes like cheese and mushroom quiche, spicy vegetarian risotto and a full-of-flavour lamb and apricot casserole served with brown rice. Salads are imaginative and delicious, and sweets range from fresh fruit salad to a marvellous coffee gâteau. Full meals Friday evening. Non-smoking area. *No dogs.* ☕

Sheffield   ★   *Toff's Restaurant & Coffee House*

23 Matilda Street, The Moor
Sheffield (0742) 20783
Map 4 C3 *South Yorkshire*

Open 10–3 (Sat till 4.30)
Closed Sun, Bank Holidays & 25 & 26 December
Mixed vegetable quiche £1.45   Rabbit, pork & chicken terrine with salads £2.95
LVs
P Matilda Way car park   ♿   **WC**

Great skill and imagination go into the cooking at this enchanting little restaurant with its white furniture and summery decor. Lunchtime brings out the very best, with superb dishes like cabbage stuffed with minced beef, wholemeal vegetable quiche and a multi-flavoured terrine of rabbit, pork and chicken. Desserts are equally good, as proved by our delectable nectarine meringue tart. Excellent tea, coffee and cakes in the morning. *No dogs.* ☕ 🍰

Shipston on Stour *Bell Inn*

Sheep Street
Shipston on Stour (0608) 61443
Map 5 A2 *Warwickshire*

Open 10–2.30, 3–5 & 6.30–9.30

Steak & kidney pie £2.95   Lasagne £2.75
LVs   *Credit* Access, Amex, Diners, Visa

P own car park   ♿ **WC**

Morning coffee and afternoon tea come with a selection of really good home baking at this lively 18th-century coaching inn. Sandwiched in between are simple, appetising bar lunches, with soups and pâtés, casseroles, lasagne and daily specials like river trout and steak and kidney pie on offer. The evening bar menu is similar. There are several indoor sitting areas and a pleasant courtyard.

Shipston on Stour *Kerry House Tea Rooms*

3 Market Place
Shipston (0608) 61224
Map 5 A2 *Warwickshire*

Open 9–5.30 (Sun from 11)
Closed Sun in winter, 1 January & 25 & 26 December

Cottage pie £1.55   Ploughman's £1.85

P Bell car park   ♿

Macaroons, flapjacks, scones and Viennese whirls are among the home-baked goodies served in this unassuming town-centre tea shop. Freshly made sandwiches are also available on a day-long basis, and at lunch-time there are salads, ploughman's platter and assorted hot snacks like Welsh rarebit and cottage pie. Honest home cooking, friendly service. Unlicensed. *No dogs.*

Shipton *Beningbrough Hall Restaurant*

By Beningbrough
York (0904) 470715
Map 4 C2 *North Yorkshire*

Open noon–2.30
Closed Mon, Fri & end October–Easter

Steak & kidney pie £2.65   Set afternoon tea £1.95

P own car park   ♿ **WC**

Self-service lunches in a refectory-style restaurant can be enjoyed by both visitors to this handsome National Trust property on the A19 and the general public (the £1 entrance fee will be returned if you are there less than an hour). Typically tasty offerings might include carrot and orange soup, savoury flans, ham or smoked mackerel with salad and home-made puddings. Non-smoking area. *No dogs.*

Shoreham-by-Sea *Cuckoo Clock*

74 High Street
Shoreham-by-Sea (0273) 453853
Map 6 B4 *West Sussex*

Open 10.30–5.30, Sun 12.30–5
Closed Mon, Bank Holidays & 2 weeks September

Steak & kidney pudding £2   Fruit pie 50p
LVs
P Ship Street car park

A quaint cottage tea shop with two tiny beamed rooms (one for non-smokers) and a small courtyard. Simple, homely fare, carefully prepared, is the order of the day, from scones, teacakes and sandwiches to lunch-time favourites like steak and kidney pudding, casseroled lamb's liver and the daily roast. Pancakes and fruit pies are popular puds, and there's a good choice of speciality teas. Unlicensed. *No dogs.*

Shrewsbury   Cornhouse Restaurant & Wine Bar

59 Wyle Cop
Shrewsbury (0743) 231991
Map 7 D1 *Shropshire*

Open noon–2.30 & 6.30–10.30
Closed 26 December

Moussaka £3.25   Chicken in pink peppercorn
sauce £2.50
Credit Access, Visa
P St Julians Friars car park   &   **WC**

This handsome building stands at the bottom of a steep hill that climbs to the city centre. The ground-floor wine bar has a blackboard menu of very pleasant dishes like mushroom and spinach soup, chicken fricassee and succulent rack of lamb with redcurrant sauce. Up a spiral staircase to the restaurant (children here only), with higher prices and a similarly interesting menu – poached salmon, cashew nut paella, gigot steak. *No dogs.*

Shrewsbury   Delany's

St Alkmunds Square, St Julians Cross
Shrewsbury (0743) 60602
Map 7 D1 *Shropshire*

Open 10.30–3.30
Closed Sun, Bank Holidays & 25 & 26
December

Spinach & bean tortilla £1.50   Flageolet bean
& vegetable casserole £1.50
LVs   **P** St Julians Friars car park   **WC**

A couldn't-be-simpler vegetarian and vegan restaurant tucked in a quiet corner beside St Julians Cross churchyard. A reasonable selection of cakes is available in the morning, and at lunchtime (no smoking) there are hot dishes like corn chowder served with good home-baked wholemeal bread, curried lentil burgers and spiced courgette quiche. Full meals by arrangement are available most Saturday evenings. *No dogs.*

Sidbury   Old Bakery

Near Sidmouth
Sidbury (039 57) 319
Map 8 C3 *Devon*

Open 10.30–12.30 & 2.30–5.30
Closed Sun, Good Fri & mid October–1 April

Afternoon tea £1.15   Coffee & walnut gâteau
70p

P street or village car park   **WC**

Jeanne Selley's spotlessly kept little tea room, its walls lined with antique bedstead panels, makes a delightful spot for afternoon tea – and there's a pretty garden for when the sun shines. A freshly brewed pot accompanies splendid scones and utterly indulgent clotted cream meringues, while other treats include rich chocolate fudge gâteau, spiced teabread and buttery shortbread. Unlicensed. No smoking.

Skipton   ★   Herbs Wholefood & Vegetarian Restaurant

10 High Street
Skipton (0756) 60619
Map 4 C2 *North Yorkshire*

Open 9.30–5
Closed Sun, Tues & 25 & 26 December

Cheese & onion pie with salad £2.25
Vegetable pancakes with hazelnut sauce
£2.45
P behind Town Hall   **WC**

Superb ingredients, careful preparation, keen service and spotless surroundings make this pine-furnished restaurant above a wholefood shop a delight to visit. Lunchtimes are especially rewarding, with appetising choices ranging from egg and sage pâté and spinach, mushrooms and rice in cheese sauce to a popular fruit and nut platter and lovely salads. Super sweets available throughout the day include Swedish applecake, chocolate gâteau and treacle tart. Unlicensed. *No dogs.*

Solihull　　　**New Entry**　　　*Bobby Browns*

165 High Street
021-704 9136
Map 5 A2 *West Midlands*

Open noon–2 & 7–10.30 (Fri & Sat till 11)
Closed lunch Sun & Bank Holidays & all 25 &
26 December
Salmon mousse £2.25　Beefsteak, mushroom
& Guinness pie £3.45
Credit Access, Amex, Diners, Visa
P Civic Centre car park　**WC**

Occupying a prime site on the high street,
this smart, first-floor restaurant offers a
tempting selection of tasty dishes. Mushrooms cooked with cream, garlic, ginger and
caraway seeds makes an enjoyable different
starter, devilled herring roes another. Main
courses include lasagne, seafood pancakes,
kidneys en brochette and apricot-stuffed
lamb noisettes, plus various ways with beef.
Lemon crunch features among some nice
home-made sweets. *No dogs.*

Southampton　　　*Lunch Break*

321 Shirley Road, Shirley
Southampton (0703) 772713
Map 6 A4 *Hampshire*

Open 11–3, Sat 9–3
Closed Sun & 3 days Christmas

Seafood pancakes £1.30　Cheese & onion
quiche 75p

P street parking　**WC**

A self-service restaurant (part of a bakery),
where Sue and Sandra keep things spick-
and-span. There's always a good selection
of fresh cakes and pastries, sandwiches and
filled rolls, plus savoury snacks (first-rate
Cornish pasties in short or puff pastry) and
delicious puddings like chocolate and pear
trifle. Extra lunchtime dishes of the day could
include quiche, filled pancakes, cheese and
potato pie and roast chicken. Unlicensed. No
smoking. *No dogs.*

Southampton　　　*La Lupa 4*

123 High Street
Southampton (0703) 331849
Map 6 A4 *Hampshire*

Open noon–2.30 & 6–midnight
Closed Sun & Bank Holidays

Pizza Lupa £3.05　Coppa Lupa £2.20
LVs　*Credit* Access, Amex, Diners, Visa

P NCP in High Street　**WC**

Pizzas are the thing to go for at this well-run
informal Italian restaurant with tiled floor and
rough plastered walls. Our Lupa was a
splendid affair made to order and topped
with nearly a dozen ingredients. Also on the
menu are pastas, salads and familiar steak,
veal and chicken dishes, with the inevitable
profiteroles or zabaglione for afters. Minimum charge of £3. *No dogs.*

Southampton　　　*La Margherita*

4 Commercial Road
Southampton (0703) 333390
Map 6 A4 *Hampshire*

Open noon–2.15 & 6.30–11.30 (Fri & Sat till
midnight)
Closed Sun & Bank Holidays
Lasagne al forno £2.70　Avocado with
Provolone cheese dressing £1.55
LVs　*Credit* Access, Amex, Diners, Visa
P car park at rear of restaurant　**WC**

'We love to spoil you' is the motto of this
noisy, colourful Italian restaurant with a menu
of firm favourites. The choice ranges from
calamari fritti to familiar steak, veal and
chicken dishes, pasta and pizzas with names
like Mamma Mia and Sophia Loren – she's
topped with artichokes, peppers, ham and
mushrooms. The tuna and butter bean salad
makes a tasty starter, and you can always
finish with profiteroles. *No dogs.*

Southampton   *Piccolo Mondo 1*

36 Windsor Terrace
Southampton (0703) 36890
Map 6 A4 *Hampshire*

Open 10–8 (Mon till 7)
Closed Sun & Bank Holidays

Salsicce alla siciliana £3.50   Home-made ice
cream £1.20
LVs
P NCP in Castle Way   **WC**

In the centre of town near the bus station and
Guildhall, this cheerful little place calls itself
pizzeria, coffee bar, tavola calda and trattoria. Pizzas are the choice of many, but there's
also plenty of antipasti and pasta, along with
a variety of fish and meat dishes (try the
splendid, meaty Sicilian sausages cooked in
tomato sauce). To finish, cakes, gâteaux and
excellent home-made ices. *No dogs.*

Spetisbury   *Marigold Cottage Tea Rooms*

High Street, Blandford Forum
Blandford (0258) 52468
Map 8 D3 *Dorset*
Open 8.30–5.30; 10–4, Sun noon–5.30
October–April
Closed Mon (except Bank Holidays),
Christmas & 1 week January
Roast beef with vegetables £3.40   Hot apple
cake with cream 85p
Credit Access, Visa
P own car park   &   **WC**

Owner Nigel Selby is also the chef at this
delightful beamed tea room in a thatched
roadside cottage. A slap-up breakfast can be
had until 11.30, and all day long there are
sandwiches, toasted snacks and baked
goodies ranging from Battenburgs and macaroons to subtly spicy hot apple cake.
Lunchtime brings salads, omelettes and
stouter fare like steak & kidney pie or roast
beef and Yorkshire pudding. *No dogs.*

Spilsby   *Buttercross Restaurant*

18 Lower Market
Spilsby (0790) 53147
Map 5 C1 *Lincolnshire*

Open 10–4.30
Closed Sun, Tues, Bank Holidays (except May
Day), 1 week December & 2 weeks June–July

Vegetarian brochette with peanut sauce £1.95
Fresh salmon coulibiac £2.60
P market square car park   **WC**

Overlooking the Buttercross in the town
centre, this is an attractive and delightfully
informal place for a snack. The dishes are all
carefully prepared, and the choice could
include cock-a-leekie soup, omelettes, Stilton and leek quiche, seafood mornay and a
roast. Also good cakes and pastries, plus a
range of home-made ice creams made with
real cream. Minimum lunchtime charge £1.60.
Full meals Fri & Sat eves. *No dogs.*

Stamford   *George of Stamford*

St Martin's High Street
Stamford (0780) 55171
Map 5 B1 *Lincolnshire*

Open 10am–11pm

Gruyère fritters £3.95   Rutland Water trout
£5.95
Credit Access, Amex, Diners, Visa

P own car park at rear   **WC**

A famous old coaching inn with attractive
bars and lounges and a walled garden. Super
snacks are provided by an extensive cold
buffet (winter lunchtime, summer both sessions) of roast meats, salmon, cheeses and
salads. Plenty of hot choice, too, from
Gruyère fritters and minestrone to lasagne,
grilled trout with almonds, and sweet and
sour chicken drumsticks. Desserts and pastries, ice creams and afternoon teas also
served. *No dogs.*

Stamford   *New Entry*   *Mr Pips Coffee Shop & Restaurant*

11 St Mary Street
Stamford (0780) 65795
Map 5 B1 *Lincolnshire*

Open 9.30–4.30
Closed Sun, 1 January, Easter Mon & 25 & 26
December
Smoked salmon quiche £2.95   Filled jacket
potato £1.95
Credit Access, Visa
P town-centre car park   **WC**

On the first floor of the china and glass shop
John Sinclair, this is a pleasant place for a
snack. Apple and sultana cake, strawberry
flan and sticky treacle tart are popular sweet
things displayed throughout the day on a fine
old sideboard, and from noon there are
savoury dishes such as sweetcorn and ham
soup, pâtés and vol-au-vents, plus sometimes a fish dish or even a traditional roast.
No dogs. 🍵

Stevenage   *New Entry*   *De Friese Coffee Shop*

71 High Street, Old Town
Stevenage (0438) 720519
Map 5 C2 *Hertfordshire*

Open 9.30–5.30 (Wed till 2), Sat 8.30–5, Sun
11–5
Closed 25 December
Ploughman's with extra mature Cheddar £1.20
Nutrocker £1.65
LVs   *Credit* Visa
P street parking

In fine weather you can sit outside; otherwise
you make your way to the back of a tiny shop
whose main claim to fame is its superb
cheeses and ice creams. The former come in
80 varieties representing eight countries, the
latter are served in single, double or triple
scoops, or in coupes – Hawaii is strawberry,
coffee and banana, nutrocker is pecan,
praline and chocolate. Freshly ground coffee.
Unlicensed. No smoking. *No dogs.* 🏷 🍵

Stockbridge   *Old Dairy Restaurant*

High Street
Andover (0264) 810886
Map 6 A3 *Hampshire*

Open 10.30–5 (Mon–Wed till 5.30), Sun 12–
5.30
Closed Wed in winter & 25 & 26 December

Clotted cream tea £1.60   Steak, kidney &
mushroom pie £3.50
P street parking   **WC**

Mrs Bray and her friendly staff are kept busy
preparing and serving a variety of snacks at
this neat little high-street tea room. Highlights
are the cream teas, with light, freshly baked
scones, but you can also have salads,
sandwiches, steak and kidney pie and things
with chips, as well as delicious home-made
cakes. More elaborate evening meals are
served Wed–Sat. *No dogs.* 🍵

Stockport   *Coconut Willy's*

37 St Petersgate
061-480 7013
Map 4 C3 *Greater Manchester*
Open 10–9.30 (Sat till 11.30), Sun 6.30pm–
10.30pm
Closed Mon, Bank Holidays & 25 & 26
December
Coconut & Caribbean bake £1.10   Date &
orange cake 45p
LVs   *Credit* Visa
P Merseyway car park   ♿   **WC**

A bright, airy vegetarian restaurant in the
centre of town and close to various shopping
precincts. Houmus with pitta bread, wholemeal quiches, nut roasts, courgette and
carrot pancakes, butter beans risotto – these
are typical tasty savoury fare, and there's
also a good choice of sweet things, including
a range of vegan cakes. They're thinking
about introducing some meat and fish dishes
in the evening. Non-smoking area. *No dogs.*

Stonham Aspal   *Stonham Barns*

Pettaugh Road, Stowmarket
Stowmarket (0449) 711755
Map 5 D2 *Suffolk*

Open 10–5.30 (till 4.30 November–April)
Closed Mon & 1 week Christmas

Uitsmijters £2.30   Sultana & whisky cake 45p

P own car park   &   **WC**

Set in pleasant countryside by the A1120, this well-run complex includes a plant centre, farm shop and a smart, modern restaurant. The lunch menu (12–2) includes excellent pâté plus ploughman's, baked potatoes and the popular uitsmijters – ham and fried egg on bread. Also salads, quiches and savoury pies in winter. Throughout the day there's a selection of good home baking such as rich fruit cake and flapjacks. *No dogs.*

Stow-on-the-Wold   *Ingram's*

Digbeth Street
Cotswold (0451) 30151
Map 5 A2 *Gloucestershire*

Open 10–5 (Sun from 2.30, Mon from noon)
Closed Sun (November–Easter) & 25 & 26 December

Chicken liver pâté £1.40   Cream tea £1.40

P in the square   **WC**

Standards remain commendably high at this pretty little tea shop, where throughout the day a good pot of tea accompanies things like scones and teacakes, chocolate slices, gâteaux and cherry pie. Savoury snacks, also available at all times, include chicken liver pâté, toasted sandwiches, salads and various quiches (tomato and herbs, cheese and onion), with jacket potatoes and more substantial hot dishes in winter. *No dogs.*

Stow-on-the-Wold   *St Edwards Café*

The Square
Cotswold (0451) 30351
Map 5 A2 *Gloucestershire*

Open 9–5.30 (Sat & Sun till 6)
Closed 25 & 26 December

Cream tea £1.75   Garlic sausage roll 40p

P in the square   **WC**

A truly bountiful display of home-made cakes crowds the small display space at this friendly café in an imposing stone building. Choose, if you can, from chocolate fudge, rock and Eccles cakes, ginger parkin, mince pies and an Australian speciality of coconut and fruit. Tasty savoury snacks include sandwiches, pâté and excellent sausage rolls, while lunchtime brings soup, salads and roast chicken. There are some tempting sweets and cream teas, too. Unlicensed.

Stow-on-the-Wold   **New Entry**   *Wyck Hill House*

Cotswold (0451) 31936
Map 5 A2 *Gloucestershire*

Open noon–2, 3–5.30 & 7–9.45

Cornish crab salad £4.75   Set afternoon tea £3.75
Credit Access, Amex, Diners, Visa

P own car park   &   **WC**

A private drive leads off the A424 to this splendidly restored manor house, whose elegant public rooms provide an attractive setting for some enjoyable snacking. Soup, steak, cold meats and goujons of sole make up a typical evening bar menu, with quiche and sandwiches among the lunchtime extras. Nice sweets. Afternoon tea in the comfortable lounge or cedar-panelled library. No children under six.

Stratford-upon-Avon   *New Entry*   *Pinocchio*

6 Union Street
Stratford-upon-Avon (0789) 69106
Town plan *Warwickshire*

Open noon–2.30 & 6–11.30
Closed Sun, 1 January & 25 December

Stuffed mushrooms £2.40   Spaghetti
carbonara £3.50
LVs   *Credit* Access, Amex, Visa
P street parking & NCP in market place   **WC**

Pop in for a pizza or settle down to a full meal in this delightful restaurant, where owner-cum-chef Gina Scimeca cooks in the Sicilian style. Besides the generously topped pizzas there's a fine parade of pasta, plus chicken and veal dishes. Mushrooms stuffed with ricotta and spinach are a speciality starter, zabaglione and mascarpone the house sweets. Very friendly service. *No dogs.*

Stratford-upon-Avon   *Slug & Lettuce*

38 Guild Street
Stratford-upon-Avon (0789) 299700
Town plan *Warwickshire*

Open noon–2 & 6–10, Sun noon–1.30 & 7–9.30
Closed 3 days Christmas & 31 December

Chicken breast with garlic & avocado £5
Banana & rum omelette £2.25

P nearby street parking   &   **WC**

The atmosphere is lively and welcoming at this smart restaurant with a pine-panelled bar and paved patio. Prime produce is prepared with skill and imagination, and daily specials could include anything from herby chicken livers to sautéed crayfish and black pudding with a mustard sauce. There are also soups, salads and lighter savoury snacks, with a boozy bread and butter pudding to finish. *No dogs.* 🌙

Stratford-upon-Avon   *New Entry*   *Truffles Olde Tea Shoppe*

The Web, 37 Shottery
Stratford-upon-Avon (0789) 292039
Town plan *Warwickshire*
Open 11–5 (Sat till 5.30), Sun noon–5.30
Closed Mon (except Bank Holidays), 25 & 26
December & 2 weeks March
Cream tea £1   Broccoli & cheese quiche
£1.95
Credit Access
P street & car park at Anne Hathaway's
cottage   &   **WC**

There's a friendly, welcoming air about this pretty little tea shop, which stands just a two-minute walk from Anne Hathaway's cottage. The choice couldn't be simpler: nicely baked scones with butter or cream and jam, toasted teacakes and brown-bread sandwiches, available individually or as part of the various set teas; and lunchtime dishes like plough-man's, salads and quiche. Unlicensed. No smoking. *No dogs.* 🍵

Stretton   *New Entry*   *Ram Jam Inn*

Great North Road, near Oakham
Castle Bytham (078 081) 776
Map 5 B1 *Leicestershire*

Open 7am–11pm
Closed 25 December

Mushroom brioche £1.80   Rutland sausage
with sweet & sour onions £2.50
Credit Access, Amex, Visa
P own car park   &   **WC**

Right alongside the A1, a very convenient stopping place comprising several eating areas. There's a good day-long choice of snacks, from muesli, sausages and scrambled eggs to steak and mushroom pie and a selection of cheeses. Also home-made ices, tarts and fruit pies plus a few extra items in the restaurant – mushroom brioche, steak, pork belly with apple sauce, barbecued chicken wings. 🌙

STRATFORD-UPON-AVON

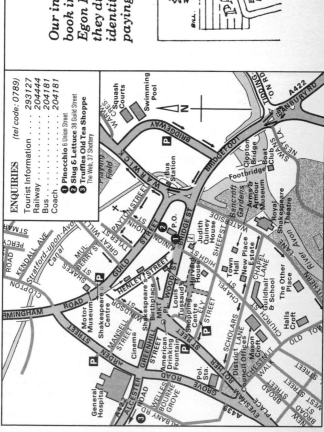

ENQUIRIES *(tel code: 0789)*

Tourist Information	293127
Railway	204444
Bus	204181
Coach	204181

❶ **Pinocchio** 6 Union Street
❷ **Slug & Lettuce** 38 Guild Street
❸ **Truffles Old Tea Shoppe** The Web, 37 Shottery

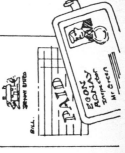

Our inspectors never book in the name of Egon Ronay's Guides; they disclose their identity only after paying their bills.

Stroud

Mother Nature

Bedford Street
Stroud (0452) 78202
Map 7 D2 *Gloucestershire*

Open 9–4.30
Closed Sun & Bank Holidays

Wholemeat pasta with spinach & cheese £2.45
Fruit crumble 70p

P John Street car park

At the back of a town-centre healthfood shop, this agreeable little vegetarian café proposes a good selection of tempting fare, much of it utilising organically grown produce. Cakes and biscuits, bhajias and samosas are joined about 11 by soup, filled jacket potatoes and quiches, and soon afterwards by a couple of hot specials like Chinese hot pot with honey and ginger. Nice salads and over 50 cheeses, plus ices and fruit-based sweets. Unlicensed. *No dogs.* ☕ 🦃

Studley

Interesting Things

8 Marble Alley, near Alcester
Studley (052 785) 3964
Map 5 A2 *Warwickshire*

Open 10–5
Closed Sun, Mon, Bank Holidays (except Good Fri) & 2 weeks Christmas

Cheese flan £1.05   Sausage & apple pie £1.05
P Leo's car park opposite & street parking
WC

All the family helps out at this wonderfully friendly first-floor coffee shop in a village near Stratford-upon-Avon. Mrs McKee prepares the splendid assortment of scones, slices, flapjacks and fruit pies available throughout the day, while from noon her range extends to include soups, sausage rolls, jacket potatoes and lasagne. Rhubarb fool and treacle tart are among favourite lunchtime sweets. Non-smoking area. Unlicensed. *No dogs.*

Sudbury

Ford's

47 Gainsborough Street
Sudbury (0787) 74298
Map 5 C2 *Suffolk*
Open 10–2.30 & 7–10
Closed Sun, Bank Holiday lunches & 2 weeks September
Broccoli terrine with yoghurt sauce £1.50 Fish soup with rouille and croûtons £1.95
Credit Visa
P Market Square   **WC**

Old church pews have been converted into booth seating at this spacious bistro, where first-class dishes are prepared by the enthusiastic owners, Jane and Gerry Ford. Consult the blackboard for the day's choice, which could include delicious smoked haddock mousse, eggs florentine and mixed grill kebab. Lunches start at noon, and before that you can enjoy superb baking (try a delectable almond tart). *No dogs.* 🦃

Surbiton   *New Entry*   *Fortunes*

4 Victoria Road
01-399 6909
Map 6 B3 *Surrey*

Open 11am–11pm
Closed 25 & 26 December

Chilliburger £3   Garlic mushrooms £1.45
LVs

P Claremont Road pay & display   **WC**

Service is friendly and the atmosphere relaxing at this classic hamburger restaurant opposite the station. Chargrilled burgers, quarter- or half-pounders, come plain and simple or with tasty toppings like chilli and red beans or garlic and parsley butter. Steaks include the T-bone special weighing in at a pound, and there are other popular favourites such as spaghetti, scampi, quiche and chicken Kiev. Sunday roast lunch. *No dogs.*

Surbiton

New Entry

Liberty Bell

158 Ewell Road
01-390 7564
Map 6 B3 *Surrey*

Open noon–2.30 & 6–11
Closed Sun & 1 week Christmas

Pork chops in red wine & coriander £5.25
Vegetarian rösti 80p
LVs   *Credit* Access, Visa
P street parking   **WC**

A busy, informal and instantly likable restaurant with a strong Edwardian feel to the decor. The menu combines a mid-Atlantic selection – guacamole, chilli con carne, burgers and steaks – with interesting daily specials such as beef and vegetable soup, lamb cutlets hollandaise and breast of chicken with a good Dijon mustard sauce. The usual range of puds like cheesecake and ice cream sundaes. Friendly, speedy service.

Sutton Scotney

Riverside Tea Garden

Bullington Lane, Near Winchester
Winchester (0962) 760353
Map 6 A3 *Hampshire*

Open 10–5.30 (Fri from noon)
Closed Tues & 25 & 26 December

Cream tea £1.45   Ham salad £2

P own car park   **WC**

A cosily old-fashioned tea shop on the old A34 where Mrs Walker carries on the tradition of her baker grandparents with some excellent home cooking. Her impeccably light scones and delicately flavoured sponges are everyone's favourite, as are the splendid fruit pies and jams she makes with fruit grown by Mr Walker in their lovely garden. Sandwiches, salads and toasted snacks available all day. Unlicensed. *No dogs.* 🍵

Swaffham

Red Door

7 London Street
Swaffham (0760) 21059
Map 5 C1 *Norfolk*

Open 9.30–5 (Sun from 11), also 7–9 Fri & Sat
Closed Mon & 1st 2 weeks January

Turkey & chestnut pie £2.95   Home-made soup with filled roll £1.75
Credit Access, Visa
P street parking   **WC**

Good, honest home cooking in a cheerful town-centre restaurant. Ploughman's, salads and omelettes provide tasty light lunches, while heartier appetites are catered for at mealtimes by the likes of lasagne, savoury pies, steak chasseur and chicken breast with walnut sauce. Sandwiches, scones and nice cakes are also available, plus vegetarian specials and children's dishes. Roast Sunday lunch. *No dogs.* 🛏

Swindon

New Entry

Acorn Wholefoods

40 Havelock Street
Swindon (0793) 39396
Map 6 A3 *Wiltshire*

Open 10–6
Closed Sun & Bank Holidays

Cashew nut lasagne £2.50   Lemon cheesecake 90p
LVs   *Credit* Access
P Brunel multi-storey car park   **WC**

Pleasing prints and posies of dried flowers decorate this self-service wholefood restaurant above a health-food shop. The menu is divided into vegetarian and seafood dishes, with noonday choices ranging from cashew nut lasagne and spicy chick pea casserole to devilled whitebait and deep-fried mussels. There are nice cakes to go with morning coffee and afternoon tea. Unlicensed. No smoking. *No dogs.*

Tarporley   *Feathers*

105 High Street
Tarporley (08293) 2812
Map 3 B4 *Cheshire*

Open 10–5
Closed Sun & Bank Holidays

Baked potato with mushroom sauce & salad
£2.50   Toasted sandwich & salad £2.50
Credit Access, Visa
P own car park   **WC**

This spotless coffee shop is just the place for ladies to recover after spending a fortune in the dress shop. For a further treat try Mrs Holloway's plump scones, lemon meringue pie or waistline-threatening chocolate cake, or lunch on home-made soup or pâté, toasted sandwiches or a hot savoury like cottage pie, lasagne or jacket potato. *No dogs.*

Tarr Steps   *Tarr Farm*

Dulverton
Winsford (064 385) 383
Map 8 C3 *Somerset*

Open 11–5.30
Closed end October–end March

Cream tea £1.50   Quiche with salad £1.95

P Exmoor National Parks car park   **WC**

Visitors to the Bronze Age stone-slab bridge known as Tarr Steps like to call in at this charmingly rustic farmhouse, where cream teas are available throughout the day. As well as lovely light scones served with clotted cream, Deborah Connell also bakes excellent sponges and fruit cakes, gingerbread and flapjacks. At lunchtime there's a simple choice of soup, ploughman's and quiche with salad, plus tempting sweets like seasonal berry fools. ☕

Taunton   *Castle Hotel, Bow Bar*

North Street
Taunton (0823) 72671
Map 8 C3 *Somerset*

Open 12–2
Closed Sun & Bank Holidays

Turkey sandwich 85p   Shell noodles with
seafood & cream sauce £2.90

P Castle Green car park   **WC**

Light lunches are served in this lofty, tapestry-hung bar, part of the renowned Castle Hotel but with a separate entrance. Smoked mackerel mousse and hot cheese and asparagus cream are typical starters, while mains range from avocado, bacon and onion flan to noodles with seafood, chicken curry and minute steak. Also salads, sandwiches and ploughman's, with cheesecake and ice creams to finish. Limited choice Saturday. *No dogs.* ☕

Tetbury   **New Entry**   *Calcot Manor*

Leighterton (0666 89) 355
Map 7 D2 *Gloucestershire*

Open 12.30–1.45
Closed Sun, 1 January, 25 & 26 December &
10 days January

Warm chicken liver salad with hazelnuts £3.25
Chocolate & pineapple mousse £2.75
Credit Access, Amex, Diners, Visa
P own car park   &   **WC**

Five or six speciality salads make up the menu in the bar lounge of this very civilised country house hotel. Presentation is impeccable, with cress and crisp lettuce leaves making a bed for succulent chicken livers with hazelnuts, marinated brill or game terrine with plums. There's a choice of two desserts or a selection of British cheeses served with walnut bread. Soup in winter. No children under eight. *No dogs.* ☕

Tewkesbury   *Telfords*

61 High Street
Tewkesbury (0684) 292225
Map 7 D2 *Gloucestershire*

Open noon–2
Closed Sun, 1 January, 26 December, 2
weeks February & 1 week November
Camembert pancake £1.95   Chocolate rum
crunch £1.50
Credit Access, Amex, Visa
P street   **WC**

A seasonal menu of one-course lunches fits
the just-a-biter's bill at this attractive little
restaurant. The choice runs from salads to
sirloin steak by way of superb spicy duck
pancake, baked trout with almonds and
chicken with a delicious creamy tarragon
sauce. The sweet choice includes cheesecake, mousses and ices. Prime produce,
herbs from the garden, good wholemeal
bread. Full menus available lunchtime and
evening. *No dogs.* 🖰

Tewkesbury   *Wintor House*

73 Church Street
Tewkesbury (0684) 292703
Map 7 D2 *Gloucestershire*

Open 10–2.15, also 3.30–5.15 Easter–
November
Closed Mon (except Bank Holidays), 25 & 26
December & 3 weeks October

Cream tea £1.50   Lasagne £2.75
P St Mary's Lane & Abbey car parks   **WC**

Set afternoon teas are served with bread and
butter, nice crumbly scones or super home-
baked cakes in this pleasant beamed restaurant. Sandwiches come plain or toasted, and
lunchtime dishes range from soup with
croûtons to salads and ploughman's platters,
casseroled chicken and grilled rainbow trout
(roast on Sunday). For sweet, perhaps meringue surprise, sherry trifle or fruit crumble.
No dogs. 🖰 🍵

Thame   *Mallards*

87 High Street
Thame (084 421) 6679
Map 6 B3 *Oxfordshire*

Open 11–3 & 6–11, Sun noon–2 & 7–10.30
Closed 10 days Christmas

Spare ribs with salad £2.85   Kidneys Turbigo
with rice £4.95
Credit Access, Visa
P Town Hall car park   ♿   **WC**

Wooden ducks gaze down benignly on customers in the cheerful wine bar section of
this smartly rustic restaurant. The menu
features such things as soups, pork terrine,
cheese platter and steak sandwich, and daily
specials could include a splendid mixed
vegetable casserole. These bar snacks are
also available at lunchtime in the restaurant
(where children are allowed), which has its
own more extensive menu. *No dogs.* 🖰 🍵

Thames Ditton   **New Entry**   *Skiffers*

High Street
01-398 5540
Map 6 B3 *Surrey*

Open noon–2
Closed Sun, Mon, 26 December & 1st week
January

Curried beef £2.85   French onion soup £1.20
Credit Access, Amex, Diners, Visa
P street parking   **WC**

They own the next-door butcher's shop, so
getting good-quality meat's no problem at
this pleasant bistro-style restaurant. Liz
Harding's enjoyable cooking spans a good
range, from French onion soup and coarse
country pâté to seafood au gratin, succulent
rack of lamb and medallions of pork with a
well-judged mustard sauce. Vegetables are
more interesting than usual (honey-roast
parsnips, carrots with raisins), and nice
sweets include Dutch apple pie. 🍵

Tideswell   *Horsmans Poppies*

Bank Square, Near Buxton
Tideswell (0298) 871083
Map 4 C3 *Derbyshire*

Open 11–2 & 6–11
Closed Mon (except Bank Holidays) & Tues

Houmus £1.55   Fish Wellington £5.35
Credit Access, Visa

P street parking   **WC**

Run with love and dedication by Su Horsman,
this charming little restaurant is the setting
for some thoroughly enjoyable home cooking. At lunchtime there are tasty quiches, pies
and salads, plus vegetarian specials like
green lentil cutlets with herby yoghurt sauce.
The evening choice (booking advisable) features slightly more elaborate dishes such as
chicken with apricots and brandy. Enjoyable
sweets from the trolley. *No dogs.* ☺ 🍵

Tissington   *Old School Tea Rooms*

Near Ashbourne
Parwich (033 525) 467
Map 4 C4 *Derbyshire*

Open 2.30–5.30 (Bank Holidays & school
holidays from 11)
Closed October–Thurs before Easter

Cream tea £1.35   Assorted cakes 40p

P own car park   ♿ **WC**

Once the village school, this bright, pleasant
tea room stands in a cluster of buildings on a
private estate belonging to Tissington Hall.
Excellent afternoon teas are the name of the
game, with lovely golden scones and thick
cream, fresh, dainty little finger sandwiches
and a small but select choice of very good
cakes such as moist apricot, and dark, rich
chocolate sponge. Unlicensed. No smoking.
No dogs. 🍵

Tiverton   *Red Fox*

Four Lanes Ends, Near Tarporley
Tarporley (082 93) 3152
Map 3 B4 *Cheshire*

Open noon–2 & 7–10.30 (Fri & Sat till 11)
Closed 1 January & 25 & 26 December

Avocado Michel £2.25   Beef & orange
casserole £4.85
LVs *Credit* Access, Amex, Diners, Visa
P own car park   **WC**

Beams and exposed brick walls provide a
characterful background at this popular restaurant in an old red-brick pub. There's plenty
of choice on the menu. There are a dozen
different pizzas (calzone has a bit of everything), enjoyable pasta dishes like lasagne
and spaghetti carbonara, plus sweet and
savoury pancakes, salads and some meaty
main courses – including pollo alla crema and
pork escalope alla milanese. Minimum
charge of £1.95 in the evening. *No dogs.*

Tiverton   *Angel Foods*

1 Angel Terrace
Tiverton (0884) 254778
Map 8 C3 *Devon*

Open 9–5.30 (Thurs till 2.30)
Closed Sun, Bank Holidays & 1 week
Christmas

Raw salad with houmus £1.65   Vegetable
crumble pie 70p
P Market Place car park

Tucked behind a shop, this tiny wholefood
café offers wholesome, imaginative snacks
and a wide range of herbal teas. Throughout
the day you can enjoy sweet things like carrot
and cinnamon cake, date slice and bread
pudding, as well as savouries such as curried
vegetable pasty. At lunchtime there's nourishing soup, popular beanburgers and tasty
pies, with local farmhouse ice creams to
round things off nicely. Unlicensed. No smoking. *No dogs.* ☺ 🍵

Tiverton ★ *Hendersons*

18 Newport Street
Tiverton (0884) 254256
Map 8 C3 *Devon*
Open 12.15–2 & 7.15–9.30
Closed Sun, Mon, Bank Holidays (except 1 January & Good Fri), 4 days Christmas & last 3 weeks August
Pink grapefruit & avocado salad £1.95   Dish of the day with vegetables £2.85
Credit Access, Amex, Diners, Visa
P market car park opposite   **WC**

A restaurant proper, but just-a-biters can order a single dish, and there's a very appealing light lunch menu. Elizabeth Ambler uses the pick of the season's produce to create dishes that are absolutely full of flavour: green summer pâté, goujons of plaice, a wonderful chicken and leek quiche, chunky Italian-style veal ragout. Delicious sweets, too, and over ten wines by the glass. Smoking only in the bar. *No dogs.* 🍷 🐕

Tolworth *Superfish*

59 The Broadway
01-390 2868
Map 6 B3 *Surrey*

Open 11.30–2.30 (Sat till 3) & 5.30–11.30 (Fri & Sat from 5)
Closed Sun, Mon & Bank Holidays (except Good Fri)
Cod & chips £2.85   Scampi & chips £3.50
LVs
P Tolworth car park to rear   ♿ **WC**

Aptly named, for the fish is indeed super at this bright, cheerful restaurant in a parade of shops. Traditional favourites like cod, plaice and haddock are beautifully cooked and served with smashing chips, good pickles and a basket full of lovely hot French bread. Scampi, sole, skate and rock are also available, and there are nice ices to finish. Friendly waiting staff. *No dogs.* 🐕

Torquay *Village Kitchen*

33 Ilsham Road, Wellswood
Torquay (0803) 22644
Map 8 C3 *Devon*

Open 9–5 (Sat till 2)
Closed Sun & Bank Holidays

Vegetable lasagne with salad £2.25   Plum & banana pie with walnut pastry 95p

P street parking   ♿ **WC**

This bright, cheerful coffee shop provides an abundant all-day selection of tasty snacks both sweet and savoury: scones and splendid cakes, plain and toasted sandwiches, salads, omelettes, quiche, hot smoked mackerel. Daily specials like chicken curry and vegetable lasagne widen the choice still further, and there are some very tempting sweets. Unlicensed. No smoking.

Totnes *Planters*

82a High Street
Totnes (0803) 865522
Map 8 C4 *Devon*
Open 10.30–2.15, also 6.30–9 in high season, Thurs–Sat in early & late season
Closed Sun, Bank Holidays & 1st 2 weeks January
Chicken mornay £3.10   Cherry mille-feuille £1.05
Credit Access, Amex, Diners, Visa
P Rotherford Square car park   **WC**

New owners since last year, but standards stay high at this bright, fresh restaurant with an open-air summer section. The blackboard menu offers a good variety of very palatable fare, from moist pâté served with home-baked bread to pizza, moussaka, vegetables au gratin and chicken in a mustard-flavoured mornay sauce. Chocolate profiteroles, meringue glacé and treacle tart are among the tasty options for pudding. Children's portions are available. 🍷 🐕

Totnes   *New Entry*   *Willow*

87 High Street
Totnes (0803) 862605
Map 8 C4 *Devon*

Open 9–5 (from 10 in winter), also 6.30–10
Tues–Sat (Fri & Sat only in winter)
Closed Sun, 1 January, Good Fri & 25 & 26
December
Coriander tofu dip £1.20   Courgette &
mushroom crumble £2.20
P Rutherfold Square car park **WC**

In the main street of town, this neatly kept
vegetarian restaurant has a special family
room and a charming little courtyard. The
two partners choose their raw materials very
carefully: cheese is rennet free, vegetables
organic, eggs free range. A typical menu
could include red chilli bean casserole with
couscous, courgette and mushroom crumb-
ble, flapjacks and a really good orange and
honey cake. There's table service at night.
No smoking.

Trebarwith Strand   *House on the Strand*

Near Tintagel
Camelford (0840) 770326
Map 8 B4 *Cornwall*

Open 10.30–9.30
Closed end October–early March

Lentil fritters with salads £2.50   Seafood
crumble £4.30
Credit Access, Visa
P street parking **WC**

Two families run this pleasant restaurant
near the beach, where everything on the
interesting menu is available at any time of
day. Avocado crab dip, lentil fritters and fresh
fettuccine with bacon and mushrooms make
tasty snacks or starters, while the hungry will
opt for main dishes like pork and lemon
casserole, vegetable gratin or a subtly spiced
curry. Sweet treats include home-made
cakes and ice creams. *No dogs.*

Trebarwith Strand   ★   *Old Millfloor*

Near Tintagel
Camelford (0840) 770234
Map 8 B4 *Cornwall*

Open 2–6 (till 5 in winter) & 7.30–9
Closed Sun eve, Mon afternoon, 25 & 26
December & 6 weeks preceding Easter

Cornish cream tea £1.75   Stuffed chicken with
vegetables £5.60
P own car park **WC**

Janice Waddon-Martyn continues to delight
visitors to her cosy country cottage with
some quite superb home cooking. Flavoursome soups, lovely light quiches and omelettes, sandwiches and ploughman's platters
all make delightful lunchtime snacks. In the
afternoon there are hot scones with jam and
cream, as well as treats like strawberry
meringues. Poached lemon sole, stuffed
aubergine and steak are typical evening
offerings. Unlicensed. *No dogs.*

Tunbridge Wells   *Buster Browns*

155 Camden Road
Tunbridge Wells (0892) 44144
Map 6 C3 *Kent*
Open Mon–Thurs noon–2.30 & 6–11.30, Fri
noon–3 & 6–midnight, Sat 11.30am–midnight,
Sun 11am–11.30pm
Closed 25 & 26 December
Special cheeseburger with French fries £3.45
Charlie Chaplin sundae £3.05
LVs *Credit* Access
P street parking **WC**

A colourful American-style restaurant full of
young people and rock music. Charcoal-
grilled burgers and French fries top the
popularity stakes, with barbecued spare ribs,
chilli and jumbo BLTs among the alternatives.
Also pasta and Mexican things, plus a variety
of ices and sundaes. Sunday brunch is well
patronised. Brisk, friendly service. *No dogs.*

Tunbridge Wells — *Delicious*

14 Mount Wells
Tunbridge Wells (0892) 47134
Map 6 C3 *Kent*

Open 9.30–5
Closed Sun & Bank Holidays

Lasagne verdi £1.75   Gâteaux 75p
LVs

P Calverley Ground multi-storey car park

Pine furnishings and a summery green decor make this busy, self-service restaurant opposite the railway station a pleasing spot for refreshment. Freshly filled rolls, quiches and salads are always available, together with over 30 different kinds of home-made cakes. Favourite hot specials, which include lasagne, macaroni cheese and Italian chicken with rice expand the choice even further during a long lunch period. *No dogs.*

Tunbridge Wells ★ *New Entry* — *Downstairs at Thackeray's*

85 London Road
Tunbridge Wells (0892) 37559
Map 6 C3 *Kent*

Open 12.30–5 & 7–11
Closed Sun, Mon & Bank Holidays

Fresh pasta with mushrooms & cheese £2.25
Brochette of lamb with date & pineapple £5.95
LVs   *Credit* Access, Visa
P street parking   **WC**

A sophisticated little brasserie-style place, beneath Thackeray's restaurant but with its own entrance. English dishes are skilfully cooked and stylishly served: typical items include potato and chive soup, mixed herb omelette, black pudding with buttered apples and pork escalopes with Stilton sauce. To finish, perhaps banana Ramsbottom, a nice concoction of bananas, chocolate and pastry. British farmhouse cheeses are a speciality. *No dogs.*

Tunbridge Wells — *Pilgrims*

37 Mount Ephraim
Tunbridge Wells (0892) 20341
Map 6 C3 *Kent*

Open 10.30–8
Closed Sun, Bank Holidays & 3 days Christmas

Moussaka £1.95   Courgette casserole £2.05
LVs
P street parking   &   **WC**

Appetising vegetarian fare is served at this bright, leafy restaurant furnished in pine. Crisp, fresh salads go down well with hot dishes like wholemeal pizzas topped with cheese and peppers, cashew paella and vegetable moussaka. There are also flavoursome soups and lots of sweet delights – including brandy mousse yoghurt and cream whip and fluffy lemon cheesecake. There's a minimum mealtime charge of £1.50. No smoking. *No dogs.*

Tunbridge Wells *New Entry* — *Pizza Piazza*

76 Mount Pleasant Road
Tunbridge Wells (0892) 47124
Map 6 C3 *Kent*

Open 11am–11.30pm
Closed 25 & 26 December
Pizza toscana £2.85   Baked mushrooms with garlic £1.15
LVs   *Credit* Access, Visa
P Crescent Road multi-storey car park   &
WC

A modern and quite stylish pizza place serving really good pizzas made with traditional or wholemeal dough. Varieties include margherita, just tomato and mozzarella; Pinocchio, with prawns, sweetcorn and fresh parsley; and alba, with mushrooms and gorgonzola. There's also a folded version filled with minced beef. Lasagne verdi for pizzaphobes; good antipasti (tuna in pâté or salad, baked mushrooms) and side salads either mixed or wholefood. *No dogs.*

Tutbury   *Corn Mill Tea Room*

Corn Mill Lane
Burton-on-Trent (0283) 813300
Map 4 C4 *Staffordshire*

Open 10–5.15
Closed Sun, Mon & Bank Holidays

Mushroom omelette £1.85   Welsh rarebit £1.65
Credit Access, Visa
P own car park   ♿   **WC**

The river Fleam, a tributary of the Dove, flows by this former corn mill just outside Tutbury, and the old water wheel is an attractive original feature. A cosy beamed room makes a pleasant setting in which to enjoy a simple selection of snacks that include scones and cakes, sandwiches, salads, omelettes and hot things on toast. Also a set afternoon tea. Unlicensed. *No dogs.*

Ullswater   ★   *Sharrow Bay Country House Hotel*

Near Penrith
Pooley Bridge (085 36) 301
Map 3 B2 *Cumbria*

Open 11–11.45 & 4–4.45
Closed 3 December–3 March

Morning coffee with biscuits £2   Set afternoon tea £5

P own car park   ♿   **WC**

To take afternoon tea in this enchanting hotel is undiluted delight: the scenery is unsurpassed, the lounges elegant and civilised, the cakes and pastries impeccably fresh. Scones rise high, sponges are silky-smooth, sandwiches are cut to order, jams are homemade. Morning coffee, which is served with an assortment of biscuits, is an equally winning occasion. No children. *No dogs.* 🍵

Upper Slaughter   *Lords of the Manor Hotel*

Near Bourton-on-the-Water
Cotswold (0451) 20243
Map 5 A2 *Gloucestershire*

Open noon–2
Closed Sun & 2 weeks January

Sole & salmon quiche with salad £4.25
Lemon tart £1.50
Credit Access, Amex, Diners, Visa
P own car park   **WC**

Paul Hackett has improved the style and standard of the light lunches served in the lounges or garden of this fine Cotswold manor house. Concise seasonal menus tempt with dishes like onion and cider soup, chicken pancakes or an exceptional sole and salmon quiche attractively presented with a lightly dressed, leafy salad. The sweet selection is being improved, and there's a good choice of cheeses. We found the service polite but not speedy. *No dogs.* ☕

Uttoxeter   *Ye Olde Pantry*

12 Carter Street
Uttoxeter (088 93) 2927
Map 4 C4 *Staffordshire*

Open 9–5
Closed Sun & Bank Holidays

Steak & kidney pie £1.95   Toasted tea cake 40p

P car park at rear   **WC**

An old-fashioned baker's shop (by the market square) fronts this simple tea room where passers-by, enticed in by a splendid window display, can sample the home-baked goodies. These include plump, buttery scones, giant teacakes, sugary jam doughnuts and lemon meringue pie – with sandwiches and toasted snacks providing an appetising savoury contrast. English breakfasts begin the day well, and set-price lunches include a roast. Unlicensed. 🍵

Walberswick   *Potters Wheel*

The Green
Southwold (0502) 724468
Map 5 D2 *Suffolk*

Open 10.30–5.30
Closed Tues & January–end March
Steak & kidney pie with vegetables £3.25
Avocado baked in ratatouille & cheese with
salad & potatoes £2.90
Credit Access
P around the green **WC**

Lesley Scott and her young assistants form
a dedicated team at this homely restaurant
by the green. Everything is carefully prepared
and delicious: baked goodies like rich fruit
cake and scones are available all day, and at
lunchtime (minimum charge of £2.35) there
are soups and savouries such as baked
avocado with ratatouille and local smoked
mackerel. Appealing sweets, and a roast on
Sunday. Table d'hôte dinner Saturday evening. Unlicensed. 🍵

Wallingford   *Lamb Coffee Shop*

Lamb Arcade, High Street
Wallingford (0491) 33581
Map 6 B3 *Oxfordshire*

Open 10–5 (Sat till 5.30)
Closed Sun & 25 & 26 December

Prawn & asparagus quiche with salad £2
Lemon chicken with wild rice £2.40

P Castle Street car park

Local artists like to stage exhibitions at this
self-service coffee shop on the top floor of
an antiques arcade. Sit beneath a ceiling
mural of sky and trees and enjoy a slice of
quiche (Stilton and herbs, prawn and asparagus or classic lorraine) with a selection of
crisp salads. Other choices include soup and
jacket potatoes, plus dips and pâtés in
summer, and hot dishes in winter. Simple
sweets, too.

Wallingford   *Lamb Wine Vaults*

Castle Street
Wallingford (0491) 39606
Map 6 B3 *Oxfordshire*

Open 10.30–2.30
Closed Sun, Mon & Bank Holidays

Quiche with salads £2.75   Tuna, cheese &
ratatouille pie £3.50
Credit Access, Visa
P Castle Street car park

A friendly and civilised wine bar where local
ladies provide the delicious food served at
lunchtime. An appetising display offers light
snacks like oak-smoked trout, Highland pâté
and bean and ham soup, plus a tasty daily
special such as vegetable pie. Excellent
French dressing accompanies the simple,
crisp salads, and there are well-kept cheeses
and a couple of sweets to finish. Non-
smoking area. *No dogs.* 🐶

Walton on the Naze   *Naze Links Café*

The Naze, Old Hall Lane
Map 5 D2 *Essex*

Open 10–5.30
Closed 1 November–end March

Ploughman's lunch £1.35   Quiche & salad
£1.75
LVs
P The Naze car park ♿

An inviting sun terrace with colourful umbrel-
las draws attention to the Woodcocks' unassuming clifftop café. If the menu is short,
everything on it is exceedingly tasty, from
scones, sausage rolls, sandwiches and light
sponge cakes to more substantial items such
as hot quiche (mushroom and pepper, tomato
and courgette) and sausage pie. Nice sweets
like bread pudding, and a smashing cup of
tea, too. Unlicensed. 🍵

Wansford-in-England   *Haycock Hotel Lounge*

London Road
Stamford (0780) 782223
Map 5 B1 *Cambridgeshire*

Open 8–2.45 & 3–11

Sugar-baked ham with salads £5.95   Seafood
pancake £3.95
Credit Access, Amex, Diners, Visa

P own car park   **WC**

The attractive riverside garden, comfortable
lounge and bar provide a choice of settings
for a snack at this popular old coaching inn.
As well as a very tempting buffet of cold cuts
and interesting salads, there are appetising
hot dishes – soup, lasagne, turkey and
mushroom pie, seafood pancake – plus
steaks, chops and sausages barbecued in
the garden when the weather is fine. Scones,
sandwiches and cakes for a satisfying afternoon tea. *No dogs.* 🍵 🍴

Wantage   *Vale & Downland Museum Centre*

Old Surgery, Church Street
Wantage (023 57) 66838
Map 6 A3 *Oxfordshire*

Open 10.30–4.30, Sun & Bank Holidays 2–5
Closed Mon & 1 week Christmas

Farmhouse soup with bread 80p   Quiche
lorraine with salad £1.75

P Civic Hall car park ♿ **WC**

Part of a converted 17th-century cloth mer-
chant's house at the heart of a fascinating
museum of local life, this delightful little
coffee shop offers splendid snacks at rock-
bottom prices. Mouthwatering baked goodies include superfresh scones and sponges,
flapjacks and shortbread, while on the savoury side there's always a warming soup, a
couple of flans, filled rolls and sausage pie.
No smoking. Unlicensed. 🍴

Ware   *Ben's Brasserie Bar*

14 High Street
Ware (0920) 68383
Map 5 C2 *Hertfordshire*

Open noon–2.30 & 6–11
Closed Sun, Bank Holidays & 4 days
Christmas

Chicken au poivre £2.95   Moules marinière
£2.45
P public car park at rear ♿ **WC**

Cooking and presentation both shine at this
friendly brasserie and bar on the site of an
old pub. Make your choice from the display
counter – quiche, Scotch eggs, super terrine,
salads – or consult the blackboard for hot
dishes like moules marinière, spicy meatballs
and fillet of fresh haddock. Sweets include
orange cheesecake with an orange sauce.
No children in the evening. *No dogs.* 🍵

Ware   **New Entry**   *Sunflowers*

7 Amwell End
Ware (0920) 3358
Map 5 C2 *Hertfordshire*

Open 10–5 (Thurs till 1.30)
Closed Sun & Bank Holidays

Carrot & lentil soup 65p   Butter bean
ratatouille £1.50

P car park next to Ware Station   **WC**

This friendly, well-run establishment is a
wholefood shop on the ground floor, a
pleasant, simple restaurant above, where the
menu includes vegeburgers, salads, jacket
potatoes and a popular risotto with sunflower
seeds, corn, peas and brown rice. Organically
grown vegetables are used whenever possible, and soya milk is offered with tea. Don't
miss the special scones filled with sugarless
jam and Greek yoghurt. Unlicensed. No
smoking. *No dogs.*

Wareham   *New Entry*   *Annies*

14a North Street
Wareham (092 95) 6242
Map 6 A4 *Dorset*

Open 10am–5.30pm; mid July–mid September
8am–10pm
Closed Sun, Bank Holidays (except August) &
1 week Christmas
Vegetable & cashew curry £1.40   Bakewell
tart 55p
P Howards Lane car park   ♿   **WC**

Wholesome vegetarian cooking has made this a very popular place. The day starts at 8 o'clock (high summer only) with croissants and coffee, and from 10 an array of tempting baking appears, from wholemeal and cheese scones to Bakewell tart and delicious ginger and apple cake. Hot items like soup, omelettes and quiche are available from midday, and the evening menu also offers savoury pancakes and ice cream treats. Unlicensed (bring your own). 🍴 ☕

Warley   *New Entry*   *Wild Thyme*

422 Bearwood Road, Bearwood
021-420 2528
Map 5 A2 *West Midlands*

Open noon–2 & 6–10
Closed Sun, Mon, Bank Holidays (except
Good Fri) & 25 December–2 January
Aduki bean & brown rice casserole £3.20
Aubergine & cashew nut timbale £3.20
Credit Amex, Diners
P street parking   **WC**

Healthy vegetarian dishes come in imaginative combinations at this modestly appointed restaurant. Mushrooms marinated in garlic, lemon and thyme and light, creamy cashew nut pâté are typically appealing starters, while for a hearty main course you might choose well-seasoned marrow and rice bake, groundnut stew or Italian beans and pasta. There are lots of interesting salads, plus pleasant sweets like banana and apple crunch. No smoking. *No dogs.*

Warminster   *Chinn's Celebrated Chophouse*

12 Market Place
Warminster (0985) 212245
Map 8 D3 *Wiltshire*
Open Coffee Lounge: 10–2.30; Chophouse:
noon–2 & 7–10.45
Closed Sun, Bank Holidays (except Good Fri)
& 2 weeks mid October
Fisherman's lunch £1.20   Rump steak & chips
£4.90
Credit Access, Visa
P own car park **WC**

Prime steaks, chops, kebabs and fish are served in the beamed cellar of this restaurant that's very pleasantly run by the Pickford family. On the ground floor is a simple coffee lounge, where you can enjoy morning coffee with home-made cakes and scones and tasty lunchtime snacks like soup, open sandwiches and ploughman's. Nice fruity pies for afters. *No dogs.* ☕

Warminster   *Jenner's*

45 Market Place
Warminster (0985) 213385
Map 8 D3 *Wiltshire*

Open 9.30–5.30
Closed Sun October–Easter & 25 December–2
January
Vegetable crumble with salad £2.45
Wholemeal Bakewell tart 95p
P street parking & large free car park at rear
WC

Standing in the main street, this is a pleasant coffee shop serving a variety of simple wholefood snacks. Pâté or houmus with toast, the day's soup, nut loaf and pizza typify the savoury selection, and there are also various sandwiches and salads. Home-baked scones, cakes and biscuits are always available, with the option of a set cream tea. Unlicensed. No smoking.

Warminster ★ *Vincent's*

60 East Street
Warminster (0985) 215052
Map 8 D3 *Wiltshire*

Open 11.45–2.30
Closed Mon lunch, all Sun & 24 Dec–6 Jan

Chicken pie £2.75   Treacle tart 75p

Credit Access, Amex, Diners, Visa
P street parking   **WC**

Excellent light lunches, faultlessly executed by Belgian-born Anne Werrell (husband Leslie acts as genial host), are a real treat at this super little restaurant. Try a single dish like featherlight spinach and cream cheese pancake, or something more substantial such as Anne's speciality pork chops with mustard cream sauce. Also salads, pies and pasta, plus gorgeous sweets. More elaborate evening meals. *No dogs.* ☺ 🐾

Warminster `New Entry` *Bar Roussel*

62a Market Place
Warwick (0926) 491983
Map 5 A2 *Warwickshire*

Open noon–2.15 & 7–9.45
Closed Sun lunch & 25 & 26 December

Tsatsiki with pitta bread £1.10   Chicken in lemon, white wine & mushroom sauce £2.95
LVs
P Market Place   **WC**

Consult the blackboard for the daily-changing food choice in this friendly and comfortable modern wine bar. Starters might include garlic prawns, tsatsiki or chicken liver pâté, while for a main course you might consider cold cuts or quiche with a salad, or go for a hot special like beef carbonnade or tasty vegetable lasagne. Good selection of cheese, and mainly home-made sweets include treacle tart. No children. *No dogs.* ☺

Warwick `New Entry` *Brethren's Kitchen*

Lord Leycester Hospital
Warwick (0926) 492797
Map 5 A2 *Warwickshire*

Open 10.30–5
Closed Sun & October–March

Eyemouth tart 35p   Ploughman's £1.50

P own car park ♿ **WC**

Mrs Robinson offers a simple but carefully prepared selection of home-made fare in this cosy tea room, where a lovingly preserved iron stove bears witness to its early days as the brethren's kitchen of the ancient Leycester Hospital. Sandwiches, open rolls, toast and salads are available throughout the day, along with nice light scones, biscuits, sponge cakes, fruit loaf and assorted slices. Unlicensed. *No dogs.* 🐾

Warwick `New Entry` *Charlottes Tea Rooms*

6 Jury Street
Warwick (0926) 498930
Map 5 A2 *Warwickshire*

Open 10–5.30, Sun 11–6
Closed 25 & 26 December & 1st 2 weeks November

Steak & Guinness casserole £2.60   Charlotte malakoff 90p
P market place ♿ **WC**

Tasty snacks can be enjoyed throughout the day at this pleasant, well-run tea shop. Toasted scones, teacakes and crumpets provide elevenses, along with assorted sandwiches, hot savouries and omelettes. The lunch choice includes soup, pâté, filled potatoes and a hot special like chicken and mushroom pie or a casserole, while at teatime there's a tempting selection of home baking to accompany a superb range of teas. Unlicensed. *No dogs.* 🐾

Warwick — New Entry — *Piccolino's Pizzeria*

31 Smith Street
Warwick (0926) 491020
Map 5 A2 *Warwickshire*

Open noon–2.30 & 5.30–11 (Fri till 11.30), Sat noon–10.30
Closed 25 & 26 December

Special pizza £3.10 (starter portion)   Lasagne £1.80
P Nibbs car park & street   **WC**

Pizzas are the big favourite at this friendly place just out of the town centre. Well-made bases are generously topped with mozzarella and tomato or your choice from a variety of other goodies, including gammon and pineapple (Hawaiian) and egg, bacon and Worcester sauce (all' inglese). Pasta dishes are available as starters or main courses, and there's also antipasto, salads and chilli con carne. Ices and simple sweets. *No dogs.*

Warwick — *Westgate Arms, Gate Brasserie*

Bowling Green Street
Warwick (0926) 492362
Map 5 A2 *Warwickshire*

Open 7.30–3
Closed Sun & Bank Holidays (except Good Fri)
Cottage cheese with fruits & salad £4.25   ½ lb burger with salad & chips £5.25
Credit Access, Amex, Diners, Visa
P own car park **WC**

Start the day with a traditional cooked breakfast or lighter continental version at this comfortably stylish coffee shop-cum-brasserie. From 10am the menu offers juicy burgers, excellent salads and double-decker sandwiches, plus tasty starters like deep-fried stuffed mushrooms and home-made soup. Finish with waffles and maple syrup or nice apple pie. Minimum charge of £2.95. *No dogs.* ☕

Wasdale — *Greendale Gallery Restaurant*

Near Wast Water
Wasdale (094 06) 243
Map 3 B2 *Cumbria*

Open 11.30–8
Closed end September–Easter

Steak & kidney pie £3.25   Chicken chasseur £3.60

P own car park ♿ **WC**

A pleasant, picture-filled restaurant offering carefully prepared, flavoursome fare to suit all appetites. Coffee is served until lunchtime, when you can have a full meal of, say, egg mayonnaise or pâté followed by fried plaice, pork chop with apple sauce or steak Diane, with hot apple pie to finish. Lighter alternatives include sandwiches, salads and omelettes, and there's a set tea later. Children's menu. *No dogs.*

Waterperry — *Waterperry Gardens Tea Shop*

Near Wheatley
Ickford (084 47) 254
Map 6 A3 *Oxfordshire*

Open 10–5.30 (till 4 October–March)
Closed 1 week mid July & 2 weeks Christmas

Lemon teacake 45p   Honey & apple cake 55p
Credit Access, Visa
P own car park ♿ **WC**

You can ponder on what shrubs or roses to buy over a cup of coffee, light lunch or afternoon tea at this simple tea shop that's part of a horticultural centre. Home-baking is much in evidence on the long self-service counter, which offers scones, shortbread and delicious lemon cake, all freshly made, along with quiche and salad at lunchtime. Eat outside and admire the gardens in fine weather. Unlicensed. ☕ 🍵

Wells   *Cloister Restaurant*

Wells Cathedral
Wells (0749) 76543
Map 8 D3 *Somerset*

Open 10–5 (Sun from 2); November–February
11–4, Sun 2–5
Closed 2 weeks Christmas

Vegetable lasagne £1.75   Date & walnut cake
55p
P market place   &   **WC**

The lovely cathedral cloisters make a splendid setting for this friendly counter-service
restaurant. Throughout the day there's a
good selection of baking, including scones,
shortbread and a heavenly apricot wholemeal
cake, and sandwiches are made to order.
Midday heralds the arrival of soup, quiche,
cold meats and salads, plus a hot special like
chicken pie and a calorific pud such as chocolate fudge cake. No smoking. *No dogs.*

Wells   *Good Earth*

4 Priory Road
Wells (0749) 78600
Map 8 D3 *Somerset*

Open 9.30–5.30
Closed Sun & Bank Holidays

Stuffed cabbage £1.30   Fresh fruit crumble
£1.10
Credit Access, Amex
P own car park   **WC**

Natural, unrefined produce is the basis for
the healthy snacks served in this delightful
wholefood restaurant with a courtyard. Moist
traditional cakes such as flapjacks, ginger
and Somerset apple dappy accompany speciality teas or pure fruit juice, and from
midday there's soup, salads, jacket potatoes,
flans (perhaps courgette and Caerphilly) and
a very good pizza, plus a hearty special and
some delicious desserts. Non-smoking section *No dogs.*

West Byfleet   **New Entry**   *Superfish*

51 Old Woking Road
Byfleet (093 23) 40366
Map 6 B3 *Surrey*

Open 11.30–2 (Sat till 2.30) & 5.30–10.30 (Fri–
Sat till 11)
Closed Sun & some Bank Holidays
Fillet of cod & chips £2.30   Halibut steak &
chips £3.95
LVs
P car park opposite   &   **WC**

The latest in a small chain of restaurants
offering, as the souvenir menu has it, 'delectable fish and chips fried in the Yorkshire
way'. Beef dripping is the medium for frying,
and the fish includes cod, haddock, rockfish
and scampi, joined by skate, halibut, whole
plaice and whole sole on the bone when
available. The French bread is good and
crusty, and sweets comprise a selection of
ice creams. *No dogs.*

Westbourne   *Hollywood!*

100 Poole Road, Bournemouth
Bournemouth (0202) 768997
Map 6 A4 *Dorset*
Open 11.45–2.45 & 6.30–10.45
Closed Sun, 25 & 26 December & 2 weeks
spring
Variously topped beefburgers £2.50   Chicken
drumsticks with salad £3.20
LVs
P street parking & nearby public car park   &
WC

Movie buffs Richard and Judy Bennett have
brought their passion for Hollywood to life at
this zippy restaurant, where film posters line
the walls, film themes provide the background music and you can even eat your
favourite film! Follow Zorba the Greek (taramasalata and pitta) with The Towering In-
ferno (fiery chilli) or perhaps The Italian Job –
home-made lasagne. There are King Kong
burgers, too, and simple sweets.

Westerham   *Henry Wilkinson*

26 Market Square
Westerham (0959) 64245
Map 6 C3 *Kent*

Open noon–2.30 & 7–10.30 (Fri–Sat till 11.30)
Closed Mon eve, all Sun, Good Fri & 25 & 26
December

Beef chasseur £4.85   Taramasalata £2.05
Credit Access, Amex, Diners, Visa
P street & car park at rear in evening   **WC**

Quite a pleasant town-centre wine bar, with
doggy prints on the walls and the pine tables
all set up for eating. The food is home-made
and wholesome, with omelettes, grills and
salads among the dishes available at both
sessions. Sandwiches and jacket potatoes
are lunchtime extras, while in the evening
blackboards announce hot specials like beef
chasseur or Swiss veal. Sweet and savoury
endings. *No dogs.* 🍵

Whitby   ★   *Magpie Café*

14 Pier Road
Whitby (0947) 602058
Map 4 D2 *North Yorkshire*

Open 11.30–6.30
Closed mid October–1 week before Easter,
also Fri till Spring Bank Holiday

Haddock & chips £2.90   Lemon trifle £1

P difficult: Khyber Pass Street   **WC**

Seafood is tops at the McKenzie family's
splendid cafe overlooking the quay: crab,
salmon and prawns for starters or in salads;
fresh lobster, hot or cold; fish, fried or grilled
and served with real chips. Steaks, ham and
turkey breast are meaty options, and there's
a wide range of excellent home baking and
gorgeous sweets. Also a long children's
menu and afternoon teas. Unlicensed. Non-
smoking area. *No dogs.* 🍵

Williton   *Blackmore's Bookshop Tea Room*

6 High Street
Williton (0984) 32227
Map 8 C3 *Somerset*

Open 9–5.30 (Sat till 1)
Closed Sun & Bank Holidays

Shepherd's pie £1.50   Fruit pie with cream
65p

P street or village car park   **WC**

A delicious array of biscuits, scones, cakes
and gâteaux tempts visitors to this cosy little
tea room at the back of a very browsable
bookshop. There are also savoury snacks,
including salads, toasted sandwiches, shepherd's pie and jacket potatoes with tasty
fillings like bacon and onion or chilli con
carne. There's a pleasant garden area for
outside eating.

Wimborne Minster   *Quinneys*

26 West Borough
Wimborne (0202) 883518
Map 6 A4 *Dorset*

Open 9.15–5.15
Closed Sun, Mon, Bank Holidays & 1 week
Spring Bank Holiday
Dorset apple cake 90p   Grilled trout with
vegetables £3.95
P Allendale Centre car park or street parking
 ♿ **WC**

The Skidmore family continue to delight
customers with their day-long menu of savoury snacks and a feast of home-baking.
Their 14th-century restaurant is just the place
for a cream tea, while if you come at
lunchtime, there's local plaice and trout as
well as daily specials such as salmon mayonnaise and chicken curry. Charming staff
are kept very busy. Non-smoking section.

Winchcombe

Pilgrims Way Coffee House

1 Hailes Street, Near Cheltenham
Winchcombe (0242) 603764
Map 5 A2 *Gloucestershire*

Open 9.30–5.30
Closed Tuesday, also Sun November–March,
2 weeks November & 1 week Christmas

Quiche & salad £1.75   Fruit cake 50p

P The Square   **WC**

Sound, down-to-earth home baking is the draw at this quaint little coffee house on the main street of the ancient capital of Mercia. The counter is well laden with a tempting cargo of flapjacks, chocolate crunch, coffee sponge, fruit cake and other goodies. Scones and teacakes provide a warm bite, and there are savoury items like soup, quiche and toasted sandwiches. Children's portions available. Unlicensed.

Winchelsea

Finch of Winchelsea

12 High Street
Rye (0797) 226234
Map 6 C4 *East Sussex*

Open 9.30–6
Closed Wednesday in winter & 25 & 26 December

Beef & vegetable pie £2.25   Bakewell tart 50p

P street parking   **WC**

Several interconnecting rooms – one featuring a fine old inglenook – make up this family-run tea shop on the main street of the village. Throughout the opening hours there's splendid home baking to enjoy, with goodies like chocolate cake and Bakewell tart being particularly delicious. Lunchtime brings a menu of steaks and gammon, quiche, scampi and a tasty beef and vegetable pie. Roast lunch on Sunday. *No dogs.* 🐾

Winchelsea

Winchelsea Tea Rooms

Higham Green, Near Rye
Rye (0797) 226679
Map 6 C4 *East Sussex*

Open noon–5.30 (Fri from 2.30)
Closed Mon (except Bank Holidays) & end October–beginning March

Cheese & prawn potato with salad £1.80
Quiche with side salad £1.80
P street parking   &   **WC**

Linda Rankin's splendid home baking ensures that the tables are rarely empty at this pretty, Victorian-style tea room. Fresh, light scones with good jam and cream, rich chocolate sponge, buttery shortbread and exceedingly morish date slice are just some of the treats in store. Sandwiches and light savoury snacks like Welsh rarebit extend the range at lunchtime. *No dogs.* 🐾

Winchester

Cloisters

12 Upper High Street
Winchester (0962) 53114
Map 6 A4 *Hampshire*

Open 9–5
Closed Sun & Bank Holidays

Roast beef £2.80   Lemon meringue pie 65p
LVs

P street parking   **WC**

Consult the blackboard menu and place your order at the counter of this unpretentious little restaurant. The food is simple and wholesome, with sandwiches and salads, cakes and puddings being available for all-day snacking. Lunchtime (minimum charge £1.50) brings the roast of the day plus a couple of other items like cottage pie or lasagne. *No dogs.* 🍵

Winchester — *Mr Pitkin's Wine Bar*

4 Jewry Street
Winchester (0962) 69630
Map 6 A4 *Hampshire*

Open 11.30–2.30 & 6–9.30
Closed 25 December

Smoked fish pie £2.50   Stilton & celery soup
90p
Credit Access, Amex, Diners, Visa
P library car park in Jewry Street   **WC**

Framed wine labels add character to this informal wine bar with an appetising counter display of cold meats and varied salads. If you prefer something hot, there are daily specials such as moussaka, chicken curry, fish pie or a quiche, and you can start with home-made soup and finish with a simple sweet. Decent cheeseboard for afters. ☺

Winchester — *Wessex Hotel Coffee Shop*

Paternoster
Winchester (0962) 61611
Map 6 A4 *Hampshire*

Open 7.30am–10pm
Closed 25 December

Catalan chicken £4.35   Swiss toast £2.35
LVs   *Credit* Access, Amex, Diners, Visa
P own car park or Colebrook Street pay &
display   **WC**

In a modern red-brick hotel by the cathedral, this smart coffee shop provides a wide range of well-prepared snacks. All-day breakfasts, burgers, omelettes, salads and steak sandwiches are typical choices, and main dishes include liver and bacon, deep-fried plaice and Spanish-style chicken. A help-yourself hot and cold buffet operates between 11.30–3. Note freshly squeezed orange juice. Non-smoking area. *No dogs.* ☺ 🍵

Windermere — *Langdale Chase Hotel*

Ambleside (0966) 32201
Map 3 B2 *Cumbria*

Open 4–5.30

Scones with cream & jam £1.70   Cumbrian
afternoon tea £3.50
Credit Access, Amex, Diners, Visa

P own car park   ♿   **WC**

On the A591 between Windermere and Ambleside lies this fine Victorian hotel, where splendid teas are served every afternoon of the year. Admire the lovely lake from the oak-panelled lounge or out on the terrace as you nibble at dainty finger sandwiches, flavoursome walnut bread, fat fruit scones with jam and cream and a selection of delicious pastries (look out for the really excellent strawberry tartlet). 🍵

Windermere — *Miller Howe Hotel*

Windermere (096 62) 2536
Map 3 B2 *Cumbria*

Open 3–5
Closed 1st week December–mid March

Set afternoon tea £3

Credit Access, Amex, Diners, Visa

P own car park   ♿   **WC**

The view from the terrace is one of the finest, adding a magic touch to afternoon tea at John Tovey's much-loved Lakeland retreat. The antique-filled lounges are delightful, too, and whether outside or in, you are sure to enjoy the scones and the walnut bread, the lovely chocolate éclairs, the mouthwatering meringues (crisp yet chewy) and all the other delicious cakes and pastries. *No dogs.* 🍵

Windsor | *New Entry* | *Angelo's Wine Bar*

5 St Leonards Road
Windsor (0753) 857600
Map 6 B3 *Berkshire*

Open noon–2.30 & 6.30–10.30 (Fri & Sat till 11)
Closed 25 December

Seafood ayillo £4   Chicken Moscow £6.60
Credit Access, Amex, Diners, Visa

P Willimu Street car park   **WC**

A friendly, relaxed wine bar run with enthusiasm by owner Angelo Delin. Food is a major feature, and there's an excellent choice of carefully cooked dishes: minestrone, mushrooms in red wine and deep-fried squid among the starters; trout bretonne, veal escalope Marsala and chicken breast stuffed with garlic butter as typical main courses. Nice sweets, too, like strawberry gâteau or Dutch apple flan. *No dogs.*

Windsor | *New Entry* | *Dôme*

5 Thames Street
Windsor (0753) 864405
Map 6 B3 *Berkshire*

Open 9–11 (Sun till 10.30)
Closed 25 December

Chilli £2.75   Steak sandwich £4.75
Credit Access, Amex, Visa
P King Edward Court multi-storey car park
WC

Friendly, informal service is a feature of this roomy, modern bar-cum-café, where a wide variety of good food is available throughout the long opening hours. The menu includes English and continental breakfast, salade niçoise, salmon mousse, omelettes and steak sandwiches, plus blackboard specials like garlic mushrooms or pork normande. Simple sweets and daily pâtisserie special. Children welcome until 7.30. *No dogs.*

Windsor | *Tracks Brasserie*

4 Goswell Hill Arches
Windsor (0753) 858090
Map 6 B3 *Berkshire*

Open noon–2.30 & 6.30–10.45
Closed Sun & Bank Holidays
Steak & kidney pie £3.25   Ham & mushroom
tagliatelle £3.60
Credit Access, Amex, Diners, Visa
P King Edward Court multi-storey car park
WC

Join the many regulars who make tracks for this friendly wine bar-cum-brasserie occupying one of the cavernous arches beneath Windsor Central Railway Station. A daily-changing blackboard menu offers a tempting variety, with taramasalata and creamy soups, chicken and mushroom pie, chargrilled steaks and pork with ginger and orange among typical offerings. Sweet tooths can finish with home-made gâteaux, ice cream or a sorbet. *No dogs.* ☺

Windsor | *New Entry* | *Windsor Chocolate House*

8 Church Street
Windsor (0753) 860157
Map 6 B3 *Berkshire*

Open 9.30–5.15
Closed 25 & 26 December
Set lunch of soup, smoked haddock with pasta
& tea £4.95   Set afternoon tea £3.70
Credit Access, Amex, Diners, Visa
P King Edward Court multi-storey car park
WC

By a cobbled pathway close to the castle, this traditional tea house combines with a shop selling hand-made chocolates and pastries. Light snacks, including sandwiches, salads and hot pies, are available all day, and at lunchtime there's a selection of set-price meals such as soup followed by cottage pie or chicken curry. There are various afternoon teas with good scones and cakes. Unlicensed. *No dogs.* 🍵

Wokingham   *Setters Bistro*

49 Peach Street
Wokingham (1734) 788893
Map 6 B3 *Berkshire*

Open noon–2.30
Closed Sun & Bank Holidays

Lasagne & salad £3.95   Liver & bacon £3.75

Credit Access, Diners, Visa
P Easthampstead Street car park   &   **WC**

A stylish, popular restaurant, where a black-board lists lunchtime specials. Among starters and main courses are chicken and leek soup, garlic mushrooms, courgette and prawn au gratin, rabbit casserole and lamb curry. There are also vegetarian dishes. All are served with market-fresh vegetables. Delicious sweets might include nectarine brûlée and Austrian plum cake. More formal evening meals. *No dogs.* ⊖

Woodbridge   *Wine Bar*

17 The Thoroughfare
Woodbridge (039 43) 2557
Map 5 D2 *Suffolk*

Open noon–2 & 7–10
Closed Sun, Mon & Bank Holidays

Soup £1.20   Spicy pork with rice & salad £3.95

P Oak Lane car park at rear   **WC**

Skill and imagination highlight Sally O'Gorman's cooking in this cheerful, relaxed upstairs wine bar. The menu changes weekly, tempting with delights like feta and courgette roulade, brochette of monkfish and king prawns with mushroom sauce or lamb's liver with gooseberries and orange syrup. Sweets are equally hard to resist – how about black cherry syllabub or honey and lavender ice cream? *No dogs.* ⊖

Woodlands   *Three Cranes Coffee Shop*

248 Great North Road, Near Adwick le Street
Doncaster (0302) 724221
Map 4 C3 *South Yorkshire*

Open 8.30–4 (Sat till 1.30)
Closed Sun, Bank Holidays & 3 days Christmas

Cherry scone 13p   Cooked breakfast £1.60
LVs
P street parking   &

The surroundings may be modest, but there's no denying the appeal of the fresh, simple snacks served at this café in a row of shops. The day kicks off with a traditional breakfast, and crispy bacon baps are one of the most popular orders. Always available is a range of good baking, including tarts, buns, scones, fruit pies and sausage rolls, plus sandwiches, plain or toasted. Unlicensed. *No dogs.*

Woodstock   **New Entry**   *Brothertons Brasserie*

1 High Street
Woodstock (0993) 811114
Map 5 A2 *Oxfordshire*

Open 10.30am–10.30pm
Closed 1 January & 25 & 26 December

Pâté £1.95   Suprême of chicken with mustard sauce £6.25
Credit Access, Amex, Diners, Visa
P street parking   &   **WC**

On the site of an old hardware store stands this busy brasserie with exposed floorboards and attractive pine furnishings. The menu is one of unusual variety: morning coffee; traditional afternoon tea; starters ranging from Russian blinis and crudités with a curry dip to tasty crab and mushroom mornay; main courses from cannelloni and garlicky sardines to mustard-sauced chicken and steak au poivre. Appetising salads and diverse desserts. *No dogs.*

Woodstock *New Entry* *Feathers Hotel Garden Bar*

Market Street
Woodstock (0993) 812291
Map 5 A2 *Oxfordshire*

Open 12.30–2.15

Chicken casserole £4.75 Deep-fried
mushrooms £3.75
Credit Access, Amex, Diners, Visa
P street parking or Hensington Road car park
WC

The bar and garden are pleasant settings for
lunch, and the good cooking and excellent
service are what you'd expect from this
splendidly run hotel. Soup of the day or fine
duck terrine precedes tasty dishes like trout
with lemon and capers, hot leek tart or
casseroled chicken in a creamy Dijon mustard sauce. Round things off with fresh
strawberries or a wickedly rich chocolate
cake. *No dogs.*

Woodstock *New Entry* *Feathers Hotel Lounge*

Market Street
Woodstock (0993) 812291
Map 5 A2 *Oxfordshire*

Open 3–5.30

Afternoon tea £3.95
Credit Access, Amex, Diners, Visa

P street parking **WC**

A splendid set tea is served in the elegant
panelled lounge of this well-known hotel in
the town centre. A selection of fresh sandwiches is followed by lovely light scones with
jam and whipped cream, shortbread and a
choice of cakes (good brandy snaps, subtly
flavoured lemon cake). China tea, Ceylon tea
or coffee accompanies. Service is polite and
courteous. *No dogs.* 🫖

Woodstock *New Entry* *Linden Tea Rooms*

52 Oxford Street
Woodstock (0993) 812373
Map 5 A2 *Oxfordshire*

Open 9.45–5.30
Closed Mon & Tues

Prawn & egg mayonnaise open sandwich
£2.80 Cream tea £1.95

P Market Street car park **WC**

Formerly known as Mawney's Kitchen, this
attractive little tea shop has enthusiastic new
owners bent on producing appetising, quality
fare. From freshly made sandwiches and
superlight scones to a lovely rich fruit cake,
all is delicious, and if you're extra hungry,
there are salads, things on toast and a
cheese or pâté ploughman's platter. Unlicensed. *No dogs.* 🫖

Woodstock *Vanbrughs*

16 Oxford Street
Woodstock (0993) 811253
Map 5 A2 *Oxfordshire*

Open 9–5.30
Closed Mon (except Bank Holidays) & 1 week
Christmas

Lasagne £4.95 Waffles £1.95

P Hensington Road car park ⅛ **WC**

A neat, attractive and very popular tea shop
named after Sir John Vanbrugh, whose
masterpiece Blenheim Palace is close at
hand. The menu is full of variety: English
breakfast until 11.30, tea cakes and croissants, sandwiches generously filled and
nicely garnished, burgers in sesame buns,
lasagne, hand-raised turkey and ham pie.
Waffles and ice cream are favourite sweets.
No dogs. 🫖

Wool

Rose Mullion Tea Rooms

3 Station Road, Near Wareham
Bindon Abbey (0929) 462542
Map 8 D3 *Dorset*

Open 9–6
Closed Mon end September–end May & all
mid December–March

Filled jacket potatoes from £1   Walnut
shortbread 35p
P own car park   **WC**

Variety's the name of the game at this
unpretentious little tea room, whose menu
runs the whole gamut from toasted tea cakes
to sirloin steaks. In between are burgers and
jacket potatoes, Welsh and buck rarebits, all-
day breakfasts and a daily special like fish
pie or moussaka. There's also a good
selection of home baking (lovely walnut
shortbread), and the Dorset cream tea is a
big favourite. *No dogs.* 🍵

Woolpit

The Bakery

Near Bury St Edmunds
Elmswell (0359) 40255
Map 5 D2 *Suffolk*

Open 10.30–5
Closed Sun & Mon

Poacher's pie £3.60   Parson's pudding £1.30

P street parking   **WC**

Scrubbed kitchen tables, quarry-tiled floors,
mellow red-brick walls, genuine old beams –
it's a very atmospheric tea shop, and the
baking is excellent. An eye-catching array of
goodies includes flapjacks and florentines,
delicious chocolate fingers and lovely macaroons. Lunchtime brings a selection of savoury dishes like fish pâté, roast Suffolk ham,
tasty poacher's pie and always a vegetarian
special. Full evening meals. *No dogs.* 🍵 🍵

Worcester   *New Entry*

Heroes

26 Friar Street
Worcester (0905) 25451
Map 7 D1 *Hereford & Worcester*

Open noon–midnight
Closed 1 January & 25 & 26 December

Mexican kebabs £5.55   Chicken escalopes
with sweetcorn & mushrooms £3.75
LVs   *Credit* Access, Visa
P Friar Street multi-storey car park   ♿ **WC**

Behind its half-timbered facade this cosy
restaurant is modern in both mood and menu.
There's a popular selection of tasty burgers,
kebabs and grills, along with pizza, pasta
and main-course salads. They've recently
added a selection of Mexican dishes like
tacos, tostados and chilli con carne. There's
always at least one vegetarian special, and
sweets range from maple nut sundae to hot
chocolate mint cake. 🍵

Worcester

Natural Break

4 The Hopmarket   Worcester (0905) 26654
Open 10–4 (till 4.30 summer), Sat 10–5
17 Mealcheapen Street   Worcester (0905)
26417
Open 10–4, Sat 9.30–5
Map 7 D1 *Hereford & Worcester*
Closed Sun & Bank Holidays (except Good
Fri)
Savoury flan 94p   Almond slice 40p
LVs
P Cornmarket pay & display   **WC**

Two simple self-service restaurants offering
freshly cooked sweet and savoury items
throughout the day. Crunchy, imaginative
salads – cauliflower and grapes in spicy
mayonnaise; sweetcorn, butter bean and
broccoli – go beautifully with tasty flans like
cheese and spinach or chicken and celery,
and there are pasties, sausage rolls and
sandwiches, too. Sweet treats include lemon
meringue pie and cherry slice. Minimum 95p
lunchtime charge. Unlicensed. *No dogs.*

Worthing   *Fogarty's*

10 Prospect Place, off Montague Street
Worthing (0903) 212984
Map 6 B4 *West Sussex*

Open 10–5
Closed Sun, 1 January, 25 & 26 December, 2
weeks February–March & last 2 weeks
September
Quiche £1.80   Honey, banana & walnut cake
60p
P street parking   **WC**

Savoury flans, served hot from the oven and
piled high with delicious fillings like celery,
ham and cauliflower cheese, are the stars of
the show at this pleasant little corner restaurant. Tasty alternatives include home-made
soup, vegetarian lasagne and stuffed jacket
potatoes, and there's also a good range of
salads (egg mayonnaise, prawn, chicken).
Finish with beautifully tangy fresh lemon
cake. Outside tables. *No dogs.* 🌣 🦃

Worthing   *Hannah*

165 Montague Street
Worthing (0903) 31132
Map 6 B4 *West Sussex*

Open 9.30–7 (Sat till 5)
Closed Sun

Vegetable lasagne £1.25   Apple & sultana
crumble 60p

P Prospect Place car park & meters   ♿ **WC**

This bright, well-kept little restaurant is
mainly vegetarian, and the owners set great
store by freshness of the food. Most of it is
available throughout the day, from excellent
cakes and pastries to filled jacket potatoes,
lentil burgers, salmon flan, delicious salads
and stir-fried vegetables. There are some
nice sweets, too, including a really enjoyable
apple and raspberry wholemeal crumble.
Non-smoking tables.

Worthing   *Mr Pastry*

8 Warwick Lane
Worthing (0903) 212780
Map 6 B4 *West Sussex*

Open 9–5
Closed Sun & most Bank Holidays

Apple strudel 80p   Tropical fruit cheesecake
75p

P Guildbourne Centre car park opposite

Martin Battrick has taken over the unit next
door to this pleasant pâtisserie in a little
shopping arcade and can now seat up to 40
hungry customers. A display counter tempts
the sweet-toothed with treats like apple and
custard creams, crunchy caramel slice, chocolate truffles and éclairs, while savoury
snacks range from tasty curried beef turnovers to sausage rolls and Cornish pasties.
Unlicensed. *No dogs.* 🦃

Worthing   *Nature's Way Coffee Shop*

130 Montague Street
Worthing (0903) 209931
Map 6 B4 *West Sussex*

Open 9.15–5
Closed Sun & Bank Holidays

Flan & salad £1.90   Lasagne £1.50
LVs

P street parking   **WC**

Located above a wholefood shop, this is a
pleasant, self-service vegetarian restaurant.
All the food is prepared on the premises, and
a regular range of jacket potatoes, interesting
salads, flans and pastries is supplemented
by a selection of specials, from broccoli
cheese and marrow provençale to lentil cake,
curry and black-eyed bean casserole. Puddings include crumbles and sherry trifle.
Unlicensed. Non-smoking area. *No dogs.* 🦃

Yarm ★ *Coffee Shop*

44 High Street
Eaglescliffe (0642) 782101
Map 4 C2 *Cleveland*

Open 9–5
Closed Sun & Bank Holidays

Cheesy prawns £3.25   Steak & kidney pie
£2.99
P own car park at rear and street parking . **WC**

This marvellous coffee shop is an ideal spot for just-a-biters. Home-baked goodies from scones to chocolate gâteau accompany an excellent cuppa, and at lunchtime there's an eye-catching array of super salads along with quiches and hot specials like mushrooms provençale or seafood vol-au-vent. Lovely cheesecake and home-made ice creams feature among the tempting sweets. *No dogs.* 🫖

Yarmouth *Jireh House*

St James Square
Isle of Wight (0983) 760513
Map 6 A4 *Isle of Wight*

Open 8.30–6
Closed November–late March

Shepherd's pie £1.35   Chocolate cake 55p

P in square   **WC**

Two attractively furnished rooms in a 17th-century building on the main square. Morning coffee is served with a straightforward selection of scones, cakes and pastries, and lunchtime savoury snacks like prawn cocktail, macaroni cheese and shepherd's pie are available starting at lunchtime until they run out. There are also rolls, toasted sandwiches and salads based on things like cheese, ham and crab. *No dogs.* 🫖

Yeovil *Clarries*

Clarence House, 5 Stars Lane
Yeovil (0935) 77841
Map 8 D3 *Somerset*

Open 11.30–2.30 & 6.30–10.30
Closed Bank Holiday lunches, all Sun & 25 & 26 December
Special pizza £2.25   Lasagne £2.16
LVs   *Credit* Amex, Diners, Visa
P Stars Lane car park   **WC**

Clarries is a smart, modern restaurant with pine furnishings, green striped wallpaper and tiles with a cactus motif. Pizzas and burgers are the choice of many, but there's a great deal more, with specialities ranging from ham, cheese and tomato crêpe to fish goujons, mushroom ratatouille and a very good and authentic coq au vin. Sweet pancakes and home-made ices to finish. Note fresh fruit and vegetable juices. *No dogs.*

Yeovil *Trugs*

5 Union Street
Yeovil (0935) 73722
Map 8 D3 *Somerset*

Open 8.30–5.30
Closed Sun & Bank Holidays

Mushroom & watercress pancake £1.85
Chicken curry on brown rice £2.15
LVs
P Peter Street car park   **WC**

Near the centre of town, this fresh, appealing wholefood restaurant features dishes for both meat-eaters and vegetarians. Jacket potatoes and pitta bread come with a tempting choice of fillings, and there's spaghetti and lasagne, chicken curry and a good nut roast. Also a children's menu (or half portions from the main list), scones, home-baked cakes and cream teas. The whole menu is available all day through. *No dogs.* 🫖

York · *Bettys*

6 St Helens Square
York (0904) 59142
Town plan *North Yorkshire*

Open 9am–9pm
Closed 1 January & 25 & 26 December

Granary mushrooms £1.50   Haddock & prawn
au gratin £3.25

P St Saviour Gate car park   ⑤   **WC**

Large windows let in plenty of light at this
attractively laid-out coffee house in the city
centre. The all-day menu is full of fresh,
appetising fare such as crumpets and cinnamon toast to enjoy with an excellent cup of
tea or coffee; sandwiches in white, brown or
granary bread; the speciality rarebits; salads,
grills and omelettes; and excellent cakes
from their own bakery. Music most evenings.
No dogs. ⊖

York · *Gillygate Wholefood Café*

Millers Yard, Gillygate
York (0904) 24045
Town plan *North Yorkshire*

Open 10–5 March–September (October–
February till 4)
Closed Sun & Bank Holidays

Carrot & onion quiche with salad £2.15
Spinach lasagne £2.15
P Gillygate car park   ⑤   **WC**

With its own bakery next door, this simply
appointed wholefood café is able to offer a
varied range of nice fresh cakes and pastries.
There are also pizza slices, mild or chilli
samosas, tofuburgers and wholewheat rolls
with various fillings. Quiche of the day comes
with a mixed salad, and for sweet you could
try apricot or tofu cheesecake. Good selection of leaf and herb teas. Unlicensed. No
smoking. *No dogs.* ⊖ 🐾

York · *Mulberry Hall Coffee Shop*

Stonegate
York (0904) 20736
Town plan *North Yorkshire*

Open 10–4.30
Closed Sun, Mon, Bank Holidays & 1 week
January

Yorkshire curd tart 60p   Prawn sandwich
£1.50
P minster car park   **WC**

The elegant setting above a china shop offers
a pleasant escape from the city's hustle and
bustle. Scones, toasted teacakes and fruit
loaf can be enjoyed with a good brew, and
there's a varied selection of sandwiches,
including pork, curried prawn and hot bacon.
Quiche, pâté and vol-au-vents extend the
choice, and there are a few salads. Nice
display of cakes on the trolley. Unlicensed.
No dogs. ⊖ 🐾

York · *St Williams College Restaurant*

3 College Street
York (0904) 34830
Town plan *North Yorkshire*

Open 10–5 (Sun from noon)
Closed 1 January, Good Fri & 25 & 26
December

Chicken & celery pie £3.25   Raised pork &
apricot pie with salad £2.40
P St Johns car park in Lord Mayors Walk

Modern furnishings blend with the old struc-
ture of this spotless coffee shop, which has
a fine courtyard for fair-weather snacking.
Good scones, cakes and pastries are served
throughout the day, with a selection of
sandwiches after 2.30. Lunchtime brings the
widest choice, including cold meats, quiche
and at least two hot specials, perhaps
lasagne or chicken and celery pie. Sweets
like banana flan end the meal nicely. Non-
smoking area. *No dogs.* ⊖

YORK

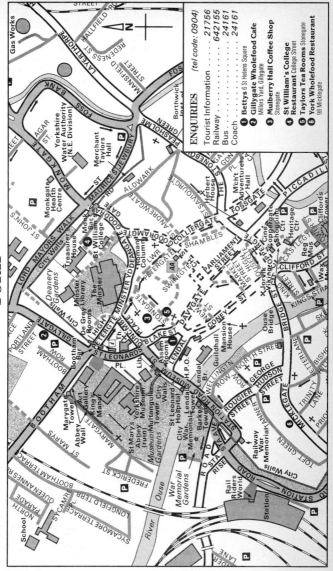

York   *Taylors Tea Rooms*

46 Stonegate
York (0904) 22865
Town plan *North Yorkshire*

Open 9–5.30 (Sun till 7)
Closed 25 & 26 December

Yorkshire rarebit £3.35   Prawn & avocado
sandwich £1.65

P minster car park   **WC**

The splendid selection of teas and coffees
sold in the shop may also be enjoyed in this
attractive tea room above. Accompanying
the drinks are toasts and tea cakes, rarebits,
omelettes and excellent sandwiches, both
filled and open. Salads and a breakfast grill
provide further choice, and the cake trolley
carries a cargo of goodies like Yorkshire curd
tart and coffee and walnut cake. Unlicensed.
Non-smoking area. *No dogs.* 🍵

York   *Wholefood Trading Company*

98 Micklegate
York (0904) 56804
Town plan *North Yorkshire*

Open 10–3.30, also 7.30–10 Wed–Sat
Closed Sun, Bank Holidays (except Good Fri)
& 10 days Christmas
Spinach roulade £3.50   Tofu & kidney bean
goulash £3.50
LVs
P car park in Nunnery Lane   **WC**

Well known for its tasty vegetarian fare, this
pine-furnished restaurant is run by a cooperative. Wholemeal quiches (perhaps cheesy
mushroom and rosemary), crunchy salads
and nice creamy soups are popular classics,
and there's always a vegan dish of the day.
Super sweets include a delicious fruit salad.
Booking is possible at night, when there's
even greater choice. Unlicensed. No smoking. *No dogs.* 🍵

SCOTLAND

Aberfeldy ★ *Country Fare Coffee House*

7 Bridgend
Aberfeldy (0887) 20729
Map 2 C3 *Tayside*

Open 10–4.45
Closed Sun, also Wed afternoon in winter, 1 &
2 January & 25 & 26 December

Cheese & asparagus quiche £1.50   Roast
beef in red wine with salads £3.50
P street & nearby car park   🚻   **WC**

Superb snacks are to be had throughout the
day at this neatly kept and enterprisingly run
coffee house with a pretty little patio. Sandwiches and toasties, quiches and pâtés,
soups and a wide variety of salads, a
marvellous array of cream cakes and gâteaux
– it's all fresh and delicious, home-made and
wholesome. Children's portions also available. Non-smoking area. *No dogs.* 🍵

Aboyne *Alford House Restaurant*

Ballater Road
Ballater (0339) 2249
Map 1 D2 *Grampian*

Open noon–6

Soup of the day 50p   Roast beef £2.90

P street parking   **WC**

A delightfully traditional little tea room in a
stone building on the A93. At lunchtime you
can tuck into warming soup followed by, say,
gammon and pineapple or a cold meat salad,
with fruit crumble for afters. Super chips
accompany hearty high teas from 4.30, and
iced fairy cakes, scones, shortbread and
chocolate crunch are delicious with a cuppa.
Unlicensed. No smoking. *No dogs.* 🍵

Arisaig *Old Library Lodge & Restaurant*

Arisaig (068 75) 651
Map 1 B2 *Highland*

Open 8.30–10, noon–2 & 6.30–9
Closed October–Easter

Home-made soup with bread £1   Beef &
mushroom casserole £2.95

P village car park   **WC**

Run in friendly, informal style, this charming
little restaurant with whitewashed stone walls
enjoys lovely views. It's open early for
breakfast, then resumes at lunchtime with
tasty dishes like onion soup (served with
super wholemeal bread), quiches (also
wholemeal), chicken casserole and fruit
crumble. The evening menu lists such things
as poached trout with chive sauce, and the
wine list is carefully chosen. *No dogs.*

Balfron *Coffee Mill*

151 Buchanan Street
Balfron (0360) 40145
Map 2 C3 *Central*

Open 10–5 (Wed till 1)
Closed Sun, 1 January & 25 December

Soup of the day 45p   Danish open cheese &
pineapple sandwich £1

P Co-op car park   **WC**

In the couldn't-be-simpler surroundings of
her tiny tea room Evelyn Warnock prepares
a selection of tasty, straightforward snacks.
Soup of the day – perhaps thick, nourishing
vegetable – could start lunch, with an open
sandwich, a baked potato or a savoury pie to
follow. Very good baking covers a tempting
range, from light scones and little fresh fruit
tarts to cream sponges and gâteaux. Unlicensed. *No dogs.*

Buckie   *Old Monastery*

Drybridge
Buckie (0542) 32660
Map 1 D2 *Grampian*

Open noon–1.45
Closed Sun, Mon, 3 weeks January & 2 weeks
October
Starter of the day £2.80   Hot dish of the day
£4
LVs
P own car park   &   **WC**

Three miles inland from Buckie, down narrow
country lanes, lies this converted chapel with
a bar where light lunches are served. Prime
local produce is used throughout the simple
but interesting selection, from flavoursome
soup and wholemeal sandwiches to seafood
salad and a daily hot dish. Enjoyable home-
made sweets to finish. Full evening meals.
No dogs. ☺

Colbost   *Three Chimneys*

Near Dunvegan, Isle of Skye
Glendale (047 081) 258
Map 1 A2 *Highland*

Open noon–2
Closed Sun lunch & November–March

Hot crab tart with salad £2.75   Skye prawns
with salad £4.25
Credit Access, Visa
P own car park   **WC**

In an old crofter's cottage right by the sea,
this cosy (and remote – check directions)
restaurant offers delicious light lunches with
a Scottish flavour. Choose from soup with
lovely home-baked bread, wholemeal pizza
wedges, hot crab tart and substantial salads
centred round local prawns, trout or cheese.
Super sweets like chilled chocolate brandy
fudge cake. More elaborate evening menu.
No dogs. ☺

Crinan   *Crinan Coffee Shop*

By Lochgilphead
Crinan (054 683) 235
Map 2 B3 *Strathclyde*

Open 9–5 (July–September till 7)
Closed end October–mid March

Open sandwich £1   Quiche 95p
Credit Access

P village car park   &   **WC**

The baked goodies are the strength of this
charming self-service coffee shop, which
enjoys a picture-book setting right by the
harbour. Scones, doughnuts, caramel slices,
fruit loaf, flapjacks . . . the list goes on and
on, and for savoury snacks there's quiche
and nice herby sausage rolls. Open sandwiches come in several varieties, and everything slips down a treat with a first-class
cuppa. *No dogs.* 🍮

Cullipool   ★   *Longhouse Buttery*

Isle of Luing, By Oban
Luing (085 24) 209
Map 2 B3 *Strathclyde*

Open 11–5
Closed Sun & early October–mid May

Prawn salad £4.95   Frozen orange cream
£1.50

P own car park   &   **WC**

Take the ferry to the enchanting Isle of Luing
and snack in style at this immaculate little
place. Audrey Stone draws on the best local
seafood for her marvellous open sandwiches
and salads (note lovely home-cooked gammon), and other delights include venison pâté
and the day's soup – in our case superb,
subtle artichoke. Fresh fruit salad and triple
meringue with cream among the lovely
sweets. *No dogs.* ☺

Dalbeattie

Coffee & Things

32 High Street
Dalbeattie (0556) 611033
Map 2 C4 *Dumfries & Galloway*

Open 10–5
Closed Sun, Mon, 1 January & 25 & 26
December

Roast beef with vegetables £3.25   Vegetable
casserole £2.95
P Town Hall car park   ♿   **WC**

A charming little high-street restaurant where
you can buy antiques and gifts as well as
enjoy some fine home baking. Look out for
the splendid fresh raspberry gâteau, millionaire's shortbread and rich, chocolaty date
slice – all delicious with an excellent brew
served in pretty china. Typical lunchtime
offerings from the daily-changing menu include a roast, fresh fish and home-made
steak and kidney pie.

Dirleton

Open Arms Hotel Lounge

Dirleton (0620 85) 241
Map 2 D3 *Lothian*

Open 12.30–2
Closed Sun, 1 January, 4 days second week
January & 25 December

Mussel & onion stew £1.10   Cold venison pie
with beetroot £3.50

P own car park   ♿   **WC**

Elegant light lunches, prepared with exemplary care, are a real treat at this comfortable
hotel lounge. Colourful chicken, apricot and
spinach terrine and asparagus mousse
served in ham cornets are typically delightful
starters, while main courses range from
home-made beef and mussel pie to pan-fried
lemon sole. Snacks include wholemeal courgette and apple quiche, and there are some
irresistible sweets like lemon sorbet with
Drambuie. ☕

Dryburgh Abbey

Orchard Tearoom

Near St Boswells
St Boswells (0835) 22053
Map 2 D4 *Borders*

Open 10–5.30 (Sun from 2)
Closed November–March

Afternoon tea £1.95   Buttered fruit
gingerbread 45p

P street parking   ♿   **WC**

Overlooking the river Tweed, this appealing
little tea shop is capably run by Fiona Lynn.
Enjoy her home-made cakes and biscuits,
fresh, light scones (cheese or plain) and
buttered fruit gingerbread with a good strong
pot of tea. Soup, sandwiches and bacon rolls
are the only savouries, but three-course
lunches and high tea can be provided if
ordered in advance. Unlicensed. ☕

Dulnain Bridge   ★   *Muckrach Lodge Hotel*

Near Grantown-on-Spey
Dulnain Bridge (047 985) 257
Map 1 C2 *Highland*

Open noon–2 (Sun from 12.30)

Gammon sandwich with cheese & onion £1.50
Raspberry Pavlova £1.05

P own car park   ♿   **WC**

The lunchtime bar snacks are outstanding at
this friendly hotel, a former shooting lodge
set back from the A938. Soups and pâtés are
particularly splendid (note a lovely light
mushroom terrine for vegetarians), and there
are superb sandwiches filled with delights
like wild salmon or gammon carved from the
bone. Delectable sweets include raspberry-
filled shortcakes with nectarine coulis. Nice
cheeses too. *No dogs.* ☕

Dumfries   *Opus Salad Bar*

95 Queensberry Street
Dumfries (0387) 55752
Map 2 C4 *Dumfries & Galloway*

Open 9–5 (Thurs till 2.30)
Closed Sun & Bank Holidays

Vegetable curry £1.50   Moussaka £1.80
Credit Access

P car park opposite   **WC**

There's a cheerful atmosphere at this bright, modern little self-service café, where the day starts with gap-fillers like egg salad rolls, buttered fruit loaf and various cakes. From midday, a good selection of appetising salads appears, together with hot lunchtime specials like lasagne, chilli con carne, curried vegetables and mushroom pie. Friendly service. Non-smoking tables. ☕ 🍵

Dundee   *Raffles Restaurant*

18 Perth Road
Dundee (0382) 26433
Map 2 C3 *Tayside*

Open 9am–9pm (Fri & Sat till 10.30)
Closed Sun, Mon, 2 weeks July & 2 weeks
Christmas

Lamb korma £3.95   Fresh fruit cheesecake
£1.30
P street & Seabrase Lane car park ♿ **WC**

A busy, bistro-style restaurant near the University. In the morning you can have a hearty cooked breakfast or take your pick from the home-baked cakes and scones. From noon a daily-changing menu offers things like spinach mornay pancake, pork schnitzel or guinea fowl with lemon sauce, along with flans, salads and good puds. Minimum charge £3 with bookings (£5 after 8). *No dogs.* ☕

Dunoon   *Black's Tea Room*

144 Argyll Street
Dunoon (0369) 2311
Map 2 B3 *Strathclyde*

Open 8.45–5
Closed Sun, 1 & 2 January & 25 & 26
December

Bridie with beans 70p   Black cherry gâteau
80p
P Moir Street car park ♿ **WC**

Mrs Black's welcoming, no-frills tea room stands right next door to her own bakery, so you can be sure that the cakes and pastries are all as fresh as can be. Wheatmeal scones, warm crumpets and a rum-laced tipsy cake are favourites, while on the savoury side there are baked potatoes, toasted sandwiches, filled rolls and half-a-dozen pies. Unlicensed. *No dogs.*

Eaglesham   *Wishing Well Tea Room*

63 Montgomery Street
Eaglesham (035 53) 2774
Map 2 C3 *Strathclyde*

Open 10–5
Closed Mon, 1 January & 25 December

Fruit scone 17p   Apple tart 25p

P street parking   **WC**

The baking is old-fashioned and excellent, the service cheerful and the prices very low at this immensely popular tea room opposite the green. The new owner has kept the same simple, successful formula – a pot of tea accompanied by scones (plain, fruit and treacle or cheese), a slice of apple pie and a plate of assorted cakes such as tiffin, date loaf, lemon sponge and chocolate-covered coconut cake. Unlicensed. *No dogs.*

East Linton   *Harvesters Hotel, Farmers Den*

Station Road
East Linton (0620) 860395
Map 2 D3 *Lothian*

Open noon–2 (Sun from 12.30)
Closed 2 weeks January

Smoked salmon £2.50   Home-baked ham on the bone with salads £3.40

P own car park **WC**

A pleasantly rustic bar in a hotel that's peacefully surrounded by trees yet only half a mile from the A1. Help yourself from the attractively displayed salad table, and then let cheerful owner Mr Lannie carve you some splendid home-baked ham or moist turkey. Hot dishes, too, like tasty minced beef and onion pie, with excellent boozy trifle to finish. Minimum charge of £2.70. *No dogs.* ⊖

Edinburgh   *New Entry*   *Brasserie Saint Jacques*

King James Thistle Hotel, Leith Street
031-556 0111
Town plan *Lothian*

Open 12.30pm–2pm
Closed 25 & 26 December

Danish open sandwiches £2.50   Cheese selection £1.75
Credit Access, Amex, Diners, Visa
P Saint James Centre NCP ⌖ **WC**

Order as little or as much as you like from the café menu of this stylish hotel brasserie. Hot or cold soups, game pâté with Cumberland sauce, omelettes (name your filling), Danish-style open sandwiches – these are typical of the appetising snacks on offer. There is also plenty of seafood (mussels, oysters, salmon) and a choice of vegetarian dishes. Scottish and French cheeses. Service is skilled and formal. *No dogs.* ⊖ 🍵

Edinburgh   *Country Kitchen*

4 South Charlotte Street
031-226 6150
Town plan *Lothian*

Open 8am–7pm
Closed Sun & Bank Holidays

Haddock in wholemeal breadcrumbs & oats £1.80   Chicken pie £2.50
LVs
P meter parking **WC**

The day starts early with croissants, wholemeal scones and sweet delights like almond apple strudel at this popular wholefood cafeteria. From 11.30 there are appetising hot dishes such as wholewheat macaroni cheese, quiches and bean stew, while healthy and delicious salads – try brown rice with ham and sweetcorn or carrot and pineapple – go beautifully with succulent cold meats. Note that each dish listed carries its calorie count alongside! *No dogs.*

Edinburgh ★ *New Entry*   *Handsel's Wine Bar*

22 Stafford Street
031-225 5521
Town plan *Lothian*

Open 11am–11pm
Closed Sun, Bank Holidays & 1 week January
Smoked Ayrshire bacon sandwich with Brie & tomato £3.40   Chocolate roulade with caramel sauce £1.60
Credit Access, Amex, Diners, Visa
P street meters **WC**

Luxurious drapes and a stylish pink decor create a sophisticated setting for talented chef Andrew Raulford's daily-changing selection of nouvelle-inspired dishes. His Scottish seafood soup is a positive triumph, and other delights include delicious feuilleté of monkfish, broccoli and courgettes in a subtle ginger sauce, lavish sandwiches and wonderfully rich dark chocolate pots. Fine cheeses, too, served with fruit, as well as excellent wines by the glass. ⊖ 🍵

EDINBURGH

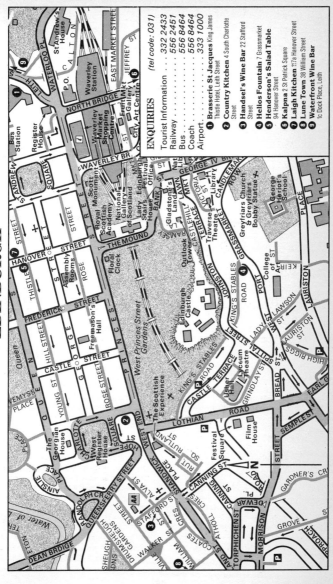

ENQUIRIES   *(tel code: 031)*

Tourist Information	332 2433
Railway	556 2451
Bus	556 8464
Coach	556 8464
Airport	333 1000

❶ **Brasserie St Jacques** King James
  Thistle Hotel, Leith Street

❷ **Country Kitchen** 4 South Charlotte
  Street

❸ **Handsel's Wine Bar** 22 Stafford
  Street

❹ **Helios Fountain** 7 Grassmarket

❺ **Henderson's Salad Table**
  94 Hanover Street

❻ **Kalpna** 2 St Patrick Square

❼ **Laigh Kitchen** 117a Hanover Street

❽ **Lune Town** 38 William Street

❾ **Waterfront Wine Bar**
  1c Dock Place, Leith

Edinburgh   *Helios Fountain*

7 Grassmarket
031-229 7884
Town plan *Lothian*

Open 10–6 (till 8 in summer)
Closed Sun & Bank Holidays
Tofu pie £2.25   Butter beans & vegetables
citron £1.95
Credit Access, Visa
P meter parking or multi-storey in King's
Stables Road   **WC**

Run by anthroposophists, staunch believers in biodynamically grown food and a dietary balance of root, leaf and grain, this simple restaurant behind a wholefood shop is really worth investigating. Splendidly flavoured pea and spinach soup and popular chestnut and pimento casserole are typical treats from the short menu, while desserts include cardamon-spiced Indian carrot cake and pear and hazelnut pudding. Unlicensed. No smoking. *No dogs.*

Edinburgh   `New Entry`   *Henderson's Salad Table*

94 Hanover Street
031-225 2131
Town plan *Lothian*
Open 8am–11pm, Sun 9am–9pm during
Festival
Closed Sun (except during Festival), Bank
Holidays, 1 & 2 January & 25 & 26 December
Moussaka £2   Dried & fresh fruits with ginger
& sour cream £1.20
LVs
P George Street meters   **WC**

A favourite with vegetarians for many years, this popular restaurant-cum-wine bar is situated below the family fruit shop. Breakfast brings muesli, fresh and dried fruit, cheese and croissants, cakes and pastries, and the lunchtime choice widens to include hot dishes like mushroom savoury bake (those generally run out by about 2.30, with a new batch arriving about 4.30). Interesting salads; sweets both healthy and creamily indulgent. *No dogs.*

Edinburgh   ★   *Kalpna*

2 St Patrick Square
031-667 9890
Town plan *Lothian*

Open noon–2 & 5.30–11
Closed Sun, 1 January & 25 & 26 December

Navaratan kurma £2.95   Dosa masala £2.50
Credit Access, Visa
P St Patrick Square & Buccleugh Street &
WC

The word kalpna means imagination, and the exquisite cooking at this splendid Indian vegetarian restaurant in the city's university area certainly merits that description. Featherlight samosas are models of their kind, and there are wonderful mixed vegetable curries, bean dishes and rice pancakes – all enhanced by the finest ingredients and subtlest spices. Finish refreshingly with delicious lemon sorbet. Set meals available. Non-smoking section. *No dogs.*

Edinburgh   ★   *Laigh Kitchen*

117a Hanover Street
031-225 1552
Town plan *Lothian*

Open 8.30–4 (till 7.30 during Festival)
Closed Sun & Bank Holidays

Tuna pâté 65p   Stovies £1.60

P meter parking   **WC**

Joan Spicer runs this basement restaurant on the lines of a traditional coffee house complete with rack of daily newspapers. The reputation for fine baking is well founded – try oatcake, carrot cake or the whisky cake that always sends customers away happy. There are also hearty soups, filled potatoes and stovies, quiches, curried vegetables and splendid salads. Charming staff and a really good atmosphere. Non-smoking section. Unlicensed.

Edinburgh   *Lune Town*

38 William Street
031-225 9388
Town plan *Lothian*

Open noon–2.30 & 6–midnight, Sat 2pm–1am,
Sun 4pm–11.30pm
Closed 1 January

Dim sum £1.10   Lemon chicken £4.40
Credit Access, Amex, Diners, Visa
P meter parking   **WC**

Good ingredients are judiciously spiced and
seasoned at this stylish little ground-floor
and basement Cantonese restaurant. Enjoy
dim sum at any time – perhaps steamed
spare ribs in black bean sauce or delicious
pork and prawn shui-mai – or opt for a piquant
main course such as squid in a garlicky
ginger sauce, chicken with abalone and
crispy, deep-fried beef. Lovely fresh vegetables and faultless rice noodles accompany.
No dogs.

Edinburgh   *Waterfront Wine Bar*

1c Dock Place, Leith
031-554 7427
Town plan *Lothian*

Open 11am–midnight, (Thurs–Sat till 1am)
Closed Sun, 1 & 2 January & 25 & 26
December

Honey-roast gammon with salad £3   Walnut
fudge cream £1
P street parking   **WC**

The atmosphere is lively and the food excellent at this immensely popular wine bar at the
Leith docks. Seafood features prominently –
poached prawns, bouillabaisse, herrings in
oatmeal – while appetising alternatives include houmus, honey-roast gammon and
beef and mussel pie. Delicious home-made
desserts or cheese and bran cakes to finish.
Eat in the charming conservatory, terrace or
cheerful bar. *No dogs.*

Falkirk   *Coffee Cabin*

Cockburn Street
Falkirk (0324) 25757
Map 2 C3 *Central*

Open 9–5
Closed Sun, Bank Holidays & 3 days
Christmas & New Year
Mince-filled jacket potato £1.25   Macaroni
cheese £1.20
LVs
P Howgate car park   **WC**

Home-baked cakes and sponges, scones
and biscuits make a tempting display at this
modest café, which stands by a mini-round-
about just below the main shopping street.
There are savoury snacks, too, including
toasted open sandwiches and jacket potatoes with fillings like mince or cheese and
onion. Also salads, daily specials like flan
and pizza and desserts such as fruit pies and
crumbles. Unlicensed. *No dogs.* ☺

Falkirk   **New Entry**   *Healthy Life*

2a Park Street
Falkirk (0324) 37186
Map 2 C3 *Central*

Open 9.30–3.30 (Sat till 4.30)
Closed Sun, Bank Holidays, 1 & 2 January &
25 & 26 December

Nut roast with salad £1.24   Seasonal fruit pie
55p
P street parking   **WC**

Eileen Clason is back in the kitchen of this
vegetarian restaurant, preparing tasty
snacks both sweet and savoury. Scones,
florentines and date loaves are among the
good baking to be enjoyed throughout the
day, and from noon there are filled baked
potatoes, quiches, nut roasts and specials
such as courgettes polonaise. Adventurous
salads (broccoli and ginger, coconut with
mixed fruit) and nice sweets like charlotte
russe. Unlicensed. No smoking. *No dogs.*

Falkland   *Kind Kyttock's Kitchen*

Cross Wynd
Falkland (0337) 57477
Map 2 C3 *Fife*

Open 10.30–5.30
Closed 24 December–1 February

Open chicken sandwich £2.20   Filled omelette
£2.30

P street parking   **WC**

Bert Dalrymple is the amiable host at this
charming little tea shop, where his wife Liz
provides all the delicious treats to enjoy with
tea or coffee. Choose from Scots pancakes
and floury scones (irresistible with home-
made jam), toffee- and chocolate-topped
shortbread and lovely nutty gingerbread.
Savoury snacks available throughout opening hours range from Scotch broth to salads,
pizzas and toasted sandwiches. Non-smoking room. *No dogs.* 🍵

Glamis   *Strathmore Arms*

Main Street
Glamis (030 784) 248
Map 2 C3 *Tayside*

Open 12.15–2 also 2.30–6 Easter–October
Closed Mon January–Easter, 4 days
Christmas & 1 week January

Kedgeree £2.95   Fruit crumble 75p
Credit Access, Amex, Diners, Visa
P own car park   ♿   **WC**

Traditional Scottish fare is served in the
restaurant of this well-run pub. Starters
include herrings in oatmeal and rumble de
thumps – a delicious concoction of cabbage,
onions, potatoes and cheese. There are
main-course casseroles, plus venison, kedgeree and a very popular cold buffet that runs
from April to October; sweets too. Afternoon
teas, with scones, Scotch pancakes, gâteaux
and fancy cakes, are an added feature in
summer. *No dogs.* 🍵

Glasgow   *Café Gandolfi*

64 Albion Street
041-552 6813
Town plan *Strathclyde*

Open 9.30am–11.30pm
Closed Sun & Bank Holidays

Gravadlax with dill & mustard sauce £3.90
New York-style pastrami £3.40

P car park in Ingram Street   ♿   **WC**

In an area of stylishly converted warehouses,
this popular café-restaurant has a strong
following among young professionals. The
menu is splendidly varied: gravadlax and
New York-style pastrami are great favourites,
and there are really tasty soups along with
hot specials like tagliatelle or vegetable
lasagne. Sweet things also span a good
range, and in the mornings appetisingly hot
croissants are available. Charming, capable
staff. *No dogs.* 🍵

Glasgow   *De Quincey's/Brahms & Liszt*

71 Renfield Street
041-333 0633
Town plan *Strathclyde*

Open 12–2.30
Closed Sun & Bank Holidays

Chicken mille-feuille £3.55   Pâté £1.35
Credit Access, Amex, Visa

P street parking & NCP in Mitchell Street   **WC**

A substantial Victorian corner building makes
an attractive setting for this self-service
restaurant and wine bar. De Quincey's,
located on the ground floor, sports much
carved wood and old tiling; Brahms and Liszt
below is more modern. Lunchtime brings a
fresh, appetising cold buffet with a varied
selection, from pâté, cheese and quiches to
honey-roast ham, salmon en croûte and
chicken mille-feuille. No children. *No dogs.* 🍵

GLASGOW

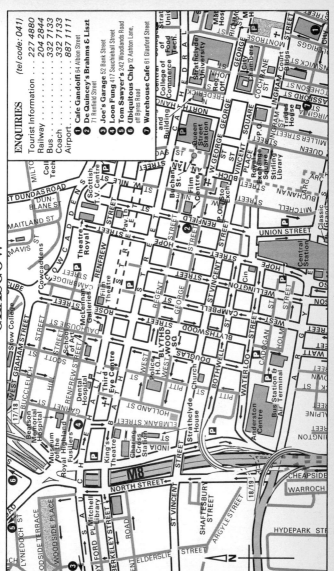

ENQUIRIES *(tel code: 041)*

Tourist Information	227 4880
Railway	204 2844
Bus	332 7133
Coach	332 7133
Airport	887 1111

❶ **Cafe Gandolfi** 64 Albion Street
❷ **De Quincey's Brahms & Liszt**
   71 Renfield Street
❸ **Joe's Garage** 52 Bank Street
❹ **Loon Fung** 417 Sauchiehall Street
❺ **Tom Sawyer's** 242 Woodlands Road
❻ **Ubiquitous Chip** 12 Ashton Lane,
   off Byres Road
❼ **Warehouse Cafe** 61 Glasford Street

Glasgow   *Joe's Garage*

52 Bank Street
041-339 5407
Town plan *Strathclyde*

Open noon–midnight
Closed 1 & 2 January & 25 & 26 December

Chicken enchilada £4.30   Chilli &
cheeseburger £3.45
Credit Access, Amex, Diners, Visa
P street parking   &   **WC**

A bright red petrol pump dominates this
American-style diner that's located near the
Hillhead/University area. You can eat the
Tex-Mex way, choosing guacamole, enchiladas and chilli, or go for meaty burgers,
pasta, club sandwiches and cripsy fried
potato skins. Pile on the calories with hot
blueberry pie or pancakes dripping maple
syrup and cream. *No dogs.*

Glasgow   *Loon Fung*

417 Sauchiehall Street
041-332 1240
Town plan *Strathclyde*

Open noon–11.30
Closed 3 days mid January

Dim sum from £1.10   Special chow mein
£4.70
Credit Access, Amex, Diners, Visa
P car park in Holland Street   &   **WC**

Popular with the local Chinese community,
this modern town-centre restaurant offers a
wide range of tasty dim sum throughout its
long opening hours. Steamed pork and king
prawn dumplings are particularly delicious,
while other choices include beef ball with
ginger and onion, turnip cake and stuffed
duck's web. The main menu offers plenty of
rice and noodle dishes. *No dogs.*

Glasgow   *Tom Sawyer's*

242 Woodlands Road
041-332 5687
Town plan *Strathclyde*

Open noon–10, Sun noon–2.30 & 6.30–10
Closed 1 January & 25 December

Chicken goujons £3.95   Chocolate mousse
£1.35
LVs   *Credit* Access, Amex, Diners, Visa
P street parking   &   **WC**

Students from nearby Glasgow University
give top marks to this lively diner-cum-bar.
Lunchtime in the bar (no children) brings an
appetising display of cold meats, pies and
salads, plus hot dishes like home-made
lasagne. In the smart modern adjoining diner,
the whole family can tuck into deep-fried
potato skins, burgers, steaks and kebabs –
and delicious sweets, too, like apple pie and
chocolate chip cookies. Smaller evening
choice. *No dogs.* ⊖

Glasgow   *New Entry*   *Ubiquitous Chip*

12 Ashton Lane, off Byres Road
041-334 5007
Town plan *Strathclyde*

Open noon–2.30
Closed Sun, 1 January & 25 December

Vegan bean soup 50p   Chicken casserole
with brown rice £2.95
Credit Access, Amex, Diners, Visa
P municipal car park (Ashton Lane)   &   **WC**

In a mews-style lane off busy Byres Road,
this popular place comprises restaurant, bar
and charming courtyard garden. The bar is
ideal for just-a-biters with its lunchtime menu
of healthy snacks – terrines and pâtés, nice
light flans, cold meats and attractive salads,
chicken casserole served with brown rice,
fresh and dried fruit salads, *no* chips. There
are also full lunchtime and evening restaurant
menus. *No dogs.* 🐾

Glasgow   *Warehouse Café*

61 Glassford Street
041-552 4181
Town plan *Strathclyde*

Open 10–6
Closed Sun & Bank Holidays

Stuffed croissants £2.25   Apple & banana
crumble 95p
Credit Access, Amex, Diners, Visa
P Albion Street car park & meters   **WC**

A new manager and a new menu for this
third-floor café in a trendy clothes store.
Deep-fried Brie and chicken liver paté feature
among the starters, while more substantial
offerings include creamy quiche, pastrami on
rye, chicken goujons and chilli con carne.
There are also salads and savoury stuffed
croissants. For sweet, perhaps banana cake,
cinnamon pastry or chocolate fudge cake.
Strong espresso coffee and speciality teas.
No dogs. 🍵 ☕

Hardgate   *Elle Coffee Shop*

35 Glasgow Road
Duntocher (0389) 76335
Map 2 C3 *Strathclyde*

Open 10–4.15
Closed Sun, Wed & Bank Holidays

Quiche with salad £1.85 Apple pie with cream
70p
Credit Access, Amex, Visa
P shopping precinct car park

At the back of a dress shop, this beamed
coffee room is made to measure for just-a-
biters. The baking is good and fresh, with
scones, fruit loaf and apple pie always in
fashion. Baked potatoes, quiche and pizza
are typical savoury snacks, and there are
salads and Danish open sandwiches. Regular sandwiches and filled rolls outside lunch
hours. Unlicensed. *No dogs.*

Helensburgh   *Original Famous Coffee House*

102a West Princes Street
Helensburgh (0436) 2005
Map 2 B3 *Strathclyde*

Open 9–5.30 (till 5 Oct–Easter)
Closed Sun end September–Easter, 1 & 2
January & 25 & 26 December

Spicy bean hotpot £2.10   Ham and pineapple
danwich £2.35
P street parking   **WC**

Everything on the menu is available all day at
this homely coffee shop behind a smart
canopied entrance, and it's all freshly prepared and delicious, whether your fancy is
for fluffy scones, Danish pastries and chocolate-topped biscuits, toasted sandwiches or
wonderful Danish open sandwiches – try
succulent turkey garnished with orange and
prune. Good hot soup, too, plus more substantial offerings like pork and apple pie with
salad. Unlicensed. ☕

Inchture   *Inchture Milk Bar*

Near Dundee
Inchture (0828) 86283
Map 2 C3 *Tayside*

Open 9–6 (till 5 October–March)
Closed 25 December & January

Home-made soup 45p   Bacon, sausages,
eggs & tomatoes £2.45

P own car park   ♿   **WC**

Kathleen McLeish is a dab hand at pastry,
and her fruit pies (apricot, blackcurrant,
cherry and apple) are deservedly popular at
this simple roadside snack bar on the A85.
Other favourites include scones and moist
chocolate cake, while on the savoury side
there are cooked breakfasts, well-filled rolls
and salads based on ham, home-roast beef,
pâté and chicken. Everything is available all
day. Unlicensed. *No dogs.*

Inverness ★ *New Entry*   *Brookes Wine Bar*

75 Castle Street
Inverness (0463) 225662
Map 1 C2 *Highland*

Open noon–10, Sun 12.30–2.30 & 6.30–10.30
Closed Sun October–April

Chicken liver terrine & mousse £2.25   Stir-fry
vegetables in pancakes £3.60
P Castle Street car park & **WC**

Superb snacks accompany a fine selection
of thoroughbred wines in this very stylish
wine bar opposite the castle. First-class
salads include coleslaw and ratatouille, and
there's an exquisite chicken liver terrine and
mousse, splendid poached salmon, tandoori
chicken legs and meat dishes, both plain and
sauced. Mushroom quiche for the vegetarian,
interesting soups and delectable raspberry
cream mousse among the sweets. *No dogs.*

Isle of Gigha   *Gigha Hotel*

Gigha (058 35) 254
Map 2 B3 *Strathclyde*

Open 10–4
Closed end October–March

Ploughman's lunch £1.75   Chicken pie £2.75
Credit Access, Visa

P own car park **WC**

The Roebuck family offer a real Highland
welcome at this peacefully placed hotel. Sit
in the bright lounge (or in the boat house
when it's fine) and enjoy splendid brown
bread sandwiches, super shortbread and
rich fruit slice with an excellent cuppa. At
lunchtime, there's soup, pâté and ploughman's, plus cold meat salads and a daily hot
dish like shepherd's pie. Nice sweets are a
feature, and cheeses from the island's own
creamery. ☕ ☕

Kentallen of Appin   *Holly Tree*

Duror (063 174) 292
Map 1 B2 *Highland*

Open 10.30–5
Closed October–Easter, also Wed in April,
May & October

Ploughman's lunch £2.50   Crêpe of game
with pineapple & green peppercorns £3.50
Credit Access, Diners, Visa
P own car park **WC**

Once the local railway station, now a delightful restaurant commanding splendid views of
Loch Linnhe. Cakes are served morning and
afternoon, while at lunchtime you can nibble
at something delicious like herby goat's
cheese pâté or pork terrine with apple
mayonnaise – or make a full meal with, say,
fillet of sole dugléré or roast lamb with
rosemary. Silky-smooth chocolate mousse
for a delicious finale. Full evening meals. No
smoking. *No dogs.* ☕

Kilchrenan   *Taychreggan Hotel*

By Taynuilt
Kilchrenan (086 63) 211
Map 2 B3 *Strathclyde*

Open noon–2.15
Closed mid-October–Easter

Quiche with salad £2.50   Fresh prawns with
salad £4.50
Credit Access, Amex, Diners, Visa
P own car park **WC**

It's certainly worth the drive up the narrow
road to this hotel on the side of Lock Awe,
where you can eat in the comfortable cocktail
bar while enjoying the sensational views. The
simple but appetising menus offers wholesome home-made soup or pâté and French
bread, quiche, superb hamburgers, colourful
fresh salads and a wide variety of sandwiches. Try the Loch Awe monster–a French
baguette stuffed with ham, cheese and salad.
No puddings. ☕

Kildonan   *Three Rowans Tea Shop & Restaurant*

Near Edinbane, Isle of Skye
Edinbane (047 082) 286
Map 1 A2 *Highland*

Open 10–5.30 (Sun 12–5.30) & from 7
Closed Sat, end October–week before Easter
except for dinner by arrangement at
weekends
Haggis with tatties & neeps £2.75   Hazelnut
roast £4.25
P roadside parking   **WC**

Midlands couple Barrie and Brenda Creed
do a great haggis with tatties and neeps at
their cosily welcoming tea shop overlooking
Loch Snizort. Other popular daytime offerings include soup and bread, both home-
made, along with toasted sandwiches,
scones and pancakes, while in the evening
there are more elaborate dishes such as
cider-poached trout, silverside and vegetarian hazelnut roast. Finish with lovely Skye-
made ice cream. *No dogs.* 🍵

Kincraig   *Boathouse Restaurant*

By Kingussie
Kincraig (054 04) 272
Map 1 C2 *Highland*

Open 10–10 June–Sept; 10–5.30 April, May &
Oct; 3–10 Dec–March
Closed 1 November–27 December

Salmon steak with baked potato & vegetables
£4   Soup of the day 95p
P own car park ♿ **WC**

Sit out on the balcony of this log cabin and
watch the windsurfers skim across Loch
Insh. Inside, the self-service counter offers a
feast of home-baking – super shortbread,
scones, fruit-packed Dundee cake – plus
appetising light lunchtime dishes like gammon, quiche, pâté and smoked mackerel with
salad. The evening menu in high season
offers a snack or a full meal: egg mayonnaise,
prawn cocktail, pork chops, sausage and
chips. No smoking. *No dogs.* 🍵

Kingussie   *Wood'n'Spoon*

3 High Street
Kingussie (054 02) 251
Map 1 C2 *Highland*

Open 10–9.30 (Sun from 12.30)

Lasagne £2.50   Venison burger £2.25
Credit Visa

P street parking & village car park nearby ♿
WC

Tourists and walkers appreciate the fine
choice of tasty fare on offer at this large,
happy self-service restaurant. Hot dishes
range from lasagne and risotto to roast
chicken and venison burgers, while on the
cold counter are competent baked quiches
and enjoyable salads. There's also a good
spread of sweet things, including carrot cake,
ice creams and lemon meringue pie. Non-
smoking area.

Kinlochbervie   *Kinlochbervie Hotel*

By Lairg
Kinlochbervie (097 182) 275
Map 1 B1 *Highland*

Open 12–1.45 (Sun from 12.30) & 2–5.30

Home-made soup 80p   Macaroni cheese
£1.15

P own car park ♿ **WC**

You can get a very decent lunch in the bars
in this agreeable modern hotel in a remote
coastal setting. Start perhaps with a nourishing broth, and go on to home-smoked ham
and salads, fresh haddock, a beefburger or
the excellent macaroni cheese that is Geral-
dine Gregory's speciality. Nice puds, too, like
coffee and brandy mousse or hazelnut slice,
and teas in the afternoon. Resident children
only. *No dogs.* 🍵

Knipoch ★ *Knipoch House Hotel*

By Oban
Kilninver (085 26) 251
Map 2 B3 *Strathclyde*

Open 12.30–2
Closed January

Home-made soup £1.50 Prawn mayonnaise
open sandwich £3.95
Credit Access, Amex, Diners, Visa
P own car park   ♿   **WC**

Overlooking Loch Feochan, this fine Georgian hotel serves very delicious lunches in either the bar or lounge. The menu couldn't be simpler, based as it is on a soup du jour (perhaps lentil and carrot), open sandwiches of rare beef, locally cured ham or prawn mayonnaise and fresh seasonal fish. Delicious home-made ices include a splendid blackcurrant sorbet. *No dogs.* ☕

Lamlash *Carraig Mhor*

Isle of Arran
Lamlash (077 06) 453
Map 2 B4 *Strathclyde*

Open 10.30–11.45, 12.15–2 & 7–9
Closed Sun, Mon, 2 weeks February & 3
weeks November

Chicken salad £1.95 Beef curry £2.50

P car park opposite   **WC**

Enjoying splendid views of Holy Island, this charming little restaurant where everything is home-made deserves its popularity. Buttery shortbread and rich treacle scones go beautifully with morning coffee, while lunchtime brings salads, omelettes, ploughman's and daily specials like cottage pie with vegetables. Round your meal off with pineapple meringue. Roast duckling and sole duglèrè are typical of the more elaborate evening menu. ☕

Lamlash *Glenscorrodale Farm Tearoom*

Isle of Arran
Sliddery (077 087) 241
Map 2 B4 *Strathclyde*

Open 10.30–4 & 7.30–9
Closed Tues & end September–May

Meatloaf platter £1.80 Danish apple pie with
cream 80p

P roadside & small car park   **WC**

Helen Driver's straightforward, honest home cooking is ample reward for tracking down this simple tea room, part of a remote sheep farm some five miles west of Lamlash. The day starts with scones, oat cakes and malt loaf; then at lunchtime there's a flavour-packed soup, delicious filled rolls and a fruit pie. Booking is essential in the evening, when the menu features more elaborate dishes such as chicken Kiev and venison in red wine. Unlicensed. *No dogs.* ☕

Largs *Green Shutter Tearoom*

28 Bath Street
Largs (0475) 672252
Map 2 B3 *Strathclyde*

Open 10–6
Closed mid October–mid March

Hawaiian toastie £1.60 Green Shutter salad
£3.60

P Promenade car park   ♿   **WC**

Picture windows command fine views across the Clyde at the simply appointed tea shop with its own bakery. Delicious cakes and biscuits are, not surprisingly, the main attraction, including rich caramel shortbread, almond tarts, fruit scones and sticky currant buns. Tasty savouries available throughout the day range from toasted sandwiches, salads and baked potatoes to home-made vegetable soup and haddock with chips. Children's menu. Unlicensed.

Largs   *Jacobite Teashop*

116 Main Street
Largs (0475) 673222
Map 2 B3 *Strathclyde*

Open 10–5
Closed Sun, 1 & 2 January & 25 & 26
December

Macaroni cheese with side salad & potatoes
£1.55   Ham & cheese toastie 80p
P station car park

Old-fashioned cakestands piled high with
home-baked goodies are the main attraction
of this traditional tea shop decorated with
gleaming brassware. Take your pick from
wholemeal scones, dainty coconut cakes,
flavoursome fruit slices and rich chocolate
fudge bars. Throughout the day you can also
get home-made soups and salads, open
sandwiches and various things with chips.
Unlicensed. *No dogs.* 🍵

Milngavie   *Famous Coffee House*

Findlay Clark Garden Centre, Boclair Road
Balmore (0360) 20700
Map 2 C3 *Strathclyde*

Open 10–5.30
Closed 1 January & 25 & 26 December

Bacon & cheese quiche £1.95   Turkey
danwich £2.45

P garden centre car park   &   **WC**

Flowers and plants decorate this smart,
modern coffee house at the rear of a large
garden centre. The all-day menu is full of
interest, with choices like hand-raised pork
and apple pie, spicy bean hot pot and
substantial open sandwiches (try cream
cheese with peaches and walnuts) ringing
the changes. Sweet treats such as Danish
pastries and scones, flavoursome gâteaux
and hot cherry tart also please. Unlicensed.
No dogs. 🍴

Moffat   *Beechwood Country House Hotel*

Off Harthope Place
Moffat (0683) 20210
Map 2 C4 *Dumfries & Galloway*

Open 12.30–1.30 & 3.30–5
Closed 2 January–2 February

Wayfarers platter £4.95   Set afternoon tea
£2.25
Credit Access, Amex, Diners, Visa
P own car park   **WC**

There are lovely valley views from this
peaceful hotel tucked into a hillside just
outside Moffat. The lunch platter brings fish,
cold meats, pâté, cheese and salads, as well
as soup, a glass of wine and coffee. For
afternoon tea there are scones with nice
home-made jam, Scottish pancake, sponge
and a very good cup of tea. Choose between
the traditionally furnished lounges and the
garden. *No dogs.* 🍵 🍴

New Abbey   *Abbey Cottage*

By Dumfries
Dunscore (038 782) 361
Map 2 C4 *Dumfries & Galloway*

Open 10–5
Closed October–Easter & weekdays Easter–
Spring Bank Holiday

Ploughman's lunch £1.70   Rhubarb tart with
cream 70p
P abbey car park   &   **WC**

To the left, a crafts shop, to the right, a simple
coffee house with prints, maps and tapestries
on the wall. Morag McKie and her young
helpers produce a day-long selection of
fresh, tasty snacks, from traditional scones
and fruit tarts to lentil soup, sandwiches,
salads, pâté and robustly stuffed jacket
potatoes. A nice little garden overlooks the
ruins of Sweetheart Abbey. Unlicensed. No
smoking. *No dogs.*

Newcastleton   *Copshaw Kitchen*

4 North Hermitage Street
Liddlesdale (054 121) 250
Map 2 D4 *Borders*

Open 9–6.30 (Sun from 10); 9–5.30 November–
March
Closed Tues, 1–3 January & 26 December

Lasagne with garnish £2.35   ½lb fillet steak
with mushrooms & chips £4.75
P own car park   **WC**

Sound, honest home cooking is the hallmark
of Jean Elliot's appealing little tea room, once
an old grocer's shop. Her simple but appetising selection ranges from hearty soups
served with lovely barley bread, omelettes
and well-seasoned burgers to chicken curry,
steaks and scampi. Toasted teacakes,
scones, cakes and biscuits for afternoon tea.
Children's menu. Evening meals Wednesday–Saturday by arrangement. *No dogs.* ♙

Peebles   *Kailzie Garden Restaurant & Tea Room*

Kailzie
Peebles (0721) 22807
Map 2 C4 *Borders*

Open 11–5.30
Closed November–March
Arbroath smokie mousse with French bread
£1.30   Gruyère cheese crêpe with vegetables
£3.20
Credit Amex
P own parking   ♿ **WC**

A converted stable by the river Tweed is the
setting for a day-long selection of snacks
and full meals at the MacGillivrays' charming
restaurant. Against a background of old stalls
and mangers, you can tuck into everything
from spicy stuffed aubergine and smoked
haddock crêpe to sirloin steak with green
peppercorn sauce and a tasty lunchtime dish
of the day. Simple sweets; cakes, scones
and set teas, too. *No dogs.*

Peebles   *Sunflower*

4 Bridgegate
Peebles (0721) 22420
Map 2 C4 *Borders*

Open 10–5.30 (Wed in winter till 2.30)
Closed Sun, Bank Holidays & Christmas–New
Year
Broccoli & mushroom pancake with tomato
sauce £2.40   Cauliflower, Stilton cheese &
walnut flan £1.95
P Edinburgh Road car park   **WC**

From midday onwards, this unpretentious
wholefood restaurant offers a tasty line in
hot vegetarian dishes. Try watercress soup
followed by cheese and lentil bake or a salad
pancake with cheese sauce for a healthy and
enjoyable lunch. Throughout the day there is
a wide assortment of toasted sandwiches
(perhaps ham and egg), salads and baked
potatoes to choose from, plus scrumptious
sweets. Non-smoking room. ♟

Pitlochry   *Luggie Restaurant*

Rie-Achen Road
Pitlochry (0796) 2085
Map 1 C2 *Tayside*

Open 9.30–5 & 6–9
Closed Sun evening & end October–March
Chicken & ham pie with salad £3   Trout in
Pernod cream sauce £5.25
Credit Access, Amex, Diners, Visa
P own car park & Rie-Achen Road car park
WC

Once a dairy, this long, beamed barn
now houses a first-rate and hugely popular
restaurant. Attractive displays of scones,
cheesecakes, gâteaux and fairy cakes appeal throughout the day, while at lunchtime
there are salads with cold meats and fresh
salmon, plus hot specials like chicken and
ham pie. The more ambitious evening selection features dishes like chicken in a piquant
ginger sauce. *No dogs.*

Powmill   *Powmill Milk Bar*

Rumbling Bridge, Near Kinross
Fossoway (057 74) 376
Map 2 C3 *Tayside*

Open 9.30–5 (Sat & Sun till 6); 9.30–8 April–
September
Closed 1 January & 25 & 26 December

Stovies £1.50   Meringues with fresh cream
50p
P own car park   &   **WC**

An unpretentious eatery in a converted farm
building by the A977. Local ladies produce
good baking in abundance for the counter
display: scones and shortbread, éclairs and
meringues, apple or rhubarb tarts, date and
walnut bread. Filled brown rolls provide light
savoury bites, and there are quiches, salads,
baked potatoes and hot specials like cauliflower cheese or a Scottish speciality such
as stovie. *No dogs.* ⊖

St Andrews   **New Entry**   *Brambles*

5 College Street
St Andrews (0334) 75380
Map 2 D3 *Fife*

Open 10–4.30
Closed Sun, Mon, 2 weeks September & 2
weeks Christmas

Leek croustade £1.20   Bramble & apple tart
55p
P North Street   **WC**

Healthy eaters are drawn to this cheerful,
pine-furnished café to sample Jean Hamilton's excellent vegetarian fare. Croissants,
cakes, biscuits and filled rolls hold the
morning stage, and midday heralds inventive
salads such as pasta and green beans with
peanut butter dressing or cauliflower with
banana, date and alfalfa. Also pizzas,
quiches, jacket potatoes and hot specials,
plus hard-to-resist sweets and Scottish farmhouse cheeses. *No smoking.* ⊖ 🍵

St Andrews   *Pepita's Restaurant*

11 Crails Lane
St Andrews (0334) 74084
Map 2 D3 *Fife*

Open 9.30–11, Sun 10.30–10
Closed 2 weeks Christmas

Scotch salmon en croûte £5.85   Chocolate
marshmallows £1.70
Credit Access, Amex, Visa
P South Street   **WC**

Lots of bustle, lots of charm and lots of good
eating in this popular restaurant. Ploughman's, pizzas, salads and lasagne are typical
lunchtime fare, served at the counter along
with a vegetarian dish and chef's specials
like pork and apple casserole. For sweet
there's fruit salad, sherry trifle and assorted
ices. In the evening it's waitress service and
extra dishes like salmon en croûte and
steaks. *No dogs.* ⊖

Selkirk   *Philipburn House Hotel*

Linglie Road
Selkirk (0750) 20747
Map 2 D4 *Borders*

Open noon–2 & 6.30–9.30

Home-smoked trout £3.75   Sachertorte £1.25
Credit Access, Amex, Diners, Visa

P own car park   &   **WC**

The charming Hill family run this delightfully
friendly and civilised hotel that's just outside
town on the A707. Tasty, satisfying snacks
from a short quick-bite menu are served to
the strains of classical music: the croque
monsieur is a particularly rich version, and
madame, with prawns as well as ham, is a
speciality. There's also pâté and ploughman's, shepherd's pie and fish cakes, along
with home-smoked trout and super-rich
sachertorte. ⊖

Stonehaven

George A. Robertson

68 Allardice Street
Stonehaven (0569) 62734
Map 1 D2 *Grampian*

Open 7–4.45
Closed Sun & Bank Holidays

Home-made soup 45p   Toasted sandwich
85p

P in Market Square   **WC**

The centrepiece of this modest little tea room above a baker's shop is a trolley laden with freshly prepared goodies to enjoy with tea or coffee. Enjoy filled rolls and baps as well as sweet treats like strawberry tartlets, doughnuts and chocolate éclairs. Simple plated salads, hot sausage rolls and pies make more substantial snacks, while lunchtime brings further savouries like soup and macaroni cheese. Unlicensed. 🍵

Stranraer

L'Aperitif

London Road
Stranraer (0776) 2991
Map 2 B4 *Dumfries & Galloway*

Open 12–2 & 5.30–9
Closed Sun & mid January–mid February

Steak pie £2.75   Roast chicken à l'Aperitif
with vegetables £4.75

P own car park   **WC**

The downstairs lounges of this jolly, family-run Italian restaurant are the place for budget-eaters to head. At lunchtime choose from flavour-packed minestrone, salads or sandwiches, or opt for something more substantial like home-made pizza, cannelloni, a steak pie or superbly fresh haddock with lovely crisp chips. Sweets are simple but delicious, the coffee good and strong. More elaborate evening meals are served in the restaurant upstairs. *No dogs.*

Strathcarron

Carron Restaurant

Cam-Allt
Lochcarron (052 02) 488
Map 1 B2 *Highland*

Open 10.30–9.15
Closed Sun & mid October–Easter except Sat
eve
Soup of the day £1.10   Salmon steak, salad &
baked potato £4.75
Credit Access, Amex, Visa
P own parking   **WC**

Overlooking Loch Carron, this spotless modern restaurant offers a wide choice of satisfying food throughout the day. Home-made cakes and pastries go well with tea or coffee at any time, while the savoury selection ranges from toasted sandwiches, quiche and honey-roast ham with salad to hearty steaks, trout and venison from the chargrill. Look out for a first-class apple pie among sweets. *No dogs.* 🍵

Tarbet

Tigh-na-Mara Seafood Restaurant

Scourie, By Lairg
Scourie (0971) 2151
Map 1 B1 *Highland*

Open noon–8
Closed Sun (except July & August) & early
October–Easter

Smoked salmon £4.50   Gooseberry crumble
with cream £1.45
P parking nearby

The name means 'house by the sea' and Essie Pearce has added a small conservatory to her cottage home, creating this delightful restaurant where delicious local seafood is served. Crab, squid, salmon and halibut need only a crisp salad as accompaniment (new potatoes, too, with hot dishes), while lighter bites include smoked mackerel and potted shrimps. Home-made soup to start, fruit crumble for dessert. Unlicensed. *No dogs.* 🍵

Taynuilt   *Shore Cottage*

Near Oban
Taynuilt (086 62) 654
Map 2 B3 *Strathclyde*

Open 9.30–6
Closed end October–week before Easter

Leek & potato soup with brown bread 60p
Wholemeal scone with home-made jam 25p

P own car park & **WC**

Lily McNaught is the driving force behind this
delightful cottage tea room on the shores of
Loch Etive. Her baking is outstanding, and
delicious wholemeal scones are accompanied by superb home-made jam. Our lemon
sponge was exemplary, too, and on the
savoury side cheese on toast is a perennial
favourite. Soup and salads are other choices
on the all-day menu. Unlicensed. No smoking.
No dogs.

Tayvallich   *Tayvallich Inn*

Near Lochgilphead
Tayvallich (05467) 282
Map 2 B3 *Strathclyde*

Open noon–2 & 6–7

Craignish mussels marinière £2.25   Jumbo
prawn salad £4.50
Credit Access, Visa

P own car park & **WC**

At lunchtime and early in the evening just-a-
biters can enjoy the best local shellfish at this
friendly, informal inn on the shores of Loch
Sween. Oysters, jumbo prawns and Craignish mussels marinière are among the favourites, and there are pâtés and
steakburgers for meat-eaters. Nice sweets
(ices, apple flan, fruit crumbles). Full evening
meals from 7pm. *No dogs.*

Tomintoul   *Glenmulliach Restaurant*

By Lecht
Tomintoul (080 74) 356
Map 1 C2 *Grampian*

Open 9–9; 11–6 in winter
Closed 1 January, December, also November,
January & February in bad weather
Roast lamb with vegetables £3.25   Apple
strudel with cream £1.20
Credit Access, Visa
P own car park **WC**

Everything on the menu is available throughout opening hours at this pleasant modern
restaurant two miles south of Tomintoul on
the A939 Braemar road. Local specialities
like smoked Spey salmon, roast venison and
herrings fried in oatmeal are popular, and
there are filled rolls, scones and flapjacks,
too. Set three-course lunch at £2.95 and high
tea at £3.60 are also available, and there's a
children's menu.

Ullapool   *Ceilidh Place*

West Argyll Street
Ullapool (0854) 2103
Map 1 B1 *Highland*

Open 9am–9pm
Closed 1 November–28 February

Scone & butter 32p   Vegan loaf 45p
Credit Access, Amex, Diners, Visa

P own car park & **WC**

Bar, coffee shop and restaurant, this friendly
place is the scene of some very enjoyable
snacking, mainly vegetarian. Breakfast gives
way at 10 o'clock to a whole range of healthy
fare, from delicious wholemeal bread and
lovely light scones to salads and hot lunchtime specials like spinach and mushroom
lasagne. Grilled sole and crab salad are
typical dinner dishes. *No dogs.*

Wester Howgate ★ *Old Howgate Inn, Coach House*

Near Penicuik
Penicuik (0968) 74244
Map 2 C3 *Lothian*

Open 11.30–2.30 (Sun from 12.30) & 6–10
Closed 1 January & 25 December
Smørrebrød of prawns with lemon
mayonnaise £2.50   Hot Danish pastry with
apricot sauce £1.70
Credit Access, Amex, Diners, Visa
P own car park   **WC**

Danish open sandwiches, or smørrebrød,
are the speciality of this delightful restaurant,
part of an old inn standing on the A6094.
Excellent nutty rye bread carries an enormous variety of mouthwatering toppings like
smoked trout with spinach pâté or roast beef
with chunky potato salad and dill cucumber.
Also more substantial Danish dishes, plus
Danish cheeses and some pleasant sweets.
Charming staff. Minimum charge £2.50. No
smoking. *No dogs.* ⊖

Whitehouse ★ *Old School Tearoom*

Near Tarbert
Whitehouse (088 073) 215
Map 2 B3 *Strathclyde*

Open 10.30–6
Closed Tues & mid October–April

Home-made soup with bread 70p   Ham & egg
pie with salad £1.95

P own car park   **WC**

Jean Curry's tea trolley piled high with
wonderful cakes and pastries is a powerful
magnet for visitors at this delightful tea room.
It's an impossible task to choose between,
say, her perfect chocolate éclairs, moist fruit
bread and fresh cream gâteaux. Equally
scrumptious savouries, served from lunchtime onwards, include soup, sandwiches and
salads, plus a masterly ham and egg pie.
Unlicensed. No smoking. *No dogs.* ⊖ 🍵

WALES

Aberaeron ★ *Hive on the Quay*

Cadwgan Place
Aberaeron (0545) 570445
Map 7 B1 *Dyfed*

Open 10.30–5; July–beginning September 10–9
Closed end September–Spring Bank Holiday

Vegetarian Greek pâté £1.25   Honey ice cream £1.65
P street parking   &

A lovely spot for a summer snack, with a delightful quayside setting and charming, attentive owners. The family bees have a hand in the business: honey ice cream is a house speciality, and there's also honey-baked ham and delicious honey Madeira cake. The sandwiches are excellent, and mealtimes bring a fine cold buffet, along with soup and hot dishes like savoury pancakes and braised steak. Ingredients are of the best quality and cooking careful.

Aberdovey *Old Coffee Shop*

13 New Street
Aberdovey (065 472) 652
Map 7 B1 *Gwynedd*

Open 10–5.30 (till 5 in winter)
Closed Mon (except July & September), 4 January–7 February & November

Chicken & almond salad £2.60   Raspberry & hazelnut meringue cake £1.15
P on the seafront   &

This popular little coffee shop stands just a stone's throw from the seafront. Fresh, tasty treats are available throughout the day, with home-baked goodies such as honey and walnut roulade and rich chocolate brandy cake dealing a delicious blow to many a diet. Open sandwiches come with various generous toppings, and there are salads, quiches and hot specials like beef casserole or devilled prawns. Unlicensed. *No dogs.*

Abergavenny **New Entry** *Coffoodles*

16 Monk Street
Abergavenny (0873) 78184
Map 7 C2 *Gwent*

Open 9.30–5, Sun 8.30–1
Closed 1 January & 25 & 26 December

Lasagne with French bread £2.45   Raspberry heaven with cream 85p

P beside St Mary's Church   &   **WC**

Scones, toast and teacakes go with coffee or tea throughout the day in this cottagy little place. A blackboard shows what's available for lunchtime consumption. The accent is on baked potatoes with fillings and salads, and specials might be lasagne, quiche, prawns in garlic or cauliflower cheese. There's a most tempting array of sweets. Packet teas and coffees are for sale, also newspapers on Sunday morning.

Aberystwyth **New Entry** *Connexion*

19 Bridge Street
Aberystwyth (0970) 615350
Map 7 B1 *Dyfed*

Open 10–4.30 & 6.30–9.30
Closed Sun & 25 December

Stuffed aubergines provençale £3.95   Pollo con prosciutto & formaggio £4.80
LVs   *Credit* Access, Visa
P street parking   **WC**

'Bistro family food' is how patronne Janet Fuerst describes the well-prepared fare on offer in this busy place. The menus are impressively varied, and you can order anything from garlic bread to lobster and steaks; at points between come pizzas, sizzling-hot tagliatelle verdi, stuffed peppers, salads, veal cutlets, even vegan dishes. Lovely rich apple tart for pud. No children under six in the evening. *No dogs.*

Egon Ronay's
CELLNET
GUIDE 1987

HOTELS, RESTAURANTS & INNS IN
GREAT BRITAIN & IRELAND

Egon Ronay's Cellnet Guide 1987 includes detailed descriptions of over 2500 of the best hotels, inns and restaurants in Great Britain and Ireland.

Restaurants serving outstanding food are awarded stars, and wine comments are included in many entries. There's an extensive section on bargain breaks and lower-priced London restaurants and hotels.

Many new features make the Guide more useful than ever for anyone who travels on business or for pleasure. Among them are

- Town house hotels
- Starred restaurants and high-grade hotels near the motorway network
- Countrywide listing of theatres

Available from AA Centres and booksellers everywhere at £9.95 or £10.95 including postage and packing from:

Mail Order Department
PO Box 51
Basingstoke
Hampshire
RG21 2BR

Caernarfon ★ New Entry Bakestone

26 Hole-in-the-Wall Street
Caernarfon (0286) 5846
Map 3 A4 *Gwynedd*

Open noon–2.30, 3.30–5 & 6.30–10
Closed Sun eve, Thurs daytime, all Mon & 1
week Christmas

Chicken & mushroom crêpe £2.40   Set
afternoon tea £2.30
P ample around castle   **WC**

Tucked under the castle wall, this is a cheerful, informal crêperie-cum-tea house with a French ambience. The chef is a man of talent, whose cakes and pastries would grace any dessert trolley. His crêpes are also excellent, and the house special has a toothsome filling of fresh spinach, succulent smoked bacon, Swiss cheese and a whole egg. Local goat's cheese salad is a popular starter, and there are daily specials based on fish. *No dogs.* 🐾

Cardiff ★ New Entry Armless Dragon

97 Wyverne Road, Cathays
Cardiff (0222) 382 357
Town plan *Mid-Glamorgan*

Open 12.30–2.30
Closed Sat lunch, all Sun, Bank Holidays & 1
week Christmas
Laverballs & mushrooms £2.20   Kidneys in
brandy £6.20
Credit Access, Amex, Diners, Visa
P ample street parking   **WC**

Take the ten-minute drive from the city centre for a super lunch at this well-run restaurant. The menu and daily specials cover a mouth-watering range, from laverballs (seaweed rolled in oatmeal with sunflower seeds, coriander and nut crunch) served with lovely field mushrooms to pigeon breasts with Szechuan pepper, vegetarian platter and superbly poached hake in samphire sauce. Tempting sweets, too. Full evening meals. *No dogs.*

Cardiff New Entry La Brasserie

60 St Mary Street
Cardiff (0222) 372 164
Town plan *Mid-Glamorgan*

Open noon–3 &7–12.15am
Closed Sun & 25 & 26 December

Spit-roast sucking pig £6.95   Lamb brochette
£3.25
Credit Access, Amex, Diners, Visa
P NCP in Bute St   **WC**

A busy wine bar with a good atmosphere and plenty of variety on the menu. Garlic pâté, snails and dressed crab are typical starters, and main courses include charcoal grills (particularly good lamb brochette) and specials like fresh salmon or roast sucking pig. Salads are self-sevice, with ten bowls to choose from. The wine list includes a dozen clarets by the glass and over 20 champagnes. *No dogs.*

Cardiff New Entry Champers

61 St Mary Street
Cardiff (0222) 373 363
Town plan *Mid-Glamorgan*

Open noon–3 &7–12.15am
Closed Sun lunch & 25 & 26 December

Stuffed chicken breast £3.25   Fish brochette
£4.25
Credit Access, Amex, Diners, Visa
P NCP in Bute St

A similar operation to La Brasserie but in Spanish, with a cellar that boasts over 100 Riojas and a dozen ports by the glass. The food system is simple and successful: starters like grilled sardines and baked mussels are listed on a blackboard, and you choose your main course – fish brochette, burger, stuffed chicken breast – from a display and have it expertly chargrilled to order. Salads are fresh and varied, and there's cheese to finish. *No dogs.* 🍷

CARDIFF

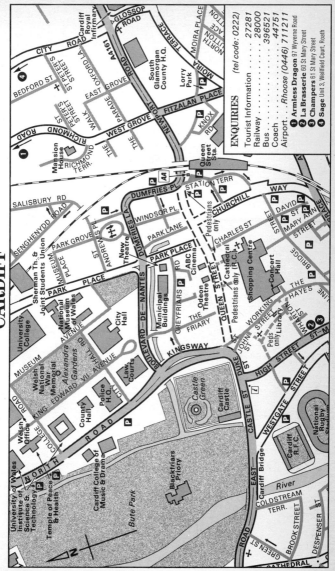

ENQUIRIES (tel code: 0222)

Tourist Information 27281
Railway 28000
Bus 396521
Coach 44751
Airport . . . *Rhoose* (0446) 711211

1 **Armless Dragon** 97 Wyeverne Road
2 **La Brasserie** 60 St Mary Street
3 **Champers** 61 St Mary Street
4 **Sage** Unit 3, Wellfield Court, Roath

Cardiff *New Entry*   *Sage*

Unit 3, Wellfield Court, Roath
(0222) 481223
Town plan *Mid-Glamorgan*

Open 9.30–5
Closed Sun & 1 week at Christmas

Leek & aduki bean casserole £1.95 Carob,
prune & apricot gâteau 75p

P limited street parking in Wellfield Road &

Tucked away in a precinct off a busy shopping
street, this wholefood vegetarian restaurant
has made many friends with its tasty cooking
and friendly ambience. Hot dishes like aubergine Parmesan or leek and aduki bean
casserole are displayed at the counter, and
there's a very good salad bar with dressings
made from sunflower oil. Home-baked cakes,
too, like carob, prune and apricot gâteau.
Open-air eating in summer. Non-smoking
section. *No dogs.*

Carmarthen   *New Entry*   *Waverley Restaurant*

23 Lammas Street
Carmarthen (0267) 236521
Map 7 B2 *Dyfed*

Open 9–4 (Thurs till 2)
Closed Sun & Bank Holidays

Vegetable lasagne with salad £1.50 Nut &
lentil burger 40p
P street & municipal pay & display car park
WC

Walk through the wholefood shop to the
restaurant section, where you can see the
tiny kitchen beyond the self-service counters.
There's a good selection of salads (sweetcorn and fruit, couscous, celery and bean
mayonnaise), along with quiches like cheese
and tomato or onion and courgette, plus
other daily specials. Nut burgers are the
best-selling line, and there are sweet things
such as oatmeal crunch and banana and
walnut sponge. No smoking. *No dogs.*

Chepstow   *New Entry*   *Willow Tree*

'The Back', Chepstow River Bank
Chepstow (029 12) 6665
Map 7 D2 *Gwent*

Open 11–5 Tues–Sun
Closed Sun eve, Mon, 25 & 26 December

Pork casserole £2.95 Fruit crumble 95p

Credit Access, Visa
P riverbank & **WC**

This small 16th-century cottage right on the
riverbank has a conservatory that serves as
a room. Here, Jeremy Hector offers a range
of scones and cakes with tea and also
creates daily specials for his blackboard
menu. Choose from soup, pâté or mushrooms in cream and then proceed to pots of
lasagne, aubergine casserole, a noodle dish
or cottage pie. Chocolate St Emilion is a
typical lovely pudding. More elaborate evening meals. *No dogs.* 🍷

Crickhowell   *Cheese Press*

18 High Street
Crickhowell (0873) 811122
Map 7 C2 *Powys*
Open 9.30–5.30 (till 5 September–Easter), Sun
10.30–4.30
Closed Sun January–Easter & 25 & 26
December
Vegetarian courgette & pasta bake with salad
£1.95 Turkey & cranberry pie with salad £1.95
Credit Access, Amex
P Greenhill Way car park & street **WC**

Tucked behind a gift shop, this simple little
coffee shop offers a good selection of home-
baked goodies to enjoy throughout the day.
Typical choices might include apricot and
coconut slice, richly flavoured fruit cake,
buttery caramel shortbread and macaroons. There's always a vegetarian dish at
lunchtime, plus soup, ploughman's, a savoury pie and some colourful, imaginative
salads. Non-smoking area. *No dogs.* 🍵

Eglwysfach   Ty'n-y-Cwm Tea Rooms

Artists' Valley, Near Machynlleth
Glandyfi (065 474) 278
Map 7 C1 *Dyfed*

Open 2–5.30
Closed Mon (except Bank Holidays), Tues,
Thurs, Fri & 1 October–Good Fri

Set tea 75p   Viennese chocolate cake £1.25

P own car park

Turn off the A487 at the sign to Cwm Einion
(Artists' Valley) in Furnace and follow winding
lanes to enjoy a delightful tea at this charming
chalet by a stream. Inside, or out in the pretty
garden, you can enjoy a lovely brew of tea
and some of Mary Mayo's very good baking:
cheesecake, raspberry torte and the popular
Viennese chocolate cake with its hazelnut,
marzipan and chocolate fudge icing all reflect
her considerable skills. Unlicensed. No
smoking. *No dogs.* 🍵

Hay-on-Wye   Granary

Broad Street
Hay-on-Wye (0497) 820790
Map 7 C2 *Powys*

Open 10–6; 9am–9pm in high season
Closed 25 & 26 December

Vegetarian mushroom bake £2.50   Set tea
from 75p
Credit Access, Amex, Visa
P street & town car park ♿ **WC**

The Golesworthys continue to welcome visitors to their rustic barn with a homely bar.
Home-cooked meals of soup, pâté, lamb and
spinach curry, lasagne, quiche and vegetarian dishes are available, together with a
teatime buffet table offering an irresistible
choice of cakes, gingerbread, cheesecake,
chocolate truffles, all with loads of cream. An
excellent cup of tea. 🍵

Hay-on-Wye   **New Entry**   Lion's Corner House

29 Lion Street
Hay-on-Wye (0497) 820175
Map 7 C2 *Powys*
Open 11–3
Closed Sun, 25 & 26 December, January &
February
Beef lasagne £3.25   Weobley cheesecake
95p
Credit Access, Amex, Diners, Visa
P municipal car park or street parking ♿
WC

Colin Thomson runs this corner restaurant
with considerable aplomb, and just-a-biters
will find plenty of tempting lunchtime snacks
served in the three rooms (one for non-
smokers) festooned with caps, scarves and
parasols. Chicken and pork pâté or garlic
snails might precede seafood lasagne, spinach and cottage cheese flan or chicken curry,
while Colin's apricot cheesecake flavoured
with tangy orange makes a smashing finale.
No dogs.

Keeston   Keeston Kitchen

Near Haverfordwest
Camrose (0437) 710440
Map 7 A2 *Dyfed*

Open 10.30–2 (Sun from 12.30)
Closed Mon except July & August, 1st week
January
Salad niçoise £2.75   Spaghetti alla paesana
£2.25
Credit Access, Visa
P in grounds ♿ **WC**

This farmhouse-style roadside establishment, which comprises restaurant, bar and
patio, is run in personal, informal style by Phil
and Clare Hallett. Lunchtime brings a decent
selection of home-cooked dishes based on
fresh ingredients. Ham and mushroom pâté
or cream of cauliflower soup could precede
chicken fricassee, a salad or a plate of
spaghetti. Sweets include the popular monster meringue. Sunday roast. Full evening
meals (plus Phil on the guitar!). *No dogs.* ☕

Llandeilo *Cawdor Arms Hotel*

Rhosmaen Street
Llandeilo (0558) 823500
Map 7 B2 *Dyfed*

Open 12.30–2 & 3.30–5.30
Closed 1 January

Lasagne £2.30   Afternoon tea £3.75
Credit Access, Diners, Visa

P municipal car park & WC

Enjoy elegant lunchtime snacks in the civilised surroundings of an antique-filled cocktail bar at this handsome Georgian hotel. Choose creamy soups and garlicky mussels among starters, with perhaps meaty lasagne, eggs indienne or a fine selection of cold meats and salads to follow. Finish with a tangy fresh fruit mousse or champagne syllabub. Afternoon teas are served in the lounge.

Llandudno **New Entry** *No. 1 Food & Wine Bar*

1 Old Road
Llandudno (0925) 75424
Map 3 A3 *Gwynedd*

Open noon–2 & 7–10
Closed Sun, January & 25 & 26 December

Smoked salmon quiche £2.60   Polish Nelson steak with cream & mushrooms £4.50
P ample street parking & WC

You'll find this convivial wine bar on a characterful Victorian street below the tram station. Kathy and Mike McCarthy respectively cook and host, both with considerable style. Smoked salmon quiche, eggs Jubilee and steak and kidney pie are typical items on a blackboard menu that is boosted in the evening by dishes like pork steak with apricots. There's an eye-catching array of sweets, from tempting chocolate cheesecake to lemon and honey crunch. *No dogs.*

Llangollen ★ *Gales Wine & Food Bar*

18 Bridge Street
Llangollen (0978) 860089
Map 3 B4 *Clwyd*

Open noon–1.45 & 6–10.15
Closed Sun & Mon September–May & 25 December–1 January

Oriental minced beef £2.60   Prawn Creole £2.60
P town-centre car park WC

Gillian Gale's super home cooking really draws the crowds, so arrive early if you want a table at this appealing panelled wine bar, where her husband Richard oversees the extensive wine list. Her ever-changing selection might include such delights as chicken liver and almond pâté, filled jacket potatoes, rib of beef and sugar-baked ham. Salads are crisp and delicious, sweets irresistible – try a home-made ice or walnut and raisin cheesecake. *No dogs.*

Llanrhaeadr *Lodge*

Near Denbigh
Llanynys (074 578) 370
Map 3 B4 *Clwyd*

Open 10–5 September–February; 9.30–5.30 March–end August
Closed Sun & Bank Holidays
Spicy beef with cheese & potato topping £1.95
Welsh rarebit £1.80
Credit Access, Visa
P own car park WC

A mother and daughter team are responsible for the cooking at this family-run coffee bar within a stylish ladies' fashion shop on the A525. Their sponges, scones and shortbread, Bakewell slices and fruit pies go down well with a good cuppa, while savoury snacks range from toasted sandwiches, ploughman's and Welsh rarebit to salads, omelettes and more substantial spicy beef hot pot. *No dogs.*

Llanrwst   *Tu-Hwnt-i'r-Bont*

Llanrwst (0492) 640138
Map 3 A4 *Gwynedd*

Open 10.30–5.30 (from 11.30 Easter–Spring
Bank Hol & mid Sept–early Oct)
Closed Mon except Bank Hols & early
October–Tuesday before Easter

Set afternoon tea £1.45   Pâté platter £1.80
Credit Access
P own car park &

Jolly owner Derek Holt bakes the champion
scones served straight from the oven at this
cosy tea room in a picturebook cottage by
the river Conway. Enjoy them with excellent
butter, jam and cream (and a splendid cuppa)
– but do leave room to sample his lovely
sponges, buttery biscuits and rich bara brith,
too. At lunchtime, you can tuck into savoury
items like pâté and ploughman's, filled rolls
and salads. Unlicensed. ☺ 🍴

Llanycefn   `New Entry`   *Llain Llogin*

Clunderwen
Maenclochog (099 13) 436
Map 7 B2 *Dyfed*

Open 10am–10.30pm
Closed 25 December, also Sun eve–Tues mid
October–mid March

Welsh pancakes with potatoes & salad £4.50
Trout with streaky bacon £4.95
P own car park & in road & **WC**

Stephen and Marion Williams keep out the
welcome mat at their homely little restaurant, which stands bright and pink alongside
the B4313. Welsh recipes are included in
the repertoire, among them pancakes with
cockles and laverbread, honeyed lamb
chops and even braised goat. Fruit pies are
regular favourites for dessert, and there are
some very good cakes and scones. Outside
eating in fine weather. *No dogs.* ☺ 🍴

Machynlleth   `New Entry`   *Centre for Alternative Technology*

Llwyngwern Quarry
Machynlleth (0654) 2400
Map 7 C1 *Powys*

Open 10–5
Closed 25 December & 1 January

Quarryworker's lunch with lentil & apple pâté
£1.20   Chick pea & fruit curry with saffron rice
£2.10
P ample &

The vegetarian restaurant and coffee house
are part of an interesting complex (admission
£1.85) in an old slate quarry north of Machynlleth. The food is particularly wholesome and
varied, with salads and pâtés in profusion,
tasty soup and lunchtime main courses like
chick pea and fruit curry. On Sunday there's
a nut roast – complete with gravy! And there
are always loads of filled rolls, brown-flour
cakes and sweets. Unlicensed. No smoking.
No dogs. 🍴

Machynlleth   *Quarry Shop*

13 Maengwyn Street
Machynlleth (0654) 2624
Map 7 C1 *Powys*

Open 9–3 & 3.30–5 (Thurs till 2pm)
Closed Sun (except Bank Holiday weekends)
& 25 & 26 December

Sweet & sour vegetables with brown rice
£1.60   Fruit trifle 75p
P street parking & **WC**

You serve yourself from a cluttered counter
at this vegetarian restaurant, an offshoot of
the Centre for Alternative Technology. The
lunchtime selection could include lentil burgers, quiche, samosas and organically grown
salads, plus baked potatoes with both vegetarian and vegan fillings. Some interesting
cakes – carrot and coconut, lemon spice, a
morish chocolate malt cake. Note barley cup,
dandelion coffee and choice of teas. Unlicensed. No smoking. *No dogs.* ☺ 🍴

Menai Bridge

Jodies Wine Bar

Telford Road, Anglesey
Menai Bridge (0248) 714864
Map 3 A4 *Gwynedd*

Open 12–1.45 & 7–9.30
Closed Sun & Mon 1 October–Easter, 25 & 26
December & 3 weeks January
Beef olives with vegetables £4.75   Spaghetti
with lentils, mushrooms & sweet peppers
£3.15
P street parking   **WC**

Order your food and wine at the bar and
choose a table in one of three cosy rooms or
outside in the lovely garden that overlooks
the Menai Straits. The blackboard menu
provides a good variety, from cream of onion
soup and grilled Jamaican grapefruit to
smoked trout, beef olives and a vegetarian
spaghetti special. Finish with blackcurrant
sorbet or apple, wholewheat and nut crumble.
No children under three. *No dogs.* ☕

Newport

★

Cnapan

East Street
Newport (0239) 820575
Map 7 B2 *Dyfed*
Open 10.30–5
Closed Tuesday & November–March (except
weekend eves & Sun lunch)
Laver bread with lemony seafood filling &
salads £3.50   Oat flan with raisin, cream
cheese & tomato filling & salad £3.50
Credit Access, Visa
P street parking   ♿   **WC**

The Lloyds and the Coopers run this cosy
wholefood restaurant, part of a Georgian
house that also has some letting rooms.
Cakes and biscuits accompany morning
coffee, while lunchtime produces delights
such as laver bread with a lemony seafood
filling or first-class quiches made with oat
pastry. On the sweet side are apricot flapjack
pudding and old-fashioned treacle tart. Fuller
evening menu and traditional Sunday lunch.
No dogs. ☕ 🐕

Newport

New Entry

Happy Carrot Bistro

5 Chartist Tower, Upper Dock Street
Newport (0633) 66150
Map 7 C2 *Gwent*

Open 10–4
Closed Sun, Wed & Bank Holidays

Baked potato with mushroom sauce £1.50
Vegetarian burger £2.25

P ample public parking

Stairs at the back of a healthfood centre lead
down to this modestly appointed vegetarian
restaurant. The chef is in view in a spotless
kitchen, producing an interesting selection of
dishes, from dense, chunky vegetable soup
to cauliflower cheese, samosas, curry and
vegetarian burgers stuffed with mixed vegetables, herbs and pine nuts. For dessert
there's banana and walnut slice and carrot
cake. Unlicensed. *No dogs.*

Newtown

New Entry

Jays

The Precinct
Newtown (0686) 25395
Map 7 C1 *Powys*

Open 9–4.30
Closed Sun & most Bank Holidays

Vegetarian lasagne £1.50   Russian pie with
egg, onion & mushrooms 90p

P street parking   ♿

Smartly kept and efficiently run, this pine-
finished restaurant stands opposite the Co-
op in a modern shopping precinct. The
emphasis is definitely on healthy eating, with
vegetarian dishes like mushroom and leek
flan and mixed bean bake being increasingly
preferred to traditional meaty specials. Also
pizzas, jacket potatoes and some delicious
sweet things like German apple cake or
mixed fruit tart. *No dogs.* 🐕

Rossett · *New Entry* · *Churtons Wine & Food Bar*

Machine House, Chester Road
Rossett (0244) 570163
Map 3 B4 *Clwyd*

Open 12–2.15 & 7–10
Closed Sun, Bank Holiday Mons & 1 week
Christmas
Stilton mushrooms on a croûton £2.45
Minted leg of lamb steak bonne femme £6.25
Credit Access, Amex, Diners, Visa
P own car park 🅰 **WC**

On the A483 just inside Wales, this delightful
wine bar is a characterful conversion of a
farm building. The menu changes daily:
starters could include ham-wrapped asparagus or enjoyable courgette and mushroom
soup, while main courses run from pepper
cod to steaks, smoked turkey and creamy-
sauced lamb. Standard puds; excellent wines
(particularly Bordeaux and Rhônes) at alluring prices. Children welcome Sat lunch only.
No dogs.

Swansea · *Home on the Range*

174 St Helen's Avenue
Swansea (0792) 467166
Map 7 B2 *West Glamorgan*

Open 11.30–3 & 6–10
Closed Mon & Tues eve, all Sun, Bank
Holidays & 10 days Christmas

Vegetable lasagne with salad £1.95   Turkey &
mushroom pie with salad £2.20
P street parking 🅰

Locals love this informal, unpretentious restaurant, where a team of five do the cooking
in rotation. Splendid raw materials, enhanced
by notably good fresh herbs, are left to speak
for themselves in such tasty mealtime offerings as home-made soup and quiche, ham
salad, burgers (walnut and cheese) and daily
specials like chicken chasseur. Beautifully
fresh sweets like peach gâteau to finish.
Unlicensed, so bring your own. *No dogs.* 🍃

Tynant · *Bronnant Tea Shop*

Maerdy, Near Corwen
Maerdy (049 081) 344
Map 3 B4 *Clwyd*

Open 9–6; 8am–8pm in high season
Closed November–mid March

Welsh cream tea £1.60   ¼lb steakburger with
jacket potato £2.20
Credit Access, Visa
P own car park 🅰 **WC**

Right on the A5, a lovely little café comprising
two rooms, one looking down on a gift shop,
the other featuring a handsome Welsh-stone
fireplace. Home-baked cakes and pastries
make a tempting display, and there are
various sandwiches, jacket potatoes and
burgers. New owners the Bethells have taken
over, and one of the changes they plan is the
introduction of more cooked lunches. Unlicensed. *No dogs.* 🐾

Wolf's Castle · *Wolfscastle Country Hotel*

Haverfordwest
Treffgarne (043 787) 225
Map 7 B2 *Dyfed*

Open noon–2

Baked potato with prawns & mayonnaise
£2.75   Hazelnut meringue with bananas £1.45
Credit Access, Amex, Visa

P own car park **WC**

Splendid snacks are served every lunchtime
in the bar of this friendly country hotel.
Freshly baked bread accompanies a steam-
ing bowl of soup, interesting salads garnish
cold cuts, quiche and locally smoked trout,
baked potatoes bulge with tasty fillings like
prawns mayonnaise or cottage cheese and
pineapple. Other typical dishes: lamb curry,
chicken and chips, rissoles with a spicy
tomato sauce. Nice sweets, too, such as
orange and lemon cheesecake. 🍃

Wrexham

Bumbles Coffee Shop

2 Charles Street
Wrexham (0978) 351044
Map 3 B4 *Clwyd*

Open 9–5
Closed Sun & Bank Holidays
Baked potato with bolognese sauce £1.75
Gammon with pineapple £2.25
LVs *Credit* Access, Visa
P municipal car park in St George's Crescent
WC

Two rooms above a gift shop, with well-spaced tables and pleasant waitress service. There's a voluminous menu of snacks, including plain and toasted sandwiches, smoked mackerel, quiche and jacket potatoes. Daily specials like leek and potato soup or steak and kidney pie widen the choice still further. The home-baking selection is equally impressive, ranging from flapjacks and fruitcake to super sultana scones. Unlicensed. *No dogs.* ⊖ ☕

We welcome complaints and bona fide recommendations on the tear-out pages for readers' comments. They are followed up by our professional team. Please also complain to the management instantly.

382

CHANNEL ISLANDS

St Anne's   *Gossip Coffee Shop*

Victoria Street
Alderney (048 182) 3485
Map 8 D4 *Alderney*

Open 9.30–4.30 (Sun till 12.30) & 7–10; June–
August 9–4.30 & 7–10, Sun 10–1 & 7–10
Closed 1 January, 25 & 26 December

Carrot cake 65p   Pizzas from £1.60

P street parking   &   **WC**

Simple, well-prepared snacks are the stock
in trade at this convivial coffee shop on the
island's cobbled main street. During the day
there's a good range of sandwiches (plain or
toasted), a selection of salads and jacket
potatoes and a hot special. Nice scones,
cakes and gateaux accompany a well-
brewed pot of tea. A pizzeria operation takes
over in the evening. Unlicensed, so bring
your own. *No dogs.*

St Peter Port   *Flying Dutchman Hotel*

Ruette Braye
Guernsey (0481) 23787
Map 8 D4 *Guernsey*

Open noon–6.30
Closed Sun & February

Toast fillet £3.90   Brill praslin £6.50
Credit Access, Amex, Visa
P own car park   &   **WC**

Jovial hosts the Deutschmanns make sure
that all appetites are catered for at this
welcoming hotel. On fine summer days you
can enjoy an open sandwich, cake or pastry
in the popular beer garden, or join in the full-
scale barbecue. Inside, lunchtime choices at
the bar range from German meatloaf and
bratwurst to omelettes, steaks and super
salads. More elaborate evening meals are
served in the restaurant. *No dogs.*

Gorey   ★   *Jersey Pottery Restaurant*

Gorey Village
Jersey (0534) 51119
Map 8 D4 *Jersey*

Open 9–5.30
Closed Sat, Sun, Bank Holidays & 10 days
Christmas

Seafood salad £6.95   Set afternoon tea £1.50
Credit Access, Amex, Diners, Visa
P own car park   &   **WC**

Top-quality seafood is the great attraction at
this enormously popular restaurant, where in
summer you can book a table in the garden.
Lobsters, crabs, squid and prawns are
served with excellent fresh salads, and there
are also cold meats, cheeses and pastries
rich with thick Jersey cream. Simple hot
dishes like soup and lasagne are served in
winter. Colin Jones heads a happy, hard-
working team. *No dogs.*

St Aubin's   *Sadler's*

1 Bank Place
Jersey (0534) 44043
Map 8 D4 *Jersey*

Open 7.30pm–10.30pm (from 6.30pm in summer)

Scallop brochettes £2.20   Monkfish in Pernod £4.85

P street parking   **WC**

There's something for everyone at Tim Sadler's cheerful, busy bistro, where the evening choice of enjoyably prepared dishes ranges from an authentic bouillabaisse to locally caught fish, deep-fried potato skins and satay. Exotic cocktails and super coffee are a bonus, and if you want to steal a march on the regulars you'll need to book. Less choice Sunday evenings. *No dogs.*

St Brelade's Bay   *Hotel l'Horizon*

Jersey (0534) 43101
Map 8 D4 *Jersey*

Open 4–6

Set afternoon tea £2.30   Crab sandwich £2.35

Credit Access, Amex, Diners, Visa

P own car park   &   **WC**

Whether you choose to sit out on the delightful sun terrace or relax in the sumptuously comfortable lounge, afternoon tea at this attractively situated hotel is a thoroughly civilised and enjoyable occasion. Freshly made scones come with local cream and butter or Jersey strawberries, the trolley displays a mouthwatering range of pastries and there are delicious sandwiches with tempting fillings like honey-baked ham and crab mayonnaise. *No dogs.* 🍵

SOLUTION OF GUZZLE PUZZLE
(on page 185)

Across 3. Bread   6. Adam   7. Sips   8, 3. French   11. Ogress   14. Rind   15. Agog   16. Ceres

Down 1. Calf   2. Pate   4. Rasher   5. Apples   9. Recipe   10. Noodle   12. Eggs   13. Sago

ISLE OF MAN

Ballasalla   ★   *La Rosette*

Main Road
Castletown (0624) 822940
Map 3 A2 *Isle of Man*

Open noon–2.30
Closed Sun

Fillet of beefburger £3   Quiche lorraine £3.50

P street parking   **WC**

Rosa Phillips cheerfully looks after guests while husband Bob works away in the kitchen creating the delicious lunches served at this charming little restaurant. Whether you choose a light snack like garlicky stuffed mushrooms, a smoked salmon sandwich or something more substantial such as hearty cassoulet or a minced steak crêpe, you're sure to be delighted. Salads and sweets are smashing, too. More elaborate evening meals. *No dogs.* 🍵 🫖

Castletown   *Castletown Golf Links Hotel*

Fort Island
Castletown (0624) 822201
Map 3 A2 *Isle of Man*

Open 3.30–5.15
Closed mid October–April

Set afternoon tea £2.25   Beef sandwich £1
LVs   *Credit* Access, Amex, Diners, Visa

P own car park   **WC**

A thoroughly traditional afternoon tea is served in this spacious hotel lounge, whose picture windows command fine views of the garden and yachting harbour of Derbyhaven beyond. Start with buttered bread and neat little triangles of sandwiches filled with, say, ham, egg and cress and lobster paste, and then move on to a well-baked scone and a choice of cakes or pastries such as chocolate cake and puff slice.

Douglas   *L'Experience*

Summerhill
Douglas (0624) 23103
Map 3 A2 *Isle of Man*

Open 12–2
Closed Sun, Tues, 1 January & 25 December

Beef bourguignon £3.15   Coffee & Tia Maria cream 95p
Credit Access, Diners, Visa
P street parking   ♿   **WC**

Very Gallic in both food and decor, this friendly, informal little restaurant does an appetising line in savoury snacks. The onion soup with lovely garlic bread is practically a meal in itself, while other equally tasty offerings include a French ploughman's lunch (with Brie), croques, quiches served with splendid baked potatoes, and three-egg omelettes. There are steaks and a daily special too, plus more elaborate evening meals. *No dogs.* 🍵

Egon Ronay's
PUB GUIDE 1987

TO BAR FOOD AND ACCOMMODATION
IN BRITISH PUBS AND INNS

- The best British bar snacks and meals
- Highly selective
- Surprising gastronomic finds at low prices
- Pubs that welcome children
- Homely, clean and pleasant bedrooms
- Excellent breakfasts

Plus pubs specially selected for atmosphere and
historic interest.

AN OFFER FOR ANSWERS

A DISCOUNT ON THE NEXT GUIDE

Readers' answers to questionnaires included in the Guide prove invaluable to us in planning future editions, either through their reactions to the contents of the current Guide, or through the tastes and inclinations indicated. Please send this tear-out page to us *after you have used the Guide for some time*, addressing the envelope to:

Egon Ronay's Just a Bite Guide
Second Floor, Greencoat House, Francis Street
London SW1P 1DH, United Kingdom

As a token of thanks for your help, we will enable respondents to obtain the 1988 Guide post free from us at a 33⅓% discount off the retail price. We will send you an order form before publication, and answering the questionnaire imposes no obligation to purchase.
All answers will be treated in confidence.

This offer closes 31 July 1987 and is limited to addresses within the United Kingdom.

---

1. Are you   *Please tick*

    male? ☐   Under 21? ☐   31–45? ☐
    female? ☐   21–30? ☐   46–65? ☐
                                          over 65? ☐

---

2. Your occupation ....

3. Do you have any previous editions of this Guide?
    1984 ☐   1985 ☐   1986 ☐

4. Do you refer to this Guide
    four times a week? ☐   once a week? ☐
    three times a week? ☐   once a fortnight? ☐
    twice a week? ☐   once a month? ☐

5. How many people, apart from yourself, are likely to consult this Guide (including those in your home and place of work)?

    male ....   female ....

6. Do you have our Hotel & Restaurant Guide?

   1985 ☐   1986 ☐   1987 ☐

7. Do you have our Pub Guide?

   1985 ☐   1986 ☐   1987 ☐

8. How many times have you travelled overseas in the past year?

   ....

9. How many nights have you spent in hotels during the past year?

   ....

10. Do you occupy more than one home? | Yes | No |

    Do you own the house you live in? | Yes | No |

11. Your car

    type .... year ....

12. What is your daily newspaper? ....

13. Which of the following credit cards do you use?

    Access ☐   Diners ☐

    American Express ☐   Visa ☐

14. What fields would you like us to survey or what improvements do
    you suggest? ....
    ....
    ....

Please *print* your name and address here if you would like us to
send you a pre-publication order form for the 1988 Guide.

Name ....

Address ....

....

Readers' comments

Please use this sheet for recommendations.
Not restaurants offering full meals but establishments of
*the type this Guide covers which serve very high-quality
food.* Your complaints about any of the Guide's entries are
also welcome.

Please post to:
JUST A BITE 1987
Egon Ronay's Guides
Greencoat House,
Francis Street,
London SW1P 1DH

NB We regret that owing to the enormous volume of readers' communications received each year,
we will be unable to acknowledge these forms but they will certainly be seriously considered.

Name and address of establishment	Your recommendation or complaint

Name of sender (in block letters) _____

Address of sender (in block letters) _____

Readers' comments

Please use this sheet for recommendations.
Not restaurants offering full rmeals but establishments of
the type this Guide covers which serve *very high-quality*
food. Your complaints about any of the Guide's entries are
also welcome.

Please post to:
JUST A BITE 1987
Egon Ronay's Guides
Greencoat House,
Francis Street,
London SW1P 1DH

NB We regret that owing to the enormous volume of readers' communications received each year,
we will be unable to acknowledge these forms but they will certainly be seriously considered.

Name and address of establishment	Your recommendation or complaint

Name of sender (in block letters)

Address of sender (in block letters)

Readers' comments

Please use this sheet for recommendations.
Not restaurants offering full meals but establishments of
the type this Guide covers which serve very high-quality
food. Your complaints about any of the Guide's entries are
also welcome.

Please post to:
JUST A BITE 1987
Egon Ronay's Guides
Greencoat House,
Francis Street,
London SW1P 1DH

NB We regret that owing to the enormous volume of readers' communications received each year,
we will be unable to acknowledge these forms but they will certainly be seriously considered.

Name and address of establishment   Your recommendation or complaint

Name of sender (in block letters) ——————————————

Address of sender (in block letters) ——————————————

Readers' comments

Please use this sheet for recommendations.
Not restaurants offering full meals but establishments of
the type this Guide covers which serve *very high-quality*
food. Your complaints about any of the Guide's entries are
also welcome.

Please post to:
JUST A BITE 1987
Egon Ronay's Guides
Greencoat House,
Francis Street,
London SW1P 1DH

NB We regret that owing to the enormous volume of readers' communications received each year,
we will be unable to acknowledge these forms but they will certainly be seriously considered.

Name and address of establishment	Your recommendation or complaint

Name of sender (in block letters) _____

Address of sender (in block letters) _____